Vernacular Religion in Everyday Life

Vernacular Religion in Everyday Life
Expressions of Belief

Edited by
Marion Bowman and Ülo Valk

Published by Equinox Publishing Ltd.
UK: Unit S3, Kelham House, 3 Lancaster Street, Sheffield, S3 8AF
USA: ISD, 70 Enterprise Drive, Bristol, CT 06010

www.equinoxpub.com

First published 2012

© Marion Bowman, Ülo Valk and contributors 2012

ISBN 978-1-908049-50-6 (hardback)

British Library Cataloguing-in-Publication Data

A catalogue record for this book is available from the British Library.

Library of Congress Cataloging-in-Publication Data

Vernacular religion in everyday life : expressions of belief / edited by
Marion Bowman and Ülo Valk.
    p. cm.
  Includes bibliographical references and index.
  ISBN 978-1-908049-50-6 (hardback)
  1. Religions—Case studies. 2. Ethnology—Religious aspects—Case studies.
I. Bowman, Marion. II. Valk, Ülo, 1962- III. Title: Expressions of belief.
  BL41.V47 2012
  305.8—dc23
                        2011020061

Typeset by S.J.I. Services, New Delhi
Printed and bound in the UK by MPG Books Group

Contents

Acknowledgements

The time lapse between the inception and completion of this volume perhaps epitomizes the joys and hardships of international scholarly cooperation! The editors would like to express their gratitude to the authors for their contributions, and to friends and colleagues for their valuable help. We particularly want to thank Daniel E. Allen for his work on English language editing for this volume, George Moore for his copy editing input, Marat Viires for drawing the maps that illustrate the articles, and Pihla Siim for her technical help. We are grateful to Veikko Anttonen for his help in devising the outline of the book, and to our colleagues at the Department of Religious Studies, The Open University in Milton Keynes, and the Department of Estonian and Comparative Folklore, University of Tartu, who have assisted us in various ways. We are thankful to our families and friends for their moral and practical support. Finally, we are immensely grateful to Janet Joyce and Valerie Hall at Equinox for their patience and enthusiasm for this project.

This book has been supported by grants from the Estonian Science Foundation (grant no. 7516 'Vernacular Religion, Genres, and the Social Sphere of Meanings') and by the European Union through the European Regional Development Fund (Centre of Excellence in Cultural Theory). We are greatly indebted to them for their financial support.

Contributors

Madis Arukask is a folklorist who works as Associate Professor at the Institute of Estonian and General Linguistics, University of Tartu, Estonia. He is also President of the Estonian Society for the Study of Religions. His main field of interest is the traditional belief of Balto-Finnic peoples, primarily Vepsians and Votes. In the last 13 years he has conducted fieldwork in North Western Russia and written articles about different aspects of vernacular religion and folklore genres there.

Marion Bowman is Head of Religious Studies and Senior Lecturer at The Open University, UK, and a past President of both the British Association for the Study of Religions and The Folklore Society. Working at the interstices of religious studies and folklore, her research interests include vernacular religion, contemporary Celtic spirituality, pilgrimage, material culture, the creation of myth and tradition, and a long-term study of Glastonbury, England, on which she has published extensively.

Ingvild Sælid Gilhus is Professor of Religion at the University of Bergen, Norway. Her interests include religion in antiquity, with a focus on ancient Gnosticism, and contemporary New Age religion. Her most recent book in English is *Animals, Gods and Humans: Changing Attitudes to Animals in Greek, Roman and Early Christian Ideas* (2006). She is book review editor of the journal *Numen: International Review for the History of Religions*.

Graham Harvey is Reader in Religious Studies at The Open University, UK, with research interests in the performance, material cultures and literatures of Jews, Pagans and indigenous peoples. His numerous publications include *Religions in Focus: New Approaches to Tradition and Contemporary Practices* (Equinox, 2009) and *The A to Z of Shamanism* (co-authored with Robert Wallis, Scarecrow Press, 2010). His current research expands upon interests in the etiquette of human interaction with the larger-than-human world.

Ágnes Hesz is Assistant Professor at the Department of European Ethnology and Cultural Anthropology, University of Pécs, Hungary. Her research includes fieldwork on the relations between the living and the dead among a Hungarian ethnic group in Romania, and she has also published on bewitchment and local festivals.

Marja-Liisa Keinänen is Associate Professor of History of Religions and Senior Lecturer at Stockholm University. Her research topics are everyday religion and gender, especially women's rituals and ritual agency in Russian Orthodox Karelia. Besides her doctoral thesis *Creating Bodies: Childbirth Practices in Pre-modern Karelia* (2003), she has published widely on these topics and also edited *Perspectives on Women's Everyday Religion*. (Stockholm Studies in Comparative Religion 35, 2010).

Judit Kis-Halas has been a Researcher and Lecturer at the Department of European Ethnology and Cultural Anthropology, University of Pécs, Hungary since 2009. She has published in the areas of traditional healing, witchcraft and magic.

Seppo Knuuttila is Professor of Folklore studies at the University of Eastern Finland. His current research interests include cultural theory, cultural localities and spatial peripheries as cultural and social constructions, and contemporary folk/outsider art. He has participated in long-term research in two North Karelian villages for around 30 years. He has also studied folk humour (Ph.D. 1992), mythic history, Finnish mentality and identity. He is the Head of Kalevala Society (2007–).

Art Leete is Professor of Ethnology at the University of Tartu, Estonia. His main research interests are related to contemporary religious changes and the development of Pentecostal and Charismatic Christian groups among the Komi people, as well as hunting practices and related beliefs. He has published several articles about Komi hunting, most of them in co-operation with Vladimir Lipin. They have conducted joint fieldwork annually since 1996 among different ethnographic groups of the Komi.

Vladimir Lipin is Research Fellow at the Department of Ethnography at the National Museum of Komi Republic, Syktyvkar, Russia. His main research topics are related to the hunting and fishing culture of the Komi people, as well as museological studies. He is the author of the first Komi ethnographic lexicon (2008) and has published a number of articles about Komi traditional culture. He also owns a traditional hunting ground near Kulymdin village.

Merili Metsvahi received her PhD from the Department of Estonian and Comparative Folklore, University of Tartu, where she now works as a Research Fellow. Her research interests include Estonian folk belief, individual-centred research in folklore studies, Estonian werewolf traditions, and women's status in Estonian society as revealed through folk narrative genres.

María Inés Palleiro is researcher in folk narrative at the Institute of Anthropology, Buenos Aires University; Professor of Methodology of Folk Research, National Institute of Folk Arts, Buenos Aires, Argentina; and Vice President of the International Society for Folk Narrative Research. She has authored over 170 articles on Argentinean folk narrative and several books, including *It Has Been a Real Case* (2004).

Alexander Panchenko is Chair of the Centre for Literary Theory and Interdisciplinary Research, Institute of Russian Literature, Russian Academy of Sciences; Director of the Centre for Anthropology of Religion, European University of St Petersburg; and Director of the Program for Sociology and Anthropology, Faculty of Liberal Arts and Sciences, St Petersburg State University. He has published extensively on vernacular religion and the history of sectarian movements in Russia and on theory of folklore.

Éva Pócs is Professor Emerita at the University of Pécs, Hungary. She is the series editor of sourcebooks on early modern religion and witchcraft and the editor of 25 volumes on religious anthropology and folklore, the latest being *Folk Religion and Folk Belief in Central-Eastern Europe,* 2009. She has conducted extensive, long-term fieldwork among Hungarian-speaking Catholics in Romania and has produced over 460 academic publications during her long and distinguished career.

Leonard Norman Primiano is Professor and Chair of the Department of Religious Studies at Cabrini College, Radnor, Pennsylvania, USA and a pioneer of the term 'vernacular religion'. He is the co-producer and co-founder of The Father Divine Project, a multimedia documentary and video podcast about The Peace Mission Movement. He is currently writing on the North American vernacular religious artist 'Sister' Ann Ameen; Roman Catholic ephemeral culture as exemplified by the 'holy card'; the international marketplace for Roman Catholic sacramental objects, such as the ex-voto; and the expressive culture of Father Divine's Peace Mission community.

Taisto-Kalevi Raudalainen is a Doctoral Student at the Folklore Department of Helsinki University, and a Lecturer at the Estonian Academy of Arts in Tallinn and the Culture Academy in Viljandi, University of Tartu, Estonia. He has done fieldwork among different groups of Finno-Ugric peoples, especially among the Balto-Finnic. His main field of interest is the construction of ethnic history and personal autobiographies within the traditional genre spectrum. His doctoral thesis concerns tradition-bound autobiographical narration among the Ingrian Finns.

Anne Rowbottom was, until her retirement, a senior lecturer in the Centre for Human Communication at Manchester Metropolitan University, UK. She conducted long-term research in the field of vernacular civil religion, on which she both published and (with Paul Henley) made a television documentary, *Royal Watchers*. After contracting CFS/ME she began researching links between chronic illness, complementary medicine and alternative spiritualities.

Tiina Sepp is a Doctoral Student of Folklore at the University of Tartu. Her research areas include Catholic and contemporary pilgrimage and vernacular religion. Since 2003, she has been researching various aspects of the Santiago de Compostela pilgrimage and has published two books on that subject.

Ülo Valk is Professor of Estonian and Comparative Folklore at the University of Tartu and ex-President of the International Society for Folk Narrative Research. His publications include the monograph *The Black Gentleman: Manifestations of the Devil in Estonian Folk Religion* (2001) and other works on belief narratives and demonology. His current research interests are connected with vernacular genres, belief systems and the social dimension of folklore in Estonia and North Eastern India.

Introduction: Vernacular Religion, Generic Expressions and the Dynamics of Belief

The development of the human sciences in the nineteenth century led to the formation of anthropology, comparative religion, ethnology and folklore – all new disciplines whose focal points lay outside the 'enlightened', 'rational' and 'advanced' realm of contemporary urban life. Anthropologists looked at non-European cultures as living examples of the pre-modern past, ethnologists and folklorists studied the rural people of their own countries as carriers of obsolete traditions, and early scholars of religious studies looked for primitive forms of religion among 'uncivilized' peoples and in historical sources, as expressions of belief that antedated the contemporary Protestant Christianity conceived to be the highest stage of religious development. What linked these disciplines was the attempt to engage with the cultures of 'others' – non-Western civilizations and 'backward' peasants – and by describing them systematically to place them within an externally conceived framework.

After nation states had been established and colonial empires had collapsed, anthropology, comparative religion, ethnology and folkloristics[1] went through periods of self-reflection and critical examination of their objects of research as they had been constructed in the context of Western scholarly discourse and social needs at the time of their formation. Defining categories such as culture, folklore or religion as reified ontological entities has lost its former attraction, because the social and verbal constructedness of concepts has become common knowledge. Former endeavours to build up disciplines on the basis of clearly defined objects of research, to establish their foundations in fundamental theories – such as evolution – and to discover timeless truths inherent to the empirical data, have become less attractive, whereas the subjective dimensions of scholarship have become more significant than ever before. The focus has been shifting to human agency in producing cultures, and to more reflexive methodologies that demonstrate awareness about 'the situated and interested character of our knowledge production' (Ritchie 2002: 445). Contemporary scholars do not think of themselves as impartial outside observers, alien 'others' who study cultures from a safe and scientific distance, but rather as partners in communication, participants in a heteroglot dialogue of indefinite numbers of voices and points of view.

Although belief in analytical categories as basic tools for producing firm knowledge has weakened, other concepts and approaches have emerged that offer alternative perspectives to those methodologies which constructed exhaustive systems of classification, transcultural taxonomies and universal definitions. Many scholars nowadays think that the goal of scholarship is not to produce authoritarian theoretical statements but rather to observe and capture the flow of vernacular discourse and reflect on it. As everyday culture cannot be neatly compartmentalized into the theoretical containers of academic discourse, it often seems more rewarding to follow the methodological credo of Lauri Honko and produce textual ethnographies (Honko 1998: 1). Rooted in whatever constitutes reality for a particular group or person, such studies allow us to see how theory is put into practice, how beliefs impact on different aspects of life, the ways in which worldview must affect, and be expressed in, everyday life.

What emerges in these studies are challenges to a number of assumptions that have operated in some discourses on religion, such as the homogeneity of belief and praxis in 'traditional' contexts, or conversely the uniquely modern nature of highly eclectic, heterogeneous personal belief systems. While agreeing with Manuel Vásquez that 'complexity, connectivity, and fluidity are preponderant features of our present age' (Vásquez 2008: 151), we get intimations that the ways in which people have expressed, maintained, articulated and negotiated beliefs in the past lack neither complexity nor fluidity. The dynamism of vernacular genres in a plethora of contexts is unmistakable.

The current book is an outcome of the 'Vernacular Religion – Vernacular Genres' symposium convened by Veikko Anttonen and Ülo Valk at the University of Tartu as part of the 15th congress of the International Society for Folk Narrative Research (ISFNR) in July 2005. At that symposium, 19 papers were delivered, ten of which have been developed into articles in the current volume; eight further scholars, with similar methodological approaches, were invited to produce articles for this joint publication, which has authors from Argentina, Estonia, Finland, Hungary, Norway, Sweden, Russia, the UK and the USA. United in the assumption that, as Richard Rorty neatly puts it, 'disengagement from practice produces theoretical hallucinations' (Rorty 1999: 94), the authors deal with beliefs expressed in a variety of local, historical, textual, virtual and performative contexts.

From Religion to Vernacular Beliefs

A range of expressions of belief is presented in this volume, in terms of genre, form and content, with careful consideration of the means of expression and the worldviews being expressed. Before considering individual chapters, however, it will be helpful to examine some of the history and key concepts forming the backdrop to these studies.

One aim of this book is to bring together scholarship from both ethnology/folkloristics and religious studies, demonstrating the value of exchanging and sharing terminological and methodological insights, and noting the impact of different academic, national and socio-political trends and assumptions on the study of belief. As Robert Orsi comments:

> Self-reflexivity within particular disciplines is most effectively done by tracking back and forth between the practice of the discipline and reflection on that practice, on its distinctive challenges and dilemmas, and the 'so called ... alternatives' to these in light of the discipline's past and its contemporary circumstances. (Orsi 2008: 138)

Early folklorists were convinced that the peasant cultures of Europe had maintained a considerable quantity of beliefs and practices with roots in pre-Christian religions. Folk beliefs thus represented the 'elder faith' of social groups and folkloristics became an auxiliary science of the history of religion (Krappe 1964: 310). Eric Sharpe described folklore as it developed in the UK in the late nineteenth and early twentieth centuries as the 'home missions department of anthropology' (Sharpe 1986: 50). Using clerical terminology and naming some supernatural beliefs 'superstitions' relied on the same opposition between Christianity as the most advanced religion, and folk beliefs as primitive survivals (see Valk 2008a). Step by step, folkloristics and comparative religion were liberated from the evolutionary model of conceptualizing beliefs as cultural survivals that could properly be interpreted only from the diachronic point of view. The two-tiered model of high and low – opposing Christianity and superstition, religion and popular beliefs, elite and the folk – was, however, deeply rooted as a cognitive pattern. Although the scheme seemed useful for understanding the conflicts and tensions within the field of study, it was nevertheless a burden because of the negative connotations of the 'folk' viewed as an isolated, uncivilized group (Mullen 2000); the difficulties of distinguishing between 'folk' and 'non folk' have caused considerable confusion (Anttonen 2004: 73). Alan Dundes saved the concept of folk in folkloristics by redefining it from a homogeneous group of illiterate, rural and backward peasants to refer to '*any group of people whatsoever* who share at least one common factor' (Dundes 1980: 6).

Don Yoder contested the tendency to pathologize folk beliefs as primitive superstitions and saw them not in opposition to religion but in a dynamic relationship with institutionalized Christianity. According to his definition, folk religion 'is the totality of all those views and practices of religion that exist among the people apart from and alongside with strictly theological and liturgical forms of the official religion' (Yoder 1974: 14). Yoder showed how the term folk religion has been used both by religious professionals and by scholars to make judgements about 'lived religion' in relation, or in contradistinction, to 'proper' or official religion, and drew attention to an enormous field of religion that frequently has been both under-researched and under-valued. In an attempt to bring this neglected area more to the fore in Religious Studies, Marion Bowman suggested that to obtain a realistic view of religion as it is lived, it should be viewed in terms of three interacting components: 'official religion (meaning what is accepted orthodoxy at any given time, although this is subject to change), folk religion (meaning that which is generally accepted and transmitted belief and practice, regardless of the official view) and individual religion (the product of the received tradition, plus personal beliefs and interpretations)' (Bowman 2004a [1992]).

Leonard Norman Primiano followed his mentor Don Yoder and criticized scholars who 'have consistently named religious peoples' beliefs in residualistic, derogatory ways as "folk", "unofficial", or "popular" religion' (Primiano 1995: 38). While acknowledging and valuing the work done by folklorists in relation to the study of religion, Primiano asserts nevertheless that 'every time a folklorist encounters religion and designates it "folk religion", he or she has done that religiosity an extreme disservice' (Primiano 1995: 38). He feels that following the two-tiered model of 'folk' and 'official' religion employed by other disciplines 'residualizes the religious lives of believers and at the same time reifies the authenticity of religious institutions as the exemplar of human religiosity' (Primiano 1995: 39). Whereas, as Yoder shows (1974), there have been many debates over and conceptualizations of 'folk religion', Primiano takes the discourse further by problematizing the category of 'official' religion. Drawing attention to the personal and private dimensions of faith, Primiano emphasizes the need to study 'religion as it is lived: as human beings encounter, understand, interpret, and practice it' (Primiano 1995: 44). All these subjective and experiential aspects are blended in Primiano's concept 'vernacular religion'. His interest is not in religion as an abstract system but in its multiple forms, related to the processes and practices of religious beliefs: their verbal, behavioural, and material expressions (Primiano 1995).

One objection to the notion of looking at – indeed privileging – belief in the study of religious life is that an obsession with belief (as opposed to praxis) is considered a highly Western, Protestant, conceptualization of what religion is (see Lopez 1998). However, while the religion with which perhaps the majority of European and Anglophone scholars have been most familiar is Christianity, the Christianity of scholarship has often been presented in terms of beliefs without due attention to the expression of these beliefs in non-liturgical settings or extra-theological discourse. In looking at expressions of belief in the context of this book, the emphasis is on the articulation of worldviews and negotiation with lifeworlds revealed and expressed in narratives, material culture and actions of different kinds.

The myths, personal experience narratives and more casual verbal expressions of belief, or material culture and actions related to, arising from or inter-related with beliefs, shed valuable light on religion in everyday life, practical religion, religion as it is lived. In this context, the stress is not on artificial expectations of theological homogeneity or 'orthodoxy', nor is it perpetuating judgements as to what counts as 'real' religion at the expense of what people actually do in relation to extra-liturgical praxis. In the tradition of folklore and ethnology, the stress, the overriding interest, is on what people in a variety of cultural, religious and geographical landscapes do, think and say in relation to what they believe about the way the world is constituted.

Many common-sense categories, widely used in human sciences and once regarded as universal, have been eroded by post-structuralist reflections on knowledge production. According to S. N. Balagangadhara, the multiple descriptions of religions in 'other' cultures transcend any definition of religion, and thus the claim about the universality of religion is pre-theoretical in nature (Balagangadhara 2005). Timothy Fitzgerald has argued that religion is an ineffective category for the analysis of Hinduism, for example, because it implies a distinction from social or secular, developing instead a typology of ritual, politics, soteriology and economics (Fitzgerald 2005); he contends that religion is a cultural construction that should be de-privileged (Fitzgerald 2000). Religion in such analyses has thus turned out to be a historical construct with roots in the theology of the Christian Reformation and distorting effects if it is applied to the study of other traditions (see Talal 1993). However, it is worth noting that others argue that 'the idea of religion needs to be challenged ... but it does not necessarily have to be eradicated' (Carrette 2001: 127).

This shift of interest from religion as systematic and coherent doctrine to its individual meanings, experiential core and expressive forms offered alternative perspectives to those, prescribed by the old two-tiered model, which had a tendency to produce closed frameworks and oppositions, such as dividing beliefs into pagan 'superstitions' versus Christian religious creeds, or Catholic 'survivals' versus Protestant faith. This ideal-typological approach is problematic, because neat schemes of classification are hardly applicable in the practical arrangement of research material. For example, it is difficult to classify folklore texts according to genre-analytic schemes, because only a few texts correspond to genres as they are defined (Honko 1989a: 17). In addition, on the theoretical level the ideal-typological approach does not reveal much because its universal categories and principles of order often contradict far more complex ethnic and emic realities. Such theoretical models tend to be normative and not flexible enough to handle the hybrid and heterogeneous forms of vernacular creativity.

One of the most influential books of the twentieth-century humanities is the *Course of General Linguistics*, by Ferdinand de Saussure, first published in 1915. This book described language as an established system of signs, whose norms rule all the manifestations of speech. De Saussure wrote: 'As soon as we give language first place among the facts of speech, we introduce a natural order into a mass that lends itself to no other classification' (de Saussure

1966: 9). According to de Saussure and his followers, systems, norms, rules and regularities offer solid scientific foundations for describing the basic aspects of language. This approach, which proceeds from language as an abstract system, was criticized by Mikhail Bakhtin and his followers, who have studied textual creativity in social context and in dialogic relationship with the words of others in both oral and written discourses. Valentin Vološinov regarded formalism and systematicity as typical distinguishing marks of authoritarian thinking focused on ready-made and 'arrested' objects – incompatible with living, historical understanding of language and its creative uses (Vološinov 1986: 78).

According to Bakhtin, 'in the philological disciplines, the speaking person and his discourse is the fundamental object of investigation' (Bakhtin 2000: 351). Primiano's thoughts about 'vernacular religion' follow the Bakhtinian approach that does not proceed from normative schemes of classification and fixed systems, but from unique cases of individual expression. If research focuses on expressions of belief in the flow of everyday life, using the scale 'official-unofficial', 'Christian-pagan' or some other etic scheme becomes irrelevant. Research thus becomes inductive, taking into account the perceptions, beliefs and behaviour of those practising it (Bowman 2004b: 127). It relies on the study of articulated beliefs, not on abstract belief systems, world religions or other forms of a *priori* knowledge.

From Belief to Genres

Primiano has commented that 'One of the hallmarks of the study of religion by folklorists has been their attempt to do justice to belief and lived experience' (Primiano 1995: 41). By not automatically privileging written over oral forms, through paying attention to different forms of narrative, by close observation of material culture and the use made of it (both formally and informally), through observing belief spilling over into diverse aspects of behaviour and by appreciating the dynamic nature of 'tradition' (characterized by folklorist Henry Glassie as 'the creation of the future out of the past' (Glassie 1995: 395)), folkloristic/ethnological studies at their best have presented a rich and nuanced picture of belief in action.

Belief seems to be an elusive category, difficult to grasp and define if we think about it as an entity in the world of ideas. Understanding becomes easier if we look at *expressions* of belief in behaviour, ritual, custom, art and music, in textual and other forms. These expressed beliefs can be reproduced, described, analysed and discussed. If beliefs are verbally articulated, they can be studied as forms of generic expression and discursive practices. Richard Bauman has conceptualized genre as 'one order of speech style, a constellation of systematically related, co-occurrent formal features and structures that serves as a conventionalized orienting framework for the production and reception of discourse' (Bauman 2004: 3). Genre has not necessarily proved to be a useful category for the classification of texts, but it has considerable power to illuminate the processes, how texts are produced, perceived and understood. As genres emerge and grow historically, they mix the voice of tradition with individual voices, and instead of being univocal, they are always ambivalent, dialogic and polyphonic. If single utterances, performances and texts are studied as generic expressions, they reveal the vast inter-textual spaces of verbal traditions and shared worldviews. Genres mould texts and constrain performances, setting limits to communication as only certain messages and themes can be expressed in certain genres (Honko 1989a: 15).

According to the Bakhtinian approach, genre is not simply a literary form, but a mode of cognition that expresses a particular worldview (Newsom 2007: 29). Both oral and written genres represent certain outlooks and orientations to social reality, which is visualized and conceptualized through the lenses provided by genres (Bakhtin and Medvedev 1991: 133–135). As culturally patterned speaking practices, genres fulfil important functions with respect to the coping with, transmission and traditionalization of intersubjective experiences of the lifeworld (Günther and Knoblauch 1995: 5). Thus genres shape individual experiences of life according to the collective patterns of traditional narratives. However, the social function of genre varies, as some of them build up poetic storyworlds and fictitious realities, such as those we encounter in cyberworld and fantasy films, while others explicitly express norms of behaviour and provide us with practical knowledge of how to cope with everyday reality.

Genres of belief have a strong orientation towards daily life, as they do not only discuss the supernatural realm but express mundane opinions and shape worldly attitudes (Valk 2008b: 153). Many narratives about supernatural experience are so strongly interwoven with the physical and social surroundings that it is easy to forget that they belong to the textual world. Folklorists call such stories legends – traditional (mono) episodic, localized and historicized narratives of past events told as believable in a conversational mode (Tangherlini 2007: 8). Legends evoke belief but also often trigger discussions and debates about their veracity (Dégh and Vázsonyi 1976). Memorates are legends that are told in the first person about the narrator's supernatural encounters (see Honko 1989b). They are reported as true stories about extraordinary or numinous experience, narrated by the witnesses themselves. Legends and memorates share similar temporal and social settings and can be distinguished from myths – 'prose narratives which, in the society in which they are told, are considered to be truthful accounts of what happened in the remote past' (Bascom 1984: 9). The categories of legend, memorate and myth represent analytical, etic categories, as they rely on clear definitions and distinct genre boundaries. Vernacular taxonomies offer different insights into the world of genres, because their borders usually remain fuzzy and the semantic fields of genre do not overlap with etic schemes of classification. Thus, vernacular uses of 'legend' and 'myth' refer to unverifiable or false stories, although through the explicit denial of their veracity, the connection of these genres with beliefs is maintained.

Another important aspect of the study of belief comes through the lens of material culture, which in this context can refer to any aspect of the material world, constructed or natural, and encompasses experiential interaction with the physical world. As David Morgan puts it:

> If culture is the full range of thoughts, feelings, objects, words, and practices that human beings use to construct and maintain the life-worlds in which they exist, material culture is any aspect of that world-making activity that happens in material form. That means things, but it also includes the feelings, values, fears, and obsessions that inform one's understanding and use of things. (Morgan 2008: 228)

This engagement with 'things' is seen in narratives in which the figures in pictures are brought into discourse, called upon as participating characters or give rise to considerable emotion. The use of food as a vehicle for sacralizing time in everyday life, the interaction with nature in the context of hunting culture or relationships with buildings and 'other than human' beings all involve belief in action.

Beliefs are multiform, appearing in various genres and expressive forms. For example, a believer can make the sign of the cross to express devotion, but the same action can take a verbal form as a detail in a legend, where an actor has to ward off the Devil. Although expressions of belief can be observed and studied, there is still something mysterious and elusive about them, as they tend to conceal more than they reveal. Beliefs have a great potential to be transformed into long narratives or elaborate rituals, although in daily life they seldom become anything bigger than short statements, expressions of modality or religious acts. Efficacy and experience are builders, consolidators and maintainers of belief, however and wherever expressed. The associative web of beliefs and intertexts, the endless realm of knowledge about the supernatural, 'the way the world *really* is' or the 'other than human' realm is only partially revealed. Each belief is a synecdochic expression of discourse, tradition, textual realm – *pars pro toto,* as the whole can only be imagined and never completely textualized.

The Contents of this Volume

Belief as conceptual reality cannot be studied outside its expressive forms, giving shape and social functions to its intangible contents. The first section of the book reflects upon different practices of vernacular Christianity in European contexts, where both individuals and communities play an active role in creating and upholding traditions of belief. **Marja-Liisa Keinänen** studies the social production of time in pre-modern rural Russian Orthodox Karelia through women's household work. Cleaning and bathing can be understood as a rite of transition from ordinary to sacred time, as purity and order were considered central properties of the sacred. Lent – the period of corporal and spiritual preparation for Easter – was marked by abstention from certain kinds of food, such as dairy products and meat. The long fast was broken on Easter morning, introducing the holidays, made special by the exceptional variety and quantity of food. Marja-Liisa Keinänen shows how women's daily activities vernacularized the church traditions and gave empirical contents to three temporal units – ferial time (*arki*), fast and holy days. **Alexander Panchenko** discusses the symbolic, ritual and narrative resources that local communities use to build up the sacred space of local shrines in Russia. He shows that the fight of the Communist authorities against Orthodox religion did not abolish vernacular religious practices but, on the contrary, fostered their diversity. Alexander Panchenko makes a distinction between three types of shrines – individual or spontaneous,

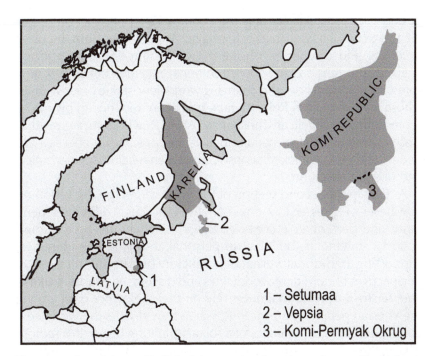

The vernacular religion and beliefs of these regions have been discussed in this book as follows: Karelia – Marja-Liisa Keinänen, Russia – Alexander Panchenko, Vepsia – Madis Arukask and Taisto-Kalevi Raudalainen, Setumaa – Merili Metsvahi, Estonia – Ülo Valk, Komi – Art Leete and Vladimir Lipin.

communal, and official. The borders of these shrines shift and their position is contested because of interaction, competition and conflicts between various groups of believers, such as local peasants, pilgrims and church authorities. Social production and control of the sacred is a process to be studied at both individual and community levels.

Judit Kis-Halas examines the practices and narrative autobiography of a Hungarian healer and diviner, whose magical activities and self-image are discussed in the context of changing belief systems. Uses of magical formulae and wax pouring connect her with traditional folk healers, her techniques for conjuring angels and preparation of angelic amulets link her to New Age ideas and praxis, while her mission as a healer brings her close to living saints in the vernacular Catholic tradition. Thus, her self-image is constructed in the context of folk beliefs and legends, contemporary spirituality and vernacular Christianity. Judit Kis-Halas also studies the healer's position in village society and the continuous reconstruction of her identity in the changing market for magic. **Anne Rowbottom** discusses practices and discourses of alternative healing in contemporary England and tensions between traditional religious belief and new spirituality. She analyses the changing worldview of one older woman whose involvement in Reiki therapy had been denounced by a vicar representing evangelical Christianity. Anne Rowbottom argues that close examination of vernacular beliefs and practices is necessary to understand the complex relationships between religion, secularization and re-spiritualization.

Articles in the second section of the book widen the discussion on how belief is expressed in various narrative practices in different generic forms and performative contexts. Belief narratives are here studied as social statements, building up personal and collective identities, supporting traditional vernacular religion or offering alternative perspectives to dominant worldviews and discourses. **Madis Arukask** and **Taisto-Kalevi Raudalainen** rely on their fieldwork data among the Vepsian people in northern Russia as they discuss the worldview and supernatural experiences of a solitary tradition bearer in a remote village, the site of a former Orthodox monastery. Her belief narratives about spirits and saints, and laments to her deceased relatives, have a strong autobiographical flavour. The article opens up personal and mystic dimensions of the vernacular world view and sheds light on beliefs as expressions of deeply rooted religious traditions in which Orthodox and non-Christian ideas merge. **Ágnes Hesz** writes about the social and religious functions of dream narratives and relationships between the living and the dead in a Catholic Hungarian-speaking community in Romania. Encounters with the dead in dreams are narrated to pass on strong moral messages, confirmed by the belief that these stories express the will and opinion of the dead, not of the dreamer or narrator. As a form of indirect communication these narratives express social norms and other important topics, sometimes too sensitive to be discussed explicitly. **Merili Metsvahi** studies the mental universe of a female storyteller, her repertoire of religious legends and her relationship with her patron saint, St Xenia. Interview, made with a woman from Setumaa, the Orthodox corner of south-eastern Estonia, reveal that traditional religious narratives acquire personal meanings as they symbolically address the storyteller's life story. In addition, religious legends can create social space for female tradition bearers who live in a patriarchal village society, where the role of women in the public sphere is marginalized.

The third section of the book examines the relations between humans, their surroundings and other-than-human beings as an essential topic in vernacular worldviews. These articles argue that symbols and images of, and interaction with, 'others' shed light on the worldview and relational mapping of the groups who share these traditions. **Graham Harvey** enhances our understanding of animism by discussing the indigenous religious traditions of North American peoples and the Maori. The article shows that indigenous religious traditions rely on ontologies and epistemologies that do not focus on the supernatural but include relational engagement with everyday things and artefacts, capable of communication, agency and desire. Accordingly, birds, fires, stones, buildings and other objects can be relational actors negotiating the joys and sorrows of being neighbours and even kin. **María Inés Palleiro** studies contemporary Argentinean legends about the dead, ghosts and haunted houses, recorded in both rural and urban settings. She discusses these stories as symbolic representations of historic tragedies and as metaphoric expressions of tensions in contemporary society. María Inés Palleiro claims that folk narrative patterns function as fictionalization devices of history and connect the fictional world with social context.

Ingvild Sælid Gilhus discusses the meaning of angels in contemporary religious discourse in Norway and their intermediary position between Christian doctrines and other traditions, such as anthroposophy, New Age spirituality and alternative therapies. Angels act in personal experience stories as helpers, although often they lack agency and appear in contemporary religious language as metaphors. Beliefs and discussions about angels in contemporary Norway reveal the dynamic relationships between self-styled 'official' and popular religion, fluctuating between dialogue and conflict. **Éva Pócs** analyses the belief system of a Hungarian-speaking Catholic village community in Romania (also studied by Ágnes Hesz in this volume) and the relevant narrative traditions about the supernatural world, which is split between divine and demonic realms. The former appears in legends about God, the Virgin Mary and the saints, and the latter in legends about the devil and non-Christian demons. These religious narratives have cognitive and emotional functions; as a normative framework they regulate everyday life. Many of these stories are book-based but have gone through considerable changes in vernacular storytelling and have acquired a more human, personal quality. Significantly, Éva Pócs notes the role of folklorists as fieldworkers in keeping alive some of these narrative traditions.

The fourth section of the book demonstrates how expressions of belief in narratives, customs and other practices build up social identities and communities and how they relate to each other. Articles in this section show the important role of belief narratives and practices in maintaining social coherence and defining the borders between ingroups and outgroups, and negotiations of identity and belonging. **Art Leete** and **Vladimir Lipin** have carried out long-term fieldwork among the Komis, an indigenous people of northern Russia whose homeland is mainly covered by forests. The article discusses the local hunting culture as a way of life and analyses the narratives and hunting practices of one hunter. Beliefs, customs and stereotypes connected with hunting are maintained through a lively story-telling tradition, which transmits the relevant knowledge and shapes the social and gender identities of Komis. The article by **Tiina Sepp** is also based on fieldwork, carried out on the pilgrimage route to Santiago de Compostela. Sepp studies the pilgrimage as a narrated journey, including miracles and supernatural encounters. Pilgrims with different religious backgrounds share the tradition of storytelling, where heterogeneous beliefs, personal experience stories and Christian legends are blended. One of the recurrent threads is the construction of the image of the 'authentic' pilgrim. **Marion Bowman** examines the ways in which two much mythologized figures, Arthur and Bridget, have been envisaged, narrated and utilized in relation to historical vernacular Christianity and contemporary spirituality in the English town of Glastonbury. Drawing on popular, individual and literary portrayals of Arthur, Bridget and Avalon, a range of expressions of belief are examined that demonstrate intertextuality and interdependence between seemingly different forms of belief and praxis, as well as the influence of previous eras of academic insistence upon the importance of cultural 'survivals'.

The final articles provide theoretical reflections on vernacular religion, discussing it from emic and etic perspectives. **Ülo Valk** explores how beliefs are maintained and constructed in contemporary Estonia, a seemingly secular and rationally oriented country, within the context of the Internet. Narratives about the supernatural evoke different attitudes and disagreements in the comments found in web portals. Discussing belief and disbelief becomes a concomitant part of transmitting legends, wrapped in the discourse of vernacular interpretations. Ülo Valk shows that disbelievers have a crucial role in reproducing beliefs and maintaining the supernatural traditions in contemporary society. **Seppo Knuuttila** discusses vernacular cognitive theories in some folk narrative genres such as myths, fairy tales and legends. He studies the imaginations of storytellers who have discussed epistemological questions, such as seeing the world through the eyes of the 'other', speaking animal languages and the possible existence of parallel worlds. The article shows the complexity and diversity of vernacular theorizing in folklore. Finally, in his Afterword, **Leonard Norman Primiano**, who coined the term 'vernacular religion', reflects upon its meanings and applications in scholarship. He emphasizes that vernacular religion is not the dichotomous or dialectical partner of 'institutional' religious forms but another concept that shifts the focus from 'religion' and 'belief' as abstractions to the power of individual creativity to shape religious lives. Reflecting more generally on the concept of vernacular religion in relation to the topics and genres discussed in the book, Primiano particularly draws attention to ambiguity, power and creativity. Primiano posits possible future trajectories for the study of personal creativity, belief and expressive culture, fittingly ending the book by reasserting the dynamism of vernacular genres and looking to the joys, challenges and contestations ahead in vernacular religious studies.

Vernacular religion in context

The chapters in this book relate to a variety of contexts: historical and contemporary; rural and urban; central, northern and western European; north and south American; Christian, non-Christian, post-Soviet and post-Christian. Beliefs explored here have been held, expressed and enacted under a range of political regimes, Christian denominational hierarchies, socio-economic and cultural circumstances. The data drawn upon are historical, archival, textual, fieldwork-generated, media-based and virtual. In exploring and testing the importance of belief and its expression, it has been important to avoid regarding any one social, political, economic, cultural or geographic context as normative.

Ullrich Kockel (2003) has claimed that the ethnological approach is 'particularly suited to studying local-level interpretations and negotiations of global processes', and our case studies demonstrate the importance of grounding the global experience in the local context. We know that Christian denominations can appear very different according to context (Calvinism in Scotland, Hungary and Zambia are obviously not the same) and similarly that aspects of contemporary spirituality, while notionally drawing on similar concepts, are evolving with very definite local traits. If part of our concern in the study of vernacular religion is with 'bi-directional influences of environments upon individuals and of individuals upon environments in the process of believing' (Primiano 1995: 44), we need to pay attention to local detail even in the midst of global and virtual developments.

Context also impacts upon identity. Rick Muir and Margaret Wetherell (2010: 4) claim that,

> identity is always both about ourselves and about how we are positioned in relation to the world. Our identities are always formed both by our own agency and by our interaction with others. Identity is always about our own personal biography and the wider collective practices in which we participate.

Individual identities are multiple and (re)narrated variously according to context, life stage and experience. In the expressions of belief studied here, identities are in some cases determined or expressed in relation to occupation, religious, ethnic or national affiliation. However, it is important to note that for some people changes of borders or regimes have resulted in shifts of 'official' identity, national or religious, which nevertheless need to be negotiated at the local and personal level through expressions of belief.

As we have already indicated, it is worth noting the importance of the academic context in which belief scholarship is conducted, whether constrained by scholarly orthodoxy, nationalist agendas or political correctness. Among the challenges in the study of belief to emerge in this volume are issues around how to use or analyse data in archives, collected under different premises, that might contain valuable information in relation to belief but lack the contextual data and thick description which we increasingly consider necessary, or conversely which might ignore important genres. This, in turn, should make us mindful of how to collect material relating to expressions of belief in ways that will make our data comprehensible and useful to future scholars, whose interests, taxonomies and analytical frameworks may in turn be very different from ours.

Dialogic methodology, which acknowledges the authority of vernacular discourse as the empirical foundation of research and as partner in producing academic knowledge, is leading scholarship towards a growing diversity of approaches. There have been recurrent attempts to subordinate expressions of vernacular beliefs to institutionalised religions, interpreting them as 'folk' deviations from religious standards or as survivals of obsolete forms of religion. In addition, there is a long history of research that tries to compartmentalize beliefs into neat systems of classification and arrange them according to comprehensive theoretical schemes. Vernacular beliefs not grounded in institutionalized truths but in individual creativity, expressed in a variety of local and social contexts and shaped by the power of tradition, present a challenge for scholars of different disciplines who need firm conceptual ground and an international theoretical language for mutual dialogue. At the same time, expressions of vernacular beliefs form rich, dynamic and inspiring source material with which to develop more flexible theoretical frameworks and new knowledge about humans as social beings. The current book, which is based on empirical data from various traditions, is a step towards this goal.

Note

1. The term folkloristics is used here to distinguish the academic discipline of the study of folklore/cultural tradition from the object of study.

References

Anttonen, V. (2004) Theory and method in the study of 'folk religion'. *Temenos, Nordic Journal of Comparative Religion* 39–40: 73–79.

Bakhtin, M. (2000) *The Dialogic Imagination: Four Essays*. Austin, TX: University of Texas Press.

Bakhtin, M. and Medvedev, P. (1991) *The Formal Method in Literary Scholarship: A Critical Introduction to Sociological Poetics*. Baltimore, MD and London: The Johns Hopkins University Press.

Balagangadhara, S. N. (2005) *'The Heathen in his Blindness …': Asia, the West and the Dynamic of Religion*. New Delhi: Manohar.

Bascom, W. (1984) The forms of folkore: Prose narratives. In A. Dundes (ed.) *Sacred Narrative: Readings in the Theory of Myth*, 5–29. Berkeley, CA, Los Angeles, CA and London: University of California Press.

Bauman, R. (2004) *A World of Others' Words: Cross-Cultural Perspectives on Intertextuality*. Malden, MA, Oxford and Carlton, Victoria, Australia: Blackwell Publishing.

Bowman, M. (2004a [1992]) Phenomenology, fieldwork and folk religion. In S. Sutcliffe (ed.) *Religion: Empirical Studies*, 3–18. Aldershot: Ashgate.

Bowman, M. (2004b) Taking stories seriously: Vernacular religion, contemporary spirituality and the myth of Jesus in Glastonbury. *Temenos, Nordic Journal of Comparative Religion* 39–40: 125–142.

Carrette, J. R. (2001) Foucault, strategic knowledge and the study of religion: A response to McCutcheon, Fitzgerald, King, and Alles. *Culture and Religion* 2 (1): 127–140.

Dégh, L. and Vázsonyi, A. (1976) Legend and belief. In D. Ben-Amos (ed.) *Folklore Genres*, 93–123. Austin, TX: University of Texas Press.

Dundes, A. (1980) *Interpreting Folklore*. Bloomington, IN: Indiana University Press.

Fitzgerald, T. (2000) *The Ideology of Religious Studies*. New York and Oxford: Oxford University Press.

Fitzgerald, T. (2005) Problems with 'religion' as a category for understanding Hinduism. In J. E. Llewellyn (ed.) *Defining Hinduism: A Reader*, 171–201. London: Equinox.

Glassie, H. (1995) Tradition. *Journal of American Folklore* 108 (430): 395–412.

Günther, S. and Knoblauch, H. (1995) Culturally patterned speaking practices: The analysis of communicative genres. *Pragmatics: Quarterly Publication of the International Pragmatics Association,* 5 (1): 1–32.

Honko, L. (1989a) Folkloristic theories of genre. In A.-L. Siikala (ed.) *Studies in Oral Narrative. Studia Fennica 33,* 13–28. Helsinki: Finnish Literature Society.

Honko, L. (1989b) Memorates and the study of folk belief. In R. Kvideland and H. K. Sehmsdorf (eds) *Nordic Folklore: Recent Studies,* 100–109. Bloomington, IN: Indiana University Press.

Honko, L. (1998) Back to basics. *FF Network for the Folklore Fellows* 16: 1.

Kockel, U. (2003) Turning the world upside down: Towards a European ethnology in (and of) England. Unpublished paper presented at 7th ESRC Seminar in European Ethnology, University of the West of England, 11 September.

Krappe, A. H. (1964 [1930]) *The Science of Folklore*. New York: W. W. Norton and Company, Inc.

Lopez Jr., D. S. (1998) Belief. In M. C. Taylor (ed.) *Critical Terms for Religious Studies*, 21–35. Chicago, IL and London: University of Chicago Press.

McDannell, C. (1995) *Material Christianity: Religion and Popular Culture in America*. New Haven, CT and London: Yale University Press.

Morgan, D. (2008) The materiality of cultural construction. *Material Religion* 4 (2): 228–229.

Mullen, P. B. (2000) Belief and the American folk. *The Journal of American Folklore* 113 (448): 119–143.

Muir, R. and Wetherell, M. (2010) *Identity, Politics and Public Policy* [pamphlet]. London: Institute for Public Policy Research.

Newsom, C. A. (2007) Spying out the land: A report from genology. In R. Boer (ed.) *Bakhtin and Genre Theory in Biblical Studies,* 19–30. Atlanta, GA: Society of Biblical Literature.

Orsi, R. (2008) The 'so-called history' of the study of religion. *Method and Theory in the Study of Religion* 20 (2): 134–138.

Primiano, L. N. (1995) Vernacular religion and the search for method in religious folklife. *Western Folklore (Reflexivity and the Study of Belief)* 54 (1): 37–56.

Ritchie, S. J. (2002) Contesting secularism: Reflexive methodology, belief studies, and disciplined knowledge. *The Journal of American Folklore* 115 (457/458): 443–456.

Rorty, R. (1999) *Achieving Our Country*. Cambridge, MA: Harvard University Press.

Saussure, F. de (1966) *Course in General Linguistics*. New York, Toronto and London: McGraw-Hill Book Company.

Sharpe, E. J. (1986) *Comparative Religion: A History.* London: Duckworth.

Talal, A. (1993) *Genealogies of Religion: Discipline and Reasons of Power in Christianity and Islam*. Baltimore, MD: Johns Hopkins University Press.

Tangherlini, T. R. (2007) Rhetoric, truth and performance: politics and the interpretation of legend. *Indian Folklife: A Quarterly Newsletter from National Folklore Support Centre* 25: 8–12.

Valk, Ü. (2008a) Superstition in Estonian folklore: From official category to vernacular concept. *Folklore* 119 (1): 14–28.

Valk, Ü. (2008b) Folk and the others: constructing social reality in Estonian legends. In T. Gunnell (ed.) *Legends and Landscape,* 153–170. Reykjavik: University of Iceland Press.

Vásquez, M. A. (2008) Studying religion in motion: A networks approach. *Method and Theory in the Study of Religion* 20 (2): 151–184.

Vološinov, V. N. (1986) *Marxism and the Philosophy of Language*. Cambridge, MA and London: Harvard University Press.

Yoder, D. (1974) Toward a definition of folk religion. *Western Folklore (Symposium on Folk Religion)* 33 (1): 2–15.

PART I
Belief as Practice

Everyday, Fast and Feast: Household Work and the Production of Time in Pre-Modern Russian Orthodox Karelia

Marja-Liisa Keinänen[*]

The church and agrarian calendars, which in the course of Christianization gradually merged, served as the basic grounds for time-reckoning in pre-modern Europe. In Russian Orthodox Karelia, the church calendar with its regular sequences of ordinary (*arki*) days, days of fast and holy days, together with fixed seasonal work periods fundamentally structured people's use of time. This is to a certain extent reflected in the vernacular names of the months and the annual *arki*, non-fasting periods, which refer to the agricultural activity of the time period, such as cutting down forest for slash and burn cultivation (*huuhta*), hay-making, sowing and harvesting.

The celestial bodies, the sun, the moon and the stars served as reference points for the daily scheduling of farm labour. The position of the sun, or the 'triple star' – three stars in the constellation of Orion – told people in northern Karelia when it was time to rise. Other daily tasks, particularly in summertime, were synchronized with the movements of the sun. At Vilho Jyrinoja's home, the house functioned as a sun clock: when the sun shone through the window by the door along a notch carved in the window pane, it was nine o'clock. When it had moved to the side window, shining straight across the floor boards, it was noon. The sun shining through the back window along the floor boards indicated that it was six o'clock in the evening. When the sun had reached the window on the women's side of the room, shining straight from the neighbour's fishing ground, it was nine o'clock in the evening (Virtaranta 1958: 247–250). Time-reckoning was not only spatialized, but also embodied, since the human body also functioned as an instrument for measuring time. When herding

* Marja-Liisa Keinänen is Associate Professor of History of Religions and Senior Lecturer at Stockholm University, Sweden.

cattle as a boy in the forest in summer, Jyrinoja (b. 1901) could tell the time from the length of his shadow. When it was the length of an axe shaft, it was noon and when it was twice as long it was six o'clock, time to go home (Virtaranta 1958: 249).

An individual's body time was also linked to the church calendar. In her autobiography, Vivi Vuoristo (b. 1905), from northern Karelia, writes that most people didn't know what year it was or the exact date of their birth, but situated themselves in the flow of time by referring to the holy day or its associated fast or *arki* closest to any particular event (Vuoristo 1983: 132–133). When a person in Olonets was asked about their date of birth, they could answer: 'Well, I was born a couple of weeks before Christmas – or so many days after the feast of Spring-Nikolai' (Taulamo 1985: 89). A child was also linked to the church calendar by its name, which was given after the saint whose day was closest to its birthday (Paulaharju 1995: 58).

However, as Nancy Munn warns us, we must be wary of reducing the concept of time to nothing more than a cataloguing of temporal reference points, or to a means of measuring duration. Since we are not only situated in time and space but also produce time and space through social action, she advocates a practice-oriented view of time. Practice-oriented scholars see action as 'a symbolic (meaningful, and meaning-forming) process in which people ongoingly produce both themselves as spatiotemporal beings and the space-time of their wider world' (Munn 1992: 106, 102, 105). This implies that the seasons, fasts, non-fast periods and holy days of the weekly and annual calendar were not only conceptual points of reference for reckoning socially and economically relevant time, but these temporal entities were filled with their time specific content and meaning by everyday human activity. Roughly speaking, people continuously produced these temporal categories and themselves as temporal beings by performing or refraining from certain types of activity at a given point of time.

However, the sporadic and seasonal nature of agricultural work and the infrequency of religious feasts, which tend to be in the focus of the studies of calendric activities, requires us to look at some further aspects of social activity if we are to study in depth the process of time production. In my opinion, women's daily work, i.e. household chores that were both continuous and repetitive, would provide a far more comprehensive basis for a study of the social production of time. The aim with this paper is therefore to investigate how women's domestic activities, largely cooking and cleaning, contributed at a fundamental

level to the production and embodiment of various kinds of time: ordinary time (*arki*), fast, and feast in pre-modern Russian Orthodox Karelia. These concrete activities also spatialize time, since they are always tied to real space.

Using folkloristic archive materials as well as folkloristic publications as source materials, the data cover the time period 1880–1930 on the Russian/Soviet side of the Karelian border with Finland, and for a further decade in Ladoga Karelia on the Finnish side of the border. For pragmatic reasons, I use the problematic term 'pre-modern' for this period of time, aware that the process of modernization was well underway on both sides of the national borders. In Soviet Karelia, the church calendar with its fasts and feasts was fiercely attacked by the anti-religious regime during the 1920s and 1930s (Keinänen 2002). In Finnish Ladoga Karelia, the modernization process had led to increasing secularization which among other things came forth in the decline of fasting and the celebration of religious holidays. In both

A – Northern Karelia (Viena)
B – Olonets Karelia
C – Ladoga Karelia

White Sea

A

B

C

FINLAND

RUSSIA

Helsinki

Gulf of Finland

St. Petersburg

Karelia is an Orthodox region on the borderlands of Eastern and Western Christianity.

areas the vernacular religion was a mixture of Russian Orthodoxy and indigenous traditions.

I will use *Karjalan kielen sanakirja* (The Dictionary of the Karelian Language) as a standard in rendering the vernacular terms, except when quoting. This means privileging the North Karelian idiom in this study.

Women's Household Chores

Although folklore collectors and authors of ethnographical literature have amply praised women's skills in cooking for fast and feast, they have shown little theoretical interest in the significance of domestic work for the creation of cultural patterns. Some feminist scholars explain this evident lack of interest in women's domestic activities by the quotidian nature of household work. Since these activities tend to deal with 'the physiological needs of the human body (sleeping, eating, shelter, etc.)', they have been perceived to be 'natural' and constant, and therefore of minor importance for historical analysis (Moore 1995: 52–53). The scholarly failure to appreciate the role of domestic work in the creation of cultural patterns may also have to do with the implicit tendency to locate the household outside the social structure, which makes domestic work appear personal and idiosyncratic (Dubisch 1991: 39–40). However, cooking and other housework not only filled basic physiological needs; they also had great religious and social significance. In Karelia, women were responsible as cooks for the household members following the diet regulations and observing food taboos. Food was central to the numerous holy feasts and rites of passage celebrations. Moreover, food was an important symbolic means of communication with the ancestors and played an important part in women's practice of charity. As Laura Stark-Arola has observed, food was also used as a social currency – a means of creating and maintaining social relationships (Stark-Arola 2001).

A further reason for the theoretical oversight of women's domestic activities in the creation of cultural patterns, was the tendency to view these activities as being '"within", or peripheral or complementary to, a system that is, implicitly or explicitly, structured by men' (Dubisch 1991: 43–44). Considering that the church calendar with its rules and regulations largely organized and steered women's household duties, especially food preparation, it is not surprising that these duties would indeed appear to be peripheral and complementary to the system created by the male dominated church. However, even though the church calendar provided the basic structure and rules for fasting and feasting, it was largely women who put the diet regulations into practice. In other words, women domesticated the official forms of religion (Sered 1992: 10). They interpreted the general rules from their cultural viewpoint accommodating them to the prevailing ecological, socioeconomic, and cultural conditions. Furthermore, women did not only domesticate ideas and practices advocated by the official religion, but even maintained and created indigenous religious traditions, weaving these different strands of traditions together into a wider religious pattern.

Cleaning and the Creation of Sacred Time and Space

In the Karelian symbolic system, the home, which has commonly been seen as representing a micro-cosmos, stood for cleanliness and order while *miero*, the profane world outside, represented disorder and filth, even immorality (cf. Dubisch 1983: 200). In Karelian popular thinking 'the gods', i.e. God, Christ, the various saints and the ancestors were the originators and guardians of sacred order. Their divine presence was materialized in the holy icons, which were in fact called 'gods'. From 'the great corner' or 'the corner of the god' they and the ancestors, who were venerated in the same place, monitored the conduct of the residents who feared that any breach of order could lead the gods to abandon the dwelling and its inhabitants. The precondition for their continued presence was the physical and moral purity of the house and its residents. Should these supernatural guardians abandon the house, the powers of chaos, epitomized in the figure of the devil, would gain free access and endanger the wellbeing of the inhabitants (Keinänen 2010: 128, 132–133).

Since purity and order were central properties of the sacred, cleaning activities were of vital importance for the creation and maintenance of sacred time and space (see Keinänen 2010: 136–140). We can view cleaning as a kind of rite of passage that ritualized the transition from ordinary space-time into sacred space-time. According to Paulaharju, the house was usually cleaned every other week but in many places in the Karelian borders every Saturday, although there were houses which were properly cleaned only before the greater holy days (Paulaharju 1983: 154; Sallinen-Gimpl 1993: 184). Cleaning and washing on Saturday or on a holiday eve can therefore be seen as a rite of passage which marked and spatialized the transition from ordinary time, *arki* into sacred time, *pyhä*. Purity and cleanliness were demanded from the physical space and the people who inhabited that space during a *pyhä* period. Because work was prohibited on Sunday, housework had to be completed on Saturday evening. Bathing hours were similarly regulated. Using the bathhouse late on Saturday evening would be the equivalent of bathing on Sunday, which was prohibited, as was bathing on the eves of greater holy days (Keinänen 2003: 249).

Bathing or cleansing were also integral parts of the rites of passage that marked existential turning points in human life, and which also implied a transition into sacred time. A newborn went through a long process of ritual bathing, a bride had her bridal bath on the eve of her wedding and a corpse was washed immediately after death. Even the soul of the departed was thought to bathe in a cup of water which was left beside the corpse for the purpose. Bathing was also an integral part of healing rites.

Cleaning also marked the transition into sacred space-time at the celebration of the commemoration feasts for the deceased. According to Akim Lomojov's description of the preparations for the fortieth day feast, all dirty clothes were washed and the house was thoroughly cleaned. The oven was whitewashed and the ceiling, walls, benches and floors were scrubbed before, finally, the house was blessed by purification with holy incense. A bed was made for the spirit of the dead with a newly stuffed, clean mattress, a clean cover and a pillow.[1] By means of cleaning, the building was turned into sacred space for the visiting dead.

The ritual nature of cleaning before the feast is particularly evident from the description recorded from one Solomanida Petrov (b. 1862):

> [On Memorial Saturday] all the dead of the family are commemorated and they'll be fetched back home for a night. Everywhere the livingroom as well as the rest of the rooms are washed. In the evening, the threshold will be washed again. ... The same goes for the door handle. This is for the dead to come. They say, 'poor things, come tonight'. If someone doesn't feel well enough to scrub the whole livingroom, she'll at least wash the threshold.[2]

Washing the threshold and the door handle twice indicates that we are not dealing with ordinary, everyday cleaning, but with the preparation of the entrance for sacred visitors. Martti Haavio's informant from Suistamo mentions the cleaning of the threshold before the commemoration feast arranged in honour of a certain dead individual, the *piirut*. During the six-week-long period of preparation, the threshold was wiped clean after each visitor. The explanation given was that the soul would then 'be able to move'.[3] The belief that the soul of a dying person would not leave through a dirty doorway, where sinful people had passed, which Haavio recorded in another context, gives a deeper explanation of the idea of a clean threshold.[4] A clean threshold can also be seen as a metonym for a pure, clean house: 'The entire house was as if holy for six weeks', i.e. during the weeks of preparation for the *piirut*.[5]

Sacred time was also differentiated from ordinary time by the prohibition against work. In particular dirty work such as cleaning and washing was strictly forbidden. These prohibitions were sanctioned by various kinds of supernatural threats or punishments. According to north Karelian Iro Remsu, it was a great sin to do laundry on Fridays (Virtaranta 1958: 721), since Friday was a day of fast that commemorated Christ's suffering. Cleaning and washing was also prohibited on Sunday, on eves of certain holy days as well as on holy days, and during some sacred, seasonal periods.

There were two significant turning points in the annual temporal cycle: one around the darkest time of the year and the other around the lightest time of the year. A variety of restrictions on work prevailed during these liminal periods. The period between Christmas and the Epiphany, called *synnynaika* or *svätkät* (from the Russian *svatki*), was characterized by merrymaking and divinatory rites. *Synnynaika* were a sacred period when the boundary to the otherworld was assumed to be open and strict purity rules were enforced. People had to abstain from chores that involved handling dirt: 'You were not allowed to wash the floors then, do laundry, or pour out dirty water outdoors.'[6] Sources from Salmi also stressed that dirty water was not to be thrown outdoors during this period, but was to be poured out in the cowshed. Any breach of this norm would have serious consequences for the entire society. It could lead to a poor harvest or to other kinds of calamities.[7] Similarly, cleaning and washing clothes were prohibited during the corresponding liminal period (*veäntöi*) at the lightest time of the year between midsummer and St Peter's day (Lavonen 1996: 201).

Food and the Production of Time in Everyday Life

At a concrete level in everyday life, food and diet were the central symbolic markers which not only distinguished the various temporal units from one another, but also served as media in the very production and embodiment of time. Mary Douglas has shown that food and meals express meaning and structure time at a fundamental cultural level. According to her findings, the variety and quantity of food permitted on any given occasion correspond to the time of the day, the day of the week, and the festival season of the year (Douglas 1984: 15).

An analysis of the semantics of Karelian time and food terminology indeed reveals that there was an intimate connection between food, meals and time. First, the nouns *arki* and *pyhä* refer to both time and food. According to the dictionary of Karelian language, the noun *arki* denoted a non-fast period or a non-fast day. It also designated ordinary, non-fasting food (Virtaranta 1968: 66–67). Besides denoting 'holy' the noun *pyhä*, also meant (1) a fast, (2) a holy day, i.e. Sunday, which nevertheless was not a fast day, as well as (3) the Eucharist, where the central element was the communion meal (Koponen 1993: 556–557).

The intimate connection between a meal and the time of the day is seen in the meal terminology, although we must keep in mind that this terminology varied locally. Depending on the day and the season, people ate three to four meals a day. They usually had a quick snack before doing their early morning chores and ate their breakfast proper at around eight or nine o'clock. Besides denoting breakfast, *murkina* is an ellipsis for *murkinapäivä*, the quarter where the sun (*päivä*) was at breakfast time (Virtaranta 1983: 373). *Lounat* denoted both lunch, and the time of the lunch, as well as the quarter where the sun usually was at lunchtime (Virtaranta 1983: 164–165). *Iltaine*, diminutive of *ilta*, 'evening' denoted also an evening meal (Virtaranta 1968: 443, 435). Since time of the day was not measured in hours, people referred to the closest meal when defining a certain point in time. Thus, people did not say 'around noon', but 'around lunch' (Vuoristo 1983: 132). This means that by eating certain kinds of meals at certain points in the day people not only structured time but produced themselves as spatiotemporal beings.

The notions *arki* and *pyhä* structured time on an even more profound level in Orthodox Karelia. As already indicated, the lapse of time consisted of the continuous rotation of ordinary time (*arki*), fast (*pyhä*) and holy days (Sunday and holy feasts). As mentioned the weekly cycle of time was divided into ordinary weekdays (*arki*): Monday, Tuesday, Thursday and Saturday, while Wednesday and Friday were days of fast (*pyhä*), which commemorated Christ's suffering. The week ended on Sunday (*pyhäpäivä*), which commemorated the Resurrection. The annual calendric cycle was divided into corresponding temporal units. There were four longer periods of ordinary time (*arki*), followed by four fasts of different lengths. *Pyhäkeski*, the period between two long fasts, started at Christmas and lasted for seven weeks until Great Lent. The spring *arki* began at Easter ending at the beginning of the fast of the Apostles. The length of this fast varied depending on the date of Trinity (*stroittša*). After the feast of the Apostles the hay *arki* began, lasting until the two-week-long fast of the Saviour (*Spoassun pyhä*) or the Mother of God preceding Dormition. At Dormition the autumn *arki* started, which in turn ended at the beginning of the six-week-long Christmas fast (*Roštuon pyhä*). Each period of fast ushered in a religious holiday that was celebrated in honour of some event in the history of Christian salvation.

In the following passage, I will examine how women structured and produced different types of time by varying and regulating the variety and the quantity of food and how their cooking contributed to the production and embodiment of religious meaning.

The Dynamics of *Arki* and *Pyhä* Food

The continuous alternation of *arki*, fast and holy days constituted time that can be seen as one of the basic elements of the God-created sacred order. It was believed that failure to fast or observe holy days would lead to a collapse of this order, which therefore was protected by strong taboos. Breaking the fast during Lent, especially on Good Friday was considered to be an 'unpardonable' sin (Marttinen 1926: 47). In the strongly dualistic thinking which, according to Leonid Heretz, characterized pre-modern Russian vernacular religion – and as far as I can see, was also very true of Karelian popular thinking – fasting became a demonstration of one's piety and allegiance to God. Those who ate forbidden food were not only seen as defying God, they were also considered to be guilty of rejecting him and of joining forces with the devil and his legions (Heretz 1997: 72–75). Some north Karelian informants saw fasting as a prerequisite for 'getting into God's kingdom' and as a way of avoiding 'the eternal flame' (Marttinen 1926: 47). A lament text from Salmi even suggests that the dead were interrogated at the gates of heaven about whether they had fasted or not. If they had not, they were denied entry into heaven.[8] One of Martta Pelkonen's informants saw the allegedly relaxed morals of the modern age as a sign that man had given the devil unbridled power. The devil reigned and tempted people to further sin, as was clearly demonstrated by their increasing failure to observe fasts and the Sabbath.[9] The devil's supposed success undermined the sacred order that was guarded by 'the gods'.

Since the observance of fasts was believed to be crucial to one's salvation, it was women's responsibility as cooks to make sure that household members did not jeopardize their fate in the afterlife by consuming forbidden substances. The *arki–pyhä*-dichotomy compelled a detailed organization of the daily household chores. Ordinary food had to be kept apart from *pyhä* food, even the utensils used for their preparation and the bowls used for their storage were kept separate. Since meat and dairy products were banned during a fast, oils and fats became the main element in distinguishing *arki* from *pyhä* food. When cooking, women had to be constantly aware of the temporal period in order to use the right type of fat and oil. They made ordinary butter (*arkivoi*) from cream, while 'butter of fast' (*pyhävoi*) was usually made of pressed linseed (*siemenvoi*). Ordinary porridge (*argikuaššah, arkihuttu*) was boiled in milk and was served with milk and butter, while during a fast porridge (*pyhäkuaššah, pyhähuttu*) was cooked and eaten without milk and butter. Milk and butter were often replaced by fish fat or water mixed with crushed berries. Milk or/and butter could be used in baking *arki* bread, buns or pastries, while *pyhä* bread was baked and smeared with oil. Depending on the period, pastries were stuffed with an *arki* or *pyhä* filling (*-sydän*) (Pelkonen 1935: 134). Milk that could not be used during a fast was processed into 'quark milk' (*pyhämaito*), which was used after the fast (Virtaranta 1958: 231).

The women brushed *arki* pastries with butter using an *arki* feather, while *pyhä* pastries were smeared with oil using a *pyhä* feather (Pelkonen 1935: 30, 66, 111, 134, 143). *Arki* food was kept in *arki* bowls (*arkiastie*), and food of fasting, in *pyhä* bowls (*pyhäastie*).

The quantity of milk, cream, and butter used in cooking correlated to the seasons and the calendric period. Since cows usually calved in the spring and only milked well during the outdoor season, fresh milk was not always available during winter months. Women might therefore be sparing in their use of cream and butter even during an *arki* period. They would emphasize the significance of a holy day or holy feast by a lavish use of these ingredients.

Thus, women could create different types of time by using different types of fats and oils. A moderate use of butter, milk and cream was typical of an *arki* period, whereas the fast was characterized by an abstention from dairy products. During a fast butter was substituted by linseed oil, fish fat or 'berry-water'. Holy days were distinguished from fast and *arki* by a lavish use of dairy products. In the following section I will focus on the Great Lent and Easter celebrations in order to examine in greater detail, and in a wider context, how food, cooking and other household chores were used to structure and embody time and religious meanings.

Lent

The Orthodox Church saw Lent as a period of corporal and spiritual preparation for the celebration of Easter. Through the Lenten weekly days of fast, which recapitulated the events of the Passion, people became spiritually and bodily involved in Christ's suffering. This bodily involvement in suffering was accomplished by reduction of the quantity of food consumed and abstention from certain kinds of food as well as from sexual intercourse. However, in order to understand more deeply the symbolic meanings of Lenten food, we have to study it in the wider context of the annual *arki–pyhä* cycle. Great Lent was preceded by *pyhäkeski*, the period that started at Christmas and was a season of excess and merriment. *Pyhäkeski* was a popular wedding period, whereas weddings, birthday celebrations and memorial feasts for the deceased were not permitted during Great Lent or Passion Week (Valmo 1935: 259). The diet of *pyhäkeski* was characterized by a relatively large variety and quantity of food, at least in contrast to the frugal diet of Lent, which expressed self-denial and piety. The more pious a person was the harder was her/his fasting (and praying). Within the Lenten period, variations in the type and quantity of food could reflect the special religious significance of a particular day or week.

Lent implied a gradual eschewing of meat and dairy products. On certain days and weeks even fish was forbidden. Since meat was given up after meatfare (*lihapyhälasku*), the Sunday eight weeks before Easter, meat dishes dominated the meatfare day menu. Thus, the variety and quantity of meat dishes set apart the meatfare breakfast, lunch and dinner from ordinary Sunday meals.

Milkfare (*maitopyhälasku*) on the Sunday a week after meatfare was the next step in the gradual transition in the Lenten diet. The week between meatfare and milkfare – the last week of the *pyhäkeski* – was a carnival period of merriment. Only the household chores that were absolutely necessary were performed during this week (Sauhke 1971: 437). Besides excessive merrymaking and various kinds of work taboos, the diet also set this week apart from ordinary *arki* weeks as well as from Lent. Meat was already excluded from the diet, but milk products were permitted during this week even on the usual fast days, Wednesday and Friday (Sauhke 1971: 431–433). According to Martta Pelkonen's survey, pancakes and 'boiled pasties' (*keitinpiiraat*) were popular foods during this week (Pelkonen 1935: 122).

Since milkfare was the last day when milk and dairy products were consumed before Easter, the menu, apart from a variety of fish courses, quite naturally consisted of a number of milk dishes. After the feasting and merry making of 'milk week', people woke up on Clean Monday, the first day of Lent. The dances, feasts and frequent social calls, typical of *pyhäkeski* and milk week, were over. Martta Kuikka from Suojärvi has described the austere tenor of Lent:

> Lent continued and the sentiment of suffering permeated the atmosphere. Old people said their prayers, made signs of cross, urging their children to follow suit. For understandable reasons, work came to a standstill during the fast and people prepared for the reception of the Great Feast with their entire mortal frame. People socialised less, talked quietly, and stopped telling dirty jokes and making booze (*kilju*).[10]

People's behaviour was thereby reserved during Lent and various different kinds of work taboos were in force. Spinning was forbidden on Monday, Wednesday and Friday. The spinning wheel and the loom had to be covered for the night and the weft and warp had to be loosened so that the Devil could not spin or weave at night.[11]

With no fresh fish available, Lenten fare largely consisted of salted or dried fish, cereals such as gruel and porridges, bread, and different kinds of pasties. Turnips, swedes, potatoes, cabbage and black radishes, prepared in a variety of ways, were common Lenten foods. Root crops and vegetables, as well as salted or dried mushrooms and conserved berries were substituted for fish during the periods when fish was forbidden (Pelkonen 1935: 132). Lenten pastries were usually filled with fish, cabbage, or slices of turnips, swede or potato. Another popular Lenten dish was *imel* or *itu*, a porridge made of flour sweetened through fermentation, reminiscent of *mämmi* in the west. A stock of flour mixed with cold water was eaten with bread on days when fish was forbidden. It was not unusual that just bread with some salt on was served instead of a meal during a fast (Pelkonen 1935: 62, 64–65, 76).

During the first week of Great Lent fasting was quite severe, comparable to the Great Week. One of Paulaharju's informants coupled the severity of these two weeks to Christ's suffering, which had been greatest during this time. 'Because it was a precious week, it should be sanctified by piety and by refraining from excesses, i.e. enjoyments, fine clothes, etc.' Ideally, food should be restricted to bread and water.[12] The great significance of the first week was emphasized by certain work taboos. According to Martta Kuha from Olonets, doing laundry and washing floors was forbidden during the first week of Lent.[13] During the following two weeks, fasting was less severe.

The fourth week in mid Lent – the week of the Veneration of the Cross – was called in Karelian 'cross bread' week (*ristileipänetäli*), and was again a precious week when fasting was stricter and even fish was forbidden. Doing laundry and washing floors was also forbidden during this week.[14] On Thursday women baked cross bread. The ways the bread was baked as well as the ritual uses of it varied locally. A common practice seems to have been to bake three loaves of bread. Sometimes they were to be baked of three different kinds of cereals: one of barley, one of rye, and one of wheat. A cross was made on the top of loaf either of strips of dough or by imprinting an image of cross with the edge of a holy icon. Most of this bread was saved in the corner of gods, or in a bin of grain until the spring sowing and/or the day when the cattle were let out. Thus, the cross bread played an important part in fertility magic. Children also carried cross bread to their godparents.

Great or Holy Week

Great week, when Christ's suffering culminated, was again a precious week – a week of intense praying and fasting. Those who for one reason or another did not observe the whole of Lent at least fasted during this week. People partook in Christ's suffering by consuming a minimum of food and by refraining from all sorts of joy: 'People tried to be sorrowful because Christ had suffered.' Martta Kuikka writes that people made their confession and took to the Eucharist either before or during Holy Week.[15]

The services of this week recapitulated the events of the Passion. The Great Week started on Palm Sunday, which was a precious holy day, in Karelia also known as Birching Sunday (*virpoipyhä* < *ru. verbnoe voskresenie*). Great Thursday or Holy Thursday was the day of purification and the day of the most thorough cleaning of the whole year. Every corner of the house was washed and cleaned. Dirty and worn out clothes were disposed of and, if possible, replaced by new clothes (Vilkuna 1978: 80–81). In addition, people purified themselves by bathing.

Pasties for Great Thursday had to be baked on Wednesday since there was a ban on pasty baking on Great Thursday. When the pasties were ready the rolling pins were hidden and were taken out again on Easter eve for baking Easter pasties.

On Great Friday or Good Friday – the day of the Crucifixion – suffering reached its peak. People shared in Christ's passion by praying intensely, and by refraining from all kinds of merriment. Work, such as spinning, grinding, mashing, washing, bathing and using an axe was prohibited.[16] According to the old church tradition, the ideal was a complete fast on Great Friday. It seems that people were familiar with this ideal: 'On Great Friday nothing was to be eaten the whole day.'[17] 'Nobody should eat on Good Friday, except children under three years.'[18] In practice the degree of fasting was related to each individual's degree of piety. Old people, especially women, fasted harder: 'Old people ate only once – some didn't eat at all. Neither my late granny nor my mother ate anything.'[19]

The Great Day and Easter Week

Easter saw a drastic shift from the austere atmosphere of suffering into one of joyful celebration of the Resurrection. After seven long weeks of self-denial, the fast was broken on Easter morning. The diet distinguished Easter week from ordinary *arki* weeks in several ways. First of all, no weekly fast days were observed. Second, the variety and the quantity of food made this week exceptional. People indulged themselves as a compensation for the long fast: 'On Easter day you have to eat seven times for the fast of seven weeks.'[20]

Cooking and baking for a holy day were distinguished from ordinary, everyday cooking and baking by ritualization. First, sacred cooking was distinguished from ordinary cooking by the point of time at which it was to be done. Christmas baking was done in the morning after midnight mass, while Easter baking had to be finished on Easter Eve, since work was prohibited on the Easter day. 'Baking on Easter was a sin (*reähkä*)' (Virtaranta 1958: 220). Second, a small change in the working routines sufficed to distinguish ordinary, everyday cooking from sacred cooking and even minute changes in routine could distinguish the cooking for different holy feasts from each other. The prohibition on using a rolling pin distinguished Easter baking from baking for other holy days. This ban also limited the choice of pasties that were standard festive food in Karelia. Women baked pasties for Easter that did not need rolling (Virtaranta 1958: 587–588). A slight difference in baking method also distinguished the pasty baked for the ancestors from that baked for the living. The pasty that was baked for the commemoration of the dead was rolled anticlockwise unlike the ordinary pasty that was rolled clockwise. During the cooking process, the food reserved for the dead was kept apart from the food intended for the living (Pelkonen 1935: 141).

The prohibition on using a rolling pin was grounded in legends that referred to Christ's suffering or described the Virgin Mary's food preparations on Easter morning. According to a legend from Salmi, neither sieves nor rolling pins were used at Easter because they were claimed to have been the very instruments with which Christ had been tormented.[21] Mari Kyyrönen from North of Karelia explained the prohibition on rolling *sultšina* pasties and boiling meat at Easter with a reference to the Virgin Mary. Mary, whose son according to a well-known legend went missing, had been cooking hazel hen and baking pasties on Easter morning, when, all of the sudden, the hazel hen flew out of the cooking pot. The rolling pin she was holding in her hand broke:

> That's why we were not allowed to roll *sultšinas* on Easter day. Old people said that it was a sin. Cooking meat was also prohibited on that day, Easter day. That was the rule! (Virtaranta 1958: 220–221)

In Vieljärvi, Olonets, women referred to Mary's interrupted baking on Easter morning, when explaining why they baked rolls for Easter instead of pasties.[22]

Even though the variety and order of dishes was pretty much the same at all feasts, it seems that each religious feast had some characteristic course that distinguished it from others. Easter, the most important holiday in the Orthodox calendar, was set apart from other holidays by the exceptional variety of dishes and quantity of food. Women baked the best pasties for Easter. The eggs, milk and cream that women had stored away during Lent were important ingredients in the preparation of Easter delicacies. In some areas, the fast was broken by eating eggs, while in some other areas it was broken by eating a kind of cheese cake (*siiroa*), which was a typical Easter dish. According to Martta Pelkonen's study, men slaughtered a fatted calf or sheep before Christmas and Easter, sometimes even a cow (Pelkonen 1935: 233–234).

The food for Easter day was carried to a church or a chapel in order to be blessed by a priest or a keeper of the chapel. Jevdokia Kunsin says that in pre-Soviet times, the *arki* food was not tasted before it had been blessed with holy incense.[23] On the Isle of Mantši, in Ladoga, women used to carry their porridge pots to the chapel before sunrise on Easter morning. The keeper of the chapel or the priest blessed the pots and purified them with holy smoke. After the food was blessed women offered porridge to each other to taste.[24] The cheese cakes mentioned above were taken to the church or chapel where they were first blessed and then offered to people who had gathered by the church. Boys brought with them small spade-shaped wooden scoops for shovelling the cake in their mouths (Virtaranta 1958: 232–233).[25] After the food had been blessed it was carried back home, where the family celebration started.

Household Work and the Creation of Time

As Nancy Munn has pointed out, 'time is not merely "lived", but "constructed" in the living' (Munn 1992: 109). Women's domestic activities, mainly cooking and cleaning, contributed to the production of space-time as well as to the embodiment of religious meaning. As we have seen, cleaning functioned as a rite marking the transition from ordinary to sacred time and space. Sacred time in turn was marked by bans on cleaning and washing. During Lent, work taboos in various ways underlined the religious significance of certain days and weeks.

Food and cooking contributed in a fundamental way to the construction of the three temporal units: *arki*, fast and holy day. In a very concrete way, food and diet not only distinguished the various temporal units from each other, but also served as media in the production and embodiment of time. Food and meals structured time at a very basic cultural level. The varieties and quantity of food corresponded to the time of day, the day of the week, and the season of the year. Different types of fats and oils, as well as their varying quantities, correlated to different categories of time, and contributed to the concretization of time. A moderate use of butter, milk and cream was typical of an *arki* period, whereas dairy products were forbidden during a fast, when they were substituted by linseed oil, fish fat and 'berry-water'. Holy days were characterized by a lavish use of dairy products.

The type and quantity of food also underlined the religious significance and meaning of certain periods of time. Lent incurred a gradual abstaining from meat and dairy products, and certain significant days of fast were distinguished from the less significant days by stricter food restrictions. The ritualization of cooking routines distinguished ordinary cooking from cooking for holy days. The holy feasts were differentiated from ordinary days and days of fast by the greater variety and amount of food.

Even though the church calendar provided the framework for Karelian time reckoning and the theological meaning of the fasts and feasts, it was women who, through their household work, concretized these different entities of time and turned the ideas advocated by the clergy into practice by accommodating them into the local ecological, socioeconomical, and cultural context. Finally, women did not only transform the official tradition into a vernacular Christian tradition, but also produced completely new traditions by intertwining these practises with local indigenous traditions.

Acknowledgement

I thank the Ellen Key Foundation for a grant that allowed me to finish this article in a peaceful and highly inspiring milieu at the Ellen Key Strand in Ödeshög, Sweden.

Notes

1. Tulomajärvi, Kolatselkä, Helmi Helminen < Akim Lomojov, b. 1874; KRA 1944: 3795.
2. Tulemajärvi, Helminen < Solomanida Petrov, b. 1862; KRA 1944: 3452.
3. Suistamo: Martti Haavio KRA 1935: 2032.
4. Suistamo: Martti Haavio KRA 1935: 274.
5. Suistamo: Martti Haavio KRA 1935: 2032.
6. Salmi: Ulla Mannonen < Martta Kuha 50 yrs; KRA 1936: 138. Salmi: Maija Juvas KRA 1935 (1938): 297.
7. Salmi: Ulla Mannonen < Martta Kuha 50 yrs; KRA 1936: 138. Salmi: Maija Juvas KRA 1935 (1938): 297.
8. Salmi Miinala: Martti Haavio < Jelena Kovero; KRA 1934: 1629.
9. Salmi, Tulema: Pelkonen Martta < Tatjana 'Höt't'i, neé. 'Jarońe'; KRA (1935), 1936: 271.
10. Suistamo: Martta Kuikka (b. 1921); KRA KJ 34: 14981, p. 4, 1957.
11. Vuonninen Samuli Paulaharju KRA 1932: 18300, 18301.
12. Vuonninen: Samuli Paulaharju KRA 1932: 18239.
13. Salmi: Ulla Mannonen < Martta Kuha, 50 yrs; KRA 1938: 11078.
14. Salmi: Ulla Mannonen < Martta Kuha, 50 yrs; KRA 1938: 11078.
15. Suistamo: Martta Kuikka (b. 1921); KRA KJ 34: 14981, p. 5, 1957.
16. Vuonninen: Samuli Paulaharju KRA 1915: 18249.
17. Salmi: H. T. Lehmusto KRA 1938: 199.
18. Vuonninen: Samuli Paulaharju KRA 1915: 18240.
19. Vuonninen: Samuli Paulaharju KRA 1915: 18249.
20. Ilomantsi, I. Manninen KRA 1916: 742.
21. Salmi: Pekka Pohjanvalo KRA 1936: 51.
22. Vieljärvi: A. Railonsala < Tarja Bottarev; KRA 1947: 3595.
23. Tulemajärvi, Haroila village: Helmi Helminen < Jevdokia Kunsin, b. 1860; KRA 1944: 3463.
24. Salmi, Mantši: Eino Toiviainen KRA KRK 154: 243.
25. Tulomajärvi, Helmi Helminen < Jogorov, Marfa, b. 1873; KRA 1944: 3223.

Archive Materials

KRA = Manuscripts at the Finnish Literature Society Folklore Archives, Helsinki.

Juvas, Maija (1938) *Kuolemaan liittyviä tapoja, itkuja ja uskomuksia.* Kerätty v. 1935 Katri Markströmiltä (56 v., kotoisin Tulemajärveltä, muuttanut aikaisin Salmiin).

Marttinen, Santtu (1926) *Uskonnollisia taikaluuloja Vienan Karjalasta*. IV, b-osa.
Paulaharju, Samuli: Praasnikkoja ym. merkkipäiviä. Vuonninen (Oulu) (1932) 18238–18406.
Pelkonen, Martta (1935) *Kansatieteellinen katsaus Salmin pitäjän vanhaan kansanomaiseen ruokatalouteen ja Salmin murteen ruokataloussanasto*. E126.

References

Douglas, M. (1984) Standard social uses of food: Introduction. In M. Douglas (ed.) *Food in the Social Order: Studies of Food and Festivities in Three American Communities*, 1–39. New York: Russell Sage Foundation.

Dubisch, J. (1983) Greek women: Sacred or profane. *Journal of Modern Greek Studies. Women and Men in Greece: A Society in Transition,* 1 (1): 185–202.

Dubisch, J. (1991) Gender, kinship, and religion: 'Reconstructing' the anthropology of Greece. In P. Loizos and E. Papataxiarchis (eds) *Contested Identities: Gender and Kinship in Modern Greece,* 29–46. Princeton, NJ: Princeton University Press.

Heretz, L. (1997) The practice and significance of fasting in Russian peasant culture at the turn of the century. In M. Glants and J. Toomre (eds) *Food in Russian History and Culture,* 67–80. Bloomington and Indianapolis, IN: Indiana University Press.

Keinänen, M.-L. (2002) Religious ritual contested: Anti-religious activities and women's ritual practice in rural Soviet-Karelia. In T. Ahlbäck (ed.) *Ritualistics,* 92–117. Turku: Donner Institute for Research in Religious and Cultural History.

Keinänen, M.-L. (2003) *Creating Bodies. Childbirth Practices in Pre-modern Karelia*. Stockholm: Stockholm University.

Keinänen, M-L. (2010) Home, the sacred order and domestic chores in premodern Russian Orthodox Karelia. In Keinänen, M.-L. (ed.) *Perspectives on Women's Everyday Religion,* 119–155. Stockholm Studies in Comparative Religion 35: Stockholm University.

Koponen, R. (ed.) (1993) *Karjalan kielen sanakirja* 4. Helsinki: Suomalais-Ugrilainen Seura.

Lavonen, N. (1996) Havaintoja hautajaisrituaalista Aunuksen Karjalassa. In Pekka Hakamies (ed.) *Näkökulmia karjalaiseen perinteeseen,* 229–253. Helsinki: Suomalaisen Kirjallisuuden Seura.

Moore, H. L. (1995 [1988]) *Feminism and Anthropology*. Cambridge: Polity Press.

Munn, N. D. (1992) The cultural anthropology of time: A critical essay. *Annual Review of Anthropology* 21: 93–13.

Paulaharju, S. (1983) *Karjalainen talo.* Helsinki: Suomalainen Kirjallisuuden Seura.

Paulaharju, S. (1995 [1924]) *Syntymä, lapsuus ja kuolema.* Kansanelämän kuvauksia 41. Helsinki: Suomalaisen Kirjallisuuden Seura.

Sallinen-Gimpl, P. (1994) *Siirtokarjalainen identiteetti ja kulttuurien kohtaaminen.* Kansatieteellinen arkisto 40. Helsinki: Suomen Muinaismuistoyhdistys.

Sauhke, N. (1971) *Karjalan praašniekat.* Jyväskylä: K. J. Gummerus. Osakeyhtiön Kirjapaino.

Starr Sered, S. (1992) *Women as Ritual Experts: The Religious Lives of Elderly Jewish Women in Jerusalem.* New York and Oxford: Oxford University Press.

Stark-Arola, L. (2001) Women and food in rural-traditional Finland. Social and symbolic dimensions. *Elore* 2. Online http://cc.joensuu.fi/~loristi/2_01/sta201.html [accessed January 17, 2011]

Taulamo, S. (1985) *Vie sinne mun kaihoni. Aunuksen Karjalassa 1941–1944.* Helsinki: Kirjayhtymä.

Valmo N. (1935) *Suomen Ortodoksinen Arkkipiispakunta. Kokoelma voimassaolevia säännöksiä Suomen Ortodoksisesta Arkkipiispakunnasta.* Helsinki.

Vilkuna, K. (1978) Vuotuinen ajantieto. *Vanhoista merkkipäivistä sekä kansanomaisesta talous- ja sääkalenterista enteisiin.* Helsinki: Otava.

Virtaranta, P. (1958) *Vienan kansa muistelee.* Porvoo and Helsinki: Werner Söderström Osakeyhtiö.

Virtaranta, P. (ed.) (1968) *Karjalan kielen sanakirja 1.* Helsinki: Suomalais-Ugrilainen Seura.

Virtaranta, P. (ed.) (1983) *Karjalan kielen sanakirja 3.* Helsinki: Suomalais-Ugrilainen Seura.

Vuoristo, V. (1983) *Ikävä omia maita. Muisteluksia vanhasta Vienan-Karjalasta.* Helsinki: Otava.

How to Make a Shrine with Your Own Hands: Local Holy Places and Vernacular Religion in Russia

Alexander Panchenko[*]

During the last decades of the twentieth century, the study of popular religious cultures in ethnology, folkloristics and historical anthropology underwent serious changes related to the crisis of dogmatic, institutional and systematic explanations of religious folklife. The changes are particularly obvious in the rejection of the residualistic 'two-tiered model' (as Peter Brown has called it) (Brown 1981) which presumes opposition between 'Christianity' and 'paganism', 'official' and 'folk' religion, 'religion' and 'magic' and so on. Furthermore, it has appeared that borderlines between various confessions and denominations, which usually play an important role in constructing and maintaining religious identity, do not impede the diffusion and interaction of practical forms of everyday religious activity. Today, folklorists and ethnologists prefer to discuss 'vernacular' (Primiano 1995: 37–56) or 'local' (Christian 1981) religions or 'religious praxis' (Panchenko 2002), on the one hand, and norms, institutions and other forms of representation and legitimization of power and social authority in the religious domain, on the other. As to the methodological strategies that dominate in the study of religious phenomena in contemporary folkloristics and ethnology, they, as a rule, proceed either from various sociological theories and approaches (elaborated by Émile Durkheim, Victor Turner, Mary Douglas et al.) or from contemporary cognitive anthropology (for example Boyer 1999: 53–72; 2001). Of course, the range of contemporary methods and explanatory modes in the study of vernacular religion is not limited by sociological and cognitive

* Alexander Panchenko is Chair of the Centre for Literary Theory and Interdisciplinary Research, Institute of Russian Literature, Russian Academy of Sciences; Director of the Centre for Anthropology of Religion, European University of St Petersburg; and Director of the Program for Sociology and Anthropology, Faculty of Liberal Arts and Sciences, St Petersburg State University, Russia.

approaches. However, these two tendencies, in my opinion, appear to be not only the most influential but also the most successful as applied to the study of religious folklife throughout various societies and cultures.

From a certain point of view, social and cognitive interpretations in the anthropology of religion may seem to contradict each other. The cognitive approach tends to minimize the social background of a certain person or community's everyday religious life. As Veikko Anttonen points out:

> Instead of posing questions on the meaning of religion to individuals and social groups, cognitive scholars study the mental operations of human beings and explain religious representations on the basis of empirical evidence of regularities in thinking and behaviour in cultures the world over. In cognitive approaches scholars are interested in clarifying how people acquire and represent the contents of supernatural agents and how they transmit them by specific religious categories and in specific forms of actions such as in religious rituals. ... Cognitive scholars study the role the human mind and its evolved cognitive machinery plays in the construction of supernatural repertoires. (Anttonen 2003: 295–296)

As to social anthropologists, they try to reduce the variety of religious phenomena to a number of models of social relations and organization. Cognitive anthropology provides a valuable and effective instrument for the analysis and understanding of the origins and basic machinery of religious practice and its representation in various cultures and societies – even without touching on the psychological or ontological explanatory models that consider personal religious experience as the principal source of individual and group religious activity. However, when we turn to immediate forms of vernacular religion observed by ethnologists, folklorists or historical anthropologists, we cannot avoid social and historical explanations. In fact, every local cult or ritual or sacred narrative should be viewed as both result and object of competition between various individuals and social groups, agents of power, discourses and so on. Thus far, specialists in folklore ethnology and historical anthropology have tried to combine both cognitive and social approaches to the study of practical forms of religious life.

In this context, I would like to discuss the problem of the symbolic, ritual and narrative resources that allow a social group or a local community to consider certain material objects to be sacred. The data for my analysis are borrowed mainly from Russian rural culture of the late twentieth- to early twenty-first centuries. First of all, it is necessary to make some preliminary remarks on the historical context of the problem. In fact, we do not have enough reliable sources to discuss general forms and patterns of vernacular religion in Russia before the first decades of the eighteenth century. Certain phenomena of the religious folklife of the Eastern Slavs before Peter the Great are well known and more or less explicable, but a vast part of the religious culture of 'the silent majority' (to use the wording of Aaron Gurevitch (1990)) seems to be missing in written sources related to both Kievan Russia and Muscovy.

The whole picture of Russian religious life changed dramatically after the seventeenth-century schism and the Church reform of Peter the Great. The latter, as contemporary Russian historian Alexander Lavrov argues, 'was intended to solve the problems which in the West were "divided" between the Reformation, the Counter-Reformation and the Enlightenment' (Lavrov 2000: 445). The main goal of the reform which, to some extent, was inspired by the Counter-Reformation 'struggle against superstitions' in Western Europe was to standardize piety and local religious practice amongst laymen and parish clergy. Although the most notable phenomena of Russian religious folklife of the late seventeenth/early eighteenth century (including worshipping of 'holy fools' (*yurodivye*) and certain miraculous icons along with canonization of new saints) were persecuted and suppressed during Peter's reign, his legislation was put into practice more or less consistently only 30 years later, during the process which Gregory Freeze has labelled the 'institutionalisation of piety'. The goal of the reform was 'to make the Church ... an efficient organisation capable of overseeing and regulating religious life' (Freeze 1998: 212). One of the most significant features of the process was an attempt to extend bishops' power:

> from the diocesan capital to the parish. One essential step was to create a new lower-echelon office, that of *blagochinnyi* ('superintendent'). In effect, the bishops replaced the elective clerical 'elder' with the superintendent appointed from above; the latter was to concentrate specifically on upholding orthodoxy and good order... in the ten or fifteen parishes under his wardship. Moreover, by the late eighteenth century, the bishop usurped the right to select and remove priests (previously the prerogative of the parish), significantly enhancing his power over parochial clergy and, indirectly, the parish itself. Finally,

by the early nineteenth century, the Church mandated the election of a lay 'church elder' (*tserkovnyi starosta*) in order to tighten diocesan control over parish funds. (Freeze 1998: 212)

However, the task of standardizing and overseeing everyday religious life in the parish was not simple. As Freeze argues:

Russian Orthodoxy was Russian Heterodoxy – an aggregate of local Orthodoxies, each with its own cults, rituals and customs. Religion, like other dimensions of life, was intensely particularistic, with kaleidoscopic variations from one parish to the next, not to mention broad regional differences. (Freeze 1998: 213)

Apart from an intensive struggle against newly recognized 'miracle-working' icons and unofficial saints, the principal goal of the Church authorities was 'to "confine the sacred" – temporally and spatially – within the ecclesiastical domain' (Freeze 1998: 221). One of the main methods here 'was to confine the sacraments to ecclesiastical territory by requiring that such rites be performed *only* in the parish church' (Freeze 1998: 222). Bishops and superintendents attempted to combat the 'superstitious' cults of holy springs and stones, miracle-working icons outside churches and monasteries, rituals performed in village chapels and so on. Parish clerics supporting such forms of religious activity were punished. To cite only one example, a typical situation took place in Setumaa, south-eastern Estonia, inhabited by the Orthodox group known as the Setu or *poluvertsy* (half-believers), in the 1780s. A local holy place existed (perhaps it was part of medieval cemetery) near the village of Saatse (Russian: *Zacheren'e*). It included a chapel, the stump of a sacred pine tree and a venerated stone cross. On the annual feast of *Il'inskaya Pyatnitca* (the Friday before St Elijah's Day), the worshippers of the shrine came to the place, brought textiles made *ex voto*, and carried the cross around the chapel. In 1784, local authorities prohibited the ritual and the cross was transferred to the parish church (Pskovskie gubernskie vedomosti *1864, No. 24, 19.07*). However, the practice of ritual carrying of the worshipped cross (it was now carried around the church) still existed a century later. It was observed and described by ethnographer Georg Trusman in the 1880s (Trusman 1890: 43).

By and large, the attempts to institutionalize rural piety in the second half of the eighteenth century appeared to be unsuccessful. At the same time, they led to the expulsion of vernacular religious practices and beliefs from the ecclesiastical domain. Rural cults relating to local holy places, unofficial saints and miracle-working icons did not disappear, rather they were moved away from the control of both secular and spiritual authorities. Although, during the next century, both higher priests and parish clergy tried to accommodate popular piety and restore official control of local shrines in the countryside, the latter often remained unofficial and uncontrolled.

The next dramatic change of Russian religious life began soon after 1917. Soviet authorities tried to combat both official Orthodox institutions (arresting and executing higher priests and parish priests, closing and ruining churches in cities, towns and villages) and popular piety (prohibiting local feasts, desecrating or destroying holy places and the relics of saints, confiscating miracle-working icons). However, the results of these activities were, to some extent, similar to those of the eighteenth-century campaign against superstitions. Again, vernacular religious practices became even more unofficial and varied. The lack of parish churches made informal and spontaneous religious practice the principal domain of rural religious life. In that way, the analysis of rural religious practice in Russia during the second half of the twentieth century allows observation of certain specific features of vernacular religion in peasant societies.

Observation of various types of local sacred places in northern Russia in the late nineteenth and early twentieth centuries allows us to talk about the wide variety of different shrines. Of course, there are numerous possible methods for their classification. In this paper, however, I would like to divide local shrines according to their social status and function. From this point of view, it is possible to single out, albeit more or less schematically, three types of shrine: (1) *individual* or *spontaneous*; (2) *communal*; and (3) *official*. What does this classification mean?

The elementary forms of local cults of holy places can be observed within some vernacular religious traditions in the Russian countryside where family and even individual shrines exist (or at least existed), which can either disappear or not after their worshipper's (worshippers') death(s). It is also possible to use the term spontaneous shrine, as proposed by Jack Santino in relation to contemporary unofficial commemorative sites in the USA (Santino 2004: 363–372).

Usually, an *individual* shrine is a separate point on the landscape (a tree, a spring, a stone, etc.) which for certain reason becomes an object of worship by an individual or a family. Stories about such holy places often tell of a dream or a vision demanding that a person makes a certain artefact *ex voto* (it may be a towel or a handmade wooden cross) and brings it to certain place. In north-western Russia, both the artefact and the ritual activity are called *zavet* or *obet* ('a vow'). Sometimes an individual or a family has a dream or repetitious dreams about a certain icon that must be placed at a certain place in the wilderness or in a special chapel to be built for this purpose. In some stories the need for the establishment of an individual shrine is explained by a certain crisis in the family: anxiety about missing or dead relatives, economic misfortunes, and so on. However, the demand for *zavet* may also be described as an amotivational order from a sacred agent or the transcendental world in general.

To illustrate these observations, I would like to recite a part of an interview recorded in 1998 with a 65-year-old peasant woman living in the eastern part of Novgorod district:

> Well, I don't know what did she dream about. Well, it was a towel. And after that, when they went berry picking, they said: 'This is an embroidered towel! How did it get here?' It dangled on a pine-tree. Well, it was brought there by mother Irina.
> *There are such dreams, then?*
> Yes, you dream about such a place, that you must do this. I had such a dream, although I did not obey it. My own dream.
> *And what did you dream about?*
> I dreamt that too, that I was praying in Fedovo, Moshenskoi [region]. Looking at the sun, I was praying there. And then ... I was looking for people or something, I turned around and I saw a fence, it was behind me. And I awakened. I awakened and said: 'Well, this is something like this. It demands a *zavet* or something'.
> *But who demands this?*
> Oh, I don't know, of course. (Panchenko 2002: 87)

I have already mentioned that individual or spontaneous shrines can disappear after (or even before) their worshippers' deaths. More often, however, such holy places soon become objects of worship for whole rural communities or groups of communities. Thus they become *communal* and meet the needs of larger groups of people. Usually, communal shrines provide various means of 'religious consumption': water from a venerated spring or well, the bark of a sacred tree, sand from a holy place, all could be used for healing purposes, for protection from sorcery and witchcraft, and so on. Sometimes a shrine is created as initially communal, although the demand to establish it is usually received by an individual. The process of communalization could be illustrated by another interview recorded in the western part of Novgorod district in 2003. According to this story, a man living in a village had a repetitious dream that he had to build a chapel and place there an icon of Our Lady Kazanskaya (presumably this was one of the icons in his house). Finally the chapel was built and came to be worshipped by people who lived in a particular part of the village:

Figure 1: Wooden cross at the site of the former chapel of Our Lady Kazanskaya. Meniusha village, Novgorod region (photograph by Alexander Panchenko 2002).

And there is another sacred place there, near the power-saw bench?
I do not know what the sacred [place] there was. But our neighbour – I lived there in the middle of the village – had a dream that he had to build a hut … a chapel. At first, he did not tell anybody about that, but then he told the priest that a man came to him [in his dreams] and asked persistently to build a chapel. The priest answered: 'Build something'. There are various kinds of chapel, there are various kinds of wood. Then he has built it and a lot of people came there. … Some rich people lived on this side near the power-saw bench. And they decided to build [a bigger chapel] a six by six square. And I remember it. It was planked from every quarter – on this side, on that side – the doors were glass, nobody did any harm to it. And there was [an icon of] Our Lady Kazanskaya. She was painted in white – this icon.[1]

After a holy place comes to communal possession, its symbolic meaning becomes more complicated and reflected in a wide range of narratives and ritual practices. Even at this level, the place can be a matter of competition between various families and/or ritual specialists. Sometimes in such cases a community or a group of communities delegates ritual authority to an individual (usually a marginal man or woman with an especially religious reputation), and therefore both rituals and narratives relating to the shrine can differ greatly within the same community. The types of competition can vary from concurrence of various plots or motifs of narratives (both memorates and fabulates) and other forms of ritual behaviour related to a certain shrine, to contradiction of belief and disbelief narratives, worship and sacrilege. It should be stressed that sacrilegious behaviour often appears to be an integral part of such local cults and can function as a creative power: it produces new narratives and ritual prescriptions, delineates and supports boundaries between the pure and impure, sacred and profane. The organized sacrilege conducted in Russian villages by local Komsomol and Communist Party members during the antireligious campaigns in the late 1920s–1930s, and in the 1960s, did not succeed in exterminating local shrines and, in my opinion, even contributed to popularization of a number of these cults. In fact, it gave origin to numerous narratives, still widespread in the Russian countryside, about the divine punishment of those who had performed sacrilege (for example Dobrovol´skaya 1999: 500–512; Shtyrkov 2006: 208–231). The situation becomes even more complicated when a local cult is recognized, approved and accommodated by Church officials. Of course, each *official* shrine is worshipped in many different vernacular ways, in spite of all attempts by church and secular authorities to unify and standardize either rituals or narratives relating to the holy place or object. What is more important, for the layman, is that such shrines represent not only sacred and supernatural agents or forces, but also the agents of official power – the state and the Church. In my opinion, this peculiarity radically changes peasants' attitudes to the shrines of this type (Stark 2002: 157–171).

However, in the following discussion, I will dwell on the first two types of local holy places in rural Russia. Comparison of the peasants' stories about the establishment of shrines of both types shows that folk narratives relating to individual or spontaneous shrines usually do not include any explicit motives of conflict between sacred agents or powers and laymen. Either a sacred personage demands that a new holy place is established, or a layman vows to make a *zavet* and to leave it at a certain place. Either way the situation presumes more or less peaceful dialogue between sacred and profane parties. On the contrary, stories about communal shrines often tell of conflicts and violence. A venerated icon, found on a tree or in a spring does not want to stay in a village and returns to its place in the wilderness. The same could occur with worshipped stones: peasants try to remove such a stone to their village, but on the way it becomes so heavy that even three horses are not able to move a cart with the stone. Then the peasants decide to return the stone to its place. When a certain old man discovers a stone cross on his field he decides to bring it home and put it in his sauna. He does this and, accidentally, breaks off a part of the cross. After this, the old man loses one ear, and a voice in a dream warns him that he must immediately return the cross to its place. Thus the community understands that the cross is sacred and begins to worship it. When St Paraskeva or the Mother of God appears in a certain place, a shepherd or a group of children tries to hit her. However, the disappearance of the sacred personage and various miraculous signs (for example, a whip turning into stone) show that the place is sacred and must be worshipped (see also Panchenko 1998).

It is possible to ask in this context whether the motives of conflict and violence in folk narratives about communal shrines are related to the very process of setting apart a sacred site and creating a boundary between sacred and profane, which inevitably involves a conflict pattern; or whether it reflects actual social conflicts and concurrence, arising as a result of communal use of a shrine? In my opinion, the second point of view is more reliable, although the modes of representation and symbolization of the conflicts are obviously related to basic characteristic features of the idea of the sacred. At the same time, certain legends exist about local shrines in which the violence is represented as the basic source of sacredness. The most striking example is a story about two saints – Ioann and Iakov Menushskie, also from Novgorod district – whose cult probably arose in the seventeenth century. According to the legend, they were children – three and five years old – who lived in a village not far from Novgorod. Once, when their parents left home, the older brother accidentally killed the younger, hid in an oven and collapsed there. The brothers were buried in the parish cemetery, but then their coffins miraculously appeared at a lake in the wilderness. Hunters who had discovered the coffins had a dream that the children were to be buried in a certain place not far from the lake. The lake and the grave of Ioann and Iakov

Figure 2: St Ioann and St Iakov, late nineteenth-century icon. Meniusha village, Novgorod region (photograph by Alexander Panchenko, private collection).

Figure 3: St Ioann killing St Iakov, early nineteenth-century icon detail. Medved' village, Novgorod region, local Orthodox church (photograph by Alexander Panchenko).

have become sacred places. Both shrines are still very popular among both local believers and pilgrims from Novgorod and St Petersburg (Panchenko 2005; Panchenko 2006: 211–235).

The history of the cult might be treated as quite specific, but not unique. Russian hagiography of the sixteenth and seventeenth centuries includes more than a dozen similar saints venerated either locally or everywhere who are known in contemporary scholarship as 'saints without vitae', 'anonymous saints', or 'saints from sepulchers' (Shtyrkov 2001: 130–155; Levin 2003: 81–103; Romodanovskaya 2005: 143–159). More important, in the course of the present analysis, is the first part of the legend that determines the specific character of its plot. The only parallel to the story of tragic death of the saint brothers in east Slavic folklore known to me is the Ukrainian story published by Piotr Chubinski in his collection *Malorusskie skazki* ('Ukrainian folktales') (Chubinski 1878: 557), published under the title 'An Oversight'. In the index of east Slavic folktales (Barag *et al.* 1978), the story is listed under 939B* ('Family Tragedy'), and the authors

Figure 4: Pilgrimage to the lake of St Ioann and St Iakov (State Archives of the Novgorod region, 1965).

of the index point to the only variant, the text from the collection by Chubinski. In fact, the story about the oversight is quite similar to the first part of the tale about the saints of Meniusha. A peasant slaughters a ram and goes away from home. His wife leaves the house as well. The older son, imitating his father, kills the youngest laying in the cradle and then hides himself in the stove. 'The mother returned and did not look at the cradle; instead, she lit the stove and the boy who was sitting there suffocated and fell into the room with the burning firewood. So she saw that the older boy had suffocated and the younger lay in the cradle knifed.' However, this story does not have any religious connotations and goes on with more tragic deaths. When the husband returns home he supposes that it is his wife who has killed the children, so he strikes her with an axe and then hangs himself.

A literary representation of the theme can be found in a story called 'A Bitter Lot' (*Gor'kaia uchast*) (1789) by Mikhail Chulkov, a Russian writer of the late eighteenth century. However, as has already been suggested by Felix Oinas, Chulkov probably used some Western sources for his story, and it is not impossible that he recalled a picture series of this tale that he had previously seen, and not the text itself, since he made some serious mistakes in the structure of the plot (Oinas 1978: 582–583). Finally, another literary version of the tale is a short story called 'The Little Lamb' (*Baranchik*) (1898) by Fiodor Sologub (see Panchenko 2009). Although the basic source for Sologub's story was a newspaper article reporting an accident that allegedly took place in Orel province in 1895 (but in fact elaborating the same folklore theme), the writer was also undoubtedly aware of the cult of Ioann and Iakov of Meniusha. Certain details of the story allow us to suppose that the story was also influenced by the so-called 'ram festivals' celebrated in Russian and Finno-Ugric villages of Karelia and Northern Russia. These festivals were usually supposed to protect cattle against sickness and bears or wolves and included ritual sacrifice of rams or bulls. It is important that Sologub implied a direct connection between the Tale of Ioann and Iakov and the *topoi* of sacrifice, the latter having no explications in the tale.

As I have already mentioned, the authors of the index of east Slavic folktales, who did not know about the cult of Ioann and Iakov, reserved a separate cluster, 939B*, for the story from the collection by Chubinski. It was, however a mistake, since European folklore includes a sufficient number of versions of this theme, listed in the tale type index by Antti Aarne and Stith Thompson under 2401 ('The Children Play at Hog-Killing'; the number in the revised version of the index by Hans-Jörg Uther is 1343*) (Uther 2004: 145–146). It is 'often presented not as a folktale but as a report of actual events that took place recently in this or that town' (Hansen 2002: 72; see also Oinas 1978: 580–583). Two versions of the tale ('How Children Played Butcher with Each Other') were included in the first edition of the Grimm brothers' *Kinder- und Hausmärchen* (1812). However, they were dropped in the 1819 edition as being unsuitable for children, although Wilhelm Grimm, who allegedly heard the story in his youth from his mother, claimed later that it had 'taught him an important lesson about caution and restraint' (Richter 1986: 1–11; Tatar 2003: 180–181, 246–247).

The first written version of the theme can be found in *Varia Historia* (XIII 2: 'How Macareus was Punished for Cruelty') by Claudius Aelian (late second to early third centuries CE). It is noteworthy that his story does not talk about children playing butcher, as in the later texts from Western Europe, but reports an imitation of sacrifice. An Arabic version of the theme, dating to the early fourteenth century, also bears some religious connotations. It tells of a man who 'slaughtered a sheep and invited Mohammed to dine with him. One of the host's two small children had witnessed the slaughtering of the animal and, wishing to show his little brother what happened, cut off his brother's head. As his mother rushed to the scene, the boy ran away in fear, falling into the bake-oven where he perished' (Hansen 2002: 80). Finally, the Sicilian folk ballad *La Donna di Calatafimi* tells about a mother of two children who went to the church after kneading dough. When she left, 'the foolish older brother took a knife and slit the infant's throat. When blood gushed out the frightened boy hid himself in a baking oven, where he fell asleep. The mother came home, quickly placed some brush-wood in the oven and made a fire. Presently she found one child dead in the cradle, the other burned in the oven. The father, thinking his wife had killed the children, grabbed the knife and killed her' (Hansen 2002: 80).

Proceeding from the variants of the young slayer's fate, William F. Hansen suggests that the tale has three subtypes. In Subtype A, the cumulative chain of deaths is extended to the maximum, and the fratricidal boy perishes by his mother's hand; she kills him in a burst of anger, while the youngest child drowns in his bath. 'In Subtype B, after slaying his brother, the boy hides in a bake-oven which his mother subsequently fires up, unknowingly roasting him. In either subtype she then kills herself from despair, or her husband, blaming her for the deaths of his children, kills her in anger, and he himself dies soon thereafter. In Subtype C the slayer is tried and acquitted on the grounds that he acted as a child, not as an adult' (Hansen 2002: 81).

Interestingly enough, tale type AT 2401/ATU 1343* has also transformed into a contemporary urban legend in which it is represented by the story that Janet Langlois have labelled 'The Inept Mother' (Langlois 1993; see also Brunvand 2001: 271; Schneider 1999). This narrative tells of a two- or three-year-old boy who resisted toilet training 'until his exasperated mother warned: "If you don't learn, I'm going to cut it off". Unfortunately, she was overheard by the boy's older sister. So one day, when the children's mother was away, the boy wet again, and the girl took up a pair of shears and cut if off' (Brunvand 1986: 72). In another version of the legend, the girl asks her mother what the strange thing is between her brother's legs. The mother answers: 'Oh, that's just something the doctor forgot to cut off'. Then the story follows the same pattern. The versions of this plot that are mostly close to the AT 2401/ATU 1343* and correspond with the Hansen's Subtype A report about the 'chain' of tragic accidents as well: while the sister castrates her brother, the mother is giving a bath to the third, newborn, baby. When the mother hears the little boy screaming in the next room, she drops the baby and runs to the scene. When she tries to grab the scissors from the girl, the girl falls on them and is stabbed. In the meantime the baby drowns. As to the castrated boy, he bleeds to death. Thus all the children of 'the inept mother' die at one time.

Although some of the European versions of this tale are not directly related to religious norms and ideas, it seems that the theme in general possesses certain moralistic and religious meaning. Noteworthy is the fact that, even its 'secular' version was used as an example in Protestant sermons in the seventeenth century (Richter 1986: 3). According to Hansen, the variants of the AT 2401/ATU 1343*,

taken together, form a kind of meditation on guilt and innocence, with which the entire story is concerned in one way or another. Often the children are said to imitate in their play the slaughtering of an animal that they have just witnessed their father perform. The guilt of one or the other parent is suggested in those texts in which the father slaughters an animal just before going to Mass. After all, the mother would not have made a fire in the bake-oven if she had not making bread that day. This behavior, which perhaps is imagined to transpire on a Sunday, seems somehow to trigger the cosmos quietly to effect the horrible punishment that ensues, suggesting that the misfortune the parent suffers is partly deserved. (Hansen 2002: 81)

It is quite obvious that the earliest known versions of the story about children killing each other in imitation of what their parents do are related to the theme of sacrifice. If one would look for relevant parallels for the theme in early Jewish and Christian tradition, it would be reasonable to mention the story of Cain (Genesis 4) and, of course, Abraham's sacrifice of Isaac (Genesis 22) known as the Aquedah or Akedah (Hebrew for 'binding') in Hebrew tradition. Although we do not know whether Aelian, or the informant who told the tale about Macareus from Mitylene, were aware of the episode, well known in both Jewish and Christian religious traditions, it is very likely that the Arabic version of AT 2401/ATU 1343* mentioned above implies some relationship with the Biblical narrative of the Aqedah. In fact, the Islamic Feast of Sacrifice (Eid al-Adha) when an animal (usually a ram) must be sacrificed, 'is to remember Ibrāhīm's preparedness to sacrifice Ismāīl and to repeat the sacrifice of the substitute that was provided to take the place of Ibrāhīm's son' (Leemhuis 2002: 125). The very story is referred to in the Koran in *Sūrat al-Ṣāffāt* (37): 100–103. It is also symptomatic that the versions of AT 2401/ATU 1343* from Western Europe usually do not talk about slaughtering a ram, rather there is a pig or a hog or unspecified animal(s). In the texts from Eastern Europe, on the contrary, the father slaughters either a ram or a goat, but never a pig. At any rate, some variants imply that the slaughtering is related to a feast, whether it is a dinner with Mohammed, or a wedding ceremony, or a Shrovetide feast in a German version (Hansen 2002: 79).

More important is the fact that a number of persistent plot details can be explained as allusions to the Aqedah, rather in its visual then textual representations. I mean, first of all, the baking oven or the stove in Subtype B, along with the firewood or brands that are so often mentioned in the narrative without, so to say, any particular reason. The only exception is the story by Aelian that takes place in the temple of Dionysos and tells of the priest's children imitating a sacrifice. It is obvious, however, that a father with a knife in his hand, a son, a ram or a lamb and an altar with some firewood upon it (either burning or not) are what one can usually see in a picture representing the sacrifice of Isaac. The list of images of Abraham's sacrifice from the third through to the thirteenth century compiled by Isabel Speyart van Woerden (1961) suggests that the scene 'was frequently painted and sculptured in Late Antiquity, at least by Christian artists' (van den Brink 2002: 140). The earliest known Christian paintings of the Aqedah are paintings in San Callisto Catacomb (Rome, c. 200 CE) and Via Latina Catacomb (Rome, c. 350 CE). The list of Jewish monuments representing Abraham's sacrifice includes painting in the synagogue of Doura Europos (244 CE) where the scene is placed 'on the most prominent place, the front of the Tora-shrine' (van den Brink 2002: 142) and the floor mosaic of the synagogue of Beth Alpha, dated somewhere around 525 CE. Both the ram, Abraham with a knife in his hand, and Isaac lying on the wood upon an altar are constantly depicted at such paintings. Although the image of the altar is varied in the earliest monuments, and it probably depended on local religious practices and traditions, Western paintings and mosaics of the eleventh and twelfth centuries usually represent an altar of oven type, which might be the best explanation for the persistence of the baking oven or the stove in Subtype B of AT 2401/ATU 1343*. I would suggest, therefore, that the very tale type could be viewed as the result of misreading or misinterpretation of Jewish and Christian iconography related to the Aqedah.

Although the example discussed above is of special interest for a historian of tale types, it is still unclear what particular social and cultural factors helped the plot of AT 2401/ATU 1343* to transform into the legend about two saint boys. Neither written accounts of the legend, nor its oral versions include any theological or moral comments on the story. Thus far, one can suggest that the cult of Ioann and Iakov Menushskie reveals some archaic semantic relationship between the image of violent death and the very concept of the sacred. In his seminal book *Violence and the Sacred*, René Girard (1977) suggested that sacrifice should be interpreted as a socially acceptable form for channelling aggression, since the latter would otherwise annihilate any community of human beings by means of a 'chain reaction' of violence. Be that true or not, it seems that mutual relationships of violence and the sacred somehow affect individual psychology and collective imagination mainly beyond human conscience and rational argumentation.

There could be, then, two possible explanations for the conflict patterns in the narratives about local shrines discussed above. On the one hand, we can assume that motives for conflict and violence are used for the expression of the counter-intuitive nature of various sacred agents participating in the establishment and use of a local shrine, in setting apart this or that material object (or point in the landscape) for ritual use. On the other hand, it is highly possible that these motives are directly related to the processes of social production and control of the sacred. In other words, I would suggest that these stories symbolically describe the history of conflicts and competition accompanying the process of transformation of a shrine from individual to communal.

The model described above represents some aspects of manufacture and consumption of the sacred in an 'elementary' form, i.e. within a rural community or group of communities. It does not seem to me, however, that a more complex environment would change the basic features of the model, since they are probably related to a number of general rules regulating religious behaviour. Although the range of sacred objects possessed by either simply organized or complex communities is variable, every human group tends to keep a kind of balance between sacred and profane. Thus, the very substance of vernacular religious culture can be viewed as the process of production and reproduction of the sacred accompanied by contests, competitions and conflicts. At the same time, the complicated nature of contemporary culture abundant in symbolic and informational resources and channels greatly changes the modes of manufacture and worship of local and unofficial holy places in both rural and urban environments.

We can say that contemporary urban culture does not simply replace peasant folklore in contemporary Russia. Sometimes, various hybrid cultural forms occur which unite motifs and elements borrowed from both rural and urban folklore. Sometimes, however, a local shrine, a ritual or a custom becomes an object of competition between different cultural groups and discourses. The situation is especially characteristic to the contemporary worship of various local shrines in the countryside. Such cults still presume competition and interaction between various groups of believers, for example, local peasants and pilgrims from big cities. Each group has its own narrative and ritual resources which allow them to worship the holy place and to use its sacred power. Sometimes, these cults are characterized by more or less peaceful coexistence of various groups of believers; in other cases, local shrines become objects of constant confrontation between such groups. However, even confronted, these groups actively exchange motifs and forms of religious narrative, types of ritual behaviour, etc. (for example Kormina 2004: 25–40).

In fact, when we talk about contemporary folklore in general, we should take into account that in societies that consist of heterogeneous social and cultural groups, practices and objects with special symbolic status are always the targets of competitive interaction between various discourses. It might also be remarked that contemporary folklore is not only the subject, but also the result, of social competition: 'the struggle for authenticity'. The emulative nature of present religious praxis is well enough demonstrated by a number of recent studies of unofficial holy places in contemporary Russian cities. One of the most remarkable examples is the cult of two worshipped stones in the national museum reservation Kolomenskoe, which is not too far from the centre of Moscow (Griva 2006: 371–383). The stones are thought to be helpful for those suffering sterility or various diseases in general and are immensely popular among some of the city dwellers. It is likely that the cult in its present form emerged a couple of decades ago due to the activities of a museum employee, who argued, without any rational proof, that the stones had once been a pagan temple. Although this tradition was invented relatively recently, field research identified at least three different groups who worshipped the stones, each with its own narratives, rituals and beliefs. Of course, every group thinks its sacred knowledge and ritual practice to be authentic and genuine. At the same time, the cult has not led to conflicts between the groups and allows a more or less peaceful coexistence between the various religious discourses that relate to the same shrine.

Does this mean that we must choose from either sociological or cognitive approaches for our explanations of vernacular religious phenomena? In my opinion, these explanatory models could be viewed rather as complementary than contradictory. Although, as Pascal Boyer points out, 'religious concepts and norms and the emotions attached to them seem designed to excite human mind, linger in memory, trigger multiple inferences in the precise way that will get people to hold them true and communicate them' (Boyer 2001: 377–378), it is also true that the very domain of religion is socially constructed and that counter-intuitive categories and agents are arranged in collective imagination according to the particular needs of various social groups. It seems to me that the study of narratives and ritual practices relating to shrines and sacred objects at the 'grass-roots' level shows most vividly how human beings and collectives exploit basic cognitive categories in the domain of social life that we call vernacular religion.

Acknowledgement

This work was supported by the Russian Foundation for Humanities, Project No. 04-04-00069a.

Notes

1. Field Archives of the Department of Anthropology, European University at St Petersburg. Tape No EU-Shimsk-03-PF-1. Novgorod district, Shimskii region, Meniusha. Recorded by Alexander Panchenko and Victoria Panchenko.

References

Anttonen, V. (2003) Sacred sites as markers of difference – exploring cognitive foundations of territoriality. In L. Tarkka (ed.) *Dynamics of Tradition: Perspectives on Oral Poetry and Folk Belief. Essays in Honour of Anna-Leena Siikala on her 60th Birthday. Studia Fennica Folkloristica* 13, 291–305. Helsinki: Finnish Literature Society.

Barag, L. G. et al. (1978) *Sravnitel'nyĭ ukazatel' syuzhetov: Vostochnoslavyanskaya skazka.* Leningrad: Nauka.

Boyer, P. (1999) Cognitive aspects of religious ontologies: How brain processes constrain religious concepts. In T. Ahlbäck (ed.) *Approaching Religion: Based on Papers Read at the Symposium on Dance, Music, and Art in Religion, Held at Åbo, Finland, on the 4th–7th of August 1997. Scripta Instituti Donneriani Aboensis* 17 (1), 53–72. Stockholm: Almqvist & Wiksell.

Boyer, P. (2001) *Religion Explained. The Evolutionary Origins of Religious Thought.* London: Basic Books.

Brown, P. (1981) *The Cult of the Saints: Its Rise and Function in Latin Christianity.* Chicago, IL: University of Chicago Press.

Brunvand, J. H. (1986) *The Mexican Pet: More 'New' Urban Legends and Some Old Favorites.* New York: Norton and Co.

Brunvand J. H. (2001) *Encyclopedia of Urban Legends.* Santa Barbara, CA: ABC-CLIO.

Christian, W. A. Jr. (1981) *Local Religion in Sixteenth-Century Spain.* Princeton, NJ: Princeton University Press.

Chubinski P. P. (1878) *Trudy̆ E'tnografichesko-Statisticheskoĭ e'kspedicii v Zapadno-russkiĭ kraĭ, snaryazhennoĭ Imperatorskim Russkim geograficheskim *obchestvom. Yugo-zapadnȳj otdel. Materialȳ i issledovaniya, sobrannȳe P. P. Chubinskim. Vol. II. Malorusskie skazki.* St Petersburg.

Dobrovol'skaya, V. E. (1999) Neskazochnaya proza o razrushenii tserkveĭ. In *Russkiĭ fol'klor.* T. XXX, 500–512. Sankt-Peterburg.

Freeze, G. (1998) Institutionalizing piety: The church and popular religion, 1750–1850. In J. Burbank and D. L. Ransel (eds) *Imperial Russia. New Histories for the Empire,* 210–250. Bloomington, IN: Indiana University Press.

Girard, R. (1977) *Violence and the Sacred* (Patrick Gregory, trans). Baltimore, MD: Johns Hopkins University Press.

Griva M. (2006) Novȳĭ kul't kamneĭ v Kolomenskom. In *Religioznȳe praktiki v sovremennoĭ Rossii,* 371–383. Moskva: Novoe Izdatel'stvo.

Gurevitch, A. Y. (1990) *Srednevekovȳĭ mir: kul'tura bezmovstvuiutschego bol'shinstva.* Moskva: Isskusstvo.

Hansen, W. F. (2002) *Ariadne's Thread: A Guide to International Tales Found in Classical Literature.* Ithaca, NY: Cornell University Press.

Langlois, J. L. (1993) Mothers' doubletalk. In J. N. Radner (ed.) *Feminist Messages: Coding in Women's Folk Culture,* 80–97. Urbana, IL: University of Illinois Press.

Leemhuis, F. (2002) Ibrāhīm's sacrifice of his son in the early post-Koranic tradition. In E. Noort and E. Tigchelaar (eds) *The Sacrifice of Isaac: The Aqedah (Genesis 22) and Its Interpretations,* 125–139. Leiden: Brill.

Levin, E. (2003) From corpse to cult. In V. A. Kivelson and R. H. Greene (eds) *Orthodox Russia: Belief and Practice under the Tsars,* 81–103. University Park, PA: Pennsylvania State University Press.

Kormina, J. (2004) Pilgrims, priest and local religion in contemporary Russia: Contested religious discourses. In: *Folklore. Electronic Journal of Folklore* 28: 25–40. Online http://www.folklore.ee/folklore/vol28/pilgrims.pdf> [accessed 17 January 2011]

Lavrov A. S. (2000) *Koldovstvo i religiya v Rossii. 1700–1740 gg.* Moskva: Drevlekhranilishche.

Oinas, F. (1978) The transformation of folklore into literature. In V. Terras, (ed.) *American Contribution to the Eighth International Congress of Slavists, Zagreb and Ljubljana, September 3–9, 1978, 2,* 570–604. Columbus, OH: Slavica.

Panchenko A. A. (1998) *Issledovaniya v oblasti narodnogo pravoslaviya. Derevenskie svyatȳni Severo-Zapada Rossii.* Sankt-Peterburg: Aleteĭya.

Panchenko A. A. (2002) *Khristovshchina i skopchectvo. Fol´klor i traditsionnaya kul´tura russkikh misticheskikh sekt.* Moskva: OGI.

Panchenko A. A. (2005) Ivan et Iakov – Deux saints étranges de la région des marais (Novgorod). In *Archives de Sciences Sociales des Religions,* 130. Online http://assr.revues.org/index2797.html [accessed 17 January 2011]

Panchenko A. A. (2006) Ivan i Yakov – strannỹe svyatỹe iz bolotnogo kraya (religioznỹe praktiki sovremennoĭ novgorodskoĭ derevni). In _Religioznỹe praktiki v sovremennoĭ Rossii._ Moskva: Novoe izdatel´stvo.

Panchenko, A. A. (2009) E'tnografiya i dekadans: k izucheniyu ranneĭ prozỹ Fedora Sologuba. _Russkaya literatura_ 2: 158–169.

Primiano, L. N. (1995) Vernacular religion and the search for method in religious folklife. _Western Folklore (Reflexivity and the Study of Belief)_ 54 (1): 37–56.

Pskovskie gubernskie vedomosti _1864 No. 24 (19.07)._

Richter, D. (1986) Wie Kinder Schlachtens mit einander gespielt haben (AaTh 2401). Von Schonung und Verschonung der Kinder – in und vor einem Märchen der Brüder Grimm. _Fabula_ 27 (1-2): 1–11.

Romodanovskaya E. K. (2005) 'Svyatoĭ iz grobnitsỹ'. O nekotorỹkh osoben-nostyakh sibirskoĭ i severnorusskoĭ agiografii. In _Russkaya agiografiya: Issledovaniya, publikacii, polemika,_ 143–159. St Petersburg: Dmitriĭ Bulanin.

Santino, J. (2004) Performative commemoratives, the personal, and the public: Spontaneous shrines, emergent ritual, and the field of folklore (AFS Presidential Plenary Address, 2003). _Journal of American Folklore_ 117 (466): 363–372.

Schneider, I. (1999) Traditionelle Erzählstoffe und Erzählmotive in Contemporary Legends. In C. Schmitt (ed.) _Homo narrans: Studien zur populären Erzählkultur. Festschrift für Siegfried Neumann zum 65. Geburtstag,_ 165–180. Münster, New York, München, Berlin: Waxmann.

Shtyrkov, S. A. (2001) 'Svyatỹe bez zhitiĭ' i zabudutschie roditeli: tserkovnaya kanonizatsiya i narodnaya traditsiya. In O. V. Belova (ed.) _Kontsept chuda v slavyanskoĭ i evrejskoĭ kul'turnoĭ traditsii: Sbornik stateĭ,_ 130–155. Moscow: Probel-2000.

Shtyrkov, S. A. (2006) Rasskazỹ ob oskvernenii svyatỹn'. _Traditsionnỹĭ fol'klor Novgorodskoĭ oblasti,_ 208–231. St Petersburg: Tropa Troyanova.

Speyart, van Woerden I. (1961) The iconography of the sacrifice of Abraham. _Vigilae Christianae_ 15: 214–255.

Stark, L. (2002) _Peasants, Pilgrims, and Sacred Promises: Ritual and the Supernatural in Orthodox Karelian Folk Religion. Studia Fennica Folkloristica_ 11. Helsinki: Finnish Literature Society.

Tatar, M. (2003) _The Hard Facts of the Grimms' Fairy Tales._ Princeton, NJ: Princeton University Press.

Trusman Yu. A. (1890) Poluvertsỹ Pskovo-Pecherskogo kraya. _Zhivaya starina_ I: 31–62.

Uther, H.-J. (2004) _The Types of International Folktales. A Classification and Bibliography. Based on the System of Antti Aarne and Stith Thompson. Part II: Tales of the Stupid Ogre, Anecdotes and Jokes, and Formula Tales._ FF Communications No. 285. Helsinki: Academia Scientiarum Fennica.

'I Make My Saints Work ...': A Hungarian Holy Healer's Identity Reflected in Autobiographical Stories and Folk Narratives

Judit Kis-Halas[*]

Introduction

In this paper I introduce the process of creating a healer's self-image by examining the case of a contemporary healer and diviner living in Rádfalva, a village in south Hungary. My inquiry is based on the narrative autobiography of this magical practitioner, named Erzsike, whom I recorded on several occasions.[1] Focusing on the integration of diverse ideologies and traditions of different origin, I highlighted certain events which are interpreted as turning points in the healer's life. Considering the magical services offered by Erzsike the healer and diviner, three major patterns of magical knowledge can be identified. First, by employing magic formulae and wax pouring[2] she diagnoses and heals bewitchment, thus seeming closely related to the folk healers still active until the most recent times in the South Transdanubian area of Hungary. Second, her activity is connected to that of the seers and diviners practising rather more in urban environments, because she reads cards in order to foretell her clients' futures or to reveal facts about their present or past. Third, her use of a certain book to conjure angels and the preparation of angelic amulets can be related to the currently flourishing methods of post-New Age/esoteric angel lore. However, her practice of magic as a whole is completely impregnated with her strong and consciously Christian outlook and mission, thus many features of her image as a healer are similar to those of the 'living saints'. Characterized by this particular mixture of magical practices, Erzsike is considered one of the 'new' type of practitioners

* Judit Kis-Halas is Researcher and Lecturer at the Department of European Ethnology and Cultural Anthropology, University of Pécs, Hungary.

who specializes in a number of spheres in order to meet the diverse needs of their village and urban clientele.[3]

Religious and Social Contexts

Rádfalva is a small village of 208 inhabitants situated in the densely populated Baranya county in south Hungary. According to medieval records the settlement must have already been inhabited in the eleventh century. The first part of its name has preserved a local landlord's name, Radó, who was the governor of the Hungarian kingdom at that time. Rádfalva is one of the easternmost villages of a particular ethnocultural region, called Ormánság. Because of its traditional material culture, special dialect, rich oral culture, and demographic peculiarities (i.e., the rapid diminishing of the 'original' population), Ormánság, consisting of 42 settlements, has been the focus of ethnographic, folklore, and sociological research in Hungary since the 1930s (for example Elek *et al.* 1936; Kiss [1937] 1979; Hegedüs 1946; Kodolányi 1960; Zentai 1983).

The broader region of south-west Hungary, including Ormánság, was among the first where the ideas of Protestantism were introduced, in the first half of the sixteenth century. The 1576 synod, held in the contemporary Baranya county village of Hercegszőlős (now Kneževi Vinogradi, Croatia) declared that the region accepted the Helvetian confession, and joined the Calvinist denomination. From that time on Calvinists were in the majority until the second half of the twentieth century. The Marian shrine of Máriagyűd in the vicinity of Ormánság, however, has remained as a local centre of Roman Catholic devotion, and even Protestants visit there for different purposes. The shrine was frequented by pilgrims from all over Hungary during the 45 years of the Communist regime, and continues to be so today. In 2010 Máriagyűd became a station of the so-called Mária route, a newly organized pilgrimage route starting at Czeztochowa in Poland and ultimately reaching Međugorje in Bosnia-Hercegovina.[4]

Demographic and social change (e.g., the settling of poor Roman Catholic serf families in the late nineteenth century; forced settlement of half-nomad Roma population after the Second World War) have entirely redesigned the religious landscape of Ormánság, and its population has become predominantly Roman Catholic, as shown by the latest census in 2001.

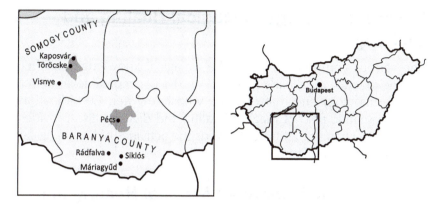

Location of Somogy and Baranya counties in Hungary.

Nevertheless, globalization and political change have opened both real and imaginary boundaries to new religious ideas. As the latest research have revealed neo-Protestant denominations (Adventists, Pentecostalists), non-Christian religions (Buddhism, Islam), sects (Jehovah's Witnesses, the Congregation of Faith), new religious movements (Hare Krishna), and New Age ideas (e.g., methods of self-improvement like brain control, or energy healing like *reiki*) appeared in the early 1990s and had rapidly gained popularity by the middle of the decade. From that time on esoteric groups with various names (like Yoga Club, Reiki Club, Spirit Healer's Club, etc.) were formed, mainly in Siklós, which is the largest town of the region. These loose informal organizations consist of 5–10 constant, and some additional 10–20, members both from Siklós and also from the neighbouring villages and smaller towns.[5] Their meetings are held more or less monthly in private apartments, where they discuss their spiritual experiences (e.g., visions, apparitions, dreams, etc.), exchange books, recommend reading or films, hold energy-sending or blessing rituals. Occasionally they attend or even organize readings by either widely known or local gurus, prophets, spiritual teachers. They also regularly organize spiritual pilgrimages to various destinations, ranging from traditional Roman or Greek Catholic shrines to sites venerated by followers of different neopagan groups or centres of new religious movements (Kis-Halas 2009: 512–515).

Local Terminology of Magical Healing and Divining

The various components of Erzsike's magical knowledge and her healing practice are clearly reflected on the conceptual level of her own terminology and that of those who know her. Consideration of the semantic field of magical healing and divining also provides insight into changing attitudes towards the activities of local magical specialists, both past and present.

Current Emic Notions of Magical Healing and Divination in the Study Area[6]

In general, Erzsike calls herself and similar healing and divining specialists, *jós* (soothsayer). At the same time she differentiates between the *kártyás* (card user) and the *viaszoló/viaszos* (wax user) and/or *viaszöntő* (wax pourer) diviners; whereas the former read cards exclusively in fortune telling, the latter are both healers and diviners who apply the technique of wax-pouring for both purposes. She regards her own method of divination and healing as *viaszolás* (waxing). In most cases Erzsike identifies *rontás* (bewitchment) as the original cause of all kinds of personal misfortune (illness, economic loss, family trouble, job problems, etc.). She often uses the notion *átok* (curse) as a synonym for bewitchment; and this terminological inter-changeability is observed in terms of the verbal forms of *megrontani* (to bewitch) and *megátkozni* (to curse) or *átkot (le) tenni/átkot megcsinálni* (to put [down]/to prepare a curse). In this sense both bewitchment and curse are regarded as real objects: there are believed to be magical paraphernalia hidden in the injured party's house which should be traced and annihilated in order to cure the patient successfully, or as Erzsike puts it *levenni az átkot/rontást* (to remove or release the curse/bewitchment).[7] Clients, relatives, acquaintances and fellow villagers univocally refer to Erzsike as *jósnő* (soothsayer, feminine) or *jós* (soothsayer, masculine) but they never apply the further definitions related to pouring wax mentioned formerly. They characterize her activity as *rontás-levétel* (removing or releasing bewitchment) or *rontás gyógyítás* (healing bewitchment), and refer to her divination practice as simple *jóslás* (soothsaying).

Former Emic Notions of Magical Healing and Divination in the Observed Area

In the South Transdanubian area of Hungary magical healers were called *javas/javos/javós* until recent times (e.g. the last decades of the 1970s).[8] Besides their 'medical' practice these healers took up the role of the main opponent of the malevolent witch (both demonic and human), and the fairy related *szépasszony* (fair woman) in the local systems of belief, and were thought to be able to heal the very specific illnesses caused by the latter, or to reverse all kinds of misfortune attributed to the former. The particular term *füves/fives* (herbalist) applied to the same type of healers is restricted only to the Ormánság area (Baranya county).[9] This notion indicates the stressed importance of using herbs in healing activity. In Somogy and Zala counties another characteristic term was formerly used: *öntőasszony* (pouring woman) which refers to the technique of pouring wax to heal bewitchment, the evil eye and fright.[10] In the Hungarian speaking area of the Carpathian basin (and also in most parts of Europe) fright, as a specific form of illness, was a collective definition applied to particular physical and/or mental conditions with symptoms like strong headache, depression, nightmares, crying. It was generally attributed to actual frightful events or to persons unexpectedly encountered (see Hovorka and Kronfeld II 1909: 208–240, 674–686). Fright could also trigger epilepsy. It was thought to be most threatening for babies and little children, but anyone being similarly in the liminal state of symbolic death (e.g. mothers in childbed, young adults shortly before marriage, brides and bridegrooms, etc.) could become potential victims. Since early modern times plenty of data have been available on fright diagnosed and cured by pouring wax or lead (see Kis-Halas 2004a: 312–319; Kis-Halas 2010a). The solidified shapes of the molten wax or lead reveals the conditions of the horrifying events or the characteristics of the person who had frightened the patient.

As opposed to summoning the human witch to the house of the victim by smoking,[11] by symbolic injury, or other means, wax-pouring was a technique for identifying bewitchment less common in the south Transdanubian area.

Research Terminology

I use the specific term of holy healer to describe Erzsike's magical practice. Éva Pócs defines holy seers as 'communal specialists with Christian connotations' (Pócs 1997: 191–192). Hungarian researchers refer to the holy seer as *szentember* (holy man) or *szentasszony* (holy woman) (for example Bálint 1942; Grynaeus 1974; Gagyi 2001) and the term is also called a living or lay saint is also used in international contexts (Boutellier 1958 201–235; Burkhardt 1994; Kieckhefer 1994). The holy seer is 'a mediator with exclusively Christian religious characteristics who communicates with the other world by dreams, visions or by adopting specific trance-techniques, and is helped by a Christian patron' (Pócs 1991: 192). In village communities holy seers occasionally practise healing, and when it overshadows their other activities they may be referred to as holy healers.[12] A *javas/javos/javós* could also have some of the holy healer's characteristics, at least based on the etymology of the term as Pócs suggests it based on her own research (Pócs 1997: 192) and the linguistic evidence supported by Pais (1975).[13] Since the Middle Ages the holy healer as a general type of magical practitioner has become one of the potential antagonists of the demonic witches, able to see and identify them and cure the illnesses they caused.

Erzsike, the Village Healer

Short Biography

At the time I interviewed her, Erzsike was a 47 year-old woman living in Rádfalva, a small village in Baranya county, south-west Hungary. About 17 years ago, after a long-term mental problem – probably depression – she gave up her profession as a hairdresser and got a divorce. Six years later, she moved with her new partner from the neighbouring village, Márfa to Rádfalva. Her adult daughter also lives in Rádfalva with her own family. Managing a small farm and owning a small plot of woodland on the outskirts of the village, Erzsike and her new family are among the village's very few well-to-do inhabitants. Her relative wealth is especially due to her profession as one of the most successful healers in the region.

The failure of repeated cures at the Neurological Clinic of the University of Pécs had prompted Erzsike to try alternative medicine. She paid a visit to an old village healer living in Töröcske (Somogy county). By the use of wax-pouring the old woman diagnosed Erzsike's illness as bewitchment, but declared her own magical abilities or 'power' insufficient to complete the healing and sent her to another 'stronger' healer living in the vicinity.[14] The second specialist, a 50 year-old man living in Visnye (Somogy county), relieved Erzsike's pains and completely healed her. As Erzsike recalls it: 'after 13 months on sick leave I was waxed by him twice and I had to believe in it, because I expected that I would faint again and I did not faint, did not faint'. Soon after her recovery Erzsike started her own healing and divining praxis.

The Many Faces of a Specialist – the Soothsayer (Reading the Cards)

Before her serious illness Erzsike worked in a small beauty salon as a hairdresser. She had an old, disabled client who was a fortune-teller. The old woman invited young Erzsike to do her hair at her tiny Pécs apartment because she had difficulty making regular visits to the salon, which was almost 30 km distant from Pécs:

> Yes, she was a fortune teller, aunt Rozika. She lived in Kertváros [the south-west quarter of Pécs with mostly huge blocks of flats], and she was crippled, and she asked me to come up and dye her hair because she could not walk.

Aunt Rozika considered Erzsike gifted in fortune telling and taught her the skills of reading cards. Following this short introduction, however, Erzsike did not start to practise as professional diviner. She did not ascribe the new skill to any particular supernatural sensibility, but to her own will-power and purposeful personality: 'I was a very practically thinking child. I always knew how to set about my aims, and I also knew that my decisions and deeds were entirely right and good.'

Her point of view corresponds to the so called inductive, interpretative or wisdom divination 'in which the diviner decodes impersonal patterns of reality' in accordance with particular divination systems (Zuesse 1987: 376). These methods can be acquired by simple learning and do not require that a diviner have special abilities to communicate with supernatural entities by mediumistic possession or through other agents.

In her own healing practice Erzsike reads cards in the first phase of defining the nature of the illness and to carefully introduce the suggestion of bewitchment when formulating a preliminary diagnosis. With this method of divination she can also reveal useful facts of a client's past and present. If the client shows even the slightest inclination towards Erzsike's suggestion, she goes further with cautious questions in an attempt to explore any former conflicts or quarrels in the client's intimate social environment that lie at the root the act of bewitchment. In the last phase of the dialogue Erzsike indicates the potential actors that may possibly be responsible for harming the patient. The broad outlines of a hypothetic bewitchment story are narrated in monologue form by the end of the card reading procedure.

[Whilst reading cards]

You have an enemy there at your workplace. You go there to do something. You go there to work. You two had a talk about some money in that house and it made you angry. You two had a dispute, or even a quarrel. You had a quarrel with someone for some papers or documents. You won't be sick any more. But your illness came from bewitchment, because you had that quarrel with that person before. Here it is! [She points at a particular constellation of cards.] They wanted to make financial troubles for you. They wanted to hide their intentions. They did not want you to realise that troublesome thing working on you. You had a quarrel with some man. You had a quarrel with this particular man.

In contrast to most fortune tellers who divine exclusively by reading cards, Erzsike applies this as a secondary method to wax-pouring. She considers the information gained from the cards less decisive than that revealed by pouring wax:

Well, wax and cards are not intimately connected to each other. Cards show me some additional facts about the perpetrator's look: the colour of the hair, the age, or the actual purpose of bewitchment. But wax may reveal whether the harming object is hidden somewhere around the house, or it shows the form of the perpetrator's face or hair-do. Generally, [the client] recognises [the perpetrator] immediately when glancing at the wax shape.

The Witch's Enemy

According to Erzsike's own confession her nervous disease was a turning point in her life:

Yes, my first illness, my bewitchment illness, came over me occasionally at that time. It came regularly after supper. It was like, as if I were epileptic. And I had to lie down and it [the attack] lasted five minutes and I could not speak or do anything. I lay and cried. I was asked to tell my problem, but in vain, I could not reply. ... I was aware of what was happening around me but I could not answer any questions. Doctors told me that I was basically neurotic. I was too nervous to work. I was just sitting around and I had not the slightest intention of doing anything. And on the top of that I was given many sedatives! They made my mental disease, my bewitchment illness, worse. And, unfortunately, I could not recover. They depressed me. I took many many sedatives and they made me more and more depressed. Then I was waxed and I stopped taking them.

A new dimension of magical tradition appears at this point of the story, namely the local system of belief. It would not be wrong to suppose, and further data from the same geographic location confirms, that Erzsike must have been familiar with the ideas of witchcraft and bewitchment as potential explanations for personal crisis situations. In this case I adopt Pócs's definition based on social and anthropological interpretations of the phenomenon (Evans-Pritchard 1935; Macfarlane 1970: 205–206):

On the one hand witchcraft is an ideology serving as explanation for personal misfortune; on the other hand it is an institution of regulating social conflicts. In the early modern age it was functioning within the tri- or quadrangular network of malefactor, victim, identifying and/ or healing specialist. According to this particular ideology – the belief system of witchcraft – misfortune is attributed to human agency, to an enemy within the community who is supposed to be able to harm (bewitch) his/her fellowmen and their households by means of supernatural abilities. (Pócs 1997: 9–10)

Nevertheless, today this ideology works exclusively on the individual level of the social network and is no longer applied to social crisis situations.[15]

Q: You mentioned before that you knew some methods of bewitching people. Can you tell me about them?
A: Well, I do not know the way they [those who harm] do it or not, and I do not even want to get to know it. Let it be enough for now that I can see the object they hid with a curse because I can release curses. I have never been involved in their [the harmers'] businesses enough to learn the ways of bewitchment. And I would not want to talk about

this particular topic, because, honestly, I only know that they pray bad prayers when bewitching, and that is all.

Q: I wanted to ask you to tell me something about bewitching or as you said cursing in general.
A: All I know is that they do it. I can tell you that they make people sick or lose their jobs. Basically, they can make splits in marriages, in jobs, in families, in relationships with children. There are many children who feel uncomfortable at home and then leave all of a sudden. All this is done by bewitching. There are many who commit crimes, steal, for example. Their brain is switched off at that moment. There are many like that.

Q: Is it brought about by bewitchment?
A: Yes, yes it is! The other thing with bewitchment is that these people have accidents, and very often! And there is always an object behind all that: one's car, one's motorbike, one's footstep has been manipulated by bewitchment. They [the malefactors] know it pretty well, which methods to apply, don't they! They know that pretty well!

In Erzsike's case witchcraft served as a latent frame of reference, first to interpret her own disease as bewitchment and later to formulate her identity as benevolent healer in contrast to malefactor witches.[16] Following the chronology of Erzsike's autobiography, the old fortune teller's instructions must have helped to make the connection between the two different layers of magical knowledge: divining by reading cards in general, and to reveal the malefactors' (witches') harmful activity. Thus Erzsike found bewitchment a potential, and credible, alternative for interpreting certain diseases which could not be cured by 'Western' or 'official' medicine:

It may happen that someone comes here and asks me because he or she is sure about having been bewitched. But it may not be the case. After looking at the cards I can tell them whether they are sick or a bewitched, or most probably both. And then I tell them that if I wax them, they will be cured for sure, or their illness would be partly relieved, at last I am not the kind of person like those who come here saying, 'I am sick. I give you some five or even ten thousand Forints to heal me.' And they come back later saying that I cheated them. I would never do that. It works like this: if that person is very ill, I will say so at the very start. I would say 'Look, you have an official disease. I may ease your pains but I am not able to heal you because it is a real sickness and I can't help you. Not even God can help you.' I suggest that this person see the doctor. There are some who take my advice and still return to me.

Yes, they come back to me. And they pay a visit here regularly. There are doctors and even psychologists among them!

With her purposeful personality, Erzsike probably realized her own healing abilities during the magical cures she underwent. In her story the healer of Visnye himself designated her as his successor by a mystical-sounding pronouncement which she only came to understand in the light of subsequent events. The prophetic sentence of the Visnye healer provided Erzsike's healing praxis with a firm basis of legitimization, as it helped her claim her own 'magical ancestor' from whom she inherited her special abilities.

> He told me that many people used to turn to him. He kept on telling me that some time he would leave me something to remember him forever. [At the moment] when he died I collapsed and lost consciousness. Then I did not wax for a long period, until a man strongly resembling him appeared at my house and asked me to wax him. I did it and I have been doing it ever since. And since then I have been able to see in the wax people's curses and the cursed objects, and also the place where these objects are hidden. And then people can find and destroy them.

The 'magical heritage story' has another version that I did not have the chance to tape. Erzsike recalled that the spirit of the dead healer arrived at her house in a whirlwind at the very moment when she started pouring the molten wax for the first time in her life. Then she saw the dead healer and suddenly felt his spirit inside her own body: 'I could see with his eyes'. She asked for the spirit's help and again felt 'him speaking with my tongue'. Apart from the general belief that wise men and women acquire magical knowledge (the ability of healing and/or clairvoyance, divining, etc.) by an initiative sickness,[17] there are some additional motifs from local beliefs (like a *javas*'s appearance in a whirlwind[18] or assuming a former healer's magical power by possession[19]) that Erzsike adapted to construct her own identity as a healer. The numerous traditional topoi about healers in Erzsike's story, for example seeing her future visitors at the moment they decide to consult her, or summoning people by concentrating on them[20] or taking over her patient's pains while healing,[21] reinforce the impression that Erzsike is strongly connected to a set of local beliefs about bewitching and healing that are quite alive as well:

> I can always feel if someone is about to come to me. I can even feel his good or evil intentions. But, if I think of someone, his face appears

to me in my mind and he will visit me in three days for sure. I can see his face because he is longing to see me.

The many curses of the people remain here. There was a time, at the beginning, when all my plans failed because the curses of the people had stuck to me. I was too quick to heal them, and their diseases came upon me first. ... It is so interesting, that when I get deep down with people's problems, I could cry all day long.

After vesting herself with the self-made image of the magical healer, Erzsike's next task was to find her place within the network of local magical specialist, who offered much the same service as hers. In the close vicinity of Rádfalva she knows of a number of specialists (among them fortune tellers, energy and spirit healers) who are also able to identify and cure bewitchment. In Erzsike's accounts rival healers are referred to in two ways, either as organized into a vertical hierarchy with the most powerful healer at the top,[22] or arranged in a horizontal bi-polar set of malefactors and healers. Erzsike proudly puts herself in the highest position in the vertical model. The extraordinarily rapid recovery period of her patients proves the efficacy of her magical healing methods and legitimates her supremacy in the local market of magical practitioners. Her pre-eminent position is also supported by the idea of an 'equal is cured by an equal': in the case of her sickness she could not be healed by the neighbouring healers, because they might have been irreversibly hurt by taking over Erzsike's illness.

What if I went to one of these healers. Honestly, they told me that it was almost impossible to wax me, because I am stronger than they are. If I went to a waxing healer, it would be in vain, because he would not be strong enough to cure me. He would fall ill of my power.

Erzsike is absolutely convinced of her rivals' awareness and acceptance of her supremacy over them:

it turned out very soon that I was the strongest in releasing bewitchment, because my patients recovered very rapidly. And people acknowledge it. If they turned to other *jósok* (soothsayers), of those I'd rather not name any, to have themselves waxed they would feel better only five months later. But if I wax them, they will feel better in two or three weeks. It happens so rapidly that it should be noticed by the patients and the other *jósok* (soothsayers) as well. I don't think that they [the other diviners] are angry with me about it. I am not angry with them, either. I think that each of us has his own ability. There is enough room for each of us.

Q: Do you often meet them?
A: Yes, I do. None of them is on bad terms with me. And why should
it be so? I tell you now there is one *jós* (soothsayer) who is envious
of my work. But I haven't heard this about the others. I know that
one of them was bad. But she is only a fortune teller who reads
cards and she can't wax, thus she could not be my opponent. She
could by no means be that. Fortune tellers are nothing more than
fortune tellers.

As a widely appreciated healer Erzsike automatically puts herself
on the positive end of the scale of healers and malefactors, thus she
is obliged to represent benevolence in public. In order to keep her
carefully constructed image she needs from time to time to identify
harmful opponents with whom she fights for the patient's health. In most
cases she accuses Jolika, a fortune teller and healer living in Görcsöny
(a village 10 km of Rádfalva) of bewitching her patients and considers
her as her most bitter enemy. Jolika offers similar magical services to
those of Erzsike; she reads cards, identifies bewitchment by pouring
wax and heals with the assistance of heavenly forces. Erzsike assumes
that Jolika has a helper of the opposite sex, a man by the nickname
of 'Békás [Froggy] Géza' who is in charge of gathering toads and frogs
for Jolika's evil practices. It is worth mentioning that the same belief
relates to Erzsike's late master, the *öntő* (pouring man) of Visnye; his
helper was a woman, a former patient of his. She used to gather toads
and the *öntő* then killed them and put their bones, mixed with a white
powder like coarse wheat, into small white sachets. His clients were
then told to deposit the sachets in particular graves where a man or
a woman was buried who once had the same Christian name as the
client's own. The *öntő* is reported to have restored the client's health
by these procedures, although the application of frog bones is strongly
reminiscent of customary methods in love magic, while the burial of
magical paraphernalia in graves refers undoubtedly to harmful practices.
Actually the whole process was considered bewitchment by the *öntő's*
magical counterpart, the *öntőasszony* (pouring woman) of Töröcske
and Erzsike had the same opinion of Jolika's alleged acts. Reflecting her
thinly concealed intention to introduce Jolika as a wicked malefactor,
Erzsike gives further accounts of Jolika's evil practices, like the so-called
feketegyertyázás (preparing black candles). Jolika and her helper gather
candles from a certain number of graves, and after melting them, the
wax is mixed with soot and a rag is put in the middle as a wick. In
Erzsike's opinion they use these particular candles in secret bewitchment

procedures. The symbolic formulation of the motives of competing healers, Erzsike and Jolika in this case, is best seen in a peculiar dream narrative, which is also telling in regard to the hierarchy of healers.

A few years ago Erzsike suffered lumbago and consequently her legs were disabled. Neither rheumatologists nor neurologists could cure her. She refused to take the pills they prescribed. She continued to receive clients, even though she did so 'crawling on the floor' by her sickbed. One night, when unable to sleep because of terrible pains she had a strange dream: seven acquainted healers appeared and offered their help. Jolika, the *öntő* of Visnye and his son, Jani, Erzsike's *jóstestvér* (brother-soothsayer) were among them.

> They stood around me in a semicircle. Jani was facing me. I turned to him and asked: 'My *jóstestvér*, tell me what my illness is and help!' 'Take the blue pills hidden in the drawer of your bedside table that you did not want to have before! You will wake up tomorrow,' Jani replied.

She woke her husband immediately and he gave her the pills mentioned. The following day she felt better, and she recovered soon after. Although her *jóstestvér* did not ascribe the sudden sickness to anyone's harmful actions, Erzsike suspected Jolika's malevolence was at work. Her suspicions had been fuelled by Jolika's visit the very day prior to her falling sick: 'Face-to-face we are very close friends; but Jolika talks unkindly about me in my absence.'

Considering the uses or abuses of magical power, Erzsike holds a rather particular view, doubtless rooted in her self-image. In terms of the opposing rules of healers and malefactors she says that the former must not harm and, in turn, those operating with evil intentions must not interfere in healing activity:

> Generally, there are *jósok* (soothsayers), who do the good things and there are *jósok*, who do the bad things. And the latter admit it publicly. But, if someone wanted to do both, it would not work.

> Q: It should not or it must not be done?
> A: There are some who want to do good to you today and then evil the next day but it does not work. It hits them back in a certain way. One is either bad or good. No one can be both.

Firmly believing that her healing ability was donated by God and Jesus Christ themselves, Erzsike defines herself as a benevolent healer who is reluctant even to mention any potential method of bewitching and condemns all those suspected of doing evil magic: 'I can get furious at bewitchment'. She of course wants to make a living, and wants to continue to be considered a healer, a practitioner of white magic, not only by herself but by her clientele as well. Nevertheless, the market for magic is balanced by the ongoing interactions between healers and malefactors meeting their clients' wishes. On the one hand malefactors 'do their job for a good sum of money', as Erzsike puts it; on the other hand healers do not help for free either: 'I am paid for healing people!' According to her rather peculiar interpretation of Christian ethics, Erzsike makes a sharp moral distinction between paying a magic specialist for evil or for benign acts. Thus, going to a malefactor is a wicked deed, but paying her (i.e., Erzsike) a large sum for restoring the patient's health or repairing damage caused by bewitchment is done for sacred purposes. She says that this money serves as a holy offering to Erzsike's patron saints, so that the patient may receive their goodwill and help in return.

Angelic Guidance – Post-New Age/esoteric Practices

Several times Erzsike told me about a certain *jóskönyv* (divination book) that she once received from an American patient. She resisted showing me the volume, but revealed certain fragments of its contents, for example the names of angels and some prayers to invoke them. She was absolutely unwilling to recall any prayers or formulae, but did give a brief summary of her angelic knowledge. According to her ideas, each thing and abstract phenomenon on earth has its own guardian angel who can be asked for help in situations connected with that particular place or area of life. At a client's special request she spontaneously invokes the appropriate angel by simply closing her eyes and concentrating on it. When the angel 'appears' she opens her eyes and on a slip of paper she draws the contours of a schematic angel figure without raising her pen. This slip of paper works as an amulet, and it should be at hand whenever that particular angel's help is required.

Erzsike's angel knowledge has been nourished by a recent, and mostly of American origin, post-New Age ideology of angels and other heavenly beings transmitted through the burgeoning esoteric literature which is available even in smaller country bookshops. In the late 1990s a certain Dr Doreen Virtue's books on angels enjoyed by far the greatest popularity on the subject in Hungary. By her own account, this American 'clairvoyant psychologist' and *angyallátó* (seer of the angels)[23] maintains relations with the transcendent sphere of the benign dead, angels and fairies.[24] She has also worked out an 'angel therapy' in order to deal with crises in private life, deepen self-knowledge, and discover personal gifts. Virtue's 'angel therapy' is a continuous inner communication with the benevolent beings of 'angelic realm' (e.g. angels, fairies and the deceased), which means first becoming aware of and then unconditionally accepting 'angel guidance' in all spheres of one's life. The simple techniques of establishing and maintaining heavenly contacts are easily attained by studying Virtue's books or participating in her 'angel readings'. Virtue's multiple personae as a specialist of heavenly communication have a distant kinship with those of medieval living saints. On the one hand she takes the role of a prophet when channelling messages from the angelic realm to the whole of mankind, covering globalization, environmental pollution or the 'forthcoming' cataclysmic events of a global cosmic change in 2012. On the other hand she takes on the more personal aspect of a seer of the dead when invoking recently deceased relatives of the volunteering participants in her workshops.[25] In addition to her magical profession, Virtue is like a guru dedicated to the angelic mission of spreading her ideas. She is convinced that psychic abilities are hidden in every person and she is committed to helping people explore and then improve them until they become an inherent part of their lives. She suggests the purification of body and mind by clearing *chakras*, a method elaborately described in many of her books, as the initial step in getting oneself ready for angelic communication. Psychic abilities and angelic knowledge can then be improved by reading her further volumes or attending the angel readings. Angelic help may be sought in any situation and/or regularly by the use of angel or fairy oracle cards either enclosed in Virtue's basic books on angel and fairy lore or in individual packages. The cards depict the different types of heavenly inhabitants wearing specific garments and with their particular attributes and symbols, and also give a short description of their functions and fields of activity. In the absence of oracle cards, some of Virtue's books may also be used to conjure up angels in a dream by placing them open next to one's bedside at night. Whether Erzsike's curious *jóskönyv* was one of Doreen Virtue's volumes or not, I do not know. From Erzsike's few asides, however, and considering her general knowledge of angels, I get the impression that she may have been given one of Virtue's early English books by an American client. Yet she must have received a detailed explanation or a rough translation of the contents in Hungarian, because none of Virtue's works had been translated and published in Hungary at that time.[26]

The Holy Healer

As I have noted above, some of the *javas* once active in the South Transdanubian area of Hungary could also be referred to as holy healers. First, heavenly helpers, which are also to be found, though less commonly, in the belief circles of the healers mentioned above,[27] are part of Erzsike's magical healing, for she communicates with her 'saints' each time she heals or divines. While executing the wax ritual she prays to Mary and Saint Anthony of Padua:

> My dearest beautiful Virgin Mary and Saint Anthony,
> Help me to save X of curses, troubles,
> illnesses, quarrels, inconveniences,
> and to bring onto X peace, health, and rest.

These saints are literally present in the form of two small statues of Mary and Saint Anthony of Padua standing on the table in the small reception room. Their overseeing of the card reading and wax pouring can be interpreted as a wordless declaration of the holy healer's solely benign intent. Nevertheless, the most important task of these saints or, in other cases numerous angels, is in each particular case to inform the holy healer of the patient's disease and instruct her what to do:

> When I am healing, the angels appear. I close my eyes, pray for that person and the angels come and tell me which part of that person's body is ill. Sweet little angels arrive, flying around me and tell into my closed eyes what I should do.

From Erzsike's point of view, there is little difference between angels and saints, and even their names are interchangeable. It is the benevolent power in their heavenly nature that seems to be more critical in Erzsike's view: 'All the holy ones I love. All saints are the same to me whether an angel or anything else. Our house, our home is full of angels.'

Erzsike makes only a gender distinction between her heavenly patrons when choosing both Jesus and the Virgin Mary as her personal guardians from the Christian pantheon, indicating that earthly gender related differences apply to Heaven as well:

> I have two patrons. One of them is the Virgin Mary. But I do not want to exclude Jesus. Jesus means the masculine for me. I think that men are stronger than women. And in this way, I love them both, somehow.

During the acts of healing or divining, by acquiring her heavenly helpers' aid, Erzsike constantly mediates between the transcendent sphere of angels and saints and the level of everyday life. In turn, her patrons support her unexpectedly with their spectacular or almost miraculous aid in her moments of need. Erzsike is convinced that traditional Christian virtues like reverence and good deeds are worthy payments for the saints' labour:

> I hope my saints will reward me for loving them, being so charitable, and helping people. They have always rewarded me so far. And, what's more, unexpectedly! This is the way saints help.

By reciting prayers and giving special offerings she not only asks for her heavenly partners' help, but very gently obliges them to co-operate with her:

> This is a mania of mine to buy flowers for my saints. I give them flowers as if I paid for their work. It is a thing like that. If the saints are rewarded, it will bring double luck then. You must have heard of giving donations to nuns or to the priest. They say then 'May God give it to you!' That is what they say, that God will give to you. And it is true. It is true.

As a matter of fact, Erzsike puts the saints to work for her clients:

> I think, if I helped someone to get a loan of eighty-million Forints within five months time, my saints here would deserve a bouquet of flowers at least. And that person then does not even care about it. There were one or two like that. I told them they did not need me to make my saints work if they were too mean to bring a bouquet.

Contradicting her firm assertion of refusing to do harmful acts both in practice and in theory, she calls on heavenly assistance when punishing her enemies, i.e., those in charge of bewitchment. She does not need to fight them herself as healers usually do with witches, and as the *javas* or *öntőasszony* once did. Her heavenly patrons are always on the alert and intervene at the right time and often without a previous request. By taking on the sacred quality of inviolability, Erzsike crosses the boundary between mortals and heavenly beings and becomes, temporarily, a living saint. When her enemies attack her holy persona, they attack at the same time her holy patrons, which brings heavenly punishment upon them.

Q: Have you ever been bewitched? When we last talked you told me something about your eyes having been bewitched ...
A: Yes. People happen to be envious of each other. There are a few who used to envy my abilities. But those loving saints must not be cursed or bewitched because saints will punish [the malefactors] doubly. Someone bewitched me ... or wanted to bewitch me. Finally I found out who did it.

Q: Did you?
A: Yes, indeed, I found out it. I waxed my own house and it revealed my enemy, who was envious of my knowledge and opposed me by [doing] evil things. Wax and cards also revealed to me that his shop, his business would go bad and that he would be hurt in a short time. That the leg of that man who did it to me would be injured. Three weeks later his shop was robbed and stock of great value was stolen. The day before yesterday his horse trampled his feet. I knew that he had done it. We had been good friends until then, but he avoids me since then. Honestly, I did nothing to him. He simply learned that I became aware of his evil acts against me. He should not have done that!

The concentrated presence of heavenly forces is perceptible both by clients and by visiting fellow healers immediately on entering Erzsike's house: the sick feel better, the nervous calm down, etc.

They [the fellow healers] do not know what it is in here, within the gates. They feel an enormous sacred defensive power in here. It is absolutely unique! They say they have never felt such thing before.

Possessed by the sacred powers of saints and angels, Erzsike's house has become a refuge for anyone, including Erzsike herself, haunted by evil supernatural forces. As a sacred place it also serves as a regenerating resource for regaining the holy healer's own magical healing power: 'I feel secure in this house and nowhere else out of here. I feel good in here.'

By her own account Erzsike informed her confessor, Father István, the Roman Catholic priest of Kémes about her transcendental experiences and her supernatural abilities. Like many female saints in the Middle Ages, the confessor helps Erzsike to accept her peculiar abilities by explaining them as a sacred gift from God. He has also supported a completely Christian interpretation of her healing activity from the very beginning, calling it a very special mission.

Priests in general do not like divination and such things because they consider it the work of Satan. But the priest told me that what I did was sacred and a good thing. He said I should not give it up because it was gifted by God.

Based on his own transcendent experiences Father István helped Erzsike to understand her initiating vision, interpreting it as a vocation from Jesus himself.

> Soon after having moved to this house, a huge light was seen inside. It appeared on the threshold in the evening, as I stepped into my room. I stepped through the light and then back again and it was still there. The other day I asked the priest what it meant. He said that Jesus appeared in the form of light at that time. He also said that I should not stop healing. He also saw Jesus once, when he was a child. He could see a great big light before him and that was Jesus. He decided to become a priest when he grew up.

Firmly believing in Erzsike's charismatic abilities, the priest himself does not hesitate to send patients who are in great need of the healing power of heavenly intervention: 'He came to me with some sick people and asked me to cure them. These people recovered faster after their operations.'

Following her confessor's advice Erzsike strives to show an exemplary behaviour to her patients, and keep her personal difficulties to herself. She is convinced that meeting a helpful and pious healer is crucial to a successful treatment to ending in perfect recovery: 'I should always be seen to be unchanged by my patients. I should always be nice with them otherwise I can not treat them.'

Erzsike's greatest desire was to be acknowledged as both a sacred and profane patroness of the village community. The erection of a statue devoted to the Virgin Mary in the front yard of her house served distinctly pious purposes. But her political ambitions have failed because she has not been elected mayor in the past three municipal elections.

> In the summer, if I recover and I have many patients, I will offer the church the money I get for healing. Yet, I would like to have a statue erected in my front yard. That would be a statue of a bigger size standing in a small arched chapel. Jesus or Mary would be standing there. My older son would build a rim where flowers or candles were put. This is my most ardent wish. ... No one would dare to take it away from here while I am still alive. I think that the village people would also be happy with it. Because they like me and I like them. I like many of them very much! I think I am too kind with them. Honestly, some of the village would like me to be the mayor. I may wait with this intention

until next year. And then if I were the mayor, I would have that statue built in the middle of the village. It would look very nice there.

Summary

In this case study I have tried to highlight the links between diverse imaginaries, ideas and beliefs in one particular healer's practice examined *in situ*. Placing the holy healer's activity and the related beliefs in a broader European context is far beyond the scope of the present study. Nevertheless, connections reach for beyond the geographical boundaries of the South Transdanubian area of Hungary.

Can one interpret some aspects of Erzsike's magical practice as a particular form of possession by the dead? Even if she denied contacting and reporting on the dead, Erzsike admitted that her deceased acquaintances and relatives appear to her spontaneously by daylight and in her dreams. Although these appearances may not necessarily involve possession, her accounts of acquiring magical power through the dead healer's apparition in a whirlwind or the arrival of the same dead healer's living alter ego have connotations of possession by the dead, or at very least interaction with them. According to Éva Pócs the motifs of possession by wind demons or by the evil or maleficent dead flying in the air is closely related to possession by the dead (Pócs 2001: 126). She also refers to the belief motif of the maleficent dead dragging the soul of the dying witch into the clouds or into a thunderstorm. These beliefs support both potential interpretations of Erzsike's versions of the stories relating to the acquisition of magical knowledge. In the first version the soul of the dead healer of Visnye, dragged by the maleficent dead, enters Erzsike's body and makes her divine by pouring wax the first time. The healer's dead alter ego's apparition in the second version reflects the belief motifs of the living/dead manifestations of certain types of wizards, but also resembles dead ancestors appearing as beneficent dead (Pócs 1997: 52–53). If Doreen Virtue is indeed the author of Erzsike's magical handbook and Erzsike's model, her practice further support to these hypotheses. Erzsike does not seem to have adopted Virtue's trance technique but, Erzsike's spontaneous visions of the dead and the initiation stories seem to indicate a temporary and immature form of possession by the dead. Indeed, the symptoms of Erzsike's mental disease (i.e. frequent headaches, depression, cataleptic states) underline this interpretation, but they also reveal connections with certain aspects of fairy belief. Illnesses brought on by the fairies and fairy possession are very similar. Éva Pócs calls possession by the fairies 'a predominant cultural variant of possession by the dead in the belief systems of the neighbouring South Eastern Europe which is closely related to divine-possession' (Pócs 2001: 128).[28] Erzsike's fairy illness which led to her acquiring magical knowledge, and the heavenly connotations of her healing activity suggest that practice is closely related to that of the 'fairy wizards', wizards initiated and under the patronage of fairies (Pócs 1989: 95–98; 1997: 184–186) who were once held to be the opponents of witches in the traditional belief systems of Hungary and South Eastern Europe.

In my opinion Erzsike does not consciously follow the traits of traditional healers in the area (the *javas*) and her activity is not a pure reconstruction of their healing practice, as with the modern esoteric *táltos*-healers whose methods are becoming more and more popular these days (Lázár 2006; Kis-Halas 2010b). She is a traditional folk healer *par excellence* who employs some fashionable contemporary methods. The most decisive features of Erzsike's magical characteristics are much closer to those of a traditional healer than a New Age specialist. She seems to have integrated the most traditional elements of Doreen Virtue's magical activity, for example the seeing of the dead and mediation between angels and men, while disregarding Virtue's prophetic manifestations and environmentalist ideology. In spite of Erzsike's seemingly old-fashioned methods and ideology, her healing and divining activities meet real social and personal needs. Due to the globalization in medicine and the boom in the market for magic, alternative methods such as reflexology, aromatherapy, energy healing and other practices have become known in the past decades, even in the remotest villages of Hungary (Kis-Halas 2007, 2008, 2009, 2010b). Some 19 years ago Erzsike introduced her very special services into this rapidly changing environment. Since her position in the local magical market requires continuous confirmation, she is obliged to constantly rearrange and reshape her image as a diviner and healer to fit her customers' demands. Nevertheless she prefers to follow traditional patterns in her activity and keeps using 'old-fashioned' concepts such as witchcraft, and traditional methods such as wax pouring.

Abbreviations for Archival Source Materials

BNA   = Baranya megye Néprajzi Atlasza (Atlas of Folk Culture in Baranya County, Hungary). Department of Ethnography, Janus Pannonus Museum, Pécs.

EA   = A Budapesti Néprajzi Múzeum Ethnológiai Adattára (Manuscript Collection of the Ethnological Archives of the Museum of Ethnography, Budapest).

MNA = Az MTA Néprajzi Kutatóintézetének Magyar Néphit Archívuma (Archive of Folk-Belief of the Ethnographical Institute of the Hungarian Academy of Sciences).

MNAt = Magyar Néprajzi Atlasz (Atlas of Hungarian Folk Culture) I–III. Hungarian Academy of Sciences, 1987. Budapest.

Notes

1. Further data is based on fieldwork interviews and conversations conducted in the villages of Rádfalva, Nagyharsány, Siklós (all in Baranya county) and in Kaposvár and Töröcske (in Somogy county) in 2000 and 2001. Furthermore, I have studied the relevant thematic groups of the healer, wise man, holy man, witch, bewitchment and divination at the Folklore Institute of the Hungarian Academy of Sciences' Folk Belief Archives. The Archive consists of publications and collections of folk belief from the Hungarian-speaking areas in the Carpathian Basin dating back to the last decades of the nineteenth century. It is currently being processed digitally and arranged into indexes of belief motifs and catalogues of belief stories and legends by a research group led by Professor Éva Pócs of the Department of European Ethnology and Cultural Anthropology at the University of Pécs.

2. A method of divination in which molten wax is poured into a bowl of cold water. The wax is cooled and takes firm shape as a pancake. The diviner then examines and interprets the 'signs' seen on the solid wax pieces.

3. Recent research revealed that contemporary practitioners of folk healing and divination are often characterized as having similarly syncretistic ideas and beliefs (see Gagyi 1988; Lengyel 1998; Mondok 2001; Pákay 2004; Párhonyi 2004; Simon 2002).

4. See, for example http://www.mariaut.hu/web/drupal63/content/mi-maria-ut (accessed 19 July 2010).

5. Tanya Luhrmann reports similarly organized formations ('magical groups') in London's esoteric milieu from the 1980s, see Luhrmann [1989] (1991): 29–38.

6. I give the Hungarian terms first, then the English literal translation in brackets.

7. This corresponds to the activity of traditional healers of the same area, reflected in belief stories, in which the healer reveals the location of certain harmful magical objects in the victim's house. Some examples: Matolay M. 1975. 09. 11–14. BNA 154 Kővágószőlős (Baranya county), Zentai T. (1983: 138) Lúzsok (Baranya county), Király L. (1995: 57–58) Gölle (Somogy county), Kis-Halas (2004b) Töröcske (Somogy county).

8. The last two traditional folk healers in Baranya county documented in ethnomedicinal and folk belief collections were Mrs János Cakó (Sellye) and the daughter of Ferenc Dallos (Szalánta). The latter was the last healer called *fíves*, while Mrs Cakó was generally referred as *javas*.

9. For further data on the *füves/fíves* see Kiss (1940 [1986] 212–213.)

10. For data on wax or lead pouring from Somogy and Zala counties see Gönczi (1905; 1914: 309–310; 1940: 200–201); Kis-Halas (2004b); for data from the Ormánság region (Baranya county): Zentai T. (1983: 170–171). For further, more or less recent, data on the Hungarian speaking areas of the Carpathian basin (the list is not intended to be exhaustive): Gyimes and Moldva regions: Diószegi (1960: 85–86); Harangzó (1998); Takács (2001: 454–457); Mezőség region (Transylvania, Romania): Keszeg (1997: 68–71); Kalotaszeg region (Transylvania, Romania): Vasas (1985: 72–73); Subcarpathian region (Ukraine): Kótyuk (2000: 88); Pákay (2004: 331–333); south-east Hungary: Polner (2002: 111–113). A forthcoming contribution to the healing of fright by pouring lead and wax in Hungarian folk medicine is by Kis-Halas (2010).

11. The *javas*, or on his/her advice, any person of the victim's family or household smoked the bewitched person, animal, or any parts of them (like hair, robe, chain, etc.) according to the *pars pro toto* principle of sympathetic magic. Soon after the procedure the potential malefactor appeared at the spot on some pretext. For data on the Ormánság region (Baranya county) see Zentai T. (1983: 139–142).

12. Living saints practising as healers in twentieth century Limousine, France see Boyon – Bertrand (1993).

13. Both *jós* (soothsayer) and *javas* are derived from the word *jó* (good), see MTESz II (1970: 267).

14. The charm recited while pouring wax by the *öntőasszony* of Töröcske (Somogy county), Mrs Nándor Fehér, Rozália Zsifkó (born in 1913) was first published by Erdélyi (1976: 133–136). The charm was still known but no longer used by the current *öntőasszony*, who is the descendant of Mrs Fehér, see Kis-Halas (2004b).

15. The same tendency of individualization is reported of current beliefs and ideas of witchcraft in Transylvania, see Györgydeák (2001).

16. For further data on witch and healer relations in the Ormánság region see: Zentai T. (1983, 148); Berze Nagy (1940 III 252–253), MNA Szilaspuszta (Baranya County) collected by Vilmos Diószegi (1961). Some data from the

Zselic region: EA 15473 Zselicszentpál (Somogy county) collected by József Hoss (1967); MNA Cserénfa (Somogy county) collected by István Velzenbach (1971); Kis-Halas (2004b).

17. Motifs about acquiring magical knowledge such as by being sick or inheriting it from a dying specialist are common in all geographical locations and can be applied to any type of magical experts. Some local examples from the South Transdanubian area: the *javas* of Sellye (Baranya county) got her mother's healing ability at the moment of her mother's death, Zentai T. 1983: 134; in Szenna (Somogy county) the *öntőasszony* was thought to take on her predecessor's knowledge by holding her hands on the deathbed, RRJM NA 1018 János Dávid (69) collected by László Fekete; the *javas* of Szigetvár (Baranya county) appointed her heiress but she did not appear at the deathbed, BNAt Mrs Bálint Kapus (b. 1914.) Kővágószőlős (Baranya county) collected by Magdolna Matolay, 1975, Sept. 9–11; the *öntőasszony* at Szilvásszentmárton (Somogy county) had to give her knowledge to her daughter in order to die. Ébner (1931: 147).

18. Dragged into a whirlwind by *szépasszonyok* (fair women), a *javas* candidate is given seeing abilities: BNAt Bogdása (Baranya county) collected by Katalin Kovács 1975, July 11. The *javas* appears or flies invisibly in the whirlwind: data from the Ormánság region by Zentai T. (1983. 68, 136–137).

19. The *öntőasszonyok* of Töröcske (Somogy county) are reputed to gain their knowledge when possessed by the former *öntőasszony* of the dynasty, see Kis-Halas (2004b). The *öntőasszony* of Simonfa is reported to acquire her abilities in the same way, MNA Mrs György Szentes (b. 1942) Simonfa (Somogy county) collected by Vilmos Diószegi (1952: Oct.).

20. More examples of the Ormánság region by Zentai T. (1983: 142, 143, 148).

21. A woman in Szaporca (Baranya county) specialized in healing the evil eye. She was reported to become seriously ill after each individual successful treatment, thus her niece had not the slightest intention of taking over her healing practice, see Zentai T. (1983: 165). The motif of the healer suffering while curing the patient emerges in connection with healers specialized in 'Saint Anthony's fire' from south-east Hungary, the Moldva and the Gyimes regions, see Grynaeus (2002: 155–156).

22. In a belief narrative collected in Kémes (Baranya county) the *javas* refuses to heal a cow because the malefactor is stronger than him, therefore he can only summon the malefactor but can not overcome her, see: Zentai T. (1983: 144). The same motif is known from a story collected in Sellye (Baranya county), Zentai T. (1983: 148).

23. I created this term on the analogy of *halottlátó* (seer of the dead), because there are no equivalents in Hungarian belief material for specialists having mediatory relations with angels. (J. K. H.)

24. Doreen Virtue's numerous biographies, published in several volumes, inform us that her seeing ability was recognized in early childhood: she was constantly seeing her deceased relatives around her. Following a car robbery in 1995, when she was almost killed but ultimately rescued by her angelic guardians, she received her first angelic message: 'Teach as many people as possible, as soon as possible, to hear their angels!', which soon became the slogan of her 'angelic' mission. See www.worldangelday.com www.angeltherapy.com [accessed 2010.01.20].

25. As far as the purposes are concerned this personal aspect of Doreen's readings strongly resembles the Hungarian *halottlátó*'s session: both procedures aim to restore the disturbed equilibrium between the worlds of the living and the dead by asking for and then fulfilling the requests and wills of those deceased.

26. Virtue (2002).

27. Considering the predominant role of God in giving healing abilities and assisting in the healing process the belief circle of the *öntőasszony* in Töröcske is unique in the region. The main motives are: God heals instead of the healer/the healer cures with God's permission, see Erdélyi 1976, 138, MNA Mrs Nándor Fehér Jr. Töröcske (Somogy county) (2001, June 28). collected by Judit Kis-Halas; God forces the healing activity on the unwilling candidate EA 3053 [JPM NA 365] Mrs Márton Zsifkó Erzsébet Kovács (b. 1878) Töröcske (Somogy county) collected by Vilmos Diószegi (1952: May); the healer's knowledge is acquired by learning a prayer, see Kis-Halas (2004b). Some further evidence of similar ideas connected with folk healers in other regions of Hungary: north Transdanubian, see Vajkai (1938: 346–349); south-east: Gryneaus (2000: 497, 2002a: 155, 2002b: 19, 25, 100); former south Hungary (now Serbia) Jung (1990: 250–251, 276–278), former north-east Hungary, subcarpathian region (now Ukraine) Kész (2000), Pákay (2004).

28. Pócs notes that the narrative tradition referring to the individual variant of fairy possession phenomena (also showing certain features of heavenly possession) exclusively concerns males (often musicians, or young lads) dragged to the fairy heavens (2001: 131–132).

References

Bálint, S. (1981 [1942]) *Egy magyar szentember. Orosz István önéletrajza.* Budapest [reprint: Szolnok].

Bouteiller, M. (1958) *Sorcieres et jeteurs de sort.* Paris: Plon.

Boyon, D. and Bertrand, M. (1993) Recourse aux guérisseurs et aux saints guérisseurs en Limousin: Approche psychologique des representations et des mécanismes permettant le persistence de ces pratiques. In N. de Belmont and F. Lautman (eds) *Ethnologie des faits religieux en Europe.*

Colloque national de le Société d' Ethnologie française, Strasbourg 24–26 novembre 1988, 193–202. Paris: Cths Editions.

Burkhardt, A. (1994) 'La radice è infetta': The case of Sophia Agnes von Klangenberg – A (False) Living Saint in Cologne in the 1620s. In *Papers of the Conference 'Healing, magic, and Belief in Europe 15th – 20th Centuries, New Perspectives, 21–25 September 1994. Woodschoten, Zeist'*, 132–144.

Diószegi, V. (1960) Embergyógyítás a moldvai székelyeknél. *Néprajzi Közlemények* 3 (4): 35–124. É. n. Viasz- és ólomöntés a magyar népi gyógyászatban. Kézirat. MTA NKI Adattára.

Ébner, S. (1931) A zselici csontrakók és 'öntőasszonyok'. *Ethnographia* XLII: 146–148.

Elek, P., Gunda, B., *et al.* (1936) *Elsüllyedt falu a Dunántúlon*. Budapest: Kemse község élete.

Erdélyi, Z. (1976) *Hegyet hágék, lőtőt lépék. Archaic Folk Prayers* (2nd edn). Budapest: Magvető Kiadó.

Erdélyi, Z. (1999) *Hegyet hágék, lőtőt lépék. Huszonöt év múlva. Archaic Folk Prayers: 25 Years Later*. Pozsony, Bratislava: Kalligram Kiadó.

Evans-Pritchard, E. E. (1935) Witchcraft. *Africa: Journal of the International Institute of African Languages and Cultures* 8 (4): 411–422.

Gagyi, J. (1998) Ica. Egy homoródalmási jósasszony és egy székelyföldi divinációs hagyomány. In *Jelek égen és földön. Hiedelem és helyi társadalom a Székelyföldön. KAM-Regionális és Antropológiai kutatások Központja*, 61–82. Csíkszereda: Pro-Print Könyvkiadó.

Gagyi, J. (2001) A szentasszony. In Pócs, É. (ed.) *Lélek, halál, túlvilág. Vallásetnológiai fogalmak tudományközi megközelítésben. Tanulmányok a transzcendemsről* Vol. 2, 171–192. Balassi Kiadó.

Györgydeák, A. (2001) A rontás szociálpszichológiája. In Pócs, É. (ed.) *Két csíki falu néphite a századvégen*. 374–418. Budapest: Európai Foklór Intézet – Osiris Kiadó.

Gönczi, F. (1905) Az emberi betegségek és gyógyításaik a göcseji s a hetési népnél. *Ethnographia* XVI: 345–61.

Gönczi, F. (1914) *Göcsej és kapcsolatosan Hetés vidékének és népének összevontabb ismertetése*. Kaposvár: Szabó L. Nyomda.

Gönczi, F. (1940) *A somogyi gyermek*. Kaposvár: Szabó L. Nyomda.

Grynaeus, T. (1974) *Engi Tüdő Vince: a legenda és a valóság. A Móra Ferenc Múzeum évkönyve 1972–1973*, 155–183. Szeged.

Grynaeus, T. (1999) Szépasszonyok és tudósok Dávodon. In K. Benedek and E. Csonka-Takács (eds) *Démonikus és szakrális világok határán. Mentalitástörténeti tanulmányok Pócs Éva 60. születésnapjára*, 189–204. Budapest: MTA Néprajzi Kutató Intézet.

Grynaeus, T. (2000) Tápai Pista ürügyén. Gyógyító egyéniségekhez fűződő legendák, mondák, narratívumok. *Néprajzi Látóhatár* IX (3–4): 495–523.

Grynaeus, T. (2002) *Szent Antal tüze*. Budapest: Akadémiai Kiadó.

Harangzó, I. (1998) *'Krisztusz háza arangyosz ...' Archaikus imák, ráolvasások, kántálók a gyimesi és moldvai hagyományból*. Újkígyós: Ipolyi Arnold Népfőiskola.

Hegedűs, L. (1946) *Népnyelvi beszélgetések az Ormánságból*. Pécs: Dunántúli Tudományos Intézet.

Hesz, Á. (2001) Kapcsolatok a halottakkal. In É. Pócs (ed.) *Két csíki falu néphite a századvégen.*, 217–243. Budapest: Európai Foklór Intézet – Osiris Kiadó.

Hovorka, O. and Kronfeld, A. (1908–1909) *Vergleichende Volksmedizin I–II. Eine Darstellung volksmedizinischer Sitten und Gerbräuche, Anschauungen und Heilfaktoren, des Aberglauben und Zaubermedizin.* Stuttgart: Strecker und Schröder.

Jung, K. (1990) *Hiedelemmondák és hiedelmek. Adatok Gombos nép hiedelemvilágához.* Újvidék: Forum Kiadó.

Kallós, Z. (1966) Ráolvasás a moldvai és a gyimesi csángóknál. *Műveltség és Hagyomány* VIII: 137–157.

Kész, M. (2000) 'Isten után gyógyítok.' Egy ugocsai öntőasszony. *Ethnica* II: 41–42.

Keszeg, V. (1997) *Jóslások a Mezőségen. Etnomantikai elemzés.* Sepsiszentgyörgy: BON AMI Könyvkiadó.

Kieckhefer, R. (1976) *European Witch Trials. Their Foundation in Popular and Learned Culture, 1300–1500.* Berkeley, CA: University of California Press.

Kis-Halas, J. (2004a) 'Amikor gyógyítok, angyalok jelennek meg a szemem előtt' Egy dél-baranyai szent gyógyító. In É. Pócs (ed.) *Áldás és átok, csoda és boszorkányság. Vallásetnológiai fogalmak tudományközi megközelítésben. Tanulmányok a transzcendensről* Vol. IV, 284–319. Budapest: Balassi Kiadó.

Kis-Halas, J. (2004b) Átformált hagyomány – a töröcskei öntőasszonyok. *Tabula* VII (2): 191–208.

Kis-Halas, J. (2007) 'Fejtetőmön arany fénygömb'. Az első lépések reiki ösvényén. Beavatás egy ezoterikus gyógyászati rendszerbe. In É. Pócs (ed.) *Maszk, átváltozás, beavatás. Vallásetnológiai fogalmak tudományközi megközelítésben. Tanulmányok a transzcendensről* Vol. V, 400–420. Budapest: Balassi Kiadó.

Kis-Halas, J. (2008) 'Ha eljönnek az angyalok ...' Angyallátók, esszénusok, beavatottak a mai magyar New Age mozgalmakban. In É. Pócs (ed.) *Démonok, látók, szentek. Vallásetnológiai fogalmak tudományközi megközelítésben. Tanulmányok a transzcendensről* Vol. VI, 243–278. Budapest: Balassi Kiadó.

Kis-Halas, J. (2009) Kortárs látók és gyógyítók. In V. Keszeg, L. Peti and É. Pócs (eds) *Álmok és látomások a 20-21. századból. Szöveggyűjtemény.*

Vol. 1, 512–538 (Fontes Ethnologiae Hungaricae VI.). Budapest: L'Harmattan Kiadó.

Kis-Halas, J. (2010a) Öröklődő tárgyak – öröklődő tudomány. A viaszöntés folklórja. (Inherited objects – inherited knowledge: the folklore of wax-pouring). In É. Pócs (ed.) *Tárgy, jel, jelentés. 'Tágy és Folklór' Konferencia Vaján, 2005 október 7–9-én,* 281–317. Budapest: L'Harmattan Kiadó – PTE Néprajz és Kulturális Antropológia tanszék.

Kis-Halas, J. (2010b) Jézus katonái a Földön és a Mennyei Jeruzsálemben. Egy kortárs ezoterikus gyógyászati rendszer. In É. Pócs (ed.) *Mágikus és szakrális medicina. Vallásetnológiai fogalmak tudományközi megközelítésben. Tanulmányok a transzcendensről* Vol. VII, 593–622. Budapest: Balassi Kiadó.

Kiss, Géza (1979 [1937]) *Ormányság. Baranya Megye Tanácsa Végrehajtó Bizottsága Művelődési Osztálya.* Pécs. (facsimile).

Kodolányi, J., Jr. (1960) *Ormánság.* Budapest: Gondolat Kiadó.

Komáromi, T. (2001) Az ijedtség. In D. Czégényi and V. Keszeg (eds) *Emberek, szövegek, hiedelmek,* 112–140. Cluj: Kriza János Néprajzi Társaság.

Kótyuk, E. (2000) *A népi gyógyítás hagyományai egy kárpátaljai magyar faluban.* Budapest: Európai Folklór Intézet – Osiris Kiadó.

Lázár, I. (2006) Táltos healers, neoshamans and multiple medical realities in post-socialist Hungary. In H. Johannesen and I. Lázár (eds) *Multiple Medical Realities: Patients and Healers in Biomedical, Alternative and Traditional Medicine. The EASA Series Vol. 4,* 35–53. Oxford and New York: Berghahn Books.

Lengyel, Á. (1998) Halottlátó Lőrinciben. *Barna Gábor Könyvtár 1,* 188–204. Szeged –Budapest: JATE Néprajz Tanszék – Magyar Néprajzi Társaság.

Luhrmann, T. M. [1989] (1991) *Persuasions of the Witches' Craft: Ritual Magic in Contemporary England.* Cambridge, MA: Harvard University Press.

Macfarlane A. (1970) *Witchcraft in Tudor and Stuart England: A Regional and Comparative Study.* London: Routledge & Kegan Paul.

Mondok, Á. (2001) Adatok egy gyógyítóasszony világképéhez. In É. Pócs (ed.) *Két csíki falu néphite a századvégen,* 242–287. Budapest: Európai Foklór Intézet – Osiris Kiadó.

Pais, D. (1975) A néző és a látó. A sámán teljesítményei közül I. In D. Pais *A magyar ősvallás nyelvi emlékeiből,* 250–253. Budapest: Akadémiai Kiadó.

Pákay, V. (2004) A tiszabökényi gyógyító. In É. Pócs (ed.) *Áldás és átok, csoda és boszorkányság. Vallásetnológiai fogalmak tudományközi megközelítésben. Tanulmányok a transzcendensről* Vol. IV, 320–341. Budapest: Balassi Kiadó.

Párhonyi, T. (2004) Egy javasasszony szerepei. In É. Pócs (ed.) *Áldás és átok, csoda és boszorkányság. Vallásetnológiai fogalmak tudományközi megközelítésben. Tanulmányok a transzcendensről* Vol. IV, 246–283. Budapest: Balassi Kiadó.

Phillips, S. D. (2004) Waxing like the moon: Women folk healers in rural western Ukraine. *Folklorica. Journal of the Slavic and East European Folklore Association* IX (1): 13–46.

Pócs, É. (1989) *Tündérek, démonok, boszorkányok.* Budapest: Akadémiai Kiadó.

Pócs, É. (1997) *Élők és holtak, látók és boszorkányok.* Budapest: Akadémiai Kiadó.

Pócs, É. (2001) Megszálló halottak, halotti megszállottság. In Pócs, É. (ed.) *Lélek, halál. Túlvilág. Vallásetnológiai fogalmak tudományközi megközelítésben. Tanulmányok a transzcendensről* II, 119–139. Budapest: Balassi Kiadó.

Pócs, É. (2002) Magyar samanizmus a kora újkori forrásokban. In É. Pócs *Magyar néphit Közép- és Kelet-Európa határán. Válogatott tanulmányok* I, 136–172. Budapest: L'Harmattan Kiadó.

Pócs, É. (2005) 'Tündéres' és 'Szent Ilona szerzete', avagy voltak-e magyar tündérvarázslók? In I. Csörsz Rumen (ed.) *Mindenes gyűjtenény I. Tanulmányok Küllős Imola 60. születésnapjára. Artes Populares* XXI, 289–308. Budapest: ELTE BTK Folklore Tanszék.

Polner, Z. (2002) *Kilenc fának termő ága. Népi szövegek Tápéról.* Szeged: Juhász Gyula Fősikola.

Simon, B. (2002) A természetfelettivel való kapcsolatteremtés technikái egy székelyföldvári parasztasszony életében. In S. Á. Töhötöm (ed.) *Lenyomatok. Fiatal kutatók a népi kultúráról. Kriza könyvek* 12, 110–129. Kriza János Néprajzi Társaság. Kolozsvár – Cluj Napoca.

Takács, Gy. (2001) *Aranykertbe' aranyfa. Gyimesi, hárompataki,úz-völgyi csángó imák és ráolvasások.* Budapest: Szent István Társulat.

Vajkai, A. (1938) Az ősi-i javas ember. *Ethnographia* XLIL: 346–373.

Vasas, S. (1985) *Népi gyógyászat. Kalotaszegi gyűjtés.* Bucharest: Kriterion Kiadó.

Virtue, D. (2002) *Angyalokkal gyógyítás.* Budapest: Mandala-Véda Kiadó.

Zentai, J. (1987) A születés, házasság és a halál népszokásai. In *A Pécsi Janus Pannonius Múzeum Évkönyve,* 30–31, 1985–1986, 325–343. Pécs.

Zentai, T. (1974) Az ormánsági 'szépasszony' helye a magyar néphitben. In *A Pécsi Janus Pannonius Múzeum Évkönyve,* 17–18, 1972–1973, 223–237. Pécs.

Zentai, T. (1983) Ormánsági hiedelmek. *Foklór Archívum* 15. Budapest: MTA Néprajzi Kutatócsoport.

Zuesse, E. M. (1987) Divination. In M. Eliade (ed.) *The Encyclopedia of Religion* 4, 375–382. New York: Collier–Macmillan.

Chronic Illness and the Negotiation of Vernacular Religious Belief

Anne Rowbottom[*]

The increasing popularity of alternative therapies is introducing many people to alternative spiritualities, often for the first time. One example of this is to be found among sufferers of Chronic Fatigue Syndrome (CFS) also known as Myalgic Encephalomylopathy (ME), a condition for which scientific medicine has been unable to produce a cure. Although many people with CFS/ME remain hopeful that medical research will eventually determine a cause and provide a remedy, their faith in science is far from absolute. Lacking a cure, many people seek alternative therapies which emphasize the holistic healing of body, mind and spirit. Those following this path often face difficulties in accommodating Christian beliefs with those of the alternative spiritualities that they encounter. The material presented in this article is grounded in my own experience of CFS/ME and of alternative therapies, including Reiki healing. This chapter is a case study drawn from work in progress. In this case study Nancy, an older woman, describes her negotiation of the tensions between traditional religious belief and her re-spiritualization through Reiki. In conclusion I argue that in Nancy's self-narrative the need for a greater under-standing of vernacular beliefs and practices can be seen.

The defining feature of CFS/ME, as provided by the medical researchers Sykes and Campion (2002), is 'chronic, severe and disabling fatigue which is made worse by physical or mental exertion. Other symptoms include impairment of short-term memory and concentration, sleep disturbance, muscle and joint pain and a profound malaise' (Shepherd 1999; Sykes and Campion 2002: 4; cf. Jacobs 1997). In other words, CFS/ME is a seriously debilitating loss of both physical and mental energy, which may last for decades. Onset frequently follows a viral infection, as in my own case, or after

* Anne Rowbottom, now retired, was formerly Senior Lecturer in the Centre for Human Communication at Manchester Metropolitan University, UK.

surgery, as in the case of Nancy whose experiences are the focus of this paper. A further difficulty for those with CFS/ME is that the symptoms, diagnosis and lack of cure do not fit the dominant model of medical practice. As a result, doctors and patients alike are confronted with the uncomfortable fact that, as Dr Anne MacIntyre (herself a sufferer and writer on CFS/ME) observes, 'you cannot go to your doctor and come away with a prescription for a drug which will cure [CFS/ME]' (MacIntyre 1998: 116). Consequently, as a report to the Government Chief Medical Officer (CFS/ME Working Group 2002) notes, '[P]atients and carers often encounter a lack of understanding from healthcare professionals. This lack seems to be associated with inadequate awareness and understanding of the illness among many health professionals and in the wider public' (CFS/ME Working Group 2002: 5). Consequently, 'a proportion of patients feel alienated from clinical professionals' (CFS/ME Working Group 2006: 6). The inability to provide a cure, accompanied by dismissiveness, incomprehension, or even disbelief (actual or perceived) have, the report goes on to suggest, a profoundly negative effect. In addition to alienating CFS/ME patients from clinical professionals 'such attitudes can also lead the patient to seek help from alternative and complementary therapists' (CFS/ME Working Group 2002: 26). This part of the report, in common with the response of many clinical professionals, communicates unease with alternative and complementary therapies and an implicit distancing of scientific medicine from other systems of healing.

Bonnie O'Connor, a folklorist and ethnographer specializing in health belief systems, compares such unease with the way the supernatural has been excluded from the domain of science in general and from medical science in particular (O'Connor 1995: 15).

In *Healing Traditions* (1995), O'Connor makes two points that are important to the current discussion. First, although the religious, the spiritual and the metaphysical are now excluded from the canon of *conventional* medicine, people still actively maintain them in their everyday lives, as part of vernacular health beliefs. Second, when people link their health beliefs with their spiritual beliefs, then such beliefs may be equated with vernacular religion. In using this term O'Connor follows the definition given by Leonard Primiano of vernacular religion as '[religion] as it is lived: as human beings encounter, understand, interpret, and practice it' (Primiano 1997: 714). One of the components of vernacular health beliefs identified by O'Connor is 'the existence of a font of healing energy (whether divine, cosmic, or marshaled from within) which is tapped by healers' (O'Connor 1995: 16). For people living with chronic fatigue, the concept of tapping into healing energy and of removing obstructions in the flow of energy through the body can be very appealing, as it is energy itself which has been sapped from their daily lives. Channelling the life energy of the universe is a central belief and practice in the tradition of Reiki healing.

Reiki is said to have originated in Japan in the 1920s through the work of Dr Mikao Usui. Mrs Hawayo Takata is credited with introducing Reiki healing to the USA in the 1940s, from where it spread into other English speaking countries. The Japanese term Reiki is usually translated as referring to 'Rei' the universal or cosmic energy and 'Ki' the life force which flows through every human being (Quest 2002; cf. Kelly 2002; Bronwen and Stiene 2003). The method of healing and the centrality of this life force energy are made clear by Penelope Quest in a widely available guidebook for Reiki practitioners. Reiki she says is 'a safe gentle, non-intrusive hands-on healing technique for use on yourself or with others, which uses spiritual energy to treat physical ailments ... However, it is much more than a physical therapy. It is a holistic system for balancing, healing and harmonizing all aspects of the person – body, mind, emotions and spirit – and it can also be used to encourage personal and spiritual awareness and growth' (Quest 2002: 3). As is apparent in Quest's description, the Reiki tradition makes a clear link between health beliefs and spiritual beliefs – a link which, following O'Connor (1995) and Primiano (1995; 1997), places Reiki healers and their clients within the practice of vernacular religion. The rest of this paper is drawn from a narrative given by 'Nancy' describing the ways in which she encounters, understands, interprets and lives out her own vernacular beliefs in Reiki healing.

Nancy was born in 1930 and was in her mid-70s at the time of the interviews. She left school at the age of 14 to work in an office and gave up work at the age of 19 when she married and raised a large family. Nancy was a devout Roman Catholic, regularly attending her parish church in an Anglo-Irish working class community. Life was not always easy as, she says, 'I had a lot of problems within my marriage'. After 25 years the marriage finally ended in divorce. Since then Nancy has lived on her own in the small town of Rowanthwaite in the Pennine hills of northwestern England.

From the mid-1960s to the mid-1970s, the most difficult period of her life, she found that turning to God through her religion failed to help her explain, or deal with, the increasingly intolerable situation of her married life and its devastating effect on her family. In discussing her loss of faith in what she refers to as 'formal religion', Nancy describes how, in seeking help for her troubles, 'I turned to God through my church, my religion, but it didn't work, it didn't help. My prayers were never answered. So that was the beginning of the fade out really. I stopped going to church regularly and would just go occasionally.' The gradual breakdown of her religious worldview led to her final break with Roman Catholicism which she identifies as occurring in the early 1970s. One day 'I felt a desperate need to call in the church, just to go and sit in the back pew and be nice and quiet and to communicate with God in a spiritual way and just to reassure myself that God was there, but when I got to the door it was locked. As I walked away, I realized that although I couldn't rely on the religion, I could still rely on myself. ... From then on I sort of turned away from formal religion.'

In common with many other Britons, Nancy no longer believes in a personal God sitting in heaven, a God separated from the world he has created and arbitrarily dispensing, or not dispensing, grace. She does not, she says, believe in a God 'who sits up there and says, "I will help you. I will not help you. I will cure you. I will not cure you."' Nancy does not experience her loss of belief in a personal God as a deprivation, but rather as a liberating reversion to feelings she had as a child that she was part of the universe, and which she says, makes her feel a whole person again. The concept of reversion, of reclaiming older and more authentic knowledge, provides a key theme in Nancy's negotiation of her changing worldview. In authenticating her new beliefs through the invocation of an older tradition, whether established or putative, Nancy follows a well-established cultural pattern for the legitimization of change.

In the early 1980s, some ten years after leaving her church, Nancy underwent surgery that probably saved her life. Conventional medicine, however, offered no remedy for the resultant symptoms of CFS/ME. Left, as she says, 'to chug along on my own', Nancy started to take vitamin and mineral supplements and listened to people talking about other remedies, especially spiritual healing. As a Roman Catholic, she reflects, 'you weren't supposed to be interested in things like fortune telling and spiritualism and spiritual healing', but when released from these strictures she felt free to pursue her interest in and need for healing, primarily by reading books and magazine articles.

Further pursuit of her interest in healing was, however, restricted by the lack of availability. The small town of Rowanthwaite is not a centre of, to use Roof's (1999) term, the alternative 'spiritual marketplace', and, not having a car, Nancy cannot easily travel to nearby larger towns. When a holistic healing centre opened in Rowanthwaite, within easy walking distance of her home, she went along to try Reiki healing. Here, from Susan, a Reiki master, Nancy not only received healing, but also went on to be attuned to receive and channel Reiki energy into herself and others. Nancy describes Reiki as 'something which is for everybody and once you are attuned to Reiki you'll never lose it. You are not a healer, you are a channel for a healing energy that is Reiki.' Free from belief in a personal God and feeling herself part of the universe she now understands spirituality to be 'given from some greater source of life energy that set the universe in motion'. Again using the concept of regaining something that has been lost, Nancy says she is, 'grateful for this spirituality again because I did have it as a child and as a young person'. It is significant to note at this point that what Nancy is describing is not an instance of a non-religious person *becoming* spiritual, or of being born again as a Christian, but what Fenn (cited in Hamilton 2001: 209) identifies as re-spiritualization, in this case into a somewhat different belief system.

As well as regaining spirituality, Nancy found that Reiki helped improve her health. This is not, however, something she has discussed with her doctor. In her experience doctors 'don't want *you* telling *them* things', nor do they deal in holistic treatment.

Consequently she says, 'my mind now operates on two tracks'. On one track there is medical science, which is useful in treating things that respond to antibiotics, or require surgery, things you cannot do for yourself. On the second track, there are things that can be treated by other means such as diet, rest, herbalism and, of course, Reiki. Again returning to the theme of regaining that which has been lost, Nancy believes that reliance on 'wonder drugs', such as antibiotics, has led to the disparaging and consequent loss of knowledge of traditional healing techniques and practices. In alternative therapies and complementary medicine she sees a regaining of this lost knowledge. It is an opinion that accords with Sutcliffe and Bowman's (2000) description of 'the re-packaging of spiritual healing as Reiki' (Sutcliffe and Bowman 2000: 11). Integrating reclaimed and re-packaged traditions into membership of mainstream religious institutions may not, as Nancy discovered, be any easier than having them accepted by medical practitioners.

While rejoicing in her re-found spirituality, Nancy found she missed belonging to a church community so, when a friend invited her to St Jude's, the local Anglican church, Nancy started attending the Sunday service. In describing what participation in the service means to her, a vernacular belief based in Reiki teaching is apparent. 'I'm acknowledging that I am part of the universe,' she says, 'and I'm acknowledging a power higher than we can image, which is the force of life.' Other reasons for attending are that 'people are friendly, it's only ten minutes walk from my home and I really enjoy the way the singing is accompanied by guitars and hand clapping'. After several weeks' attendance Nancy's sense of belonging was seriously disrupted by the views of the vicar, an evangelical Christian. She listened in shocked disbelief to a sermon in which alternative therapies, including Reiki, were denounced from the altar steps. 'The vicar said, "Reiki's come through Hinduism and they believe in lots of gods, so that's dodgy to start with. And anybody who is bothering with Reiki must give it up. You must repent. And if you come to see me I will help you repent." So I'm sat there, someone who practices Reiki and I just couldn't believe what I was hearing. I felt like I was sat in a church in the seventeenth century being pontificated at.'

The vicar's denouncement encapsulated everything Nancy finds offensive in formal religion: '[T]he indoctrination that only if you do *this* will your soul be saved'. In contrast she finds Reiki 'to be kinder and gentler. It is not frightening you with what will happen if you don't do this or that. Everyone has it in their own hands to bring themselves healing and comfort, so it offers strength and health and happiness, because you are healthy if you are happy. You are controlling yourself, not being controlled from the outside.' Nancy also identifies a contradiction in the vicar's position, again utilizing the concept of reclaiming suppressed knowledge and tradition. 'Christianity', she argues, 'is *based* on Jesus' miracles, including the laying on of hands to give healing, as well as visions and voices. Yet once Christianity got established as an *organized* religion, *we* haven't got to bother with these things any more. They are said to belong to the past, not the present, and they are made taboo.' Nancy identifies these taboos as man-made restrictions, which act as obstacles through which 'we lose touch with the really spiritual'. As a vernacular believer Nancy presently faces the dilemma of whether to continue to attend

St Jude's. On one hand, she feels that as she benefits spiritually and socially from attending she can carry on and keep her beliefs and practices to herself. On the other hand, she feels 'if you cannot say what you believe we might as well be living in a dictatorship'. How this conflict will finally be resolved still remains to be seen, but at the time of writing she rarely attends the Sunday service.

As discussed earlier in this paper, O'Connor's (1995) work on healing has shown how the boundary between the sacred and the secular has been drawn between science and religion. The significance of this for the study of healing is that when this boundary is applied to medical science, the treatment of illness then becomes separated from religious and spiritual beliefs and practices. Drawing boundaries between the sacred and the secular, as Fenn (cited in Hamilton 2001: 179–181) argues, is part of the process of the secularization of society. Although this may now be taken as a fairly commonplace argument, what is interesting about Fenn's argument is his insistence that the process of secularization has to be understood as being *contested*. Secularization, Fenn tells us, has to be viewed not as a linear progression, but rather as a process of struggle, dispute, conflict and negotiation. Furthermore, this process has to be recognized not only as a struggle between religion and secularization, but also as a struggle between religion, secularization and *re-spiritualization*. Nancy's story provides an interesting case study of one woman's lived experience of this three-fold contestation.

Involvement in alternative and complementary healing often invokes criticism based on stereotypes of middle class narcissistic consumerism. In response to such criticisms Heelas notes how alternative and complementary healing, 'very often encourages people to make contact with the spiritual realm, and – given what is often at stake, namely being healed – is surely more than a consumer item for many of those involved' (Heelas 2000: 243). Fuller similarly argues that those with unconventional spiritual practices are not necessarily narcissistic. 'Their greatest spiritual need', he concludes, 'is to view life with a sense of wonder, to feel connected with the sacred meanings and powers that permeate everyday life' (Fuller 2001: 174). In this respect, Nancy's case study supports both Heelas and Fuller for, as a state pensioner and highly imbued with the Christian and maternal ethic of putting others before herself, she has neither the income nor the disposition to fit the dismissive stereotype of narcissistic consumerism. As described above, her interest and involvement lies in the re-discovery of the spiritual. One case study cannot, of course, be in any way conclusive, but it does highlight the need for an understanding of the way people actually live out their beliefs in daily life in order to fully understand the contested processes of secularization. In other words what is needed is, as O'Connor (1995) and Primiano (1995; 1997) insist, a greater understanding of the role of vernacular spirituality. Nancy's story also serves to highlight one of the difficulties encountered in undertaking such a study. Nancy uses Reiki only on herself, her family, and a few friends and, as no commercial transactions are involved or sought, her beliefs and practices remain in the private rather than public sphere. In addition, the largely hidden nature of Nancy's beliefs is compounded by a reluctance to talk to people about her beliefs and practices – a reluctance reinforced, on her return to churched religion, by her experience of the Vicar's sermon denouncing Reiki. Consequently, like much alternative re-spiritualization, Nancy's beliefs and practices remain publicly muted and statistically invisible, leaving a whole dimension of spirituality omitted from the data on religious belief. Heelas identifies one of the great challenges facing social science as ascertaining 'whether people find "new" sources of significance for their lives when traditional, long-standing formations … lose their hold' (Heelas 2000: 237). Nancy's story not only suggests that they do, but that a greater understanding of vernacular spiritual beliefs and practices would both be of value to the Christian churches and also to the practice of scientific medicine.

References

CFS/ME Working Group (2002) *Report to the Government Chief Medical Officer.* London: Department of Health.

Fuller, R. C. (2001) *Spiritual but not Religious: Understanding Unchurched America.* Oxford: Oxford University Press.

Hamilton, M. (2001) *The Sociology of Religion* (2nd edn). London: Routledge.

Heelas, P. (2000) Expressive spirituality and humanistic expressivism: Sources of significance beyond church and chapel. In S. Sutcliffe and M. Bowman (eds) *Beyond New Age: Exploring Alternative Spirituality*, 237–154. Edinburgh: Edinburgh University Press.

Jacobs, G. (1997) *Chronic Fatigue Syndrome.* Dorset: Element.

Kelly, M. J. (2002) *Degrees of Reiki.* Twin Lakes, WI: Lotus Press.

MacIntyre, A. (1998) *ME a Practical Guide.* London: Thorsons.

O'Connor, B. B. (1995) *Healing Traditions*. Philadelphia, PA: University of Pennsylvania Press.

Primiano, L. N. (1995) Vernacular religion and the search for method in religious folklife. *Western Folklore (Reflexivity and the Study of Belief)* 54 (1): 37–56.

Primiano, L. N. (1997) Religion, folk. In Thomas A. Green (ed.) *Folklore: An Encyclopedia of Beliefs, Customs, Tales, Music, and Art*, Vol. I. Santa Barbara, CA: ABC-Clio Inc.

Quest, P. (2002) *Reiki for Life: The Complete Guide to Reiki Practice for Levels 1, 2, & 3*. London: Piatkus.

Roof, W. C. (1999) *Spiritual Market Place: Baby Boomers and the Remaking of American Religion*. Princeton, NJ: Princeton University Press.

Shepherd, C. (1999) *Living with ME*. London: Vermilion.

Stiene, B. and Stiene, F. (2003) *The Reiki Sourcebook*. Winchester: O Books.

Sutcliffe, S. and Bowman, M. (2000) Introduction. In S. Sutcliffe and M. Bowman (eds) *Beyond New Age: Exploring Alternative Spirituality*, 1–13. Edinburgh: Edinburgh University Press.

Sykes, R. and Campion, P. (2002) *The Physical and The Mental in Chronic Fatigue Syndrome/ME. Principals of Psychological Help*. Bristol: Westcare UK.

PART II
Traditions of Narrated Belief

Autobiographical and Interpretative Dynamics in the Oral Repertoire of a Vepsian Woman

Madis Arukask* and Taisto-Kalevi Raudalainen

Introduction

Vepsians are the easternmost of the Balto-Finnic people residing in north-west Russia. Today there are less than 10,000 speakers of Vepsian living in separate groups in the Leningrad and Vologda oblasts and in Karelia, on the south-eastern coast of Lake Onega. The neighbours of Onega Vepsians are the Karelians, who speak Livvic and Ludic dialects similar to the Vepsian language. Today in everyday life Russian is dominant as the common language and Vepsian is used only by the older generation. Popular Orthodoxy, containing pre-Christian animistic components, has a central position in the worldview of the Vepsians. The present paper is based on a fieldtrip made to the Onega Vepsian villages of southern Karelia in July 2005, and concentrates on the religious worldview of one particular informant.

The authors of this chapter arrived quite accidentally in Yašozero, a forest village about 80 kilometres from Petrozavodsk and 17 kilometres from Šokša (see the map). As late as the 1930s the village had been home to 25 families. Today only one house remains, the rest having been cut into logs for heating, burned down or removed to be reconstructed elsewhere. In their place stands a hunting base for the nouveau riche. A similar fate has befallen several other Onega Vepsian villages, such as Hapšon, Kir'ik, Kuślega, Meccantaga, M'ägots-Šoutar', Rugižjarv, Vanhimanśelga, Vehka, Voimäg'i and others. The assimilation process of Orthodox Vepsians in the so-called inter-lake region of north-west Russia, including various districts bordering on

* Madis Arukask is Associate Professor at the Institute of Estonian and General Linguistics, University of Tartu, Estonia.

Taisto-Kalevi Raudalainen is lecturer at the Department of Folk Art and Cultural Anthropology, Estonian Academy of Arts, Tallinn and the Culture Academy in Viljandi, University of Tartu, Estonia.

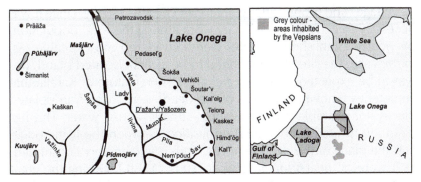

The Vepsians are a Finno-Ugric people. The railway on the map connects St Petersburg with Murmansk in the North.

the White Lake, Lake Ladoga and Lake Onega, has, of course, been going on for centuries. The only remaining native inhabitant that we found in the village of D'azar' (Russ. Yašozero) was Maria Anisimova (b. 1925), whose repertoire we attempt to describe and analyse below. In addition to analysing the oral history expressed through Maria's personality and carrying out a traditional folklore genre analysis, we will also focus on the problems associated with the scientific modelling of a popular (religious) worldview.

Interchanging Symbols of Power in Local Consciousness

As recently as the first three decades of the previous century, this currently deserted village was teeming with life. While Yašozero's monastery was at the peak of its power, the village was home to some couple of hundred monks and people closely connected with the monastery. According to a legend, the founder of the *Blagovesčenskii* (*Presvjatoi Bogorodicy*) monastery was St Iona (d. 1629), who first lived here as a hermit monk. Like Alexander of Svir (d. 1533), another saint from this area known all over Russia, Iona was probably a Vepsian. The legend also says that Alexander was Iona's mentor, although the most cursory glance at their lives suffices to tell us this can in no way be possible. In the forests near the monastery it is still possible to see a cave where Iona is said to have spent the last years of his life.[1] Some reports indicate that an earlier pagan cult site (Russian: *kapishche*) was located on the site of the monastery. The sites of hermitages and monasteries were never chosen casually: since it was necessary to carry out missionary work among the local population, previously established cult sites were considered most suitable. As, in this case, the site also happened to be a small isolated island, this was to be expected.[2] It is also a characteristic feature of Karelia that cemeteries (known as villages of the dead) were located in isolated places, for example on lake islands – that is, across water. This has been interpreted as a cultural opposition between the living origin and the place of the dead relatives. Thus, the cemetery constituted, as it were, a 'near-Tuonela' (Siikala 2002: 123ff.). During the great changes of the 1930s, the cemetery was relocated from the island to be directly next to the village, an act that perhaps considerably weakened this opposition. However, when we visited the cemetery with Maria, she still took us to her old family burial place, separated from the rest of the world, as it is characteristic of the Vepsians, by a fence made of horizontal poles.

Yašozero received pilgrims throughout the year, and it was customary for them to make a promise or oath (Russian *zavet*) that they would compensate the monastery with labour in return for what help or relief the saints would give in response to their own, or the monks', prayers. Frequently, the Karelian monasteries also received the weaker youths from the local area who were thus introduced

Figure 1: Ruins of the monastery of St Iona of Yašozero close to Maria Anisimova's house (photograph by Madis Arukask).

to monastic life and work, bringing blessings upon themselves and their families.[3] Among the Livviks, in Aunus Karelia, the tradition of staying in the monastery for a while and working there was known as *jiäksentä, jiäksimine* (see Järvinen 2004: 46; also Kilpeläinen 2000: 243–245; Stark 2002: 41–42, 160–164). Such arrivals found accommodation at the inn next to the monastery and work in the gardens, forest and fields. Real crowds arrived in Yašozero in early autumn, around the commemoration day of the local patron saint and the monastery's founder (22 September or 5 October according to the Julian calendar[4]). Since St Iona of Yašozero was widely known and respected, a special steamer line was set up in the closing decades of the nineteenth century, making two or three trips per week there from St Petersburg. A separate port was built on Lake Onega, 26 *versts*[5] from the monastery, to take care of the transportation of pilgrims from St Petersburg to Yašozero Monastery. Maria's contemporary Dunja Nikonova (b. 1915) remembers:

> Iona was born in Šokša. Rich people came from Petrozavodsk and built a monastery here. The walls and floors were made of marble. Next to it, there stood a long house. Tables downstairs, (bed)chambers upstairs. Built of wood, but with corners made of brick. One took a vow, and then one had to work in the monastery for a month. In the corner, there was a small monk's cell where lived a monk (who dealt with the pilgrims). Pilgrims came and lived there. However, the monks themselves lived downstairs. When your legs ached, for example, you came and worked for the monastery for a month or two, without pay.

The monastery's architectural ensemble, dating in the most part back to the middle of the nineteenth century, has been ranked second only to Valamo monastery as probably the most famous and outstanding monastery in Karelia for its imposing beauty and power. This is not to be wondered at, since the monastery received donations not only from the merchants of Petrozavodsk and St Petersburg, but also from the high clergy of the Solovetski monastery and even from the Tsars.

Today nothing remains of the magnificent monastery complex but a few crumbling walls. And, of course, the very diverse memories that we were still able to record from the few people surviving from that period. Dilapidation began during and immediately after the years of War Communism (1918–1920) and the plundering of monasteries in the 1920s; next came the 1930s with the atrocities of the Gulag, during which both local clergy and the homegrown Vepsian intelligentsia were repressed (see, for example, Salve 1997: 158–159). One of the many detention camps of the region was located in this monastery. The last blow was dealt by the cynicism that manifested itself as post-war socialist egalitarianism and atheism. Before the monastery fell into ruins completely it was home to a centre for juvenile delinquents.

Against this background it is not in the least surprising that Maria, who in the 1940s even held the post of collective farm chairwoman in the monastery village, was acutely opposed to Soviet power and communist ideology. Even though she speaks Russian most of the time and is part Russian in origin (her father was born in a partly Russian-speaking village), she nevertheless freely condemns Soviet ideology and its cynical executors. An honest and straightforward person, she is also suspicious of the creation, in the 1990s, of a Vepsian ethnic parish, an entity called into being by the efforts of Vepsian national activists but which has remained largely an empty form.[6] Interestingly, although she remained something of a bystander in the Vepsian 'reawakening' of the 1990s, she is sharply critical of the destruction both of places and of ethnic groups that occurred in the previous decades and which still occurs. Such sharp criticism is not to be heard around the village, because when the authorities are close, these topics can only be hinted at. And even though critical views may exist in the form of oral discourse, without the support of a written culture they are bound to perish.

Unfortunately, we failed to ask Maria what she thought about the procession held in Šokša in 2004, on the commemoration day of St Iona, and about the fact that Iona was declared 'the patron saint of Vepsian lands'. A report published on the Internet has the following to say:

> Beginning with 2004, the Saint's commemoration day is declared a national holiday for the Vepsian parish of the Republic of Karelia. A national holiday for the Vepsian nation …

> ITAR-TASS reports

> Karelia's leader Sergei Katanandov sent a message of congratulations, saying: 'Iona of Yašozero is the spiritual protector of the Vepsian lands. The elevation of his commemoration day to the status of a Vepsian national holiday testifies to the fact that he now enters our lives once again to help people perfect themselves and do good.'

Unfortunately these words, resorting to such remote history in order to achieve greater communal integration today, are revealed as 'showcase politics' as soon as we take the briefest of glimpses at what is really going on in the 'Vepsian ethnic parish'. Although spoken of as the 'Vepsian national saint', Iona is, in fact, venerated as an important saint all over Russia.[7] Likewise, there is no escaping the 'symphony' of the state and the church when speaking about Iona, since in Russia the church has always acted in the service of unification (see also Salve 1997: 154–156).

After all, the Vepsians' former pagan sanctuary on the island in the lake was also drawn into the sphere of the Christian world order in the context of an imperialist conquest. Despite the fact that in the mid-1990s minority politics in Karelia was characterized by a certain measure of legislative constructiveness and capacity for dialogue, the current political atmosphere of pragmatic unification has, as the Vepsian intellectual Zinaida Strogalschikova put it, pushed the native peoples back into the role of foster children that has so customarily been attributed to them. They are not afforded subjecthood but regarded as minions of the central power (Strogalschikova 2006).

The Environment in the Monastic Village and Maria's Personality

The accurate focus and density of the information that Maria was able to impart to events of the recent past was amazing. She identified settlements that have been Russian-speaking for several generations as one-time Vepsian hamlets, thus proving to be a remarkable carrier of local memory. Whereas for decision makers the monastery of Yašozero and its founder Saint Iona are mere cultural monuments, images from icons or means of present-day integration and politics, for Maria they are organic components of everyday life. In this section we shall survey the components that made up Maria's mental space at the moment of our accidental meeting. Maria's performances came either in response to our interest or as largely auto-communicative associations/moods (abjection, grief, fear, condemnation, commemoration, remembering). Taken together, they express one possible idiolect of Vepsian-Russian orthodox folk piety.

It was not the aim of our unplanned meeting to chart an Onega Vepsian monastic village's culture in its entirety, still less so to reconstruct 'the days of yore'. Indeed, we had practically no idea of the village's onetime cultural entirety. All we had were the fragmentary tales, collected during our 2004 expedition, of the wealth once accumulated by logging and stone-quarrying. Tales that also told of the series of topoclastic reorganizations that then befell the region, amongst which we could, in temporal order, mention: secularization and national-ization during the Russian Civil War (in 1918–1920), condemnation as kulaks, the foundation of collective farms, annexation by Finland during the Second World War, the post-war deportation of the whole ethnic group into the oblast of Vologda, the Stalinist prison camp era, the closing down of small collective farms in the 1960s and 1970s and the final abolition of collective farms in the 1990s, after which there followed only ruin and perdition. Thus, we had mainly heard about the Soviet era and about how people learned to live after the great collapse. It was wonderful, therefore, to suddenly be pulled into another world in which a seemingly different language was spoken and where creatures moved, about whom the rest of the world had hardly any knowledge.

In connection with Maria's personality, the issue of so-called complementarity of roles is raised: a person talented and competent in one field is usually talented and competent in a wholly different one as well. In Maria's case, we can see that she masters not only the various usages of the oral tradition but also those acquired from areas

Figure 2: Maria Anisimova in her kitchen (photograph by Madis Arukask).

of culture more usually associated with literature. At the same time, it was possible to see in Maria a somewhat eccentric person who, in a traditional society with relatively fixed models, has taken on herself the role of a synthesizer, an interpreter, even a re-shaper, without fearing marginalization.[8] She has her own experiential attitudes, and she seldom expresses herself using indirect speech. She is both a sovereign carrier of the tradition and its interpreter. (For a discussion of these topics see, for example, Goody 1977: 17–35.)

During her earliest years Maria already had a multiple identity, since her father came from the nearby village of Zalesye (Meccantaga), the inhabitants of which reportedly considered themselves Russians. Maria's husband – who came from Kuślega – also considered himself a Russian, even though he too had Vepsian blood in his veins. Creolization, bilingualism and multiple identities have been characteristic of these parts for several generations. Maria, however, had a relatively exemplary education for her generation (which in itself does not mean reading widely) in that she attended a village school (in Matveyaśelga) for four years and continued for a few months at school in the market town of Šokša. In 1940, when Maria turned 15, she was taken away from school because she was needed at home to take care of her younger siblings. Her mother gave birth to another baby, but died in the same year, her father was recruited into the army and thus, during the war, Maria became the head of a large family. Thanks to her relatively good education, she soon rose to become chairwoman of the collective farm. On the other hand, we also know that by placing Maria in this position during the war-time famine, the older members of the community were cleverly escaping the direct stresses of Stalinism themselves and the responsibilities of fulfilling national economic plans (perhaps with the cajoling promise: 'You'll be drinking tea, the others will do the hard work').

Maria's mother, however, was a Vepsian from the village of Vehručei (Vepsian *Vehka*) about 40 km from Yašozero. She came from a large wealthy family that won additional prestige from the fact that one of its daughters had married into the monastic village. In addition to a better standard of living, the monastery brought great prestige to local life. (Facts backed up by several icons acquired by Maria's ancestors, items which the great majority of people could not afford.) The monastery, a haven where people sought relief from both bodily and spiritual ills, was revered in hamlets far and near. Its dedication to the local saint cast a holy glow on the local lay inhabitants as well. Even the dead resting in the monastery's cemetery could enjoy privileged status, since they could expect to rise again in such a holy place, where the monks prayed for God's grace and blessings day and night. A significant role was played by the bilingual environment of the monastic village. In the religious sphere, the Vepsian language has undoubtedly been under huge pressure from Russian, the language of the liturgy. However, Russian has had an impact on Vepsian usage in various other spheres as well, a feature characteristic of multicultural environments in general.[9] Russian was the *lingua franca* of pilgrims arriving from nearby villages, from more distant parts of Karelia, from Petrozavodsk and even from St Petersburg; according to Maria, another reason why Russian was more frequently used was the Russian village near by. In spite of that, the everyday activities of the village were largely carried out in Vepsian. Maria is far from considering herself unambiguously a Vepsian, connecting her 'Vepsianness' mainly with her mother tongue and her childhood. Yet at the same time, she does not consider herself a real Russian either. Regardless of the facts that with her loved ones she speaks only in Russian, and that Vepsian has not been spoken in the village for decades now, her 'mother's tongue' has not fully disappeared from her life. In spite of underusage and other levelling factors, the Vepsian tongue has remained emotionally close to her:

> While there were still many people living here, I, too, spoke Vepsian. But nowadays, there is not one person left any more. Who should I speak to? These folks here understand nothing! They even laugh at me when I speak it (on my own).

On the basis of Maria's attitudes, we could rather say that her first identity is that of a Christian, *risttu*, the Vepsian word for human being. Thus, the issue of ethno-confessionality is raised. In earlier times, people in this area used to identify themselves mainly through confessional adherence, and thus, Vepsians have never directly opposed themselves to Karelians, Russians or Livviks, making it easier to incorporate them into larger groups of Orthodox believers.[10] But within the coordinate system characteristic of modern times, ethno-confessional self-identification, as well as national self-identification, has to do with the discourse of power.[11] In the eyes of the power centres, which in this part of the world were of course represented by monasteries, the ideal peasant was, first and foremost, an obedient Christian (the Russian *krest´yane*, 'peasants', is equal to 'Christians').[12]

Their education, however, was not limited to just the liturgy, catechesis and religious dogmas, but also involved numerous other narratives rooted in the monastic culture: the legends of the saints, apocryphal texts, etc., with which Karelian popular culture has been imbued (see Järvinen 2004: 231–248). In the early days of putting the new power ideology into practice, working communes were first established in the monasteries in the 1930s, which were soon followed by detention establishments of a stricter regime aiming to shape 'new human beings' by means of an apparatus of violence. This was a cataclysmic event for the Christians, since for centuries monasteries had represented something completely different. Dogmatic in its principles, but paradoxically exercising a fructifying influence on oral tradition, monastic culture found its antipode in a worldview which unambiguously ruled out all interpretations.

Finally, it must be pointed out that the local inhabitants' image of both themselves and of recent history was significantly influenced by the Finnish annexation (from July 1941 to June 1944), as a result of which their attitude towards the Finns is radically different from that apparent in Soviet propaganda. Their attitude towards the central power has been coloured by their forced evacuation, after the Finnish army had been driven out, into the oblast of Vologda, where they had to stay for two years (from autumn 1944 to December 1946). Ethnic policies that were based on fear and surveillance are not an important issue on the banks of Onega today, since written culture has not been particularly emphatic about it, whereas memories of oral stories fade quickly under general censorship. So much greater, therefore, was our surprise to hear such views, critical of topoclasm, loyal to religious values and the Vepsian language, expressed by Maria as part of her critical attitude towards Stalinist ethnic policies, all inclusive repressions, or Russification.

Genre Analysis: Worldview or Personal Composition in Performance?

Maria's Spirit Experiences Versus Her Prayers

In anticipation, the theoretical opposition between 'imagistic' and 'dogmatic' religious practices, forwarded by Harvey Whitehouse (2004: 195–196, 199), might lend colour to the following. The former are based on (often charismatic) experiences shared within small communities. In one of her publications, Estonian folklorist Kristi Salve has also indicated that while Orthodoxy does not favour vernaculars, and the liturgy is always based on dogma, the Vepsians have nevertheless used their own tongue to express their religious experiences, filtering the originally 'foreign' experience through the prism of their personal notions, practising this in the vicinity of their homes, in the cemetery, in smaller chapels and even in the forest (see Salve 1997: 154). Thus, religious truths have continually been adapted and translated from their liturgical and dogmatic environment into a very different contextual setting. In the relatively small communities of the Vepsian village clusters, it is possible to observe the domination of imagistic religious representations (revelatory and augural dreams, stories of the appearances of saints, prayer incantations,[13] spirit memorates, etc.) over dogmatic ones. The prevailing memory type, in religious materials, is episodic (or implicit) memory which draws not on 'dry' routine institutionalized knowledge but on personal experiences, autobiographical events. Either explicitly or implicitly, the autobiographical is present in everything that Maria speaks about. It is therefore possible to speak about the reciprocity between the communally shared and the personally experienced: what is being told is simultaneously both a personal experience and a pattern prescribed by the narrative genre.

Analysis of Maria's repertoire also revealed signs of 'Vepsian-style Christianity', as Kristi Salve, for instance, has tried to describe it (Salve 1997). Occasionally, in her mixed Vepsian and Russian speech, Maria talks to St Iona and probably also to other saints who appeared in the icons recently stolen from her. The prayer incantations form a kind of formulaic communicative code modulated according to the situation. Maria's numerous religious experiences – encounters with spirits experienced in childhood, dreams and revelations that began when she was on the threshold of adolescence – are recorded in her memory as being Vepsian-based. Her later dream experiences, however, mainly occur in the Russian language.

Maria's use of language allows us to gain an understanding of, among others things, how liturgical language use has penetrated the monastic village's vernacular language sphere, for example, in the form of numerous everyday prayers addressed to St Iona: 'Iona of Yašozero, help me, a foolish mortal. I can't remember where I have put my herdsman's horn. Help me find it. And I do find it. So it is true that Iona gives help!'

Prayer dialogue with Iona seems to be so habitual for Maria as to lead to a tentative view of Iona as a kind of alter ego through whose sanctified person various personal and communal crises of different degrees of complication are overcome. Prayers – and the treasure trove of legends relating to the saints in general – may be characterized as a peculiar kind of ethno-strategy for crisis management (see also Järvinen 2004: 135–144).

Iona has stood by Maria's side as a real being ever since she was a child, both as a life-size icon in the monastery, as pictured in the icons painted on wood that she inherited from her mother and grandmother, and as a living and moving creature on a forest path (see below). Maria goes to the ruins of the monastery, to light a candle for him there, not only on St Iona's day (22 September), but also on 19 August (the feast of the Transfiguration of Christ (*spassu*), thus observing a tradition handed down through generations: 'Each *spassu* I go to the monastery ... and I light a candle for Iona there. And there the candle burns.'

The community of saints headed by Iona is something very human and real for her. The Transfiguration of Christ, as we know, celebrates the transfiguration of Christ in his resplendent robes into a shape approachable by an ordinary Christian. Isn't this precisely the defining characteristic of 'Vepsian Orthodoxy'? The saints are accompanied by the Mother of God who used to watch over Maria out of the corner of an icon, depicted in the likeness of her appearance in Kazan, until the day when thieves disguised as monks robbed her of the images:

> That's who they pray for, in church. Pray on, pray! Let them hide ...
> But from me, the Mother of God [icon] was stolen. A beautiful Mother of God it was, it cost a lot of money. They took it away from me, my Mother of God of Kazan. A hundred years old it was, my great-grandmother bought it.

Examining next the memorates represented in Maria's repertoire, a dynamic relationship between prayers and experiential tales can be observed (see Figure 3). In Maria's memorates of getting lost and of revelations, the *metshiiŕe* or 'forest spirit', as a representative of the abjective (unwanted) power, is clearly opposed to the St Iona of her prayers as a representative of 'Christian power'. This is particularly manifest in tales of going to the forest (to pick berries), to the sauna (to wash) or to some forest pasture (to herd cattle). All the above places involve the presence of an abjective liminal power. Iona's name is

Figure 3: The genre-spectrum used by Maria Anisimova (b. 1925) during 'composition in performance'.

mentioned most frequently in the prayers said before entering these places. When going to the woods, to the sauna or to the graveyard, one should never call a forest or sauna spirit (*kil'bet-emag*) by name nor – more dangerously – use strong words or behave in a boisterous manner. If anything of the sort should nevertheless happen, one must say the following incantation, just in case: 'Oh, creature of the wild, catch yourself, you – and get lost on your forest paths!' On St George's day, when cattle were turned out on to fresh pastures for the first time in the year, housewives were wont to beseech the patron saint to protect their cattle, using a brush made of bristles[14] as an additional magical tool:

> When the animals go out to the woods, then one of such [a brush made of bristles] is taken. And the housewife must say: 'I leave you in the woods, in the care of the dear god. The wood will attract you – but

you will come back home.' (Report from Anastasija Ijudina, Kaskeza village 2004)

Similarly, when going out on to the lake one must strictly avoid mentioning the spirit of the lake (d´arvhiin´e, d´arvud-ižand). Uttering his name may cause one to meet him, usually with fatal consequences. Maria also says that the houses that are haunted (Veps. *glumitab*) are precisely those where relations with the house's guardian spirit are not harmonious: 'There are all kinds of ghosts, some dance, others sing or cry … It sounds as if a host of people were coming, but [when you go to see] there's nobody there. I cross myself – and it all vanishes!' But should the haunting continue after crossing oneself, then the prayer of Almighty Trinity must be said: *Vo imya ottsa i sỹna, Sv. Dukhu. – Amin'! Amin'! Amin'!* 'In the name of the Father, and the Son, and the Holy Ghost. Amen! Amen! Amen!'

Whereas it is generally felt that Christ himself cannot and should not be bothered with all sorts of everyday problems, Iona appears to be handy in all manifestations of trouble or disorder, even the most insignificant. In Vepsian village Christianity, as Kristi Salve has observed (Salve 2005), it was common to beg the help of the saints in quite trifling matters. This, too, gives proof of a certain degree of secularization of the saint(s), of a notable transformation and extension of their functions as compared to the Christian canon (cf. also Stark 2002: 124–133). The saints as sacral actors are not elevated by 'the nimbus of the dogmas', but rather are accompanied by 'the smell of birch-bark'. It is noteworthy that saints usually appear in the context of beginning something or crossing some border. Maria, for example, invokes Iona's help before going into the woods to pick berries. It is the mother, however, who is particularly anxious, warning her children not to say the name of the forest spirit, not to quarrel or bandy words with each other. As Salve has written: '[a]ny violation of forest's laws … – disrespect, noisy behaviour, etc., alongside with other negative consequences – could result in getting lost' (Salve 1995: 419).

> Give us berries, give us cowberries. Lead us to a place rich in berries, dear god. Let us pick many [berries]. But also keep us on the right path, watch over us on our way home. See to it that we do not lose our way. That we always know where to find our home … [Mother told them:] Children, take care, don't speak foolishly in the forest. You mustn't do that. Keep to God's ways. Then you will find berries, too. Don't stay long in the forest. Come home before dark … You mustn't say: 'May the forest spirit have you.' If you say so, you'll lose your way at once.

In a similar manner, the men invoked Iona before they went fishing, although he was especially helpful when a person lost their way in the woods:

> God, our Lord, set us back on the right path. And immediately we find the path. I look – and lo, the path is there.

> Iona of Yašozero, let us find our way back home.
> I always invoke Iona. Iona is my patron saint. And all my prayers I address to Iona. Whenever I do anything, I always say: 'Dear Iona.' And my daughter said, too: 'Mother, I pray to Iona. Whatever happens, I always pray to Iona.'

We have repeatedly seen that in Maria's performances, the whole spectrum of narrative genres acquires an autobiographical colouring. The basis of the particular flexibility, dynamics and vivacity of a coherent traditional representation lies in the fact that the tradition lives thanks to unique experiences, while nevertheless maintaining a recognizable generality. It is quite possible that Maria had related (verbalized) several of these experiences only a few times previously in her life. In any case, they are textually neither very fluent nor crystallized. It is also noteworthy that when narrating them, Maria vacillates between two languages – additional proof that in the process of textualization, she does not tend to use clichés. The dominant feature is immediate experience.

The guardian spirit of the house must be treated with particular respect. Relations with him can be improved by invoking *d'umala* (or *boženka*) or 'the dear god' St Iona. It seems that the *spiriti loci* are here subordinated to the supremacy of the patron saint and can be propitiated by invoking Iona at the right moment. The guardian spirits of places appear whenever borders are crossed, an act that, in itself, gives occasion to invoke the help of the saints. The patron saint appears to have taken the role of mediator in the relations between the inhabitants of the monastic village and their local spirits, whereas the classical belief in spirits presumes an immediate relationship with the spirit through offerings or sacrifices (for example offering the first and last sheaves, offerings before threshing or to the barn spirit or the offerings made when buying the land for a house, offerings to the water or forest spirits, etc.). Giving and offering establish contractual relationships and compel the participants in this relationship to share (Mauss 1967: 10–16, 78). Until recently, this kind of spirit belief based on reciprocal exchange was characteristic of the central and south Vepsian areas, where the influence of the monasteries was weaker. In the area surrounding the monastery, the relationship of direct exchange with spiritual beings seems to have been replaced by the patronage of St Iona, to whom the fulfilled promises (Russ. *zavet*) are made.

Do people, then, no longer try to come to an agreement with the spirits, attempting instead to control them? The answer to this, is that this is not quite the case. They are still the masters of all places, even though they remain passive as long as no social or religious norms have been breached, for example by crossing the borders between different areas at the wrong time or in the wrong place (see also Jürgenson 2004). Concerning the tales of losing one's way, for instance, it can be said that when a person loses his or her way physically, they have usually also lost their bearings normatively. Getting lost physically is always experienced psychically, as obviated by alterations in the state of consciousness.

Kristi Salve says:

It should also be mentioned that children have been basically the ones who have seen their misleaders. In the majority of cases the misled person sees none, although knows that he is in the power of fairies. Also in case of blows, dragging or even carrying the victim, the perception has been predominantly tactile. (Salve 1995: 421)

Thus Maria, too, emphasizes in the tale of losing her way that she had been right next to the forest spirit and that it had felt unpleasant, but has nothing to say about the appearance of the forest spirit (*lešii, mechiin'e*). The spirit led her astray shortly before the first snow of the year fell; after the snowfall it would have been far more difficult to find the path. Finally, Maria managed to find her way to the village of Šokša, from where she could send home a telegram saying that she was alive.

In order to get a better idea of the narration (textualization) situation, unfolding in the form of an interview, let us examine a somewhat longer presentation of the so-called 'spirit discourse' (most of the omissions are either repetitions or passages impossible to understand, and less frequently excursions away from the thematic axis):

Well, with the domestic spirit you have to go to her and ask for forgiveness. Address her with prayers. But if you just pass by, that is bad. Then the house will be haunted. There are many such houses.

You said that there was a housewife in the house, a mistress?

Yes, a mistress. A housewife ... This is perfectly true. Many do not believe it, but I have seen her with my own eyes. I am afraid of her, all the time. All the time I pray to the saint and cross myself: 'Help me, God, in all my sorrows. Give me good health, let my works be fruitful.'

But what does this domestic spirit look like?
What does it look like? Well, how shall I put it? It's very hairy. And growls like Baba Yaga. Quite ugly to look at, that's what it's like ... And in the forest there is a spirit, too. My mother once said: 'May the forest spirit have you,' when my brother went fishing. And it took him!

Maria's tale of losing her way:

But I was caught by the forest spirit – disgusting! We went right side by side ... Then my mother received the telegram, delivered by carriage. I was lost for three weeks [perhaps she means three days?] They missed me there, but they could do nothing. They prayed. They searched. 'We thought you were dead somewhere. Or drowned in the lake.'
... I quarrelled (with my father). I was about to leave the lakeside, or the swamp. I headed towards home ...
Father told me: 'Don't go to pick cranberries, today.' 'I will go', I said. He replied, 'no, you mustn't go, the cows need to be looked after.' I said, 'I won't stay long. I'll be back soon.' But what do you know ... around ten o'clock in the evening of October 29, three days later, the first snow fell. If I hadn't found my way then, I couldn't have ... the snow would have fallen and ... they searched for me from the opposite side of the lake. But I was on the other side. So what do you know.

But what did you have to do then?
I turned all my clothes inside out and prayed [probably to St Iona]: 'Dear God, send a human being to me ... Let me go along a path. Find a path for me. I quarrelled. Please, forgive me for this. Take the sins ... take the evil upon your shoulders. Give me ...' I turned around, and lo! There was the path ... I had been circling on that spot for a long time. I walk and I walk and I walk, and still I come back to the same spot. Where, then, is the path? Dreadful. But I was not afraid. No.

These memorates also show that losing one's way or suffering a misfortune always occurs after some breach of the norms. One may have raised one's voice in the wrong place or at the wrong time, or one may have quarrelled or disturbed the spirits' peace of mind in some other way. The consequences are serious and the only way to avoid them is to invoke the patron saint (*d'umal, boženka*) through prayer. The spirits are like attentive neighbours, making a mental note of even the smallest misconduct. Apparently it is impossible to do anything inconsequential. Chance occurrence does not exist – all deeds are noticed and remembered, until at some later date they are either rewarded or punished. '(P)eople may forget a lot, while fairies hear everything and miss nothing,' as Salve (1995: 422) sums up. Thus, one must always keep in mind not only the community of humans, but also that of the spirits and the saints. The following revelation occurred immediately before Maria was orphaned and had to take up the role of housewife to a large family, an incidence well in accord with the belief that spirits do, indeed, appear only to the happiest or the unhappiest of humans, never to ordinary people (see Salve 1995: 417).

> One day I go to the sauna and see an old man standing there. A small man, hairy, too. Neither the mouth nor the eyes could be seen. He goes into the sauna like a priest, all hairy. No eyes or anything.
> I ask him, 'what did you come here for? ... Do you portend good or evil?'
> He tells me, 'do not fear. All will be well.' (You always have to ask that.)
> I return, 'what if something evil will happen – you look so terrible.'
> 'Do not fear, I shall leave at once.' And he went away.
> I went to my Granny and told her, 'there was that kin in the sauna.' 'You must have used strong words,' she said to me. 'No, I didn't,' I said, 'not one.' And no evil befell us, nothing indeed. All went well.

The autobiographical element also plays an important role in the part of Maria's religious repertoire that does not directly concern her own experiences. In the following passage, Maria talks about what happened to her brother, who was killed in the first months of the Second World War. She connects her brother's death to the night when their mother had allowed him, aged 14, to go to the sauna to wash. From that night on her brother appears to have lived under the sauna spirit's curse, because traditionally entering the sauna after midnight was forbidden. Thus, Maria would seem to be dividing the blame between the two sides:

> Mother says: 'Oh, one doesn't go to the sauna at midnight. Go, wash quietly, be silent. Don't you make any noise.' But brother goes in, washes, whisks himself with birch twigs ... And all of a sudden one comes that looks like a bear (roaring). Brother leapt down from the platform and ran towards the house, naked: 'Mother, there are bears in the sauna.' Mother hurriedly began to cross herself (praying) ...

In the morning she went to see. Everything looked as it usually did. Then brother was taken into the army and killed. All that happened before he died.

Thunder

Special mention should still be made of the abjective force holding perhaps the most powerful position in Maria's consciousness. This is thunder. Among the Vepsians, the concept of God is closely related to thunder, after all, thunder in the Vepsian language is *d'umalan d'uru*, the thunder of God.[15] Maria also has a personal association with thunder because her childhood home burned down after a lightning strike, a memory constantly fresh in the uppermost layers of her consciousness. She never mentions the name of Iona in order to avoid thunder, the most powerful of natural phenomena. In fact when dealing with thunder, Iona appears to be an insignificant and minor actor. Could thunder, then, be something equal to the Christian God himself? Although we allowed ourselves no such speculations when talking to Maria, her tales make it obvious that it would be hard to imagine something still more powerful and inevitable. A long period of humid weather worries her:

> I look and see that the sky is quite black … I fear greatly. I cover all the mirrors. My home burned down because of lightning. One must be very wary of globe lightning … but in August we have a real feast of it. It keeps thundering all the time. But when it thunders, you must cover up all windows and mirrors. You must put a glass of milk on the windowsill and hide all your cutlery.

Dreams, the Dead and the Lamentation Code

The communities of spirits, mentioned above, and the saints are supplemented by the regularly commemorated host of deceased relatives. In Karelia, a cemetery forms a completely separate sphere where ritual reality is largely subordinated to the decrees of the relatives who have passed into the other world. What goes on there doesn't really fit into either of the two spheres, neither that of the monastery nor that of the forest. It would seem that in the graveyard there reigns a third, comparatively independent, space-time where contact is made with the dead through the use of the lamentation code. In Onega Vepsian regions – and Karelia, in general – the ecclesiastical feast calendar is woven through with communication between relatives; the community of the deceased is involved in this communication in a most natural manner. The so-called *stolan praznikad* – the feasts of the patron saints of the local chapels or churches – have also served as pretexts for regular family meetings, crossing the border between the living and the dead. (See Table 1 – compiled according to Vinokurova 1998. See also Salve 1997: 13; Järvinen 2004: 199–205.) Through this religious practice, probably the closest ritual to people's hearts, family coherence was maintained and it should not be considered impossible that precisely this consolidating habit could be the reason why certain old, unofficial, tribal names are remembered in this region even today.

Table 1. Onega Vepsian village feasts (*stolan praznika's*) according to Irina Vinokurova (1998)

Šokša	May 9	*Kevaz-Mikul* (springtide feast of St Michael, the Church of St Nicholas the Miracle Worker, 1645)
	June 29	*Pedru* (St Peter)
	Oct. 1	*Pokrov* (feast of the Protection of the Holy Mother of God)
	Dec. 6	*Talv-Mikul* (winter feast of St Michael)
Šoutar'	April 23	*Kevaz-Jürgi* (Springtide feast of St George)
	July 20	*Ilja* (St Elijah, Church of St Elijah, 1585)
	Nov. 26	*Talv-Jürgi* (autumn feast of St George)
Mäg´i	July 20	*Ilja* (St Elijah)
Kaskeza	Aug. 15	*Uspenja* (Assumption of Virgin Mary)
Meccantaga (Zalesye)	July 7	*Iivan* (St John)
Matvejašelga	Sept. 27	*Voznesenja* (Elevation of the Life-Giving Cross)
D'azar' (Yašozero)	Sept. 22	St Iona's commemoration day
	Aug. 19	*Spassu* (The Transfiguration of Christ) in the churches of the Annunciation of the Virgin and of St Nicholas the Miracle-Worker, 1675
Süvarinniska (Voznesenye)	Oct. 1	*Pokrov* – the feast of Protection of the Holy Mother of God (the churches of the Annunciation of the Virgin and of St Nicholas the Miracle-Worker, 1654)

The traditional material focusing on dreams and apparitions legitimizes the appearance of the other world to the living. Although the homecoming of the dead is not laudable in itself, their appearance in the dreams of Onega Vepsian women is practically compulsory, explaining why in most villages there have been very sensitive dreamers, and, in parallel, dream interpreters enriching these visions with culturally and contextually coherent meanings (Kaivola-Bregenhøj 1993: 211). Thus, depending on the circumstances even revenants can be experienced in a positive way in these regions. '"Reality" flows into the dreams and dreams are connected to "reality" in a stronger, more aware and more public manner than we usually see, in our own culture' (Järvinen 2004: 191).

Maria's representations of various tales of appearance – and also, of course, of various lamentations – echo a mentality in which the limen between this and the other world may be strongly marked, but can nevertheless be crossed from both directions. Depending on the circumstances and the context, such contacts may be regarded as good or ominous. Thus, the border separating this world from the next, the living from the dead, is a matter of continuous negotiation. In general the border is obvious and well defined; occasionally, however, it turns out to be surprisingly subtle and distinctly permeable. The same kind of strong ambivalence is evident in the texts of the lamentations themselves. It is noteworthy that on the one hand, Maria declares that the appearances of her husband have given her joy; on the other hand, she nevertheless pleads with him to stay in the realm of the dead. When describing the revenant, she takes the whole phenomenon as a matter of course; at the same time, however, she considers it necessary to go to the monastery's ruins to light a candle, and to draw a strong line between this world and the next with her prayers. A careful reading of the lamentation texts presented in the Appendix will reveal several similarities, both fundamental and verbal, between the following narrative fragments and the lamentations.[16] The fragments appear to present a prose commentary on the poetic dialogue of the lamentations. Here, the whole ambivalence of communicating with the dead becomes manifest. Its openness to dialogue is combined with an abjective position, expressed with particular clarity in the prayer incantations.

> He comes and seems to be placing a glass [on the table]. He seems to be putting logs into the stove. I lie in the bed and I smell smoke. I get out and go to see – nothing.

Sometimes it feels as though he is going to bed. But I ward him off. I wake up and there's nobody there ...

Then he seems to be leaving. He opens the door and closes it. Oh my, oh my, oh my. Again I go to see whether the door is locked. If the door is not bolted that means there must have been someone here ... I go to see, but I am very scared. I go and I see that the door is bolted ...

'Did you come here again to frighten me, old man? Don't come. Sleep where you are. Once you got there, stay there and sleep. You were led to the other side – here, I have nothing left at all ...'...

He walks and walks around and I think: 'My Lord, who is it walking there?' But there's nobody ... 'Old man, did you come again? Go away to your home.'

I went to the church and lit a candle there, then it became less frequent ...

What was it that I said: 'Through shining prayers, through the firmness of St Nicholas, the cross of St George, with the help of the blue heavens – Amen. Amen. Amen.' And everything passes. I cross myself and I say ...

throughout the day I must keep my doors closed and I must pray.

But they say that some even come to stay the night. That is wrong. You just have to go to bed, fearing your God; with God. 'God, our Lord, save and protect me. Save me from evil. Save me from evil people. Save and protect and be gracious.'

Yet Maria's attitude towards her father's appearances in her dreams is very positive. All in all, there have been three such appearances: during the Second World War, after the war and 40 years later. Indeed, it is characteristic of husbands and fathers to appear on important commemoration days (see also Järvinen 2004: 192, 200). The dream appearances of mothers have generally been considered ominous in Karelia, probably because for her daughter a mother will always remain a representation of authority, with both positive and negative associations (Järvinen 2004: 202). As illustrated below:

The appearance of your mother in a dream does not signify good. But if you see your father, this is a good sign. I tell my mother: "'Don't come to me [in dreams]. You don't bring me anything good, only heartaches.' But my father appeared to me when the war ended. And when 40 years had gone by. But when I first saw him, the war was still going on.

Throughout her life, Maria has been a great dreamer of portentous dreams (Russian *snit'sya*, 'have a dream'). Even during our brief contact, we counted a number of them dealing with different subjects: (1) Maria's father, killed in war, came home to stroke the children's heads; (2) four charred logs and the four family members who died during the war; (3) the disappearance of the village; (4) the failed washing that foretold her husband's death; (5) Maria's teeth breaking and head itching that foretold her daughter's unfortunate death, etc. Yet according to popular belief, not all dreams come true, only those seen on Thursday and Friday nights. Let us now examine, as an example, one of those portentous dreams, the one foretelling the death of four near relatives. In the dream, the father, a casualty of war, appears to Maria carrying half-charred logs into the yard to replace four rotten logs in the wall:

> The war is going on and I dreamt that father brought home half-charred logs, six metres in length. He carries them up to the house – two and then again two logs. And I say, 'Father, why did you bring these logs beneath the window, they are charred.' And he says, 'Don't you see that four logs in the wall are rotten, they must be exchanged.' And when the war ended, father was dead, mother died, the brothers were killed … Four dead ones.

Central to Maria's dream repertoire, there is yet another portentous dream foreshadowing the disappearance of the village and the fact that only Maria's solitary house remained standing:

> I went to the lake to do the washing. In the old days, we had yokes for carrying pails. I went carrying the yokes to rinse the washing. Goodness gracious. I came back and saw that everything seems to be turned upside down. Where are the houses? There's only one house left … That's true – that is what I saw. Not a house left standing anywhere. I told this dream to my Granny. And it's come true, too. Some people have died, some were taken away to live with their daughters, some just packed up and left. I did, indeed, stay alone. I could never have believed it – that I would be left alone living in a solitary house. All the other houses were torn down. That one over there was struck by lightning and burned down.

Lamentation in the Cemetery

Maria's husband died a year before our meeting, her daughter half a year before. Left alone and bent under her double grief, she practised commemoration on a daily basis. Sitting alone on the bench in front of her house, she recited words of lamentation which she was quite happy to repeat, upon our request, even outside the ritual environment. Her special emotional state may also have been one of the reasons why she took us to the family burial ground, where she broke into a powerful lamentational conversation with her loved ones (about this performance cf. Arukask and Lašmanova 2009).

In the old days, the cemetery was situated next to the monastery, across the lake, but after the monastery was turned into a prison camp in the 1930s a new burial ground was located in a small grove near the village. It is there now, situated in many ways on liminal ground; on the threshold between the wood and the village, between this world and the next. When approaching the graveyard, we put a somewhat careless question to Maria concerning the *mechiin̄e* ('forest spirit'). She quite obviously avoided answering the question and took care not to mention the name of the forest spirit, who represents everything sinister and evil, in this liminal situation.

About 10 metres before the grave, a couple of minutes before beginning her lamentation, Maria called out to her husband, thus marking her entrance into ritual space-time: 'Fedka, where are you? Wake up ... Good day, dear Daddy. Christ has risen, all the deceased have come.'

In this way, she prepared to meet her husband, face to face, since during the lamentation, the deceased one rises before her eyes as though alive. First she quickly trimmed the grave, and then a marvel-lously lengthy lamentational recital began. Maria pressed her forehead against the burial mound, which still stood high. She seemed to be uttering the words of her lamentation straight into an imaginary hole in the ground – but then the *voik* (Veps. 'lament') was, indeed, addressed to those in the nether world. She addressed her deceased husband as if he were alive: she asked him to take her greetings to other loved ones, urged them to comfort each other, to go fishing and enjoy fish soup together, as they did when alive. Maria asked her deceased relatives to forgive her for not being able to go to all their graves and recite lamentations there. Instead, she said, she commemorates them each morning with tea and biscuits. Maria praised the wellbeing of the dead and recalled the dignity of their funeral tributes. In contrast, she emphasized her own miserable condition, her great grief and spiritual suffering. At the end, she reached the conclusion that life in this world is worth nothing; now it is nothing but a waste of time and

Figure 4: Maria lamenting on the grave of her husband at the partly deserted cemetery (photograph by Madis Arukask).

has no joy to offer her. The only joy left to her – as Maria paradoxically realized – was lamenting itself. Several times she asked the deceased not to bother her in her daily life, not to come visiting her at home, since they now have 'their own discretion' in their realm.

When Maria raised her head, it could be seen that she had poured all her strength into the lamentation. The imaginary journey to her departed loved ones had exhausted her, draining her of what vigour she had left. At the same time, Maria was able to stick to the limitations of the genre, in her lamentation recital, and she did not lose control of her psychophysical being. The intenseness of the lamentation code, its clear difference from ordinary speech and its power to alter consciousness are the agents that enable the person undergoing the experience to push her voice across the boundary and to reach the dead. A nonagenarian woman has indeed claimed that in the old days, women could *voikta* (lament) until they lost consciousness. The imaginary act of crossing the border requires extreme physical effort in order to establish contact and maintain a conversation. That physical effort appears to transform the spiritual experience of border crossing into a real, physical, act. This is precisely the border marked by the loss of consciousness (fainting). The physical (that which is experienced through the senses) flows into the metaphysical (that which is experienced supersensorily) and the body acquires the significance of a threshold. Something of the kind could be observed in Maria's lamentation behaviour. All in all, her intense and almost unremitting lamentation lasted for more than half an hour. During the brief pauses, she easily switched back to ordinary speech, letting us for example know of her exhaustion. As soon as she switched back to ordinary speech, the contact with the nether world seemed to snap. The first recital for her husband lasted for almost 20 minutes, with the briefest of pauses. Her second lamentation, of which the beginning was dedicated to her daughter, and the continuation again to her husband, was of equal length. Thus, Maria's lengthy and emotionally exhausting recital in the cemetery took on quite epic dimensions. Taking into account the oppressive heat of the day, it was quite a formidable achievement for an 80-year-old.

In Place of a Conclusion: Reflections on our Experience, a Deconstructionist Re-reading of Maria's Worldview

So far, we have hopefully been able to describe Maria's solitary world and her vernacular conviction in its holistic integrity, 'as it is lived'. The different spheres of Maria's religious life have proven relatively easily divisible and differentiable, without shattering an illusion of continuity. In a sense we had what could be described as ideal laboratory conditions in which to study our subject, a person whose daily life is no longer disturbed by continuing human relationships and who was very willing to open up a concentrated worldview to us. This is, indeed, an ideal situation. One which could very easily become of interest to, for instance, students interested in traditional folk belief, or indeed to any of the constantly touring specialists who, year in and year out, make use of 'good informants', at the same time reinforcing them in, and even limiting them to, roles designated for them by ourselves.

At the same time, all this is rather circumstantial. Naturally we didn't start out on our fieldwork in the Onega Vepsian areas without previous knowledge or attitudes, made up of a certain combination of relevant professional knowledge of the region's history, vernacular culture and research history.

Thus, the analysis has so far been influenced by certain discursive choices, and describing our experiences through them we have perhaps succeeded in making plausible claims about Maria's reality. Yet we must acknowledge that the results of our short observation of this reality are relatively fragile, involving, to a considerable extent, what we wanted to believe and wanted to see, as well as Maria's aptitude for pinpointing the focus of our interests in full flight, as it were, and easily adjusting her descriptions to our expectations. Therefore, we should set out methodically to patch the more sparse areas of this holistic ideal model, presented here through the prism of what we wished to see. We are in danger of slipping into a position similar to that of the Karelianism among Finnish nationals at the beginning of the twentieth century, who in their unbalanced Kalevala enthusiasm distorted the predominant reality of Orthodox folk piety, first to satisfy themselves and then their audiences; or into the situation of the Russian historians, compelled, in their imperial discourse, to ignore even the modest role played by native peoples in the history of the eastern Slavs.

The dimensions of Maria's world, and particularly the part of it which we were able to focus on during our brief stay, are naturally not comparable to those of a fundamental treatment of any period, ethnic group or chain of events. All the more amazing, even for ourselves, was the illusion of a continuum that opened up through Maria's performances. Wouldn't it then be wiser here to use, instead of a 'unifying world vision', a model of different discursive series (cf. Foucault 2001) that refer, in their diffuse co-action, to the natural breaks in a person's life? Vernacular thinking is rather characterized by discontinuity. In this light, a sceptical attitude arises towards vernacular belief as a 'syncretic system'. Leonard Primiano has said that vernacular religion as a theoretical approach is the study of religious peoples' belief systems (Primiano 1995: 51). However, one should be very clear whether by 'system' we understand the meaning to be: (1) an explicit grammar or rather, perhaps, admit that; (2) speaking about religion and a world image we can use the word 'system' only metaphorically, or (3) we should tend even further towards a more changeable or dynamic conglomerate.

An encounter between cultures always involves a certain amount of stress. In a fieldwork situation it is possible, as a researcher, to speak about a double amount of stress: in addition to the human effort to understand a situation, the researcher feels a professional commitment to scientifically chart what he sees and experiences, which, in essence, always constitutes a system-building effort. This urge has deep roots in tradition, going back at least to the beginning of the twentieth century with its functionalist ideas of a culture as a whole. Thus, a good researcher is one who can, in addition to solitary phenomena, also present an analytical survey of the research object's genre and tradition system, as well as sketching holistic, tradition-ecological and other similar models.

Certainly we shall have to review the concept of a worldview, as even in the case of the 80-year-old Maria's reflections we have dynamic mental process(es) undergoing organic transformations over time. She could be seen continually adjusting her experiential knowledge to new phenomena, including our entrance over the horizon of her experiential world. Or perhaps we should speak here about a 'creative groundlessness', a strategic survival adaptation in which the established traditional and personal points of reference (the dominant position of Iona described above, the *mechiińe*, thunder, etc.), are seconded by an ability to interpret huge creative potential. Symptomatically, Maria's performances involve playing with both our and her own experiences, although there is also an openness to interpretations and compromises arising from the situation. Each representation of the tradition is also a unique personal experience, an interpretation departing from the currently valid conjuncture.

We should also ask which probable dominants and areas of density (cf. Foucault's *positivities*) in Maria's self-expressive utterances have so far remained in the background in our analysis? Possibly because of our own discursive preferences, we gleaned a strong sense of Maria's inner protest against the authorities that have neglected her, and against administrative carelessness. At the same time Maria has come to terms with the existence, in her immediate neighbourhood, of the hunting base that now keeps her alive. Walking from her house to the base, she may curse the bar placed across the old village road that blocks her way, but a moment later she receives, with satisfaction, her daily rations from the men working at the base (the 'foreign locals'), plays cards with them and uses their sauna. In a similar way, Maria's attitude to the ruined monastery complex is complicated; it certainly means much more to her than merely being Iona's home. It probably has strong associations for her with the period of collective farms (when

Maria, a young woman of 18, had to be the farm's chairperson during the famine of the 1940s), or with the thieves disguised as monks who only recently took away her venerated icons and household possessions, under the pretence of piety. It also seems that being an attentive person, Maria was able to generate a lot of 'density' spurred by her wish to participate in the fieldwork partnership, in order both to please us and for the stimulation it afforded her. With the so-called bad informants, this kind of illusionary continuum is generated with far greater difficulty, as is well known.

Now, if that continuum can be breached or its generation be hampered by the mere inevitabilities of human life, its essential correctness in general might be called into question. Human life might then be treated not so much as a system of rules, albeit in the process of formation, but rather as a process of permanent mutation. The study of life stories, personal identities and beliefs could then be seen as the study of the plurality of voices – in part inner, in part interpersonal – engaged in a dialogue. For the most part, these voices give us a hint of changeability, a hint that the outlines of the continental shelves are forming out of permanently transmuting convictions, rather than the feeling that epoch-making convictions have been shaped once and for all and will now remain for ever the immutable. While established religions are – as one would expect – explicit grammars, systems characteristic of literate cultures, their assimilation of vernacular religions (by merely resorting to the epithet 'syncretic', for example) may seem to be not only oversimplifying the matter, but even misleading. It seems that for our informant several parallel worlds exist, which remain in some sense autonomous but which are nevertheless interrelated and which we have called here conglomerates.

Thus, Maria's world could be described through the models of genre system and a holistic worldview that offer the joy of recognition to a student of folklore; although they can also be described as a process of permanent mutation, polemicizing with the former. The latter view arose from a steady feeling that even the best models cannot cover that something that always remains between the lines – the momentary creativity of the informant, his or her playfulness, the ability to adapt to the situation and to the researcher, and the unexpected transitions between controversial positions. Whether we speak about the 1950s or the 1990s, we nevertheless find constructs specifically adjusted to the context of the period lacking similarity to the supra-narratives

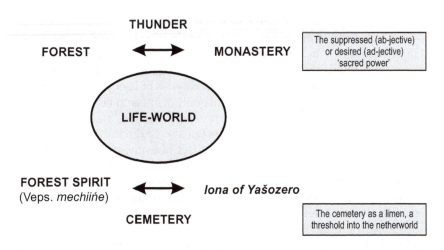

Figure 5: An attempt to schematize Maria's world view: the four sacral areas in Maria Anisimova's world view.

that create 'continuity' and historical coherence. For us, the strangers incidentally staying with her, Maria offered a colourful example both of the monumental omnipotence of human destiny, and also of the conglomeratic latency of orientation in new paradoxes.

Acknowledgements

This research was supported by the Estonian Science Foundation (grant no 7385) and by the European Union through the Regional Development Fund (Centre of Excellence, CECT).

Notes

1. According to hagiographers, such cave monks are in no way extraordinary in north Russian monasticism; the hagiography of Alexander of Svir, St Iona's spiritual teacher, shows that he, too, had spent a year as a cave hermit before founding the Monastery of the Holy Trinity.

2. What did this missionary work actually involve? Concerning the monastery of Valamo, for instance, we have a report saying that in 1408, the monastery's founder monk Sergii received an armed company from archbishop Ioan II, in order to strike a decisive blow against the 'Chuds of Korela' and to banish them from the main island (see Sorokin 1997: 189). It is obvious that the islands of Valamo in Lake Ladoga, the islands of Kizh in

Lake Onega (the name of which comes from *kizha*, a place to hold sacrificial festivals), and the island in Lake Vodla had been held sacred by the local Balto-Finnic tribes. In addition, this region was also crossed by the trade routes from Korela through Svir and Lake Onega to the upper course of the Volga. Pagan sanctuaries, like the monasteries of later date, were often located on islands. In all likelihood, the majority of fifteenth-century Karelians and Vepsians already considered themselves Christians, and had, on the same islands, not only pagan sanctuaries but also Christian chapels (see, for example, Istoriya Karelii 2000: 29). That fact notwithstanding, they were frequently treated as pagans, since they had retained various 'superstitious practices', as can be seen from a letter written as late as 1534 by Makarii, the archbishop of Novgorod, on the 'uprooting of pagan beliefs' (see, for example, Istoriya Karelii 2000: 29–30).

3. Among the Livviks of the Aunus Karelia area, the tradition of living and working for a period in the monastery there was known as *jiäksentä*, *jiäksimine* (see Järvinen 2004: 46; Kilpeläinen 2000: 243–245).

4. In the Russian Empire the replacement of the Julian calendar with the Georgian took place at the beginning of 1918. The Russian Orthodox Church did not follow this change and continues to celebrate its feasts according to the Julian calendar today.

5. The *verst* is an obsolete measurement equating to approximately 1.1 kilometres.

6. One of the main reasons for the assimilation of the Vepsians has, throughout history, been their administrative fragmentation.

7. St Iona was doing his missionary work during the reign of the expansionist Ivan the Terrible, a time when reinforcing Russia's peripheral areas against the military ambitions of Sweden was particularly topical.

8. The role assigned by traditional societies to the eccentric (to witches, healers, dreamers and dream interpreters, or the bodily or mentally deficient, etc.) has mainly been that of a marginal person empowered by the supernatural. A role which, however, carried with it the power to influence the centre.

9. The absence of an operating written language is also obviated by a report from Kaleigi, from the year 2004: 'The Vepsian tongue has few words.'

10. Thus, for instance, the assimilation of the Vepsians with the Karelians, and the advent of the neighbouring group of Ludians, came about in addition to the assimilation of the Vepsian community living by the Svir, etc.

11. Even the self-appellations of the neighbouring Livvi of Aunus (Olonetsian Karelians) and the Ludians came from the time when, subjected as tax payers to the Novgorod Slovenians and baptized, they were clearly distinguished from the Saami living further north and from part of the Vepsians. Such allies of Novgorod were called *po-ljudje* (humans/people),

to distinguish them from the 'savage/disloyal' tribes – whence the ethnic group took its name.

12. In the Vepsian lexicon, this process is strikingly described by the fact that the Balto-Finnic root signifying a human being, *inehmoi*, means lazy or suffering human being (see, for example, Laakso 1999).

13. These could be described as improvizational prayer formulae that have partly sprung up from literary forms, except function, in an oral environment.

14. Stiff animal fur, for example from a pig.

15. Among the Balto-Finnic peoples, as among ancient Balts and Germans, thunder was a semi-personified deity (*Ukko, Jumala*) who later partly overlapped with the Christian God (Siikala 2002: 203–208). In order to scare off evil powers or punish the oath breakers, thunder wields his bolt of lightning. The birch bark letter, No. 292, written in the Baltic Sea Koine, approximately thirteenth–fourteenth century (see Laakso 1999: 550) bears testimony to this fact, although it must be noted that the letter allows several hypothetical readings (for example Laakso 1999: 531–535).

16. It must be said that due to lack of space, the lamentations recorded as spontaneous performances are not published in the present paper in their entirety (the lamentation situation lasted around 40 minutes). In the Appendix, however, we present the lamentations that were performed upon our request after the visit to the cemetery, inside the house, and that were taken down by hand. These are, as it were, a condensed version of what had been performed in the cemetery.

References

Arukask, M. and Lašmanova, A. (2009) Määratledes ennast suulises esituses. Äänisvepsa naise itk oma mehe haual. *Mäetagused* 42: 55–76. Online http://www.folklore.ee/tagused/nr42/itk.pdf [Accessed 17 January 2011.]

Foucault, M. (2001) *The Archaeology of Knowledge*. London: Routledge.

Goody, J. (1977) *The Domestication of the Savage Mind*. Cambridge, London, New York, Melbourne: Cambridge University Press.

Istoriya Karelii (2000) *Istoriya Karelii v dokumentakh i materialakh (s drevneĭshchikh vremen do nachala XX veka)*. Petrozavodsk: Petrozavodskiĭ Gosudarstvennyĭ Universitet.

Järvinen, I.-R. (2004) *Karjalan pyhät kertomukset: tutkimus livvinkielisen alueen legendaperinteestä ja kansanuskon muutoksista*. Suomalaisen Kirjallisuuden Seuran toimituksia 962. Helsinki: Suomalaisen Kirjallisuuden Seura.

Jürgenson, A. (2004) Eksitaja jälgedel. In *Setumaa kogumik* 2. Uurimusi Setumaa arheoloogiast, geograafiast, rahvakultuurist ja ajaloost, 126–149. Tallinn: Arheoloogia Instituut/MTÜ Arheoloogiakeskus.

Kaivola-Bregenhøj, A. (1993) Dreams as folklore. *Fabula* 34 (3–4): 211–224.

Kilpeläinen, H. (2000) *Valamo – karjalaisten luostari?: Luostarin ja yhteiskunnan interaktio maailmansotien välisenä aikana. Suomalaisen Kirjallisuuden Seuran toimituksia* 799. Helsinki: Suomalaisen Kirjallisuuden Seura.

Laakso, J. (1999) Vielä kerran itämerensuomen vanhimmista muistomerkeistä. *Virittäjä* 4: 531–555.

Mauss, M. (1967) *The Gift: Forms and Functions of Exchange in Archaic Societies.* New York: The Norton Library.

Primiano, L. N. (1995) Vernacular religion and the search for method in religious folklife. *Western Folklore (Reflexivity and the Study of Belief)* 54 (1): 37–56.

Salve, K. (1995) Forest fairies in the Vepsian folk tradition. In M. Kõiva and K. Vassiljeva (eds) *Folk Belief Today,* 413–434. Tartu: Estonian Academy of Sciences, Institute of the Estonian Language and the Estonian Museum of Literature. Online http://www.folklore.ee/rl/folkte/sugri/vepsa1.html [Accessed 17 January 2011.]

Salve, K. (2005) Vepsäläisestä folkloresta. In L. Saressalo (ed.) *Vepsä: maa, kansa, kulttuuri.* Tampereen museoiden julkaisuja 81. Suomalaisen Kirjallisuuden Seuran toimituksia 1005, 85–115. Tampere: Tampereen museot; Helsinki: Suomalaisen Kirjallisuuden Seura.

Salve, K. (1997) Vepsa õigeusk: ka metsas võib palvetada. In *Lee 4. Ümin. Eesti Rahva Muuseumi Sõprade Seltsi väljaanne,* 153–169. Tartu. Online http://www.folklore.ee/rl/folkte/sugri/vepsa/palve1.htm [Accessed 17 January 2011.]

Siikala, A.-L. (2002) Mythic images and shamanism: A perspective on Kalevala poetry. *FF Communications No.* 280. Helsinki: Academia Scientarum Fennica.

Sorokin, P. E. (1997) Vozniknovenie Valaamskogo monastȳrya i formiro-vanie ego topografii. In A. N. Kirpichnikova, E. A Ryabinina and A. I. Saksa (eds) *Slavyane i finno-ugrȳ: arkheologiya, istoriya, kul'tura. Dokladȳ rossiĭsko-finlyandskogo simpoziuma po voprosam arkheologii.* Rossiĭskaya akademiya nauk. Institut istorii material'noĭ kul'turȳ; pod redaktsieĭ, 186–195. Sankt-Peterburg: Dmitriĭ Bulanin.

Stark, L. (2002) *Peasants, Pilgrims, and Sacred Promises: Ritual and the Supernatural in Orthodox Karelian Folk Religion. Studia Fennica Folkloristica* 11. Helsinki: Finnish Literature Society.

Strogalschikova, Z. (2006) Naisen voima auttaa kansan jaloilleen. *Carelia: Karjalan Tasavallan Kansallisuuspolitiikan Asiain Komitean, Inkerin Liiton, Karjalan Rahvahan Liiton ja Vepsän Kulttuuriseuran kulttuurilehti* 2006/1, 152–157.

Vinokurova, I. (1998) Äänisvepsän kirkkopyhät: perinteet ja nykyaika. In Hakamies, P. (ed.) *Ison Karhun jälkeläiset*. Suomalaisen Kirjallisuuden Seuran toimituksia 697. Helsinki: Suomalaisen Kirjallisuuden Seura.

Whitehouse, H. (2004) Toward a comparative anthropology of religion. In H. Whitehouse and J. Laidlaw (eds) *Ritual and Memory: Toward a Comparative Anthropology of Religion*, 187–205.Walnut Creek, CA: AltaMira Press.

Appendix

Lamentational recitation written down in Maria's kitchen:

1. Maria's lament for her husband:

You pass through the wide gates
With locks forged of iron
The guards are stern.
There is no coming back:
The gates are narrow.

It is me, your sweetheart, coming to greet you
Coming to your bleak grave,
Stop and let me know, how is life over there?
We sent you away from here as best we could.
What a pity we could not have you here longer,
Although you stayed one last summer.
You left me here, alone with my bitter grief.

Nothing can give me joy in this life any more,
Nothing I do makes sense to me.
Everything seems to be crumbling, after you left,
Nothing I start gets going.
Nobody comes to offer me help,
I don't hear a single good word of greeting.

But lie in peace on your feathery bed,
Lie in peace on your bed soft as pillows.
You have everything you need there.
Tell your dear father
Of my misery.
Go a-fishing, as ever, and enjoy the catch!

Time and again you appear in my dreams,
I wake up and it has all been a dream!
This gives me great joy …

May God give me days of life,
and good health.

As long as my legs still serve me, I will always come to see you
And commemorate you each morning with hot tea.
Rest in peace and do not disturb me.
You have passed into the next world, unto your own power
May the earth be as light as a feather upon you all.

Amen! Amen! Amen! – May none of you come back visiting: that is
not good!

2. Maria's lament for her daughter, buried in Novaya Vilga, a village
too far away for anyone to take flowers or commemorate her:

My dear, you have gone to a strange land,
Nobody wakes you, nobody comes to remember you,
Nobody trims your little grave.
Mummy cannot come
And find you there.
Thousands are buried over there …

She was a good daughter – it simply hurts!
I'll set up a gravestone for her …

It strangles me, like a stone set on my chest,
It is as if you were cut off!
So I sit and lament on my bench.

3. Maria's lament for her mother:

I curse myself:
'Mother, why did you bear me, poor thing, into this white world?
Never have I seen any good in it.
I buried you, then I buried my husband, then my daughter.

Alone I wait in my village,
The only one left in my house.
There is no one to greet, no one to come to see me –
I'm no longer living, I just waste away in this white world!
I can't bear to look at this white world!
Lamenting, I comfort myself with tears. –
That is my only joy!
There is no beauty in this white world ...'

Hidden Messages: Dream Narratives about the Dead as Indirect Communication

Ágnes Hesz[*]

Among the Csángós of Gyimes, a Hungarian community living in Romania,[1] it is not rare for people to dream about their dead relatives and acquaintances. These dreams provide one of the main channels for communication between the living and the dead, and thus are central to the cult of the dead: they maintain and regulate the relationship between the two groups, reinforce or mould ideas about the afterlife, and make people observe rituals related to the dead. (cf. Järvinen *et al.* 1996; Järvinen 1998). In this article however, I will focus on the communicative aspects these dreams have within the living community, when narrated to others. My arguments are based on an eight-month fieldwork trip among the Csángós.[2]

To understand the communicational significance of the dream narratives, a few words have to be said about the local discourse. In Gyimes – as in many other close-knit communities – there is a communicational paradox. On the one hand there is an expectation that people should mind their own business and shouldn't care about others' affairs. On the other, they have to be informed about village affairs in order to effectively negotiate social relationships and their positions in social space. Thus, as everyday conversations show, communication does centre on the acts and problems of fellow villagers. To solve this paradox, people in Gyimes tend to express themselves indirectly. The characteristics of indirect speech were defined by Donald Brenneis as follows: the speaker means something other then what he literally expresses, and though his wording is neutral, he conveys moral judgement, which has to be deduced by the audience. Indirectness comes from different factors: from ambivalent wording, from the use of substitute words, from the use of reported

* Ágnes Hesz is Assistant Professor at the Department of European Ethnology and Cultural Anthropology, University of Pécs, Hungary.

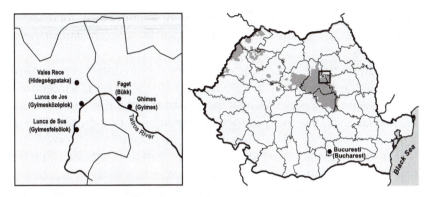

The belief narratives of the Gyimes region in Romania are studied by Agnes Hesz and Éva Pócs in this volume.

speech, or from telling things to people other than the real target of the message. Certain situations may also lend special connotations to what is said, thus meaning more than the literal expressions. The goal of speaking in an indirect way is to make the speaker unimpeachable for what has been said (Brenneis 1987: 504–507). Speaking indirectly thus resolves the opposition between the norms of discretion and the avoidance of conflict, and the need for violating these norms. In what follows, I will argue that dream narratives about encounters with the dead represent a unique form of indirect communication and thus express messages which, owing to local etiquette, are not really proper to utter in any other form.[3]

Dream Narratives as Indirect Communication

The indirectness of dream narratives is partly due to the fact that these accounts are essentially considered as messages from the dead, thus, on the merely textual level, they express the will and opinion of the dead person, and not of the dreamer or narrator. The speaker plays the part of mouthpiece for the dead person and is thus able to cover his or her own communication. All of this has some very important consequences for the authenticity of the texts. As manifestations of the transcendental sphere, in the eyes of the listeners they convey a higher degree of reality and authenticity than other expressions (cf. Fabian 1966 quoted by Tedlock 1987: 22). At Hidegség, although there are significant exceptions which I shall discuss later on, dream narratives about the dead are usually given credit. This way the speaker, by hiding their message behind that of the deceased, legitimizes it, increasing the chance that the communicational act will be successful from their perspective.

In addition to the above considerations, dream narratives are also indirect in the sense that – in accordance with the speaker's intention – on occasion they may mean far more than the text itself reveals. On the textual level, the main framework for interpreting dream visions of the dead is the way the Csángós conceptualize their relationship to their dead. In accordance with the teachings of the Catholic Church, the living have to take care of the dead in order to give them assistance in expiating their sins and to help them into heaven. They do so in return for life, upbringing and property. In a similar way to the practices in the Middle Ages and in some contemporary parts of Catholic and Orthodox Europe (Douglass 1969: 133–134; Kenna 1976: 23–28; Danforth and Tsiaras 1982: 124; Goldey 1983: 14; Cátedra 1992: 247–254; Geary 1994: 77–94; Schmitt 1998: 33), there is a strong connection between inheritance and the obligation for commemorative services, especially if the inheritance involves the house and personal property of the deceased. Methods of caring for the dead follow the teachings and practices of the Catholic Church: prayers, masses and alms giving, and providing a decent funeral. Neglecting the dead results in attacks on the living or on their property by the dead. Accordingly, any type of appearance of the dead is usually seen as a sign of dissatisfaction and the majority of the dream narratives expressing the intentions of the dead move along this line: they inform the dreamer that the dead person needs something, their memory has been insulted or the living are not acting according to their will or liking.

At the same time, this interpretative framework also gives rise to the possible secondary meaning of dream narratives. Since the appearance of the dead and their good or bad fortune largely depend on how far their living relatives live up to the obligations towards them, dream narratives may be used to express approval or criticism. Thus they may be applied to establish or ruin one's reputation, as well as to manipulate public opinion in conflicts, or even, as we will see, to reach material ends.

However, not all dream narratives are apt for such purposes. Those dream narratives, for example, in which the dead appear to their own relatives rarely take up such functions (around 70% of the 134 narratives I recorded) as opposed to those in which the dreamer sees a dead person outside of their close family, or the narrator is different from the dreamer. It is also true that narrating dreams can have many purposes other than conveying secondary messages. People from Hidegség often relate their dreams simply to share a stirring experience with others or to try to figure out together what the dead person wanted and why, if the dream itself was not very clear. Among the texts in my possession there are around 22 examples, i.e. one-sixth of all cases, in which the contents and the conditions of narration render it certain that the dream was used in order to convey some sort of message.

Now, let us see what sort of messages are transmitted by the people at Hidegség, how these are expressed and what the people are trying to attain by relating their dreams.

Hidden Messages

Before analysing the way in which dream narratives are used, it is essential to describe the types and generic characteristics of this – formally very varied – group of texts. In an essay examining the process whereby the dream experience becomes a text, Judit Gulyás distinguished three types of dream narratives, according to the level of text formation: (1) texts resulting from the first recollection of the dream experience; (2) *memorate* type dream narratives; and (3) dream narratives in folklore genres using narrative poetics (Gulyás 2007: 213).

In Gyimes, practically all instances are *memorate* dream narratives,[4] or more precisely, this is the type most easily accessible to the fieldworker, as (s)he is rarely lucky enough to hear a fresh, first-hand dream verbalization. *Memorate* type dream narratives have two further sub-types in everyday speech situations in which the difference comes largely from one type being more elaborate than the other. The first type contains texts which attempt to do nothing more than relate a dream experience: the dreamer describes the dream in a concise fashion in one or two sentences and the interpretation is usually done jointly by those present. These communications usually take place directly or shortly after the dream experience, on one or several occasions. Although it is difficult or even impossible to prove empirically, this is how the majority of dream experiences about the dead come to the surface and this sub-type is soon forgotten both by the dreamer and their audience.

However, dream experiences which proved particularly significant for some reason become fixed in texts that belong to the second type of *memorate* dream narrative. These narratives may often include a brief recapitulation of the dream experience, the antecedents of the dream, its circumstances, interpretation and conclusions. There have been several excellent attempts in folklore research to establish the structural scheme of recorded dream narratives (see for example Barna 1998: 342; Kaivola-Bregenhøj 1998: 356). However, when we examine the formal characteristics of dream narratives, we must bear in mind the fact that in their natural medium, i.e. everyday communi-cation, they do not have a permanent and final structure. Whenever the Changós consider a dream particularly significant, be it their own dream or someone else's, they tell it in varied circumstances to varied audiences and with different aims. These factors influence the sort of details they cover in the context, the sort of commentaries or the thing they emphasize, as well as the interpretation of the dream itself. In other words, the form that the dream narrative takes from occasion to occasion depends on the speech situation in which it is uttered.

From the perspective of our subject all this had to be emphasized because the dream narratives on which this research was based were noted down in interview situations, except for a few lucky occasions. Consequently the texts differ considerably from the way in which locals tell their dreams to each other. The fieldworker being unfamiliar with the life of the village and with local beliefs, ideas and practices does not have the stock of knowledge possessed by the local people. Therefore informants have to supplement their narrative with bits of information that are superfluous from the locals' point of view, in order to make their accounts clear to the visitor. Narrative formation is also influenced by the fact that the dream narratives related in the interview had come into focus in the context of different questions and were intended to confirm various ideas or customs regarding the dead. Thus the communicational aim was different from the conversations of the locals.[5] As a consequence the narratives are interspersed with explanations regarding customs and ideas, as well as remarks pointing out how these relate to the dream experience. Similarly, the accounts offered to me often included characterizations or judgement of those involved, believing that not being familiar in the village, I would be unable to make the right conclusions on my own.

Thus, some of the recorded dream narratives were not sufficiently indirect. At the same time, these explanations, appended merely for my benefit, often proved useful in revealing why stories of this kind are told. Analysis was made easier by the informers describing the context of the dream, explaining who the dreamer was and who was the listener for the resulting narrative.

The dream narrative in my first example is of this kind. I heard the narrative, which expresses criticism about a relative who did not sufficiently promote the memory of a dead person, from an old woman, Ágnes Takács,[6] who narrated several of her dreams to me when speaking about rituals regarding the dead. The text quoted below was the second dream narrative told during our interview.

> There was a nice guy called Dezső Péter in Kápolna, and he was already dead. We were visiting each other frequently. And there was a mass [for him]. His mother was so stingy, his widow paid for the mass, but his mother secretly went to the priest and added all the family dead to the list [of names for whom the mass was celebrated]. The rule says that the first mass, the one said six weeks after one's death, should only be celebrated for that single person. And she had added all her dead to the list. So the mass was said, and the next day I was going to Kápolna, and I met with one of his good neighbours, and she said to me, listen Ágnes, she said, Ágnes last night I've dreamt of Dezső Péter. He had an empty backpack with him, he opened it for me, she said, and there was nothing in it but a small piece of bread and three small, tiny pieces of garlic. And I said ... and Ágnes said to me that the dead one told her he was left with nothing, for the others took everything [the family dead took the rest of the food given as charity gifts for the sake of the dead]. And I saw exactly the same dream that night, these three pieces of garlic, this man, and this small piece of bread and that backpack.

The text reveals that this dream experience was shared and discussed by two women who met in the street and who had both been on good terms with the deceased. The dream experience had given a legitimate base for them to condemn the mother of the dead person who had not respected an important local clerical practice. The fact that the custom was not followed obviously caused consternation among those present at the mass, and it turned into disapproval when the dream revealed the consequences of this breech of rules. The complaint of the deceased, 'I was left with nothing, they took everything,' refers to the idea that the beneficial effects of the mass are shared by all the dead mentioned during the ceremony. The fewer persons noted at one mass, the greater the extent to which the dead person's sufferings are eased. The complaint against the mother, not made explicit in the narrative, was that she – behaving in a very unmotherly way – had put her own financial interests before the well-being of her son, when she had tried to fulfil her obligation to her own dead at the expense of her daughter-in-law.

At the very beginning of the narrative Ágnes Takács declared that the mother's behaviour was evidence of shortcomings in her character, namely of her meanness. The narrative she told me and the explanation she gave about the order of the sixth-week mass differed (in all probability) from the narratives passed down among the people of the village. In this case, she had to emphasize the deviation of the mother's behaviour from local norms, in order to guarantee the correct interpretation of the dream.

Dreams about the dead, as I have already mentioned, partly owe their effectiveness to the fact that they assure the legitimacy of their contents, since they are accepted as true manifestations of the transcendental sphere. This is even more true of this particular example, as both women had the same dream at the same time, which proved, or at least had the capacity to prove, the truth value of the dream contents – both to them and to their later audiences.

The text in the next example contains essentially the same accusation – that of meanness and neglect of the deceased person. The only difference is that here the dreamer, a young woman, related her dream to the very person at whom it was targeted. She told her dream to me when we were talking about giving alms to the dead. She also added explanations to her dream narrative to aid correct interpretation.

> You know, our neighbour down there, the old man, I didn't know him. He died in the year I moved here. And his wife was a smart one, I don't know, somehow she was a strange woman. And I saw in a dream that I was having coffee with the mother-in-law of the woman who visited us yesterday. And in my dream the curtains had been taken off, and the light was switched on in the room while it was dark outside. And once I happened to look at the window and saw that a grey old man with a white moustache was standing there. And I, in my dream, I asked: Aunt Erzsi, Aunt Erzsi, I asked, hey, isn't it Uncle Gyula? And she said yes, it is him, little Kati. And that man, he spoke to me, he said: little woman, please give me a cup of coffee. Because Anna [his wife] has enough coffee, but she never gives a cup of coffee for me. The next morning, when I woke up, I went down to the old lady. And I told

her: Godmother, I saw Uncle Gyula in my dream this night. I did not know him personally, but I saw him in my dream. And how did you see him? she asked. And I told her that he had asked a cup of coffee from me. Because nobody gives him any – though the old woman had plenty, because she liked all sorts of things, but ... And she looked at me and admitted: it is true. That I don't give a cup of coffee for the sake of him. (female, 32)

For all the people in Gyimes, the message of the narrative should have been clear: the widow was a stingy person (a serious flaw in character), which is proved by her neglect towards her husband. In the narrative told to me, the dreamer did not say the word 'mean' or 'stingy', but at the same time, she tried to make the suggested meaning clear for me. In introducing her dream experience she used the words 'strange' and 'smart' to characterize the widow. These words, just like the word 'interesting', not mentioned here, are usually used to characterize people who for some reasons don't live up to the norms of the community. At the end of the narration she made her point more straightforward by declaring that it was not for lack of money that the widow neglected the deceased. In fact, by saying that 'she liked all sorts of things', the informer also hints that the woman was far from mean toward herself – in fact she was particularly selfish.

The dreamer also tried to underline the authenticity of the narrative by repeatedly declaring, both in the original context of the narrative – that is, when she told it to the widow – and during our interview that she had never known the deceased personally. Thus she tried to exclude a commonly accepted explanation for the origin of certain dreams, according to which people may dream about a particular dead person if they think of them or talk about them during the day. In addition, the reaction of the widow, who admitted the neglect, also substantiated the truth content of the dream. The facts that she received the message in a positive spirit and offered the dreamer alms proved that she did not consider the warning an insult. Any other form of criticism would have led to a conflict: the indirectness of the dream was the only acceptable means for letting the widow know about her own – and probably the entire neighbourhood's – disapproval.

Neglect is not the only transgression attacked in dream narratives. They are also used for reprimanding people who fail to come to terms with their loss and engage in prolonged or ostentatious grief.[7] The following narrative was related by a young woman when I asked her about communication between the living and the dead.

Q. And can they [the dead] signal to the living or appear to them or anything like that?

A. No. Well, there are these cases like when, you see, a young lad – he'd been the same age as my husband and had died – and his mother mourned for him and wept for a long time. What happened, you see, was, well, he was killed and then one of my husband's cousins saw him in a dream and the dead man said to him 'tell my mother not to weep any more' because, he said, he is standing so deep in water in the other world that he really cannot stand it any longer. His mother, wherever she went, she would walk along the street and cry, she cried at home or any time, and just kept weeping for her son. And then [the dead man] said she should not cry for him any more because he cannot stand it any longer. (Female, 36)

Dream narratives where the dead complain that they are standing in water as a result of exaggerated grief are quite common in the village. The notion itself is a belief legend motif well known throughout Hungarian-speaking areas.[8] In Gyimes, dream narratives of this kind are indeed used with a normative intent. A widow I met with wept a little when speaking about her late husband, but also noted that she had been warned that she did harm to the deceased by lamenting so much.

Here a woman told us that her husband had died and she cried about him a lot, and she said that [the dead man] went home and she saw him in a dream saying, 'don't cry for me any more for I cannot rest'. They tell me the same, but mine [her late husband] has not come home yet. (Female, 73)

In the cases mentioned above the dream narratives served to mediate negative opinions about the behaviour of the living towards the dead. Dream narratives, however, can also be used to regulate public discourse. The following dream narrative, for example, can be seen as an attempt to stop people gossiping about a dead person and their relatives. I heard this account from an old couple who were not close to the deceased or to the dreamer. In their account the story was used to illustrate the idea that it is wrong to speak in ill terms about the dead.

The dream narrative centred around a woman who – together with her husband – died in a tragic accident a few years before my fieldwork. The event stirred the village deeply and people soon began a rumour that the cause of the couple's 'miraculous'[9] death was that someone had 'had a mass served upon them'. This means that an

Orthodox priest was hired to serve a curse mass which, it is believed, only takes effect on sinners, and as such can be seen as a kind of divine judgement. Thus if the idea occurs that someone had fallen victim to such a mass, it is equivalent to declaring (again, indirectly) that the person had done something against the expectations of the community or the laws of God. The woman who had died in the accident was held in the village to be an unreliable business partner. People supposed that her death was triggered by someone she had cheated. Shortly after the tragedy, presumably at the time when gossip about her was most intense, the young daughter of the woman's sister-in-law saw the woman in her dream.

> A: The daughter of her sister-in-law saw one night in a dream that she spoke with this woman taken by the flood ... with Julia. And Julia told her: go and tell all the neighbours not to speak about me, for I cannot rest.
> B: That the neighbours should not talk about her anymore.
> A: Don't speak about me anymore, she said, for I cannot rest. The little girl saw this in a dream, and the next morning related what she has seen. That Aunt Julia asked her to tell everybody not to speak about her for she couldn't find her rest. (A: male, 69; B: female, 67)

I have already mentioned that the message of the dream is in harmony with the idea that the dead cannot rest if they are talked about – particularly if this is done in an unfavourable tone. In this case, however, there was more at stake than the dead person resting in peace. The sin that was attributed to her and the curse on her had stigmatized her closest family. Passing on the dream narrative was probably aimed at halting this stigmatization process. Moreover, it was done by presenting the gossiping people as transgressors against the norm, claiming that they violated the rule that one should be respectful towards the dead. In fact if we also take into account the widespread idea that the dead can take revenge on those who offend them, the dream can also be seen as an implied threat.

While in the previous case those who related the dream wanted to deny that a mass had been served on the dead, and thus defend her reputation, in the following story the dream narrative gave ground to raising the charge of bewitchment.[10] In this case bewitchment is mentioned with the aim of acquitting the deceased. The narrative is about a suicide; the dream was experienced and related by a woman who was once very close to the deceased.

Well I had a dream. She [the dead woman] was laying in state, you know. And we were standing by the side of the coffin and the priest was doing the ceremony of burial and Erzsi, the dead woman who hung herself, suddenly sat up and said, quite clearly, 'Mary has resurrected me'. And so she [raised] her head and sat up. She said, 'Mary has raised me, I am not dead'. So this must have been a dream, even though I never have dreams but this was not real so it must have been a dream.

Q. And what does it mean?
Well, to me it means that the Virgin Mary, for in her life she had prayed a lot to the Virgin and all that, so she is helping her soul, you see, and so she will be free after her death. And it is possible you know, for only the Good Lord knows this, that she did not do it out of her own free will but someone had done it to her by *fermeka*.[11] Because, you see, that also happens sometimes that someone has someone else killed by *fermeka*, to make it a hundred percent sure that they die. And if it was done by *fermeka* then the Good Lord will free her soul because only the Lord knows that, we don't. (female, 36)

This dream narrative should be interpreted in the context of local beliefs regarding suicides which – in accordance with the teachings of the local priest – are especially harsh regarding the fate of the person: they face eternal damnation. However, in this dream narrative the woman who has hung herself sat up in her coffin and stated that she had been resurrected by the Virgin Mary. An explanation for this contradiction is offered by a common belief within the community. According to this, suicides do not count as sinners if their act was an escape from an untenable situation for which other people are responsible. This was the case if the person suffered regular humiliation from his or her spouse or family, if he or she was restricted in her freedom or became innocently entangled in some serious conflict. In this case the dead woman's resurrection by the Virgin was regarded as a proof of her innocence, which made the dreamer ponder that her god-daughter might have committed suicide because someone had bewitched her to do so.

This dream narrative had several possible consequences. On the one hand it could improve the appraisal of the dead person, second it could open the way to identify the persons responsible and, lastly, those who knew or thought they knew the antecedents of the accident may have sensed it as implied accusation. In another part of the interview not quoted here, the narrator and a third listener (another woman who took part in the conversation) talked of the former conflicts and enemies of the dead woman, and enlisted a number of theories as to who might be implicated in the case and in what ways.

A similar message is conveyed by the following dream narrative in which a woman related two dreams she had had about a neighbour who had committed suicide.

> I have seen him (the man who committed suicide) once. Here we had an old barn, because we lived close, our houses were just close, his and ours. And then it was here in the barn, there was a middle wall, and in my dream I entered the barn, and a hand grabbed me through the middle wall. And I was very scared because I saw that it was him. And then I started to scream and ran out, and stopped at the door. And then he laughed at me. He said, you were scared, weren't you, but you shouldn't be. And then later I saw that we were at the cemetery. This dream, these two dreams, I will never forget, though I saw them long ago, more than thirty, thirty-three years ago. And there he was coming from the cemetery bringing a handful of flowers. And then I knew he was dead, and asked him, Tibi, how come that … and he was at a beautiful place, among beautiful flowers. How could you get here, you have hanged yourself, haven't you? And he said, 'God has forgiven me because I was innocent'. Because he wasn't wrong, others blamed fraud on him, and then he told me that 'God has forgiven me because I was innocent'. And he was at such a nice place, among flowers, among plenty of beautiful flowers. (female, 57)

During the account of the second dream the dreamer had indicated that she was aware in her dream that her neighbour had committed suicide. Thus she was surprised to see him in a lovely place with flowers in his arms which, in terms of the motifs of dreams about the dead, clearly means that the deceased had gone to heaven. The contradiction between the view of the local church and the salvation of the deceased is explained here by the dead person himself: his sin was forgiven because he was innocent. The informer had already told me about the conflict which led to the person's suicide earlier and thus in the dream account she only made a brief reference to it, making it clear why the deceased is not responsible for his own death. According to the story the dead person, who had worked in a shop, had been accused of making the shop unprofitable. The man, who had already considered himself unfortunate because his wife had left him, saw no other way out of this troubled situation than to hang himself. In the eyes of the dreamer, the dead person's message from the other world unequivocally proved that the deceased had been innocent of the accusations and the responsibility for his death rested upon those who had driven him into this impossible situation. By sharing the dream with others, the dreamer could influence the public judgement of the event in a positive way, since the fact that the message was revealed in a dream by the dead person himself increased its legitimacy. On the other hand, the dreamer expressed her solidarity with the family of the deceased who must have experienced the dream as reassuring in a number of ways: it cleared their loved one of the charges and reassured them of his heavenly salvation.

The next dream narrative is also related to a conflict situation, this time to an inheritance debate. Dreams of this kind are not rare in Gyimes, because last wills differing from the inheritance law are usually expressed only orally, which results in a great number of conflicts regarding inheritance. In debated situations, dreams in which the dead express their final will or voice their disapproval over the way in which their assets had been divided are also suited to influence public opinion.

The following two dream narratives were related by an old woman when she, her husband and I were talking about the dead and dreams in general. The narratives have to be interpreted in the context of an ongoing conflict of inheritance in her family. The narrator's mother-in-law had remarried after the death of her first husband and moved to her new husband's home, leaving the first husband's estate to her children. This marriage was childless and since her husband had no children of his own either, she also wanted his belongings to be inherited by her own children – notably the dreamer's family. However, the mother-in-law died before her second husband who in the event did not go along with her wish and left his estate to his own relatives.

> Once I saw her [her mother-in-law] in a dream and she asked me that Margit, she said, did Uncle Imre give you something from my property [as inheritance]? Because Uncle Imre, her second husband had no children and the old woman wanted our family to inherit the property. So. And they had a testament about this. And then, we took care of the old man, but then he was turned against us by someone, and his relatives took care of him instead of us. And then time went by and my mother-in-law asked me in a dream: Margit, did the old guy give you something? From the property? And I said, to us he gave nothing.

And then she started to swear. She said, he didn't give anything, and I said, he didn't. I saw it very clearly, we spoke with each other like that and then I woke up. (female, 56)

Although according to the dream narrative the dead person was outraged to find out that her wish was not fulfilled, the husband had in fact followed the local customs when he left his estate to the people who had tended to him in the last phase of his life. Thus he can only be accused of not having respected the dead person's last will. The idea that it was a mistake to leave his property to his own relatives was meant to be supported by another dream related in a later stage of our conversation.

Then I also saw that she [her mother-in-law] said that: I have plenty of food because I'm given so much – for it is said that if you give something for a dead person in God's name then she will not suffer from distress in the other world. And then she said that the old man [the mother-in-law's second husband] asked her: 'give me some, too, Anna', to which she replied: 'I won't give you any, let the people who received your fortune give you food!'

Although the narrator has not directly stated it, the dream, by showing the mother-in-law's husband's distress, proves that the inheritors did not properly represent the interests of the deceased and were not paying enough alms for him.

By relating these two dreams, then, this woman was suggesting two things. The first dream proved that the original testimony, in harmony with the mother-in-law's will, made the dreamer's family the rightful inheritors, and that the husband had transgressed the norms when he did not respect his wife's last will. The second dream clearly compared the conflicting parties with a result favourable for the dreamer's family. The mother-in-law's prosperity in the other-world showed that the dreamer's family acted as a fair exchange partner, and appropriately tended the deceased in return for inheritance, while the husband's relatives had proved ungrateful. Thus – the suggestion goes – the husband would have fared better if he had refused to turn against the dreamer's family and made his last will in harmony with his late wife's wish.

Dream narratives can also be used for expressing favourable opinions. Narratives about the deceased person doing well in the other-world indicate that the community, or at least the dreamer or narrator, considers the attitude of the relatives towards the dead person and the quality of their grief as adequate. In the following story the dead grandfather of my informant was seen in a dream by a young girl living next door.

> Here was Juliska from next door, she was a little girl and she told me, 'Godmother, I have seen old Pali in my dream'. But she had been as young as little Emma [the narrator's granddaughter] when [the narrator's grandfather] died. A bit older. And she said, 'I saw Granddad in my dream. Uncle Pali in my dream.' And I said, 'How did you see him, Juliska?' And she said 'I saw him and he said, "Juliska I am doing so well here and I have got everything and I am really very well".' (female, 62)

Later in our conversation it was revealed that the narrator attributed her grandfather's well-being to two things. On the one hand, and this was partly prompted by my question, she believed it was due to the considerable quantity of alms paid in his favour; and on the other hand to the deceased having lived a very religious life: as the narrator told me, he had never cursed God and kept fasts strictly. The dream of the little girl next door proved all this, which shows that the neighbourhood had a favourable opinion both about the dead person and his family, and they let them know this.

The Efficiency and Authenticity of Dream Narratives

After analysing the above examples we may just ask how effective dream narratives about the dead are as means of communication – in other words how powerfully can they influence public opinion. Regrettably, we can answer this question only indirectly. One reason for this is that it is impossible to map the spreading of various dream narratives. However, the very fact that almost half of the dreams I collected came from second-hand narrators, i.e. not from the dreamer himself or herself, proves that the Csángós tend to share their dreams when visiting each other or meeting in the street.

On the other hand, it is also hard to establish how far the Csángós consider these accounts as true. Dream narratives as texts based on a dream experience are usually attributed the same degree of reality as waking experience. This means that there is a high chance of attributing truth to the contents of dream narratives – but this does not extend to everybody in the community. Some people deny the reality of the dream experience in general; others are only suspicious about the contents of certain dreams; in fact even one and the same person can voice different opinions at different times. What can be pointed out in general is that compared to other types of dreams, those about the dead are considered true more frequently than, for example, presaging dreams. This is even true of people who otherwise claim not to believe in dreams.[12]

In other words, we can declare that the characteristics of the genre positively influence the degree to which the contents are given credit. Yet, when the truth value of a dream is judged, the person of the dreamer – whether (s)he is generally held to be trustworthy or not – as well as the context of narration, and the supposed motivation of the narrator are important points of consideration (cf. Fine 1995: 126–128). For instance, several people have mentioned that in the case of certain dreams and certain narrators the suspicion may arise that the story serves pecuniary self-interest. The following quote is from an old woman who hoped to support the authenticity of a dream she had related by quoting a negative example (in the dream she told me the Virgin Mary was trying to divert a young woman from having an abortion):

> Well, I don't know [she laughs]. Because some people – if someone who had nice head scarfs or nice clothes dies – say: 'I saw a dream and she promised to give me that beautiful dress or head scarf.' But not me, not me. I saw this clearly, my aunt told me that it was true. (female, 70)

The suspicion that the dream narrator may be using the story to serve their own ends does not necessarily mean that the audience will consider it untrue. The following case, which took place all but under my very eyes, illustrates the ambivalence of judgement about dream narratives and the dilemma that the Csángós come to face regarding dream narratives. The example also shows the power of faith in the transcendent origin of dreams and of notions about the dead.

During the time of my fieldwork a man who had lived in great hardship died after being ill for several months. The family needed considerable financial assistance to be able to give the dead person a sufficient funerary ritual. The funeral clothes for example, were donated by one of the nephews of the deceased who also happened to live next door, and the two families were engaged in a complex exchange relationship. Shortly after the funeral, however, the nephew's mother had a dream in which the dead person appeared naked. According to the dream interpretation of the community this clearly meant that the deceased needed clothes in the other world – and the relatives had to give somebody some clothes as alms. The dreamer related the dream to the relatives without delay, who in response gave the dreamer's son a piece of fabric large enough for a suit. I found out about the whole story in a roundabout way, from one of the neighbours who had actively taken part in organizing the funeral.

> I don't know if I have told you that when Péter was buried, his funeral costume was provided by Zoltán. It was the wedding costume of Zoltán, you know. And then Margit [the mother of Zoltán] said she saw Péter in her dream and he was stark naked. You know. And then, I don't know if she told this to Aunt Mari or someone else, but Aunt Mari had enough textile for a costume. You were not there this morning as she brought it, were you?
> No.
> And then she said that it must be given to them, in order to reciprocate the costume, not to accept it as a charity gift. And they gave it to Kati [Zoltán's wife]. They gave it to her, to prevent him [Péter] from being seen naked. (female, 32)

The reaction given by the relatives of the deceased indicates that they interpreted the dream on two levels. On the one hand they considered it as news about the dead person in the literal sense and by donating clothes they tried to meet the needs of the deceased without delay. For this, however, they could have chosen anybody as beneficiaries – the bliss of the deceased would have been served equally well had the gift been given to anyone else. That they chose the family of the dreamer without any hesitation, indicates that they also attributed a secondary meaning to the dream: they considered it as a reminder that they ought to return the considerable assistance they had received. It was revealed in later conversations that the relatives of the deceased have to a certain extent doubted the authenticity of this dream experience. However, there were two reasons why instead of ignoring it, they acted in accordance with what they believed to be the dreamer's wish. Had they not returned the help they were once given, their relationship with one of their chief allies and exchange partners might have taken a turn for the worse. Second, respect for the deceased prevented them from brushing off the issue by claiming that the dreamer had simply invented the dream. The family did not take the risk that if the dream did happen to be true, their dead family member would be left to suffer.[13]

Conclusion

With the cases cited in the paper I have attempted to show the communication potential of dream narratives regarding the dead, and that this potential was mainly due to them being a form of indirect communication. The last example proved how effective these narratives are, despite occasional doubt surrounding them, and also offered a glimpse into the mechanisms through which they operate. The family of the deceased primarily handled it as a message from the dead man, and not as a message from the narrator. On the other hand they understood the connotation of the message which referred to the return of the gift they got from the dreamer/narrator's family. For the narrator the form of the dream narrative was the only way to express her request – had it really been her intention to ask for a compensation – since the etiquette of exchange relationships in Gyimes prohibits anyone openly asking for a return. Thus, the fact that the message appeared in a dream narrative made it expressible on the first hand, and on the second, it considerably increased the chance of it being heard.

Notes

1. The Roman Catholic Csángós of Gyimes live in the Tatros valley in the eastern Carpathians, and are not to be mistaken for the Csángós living in Moldavia. There are a considerable number of Orthodox Romanians living in the region as well, and as a result of the same ecological and economic conditions and intermarriage, there are no significant social and cultural differences between the two groups (except for their religion).

2. My fieldwork was financed by the OTKA programme (No. 49 175) of the Hungarian Academy of Sciences, while further research was supported by the Alfred Toepfer Stiftung FVS (2004–2005) and the Collegium Budapest Institute for Advanced Study (2005–2006).

3. My conclusions are in many ways in line with those of Leea Virtanen. Based on a survey executed in Finland in the late 1970s among university students and readers of women's magazines she listed six possible reasons for relating a dream. One of them is when the dreamer uses the dream account, for example a narrative about imminent disaster, to communicate his or her opinion about other people's behaviour, or to influence the

behaviour of others. In addition, Virtanen points out that similarly to gossip, dream accounts are suited to expressing emotions, e.g. anxiety, fear, hatred or attraction, which the dreamer or gossiper is reluctant to admit, perhaps even to themselves. The reason for this is that in the cases of gossip or dream accounts the narrator does not have to take direct responsibility for whatever is stated, since they appear as mediators rather than sources of the information. (Virtanen 1989: 144) Virtanen's examples however are different both in content and social context from the cases discussed here.

4. The phrase, proposed by Judit Gulyás, arises from regarding dream accounts as the same narrative types as folk belief *memorates* (Tüskés-Knapp 1998: 371–327). This is based on the idea that both dream accounts and belief narratives describe encounters between humans and the supernatural (cf. Dégh 2001: 34–44).

5. Although in local debates about the dead and the afterlife these dreams may also be used as arguments for the credibility of certain ideas.

6. All the names used in the paper are pseudonyms.

7. Ostentatious grief that does not calm down even after a long time is harmful for the mourner and also for the entire community because, by refusing to accept death and the response culturally given to it, ultimately questions the religious value system and worldview of the community (Berta 2001: 214).

8. Körner B. III. 22 (Körner 1970: 62).

9. 'Miraculous' in this case means 'unnatural, supernatural'.

10. In contrast to curse masses, supposedly celebrated by Romanian Orthodox priests, bewitchment could harm anybody, guilty and innocent alike. It is thus a more generally accepted explanation for misfortune.

11. Fermeka is the local term for bewitchment.

12. Virtanen reports a similar phenomenon (1989: 142).

13. I do not want to suggest that the Csángós readily invent dream narratives in order to manipulate others – even if the Csángós themselves occasionally doubt the authenticity of certain dreams. There are other – more subtle – reasons for the correspondence between the intention of the dreamer and the dream narrative: the formation of dreams and dream narratives is determined by the subconscious, thus the dreamer's opinion and emotions may well influence the dream experience itself, and these same emotions, coupled with the dreamer's motivations make their similarly subconscious effect on the interpretation of the dream and the formation of the narrative. (Kaivola-Bregenhøj 1998: 352).

References

Barna, G. (1998) Az álmok szerepe Orosz István életében. In É. Pócs (ed.) *Eksztázis, álom, látomás. Vallásetnológiai fogalmak tudományközi* megközelítésben. Tanulmányok a transzcendensről I, 340–350. Budapest: Balassi Kiadó/Pécs: University Press.

Berta, P. (2001) A túlélők teendői. A posztmortális szolgálatok rendje késő középkori városaink vallásos közösségeiben. In É. Pócs (ed.) Lélek, Halál, Túlvilág. Vallásetnológiai Fogalmak Tudományközi Megközelítésben. Tanulmányok a Transzcendensről II, 213–238. Budapest: Balassi Kiadó.

Brenneis, D. (1987) Talk and transformation. Man 22 (3): 199–510.

Dégh, L. (2001) Legend and Belief: Dialectics of a Folklore Genre. Bloomington, IN: Indiana University Press.

Fine, G. A. (1995) Accounting for rumour: The creation of credibility in folk knowledge. In R. Bendix and R. Levy-Zumwalt (eds) Folklore Interpreted. Essays in Honor of Alan Dundes, 123–135. New York and London: Garland Publishing.

Cátedra, M. (1992) This World, Other Worlds. Sickness, Suicide, Death, and the Afterlife among the Vaqueiros de Alzada of Spain. Chicago, IL and London: The University of Chicago Press.

Danforth, L. M. and Tsiaras, A. (1982) The Death Rituals of Rural Greece. Princeton, NJ: Princeton University Press.

Douglass, W. A. (1969) Death in Murelaga. Funerary Rirual in a Spanish Basque Village. Seattle, WA: University of Washington Press.

Geary, P. J. (1994) Living with the Dead in the Middle Ages. London: Cornell University Press.

Goldey, P. (1983) The good death: personal salvation and community identity. In R. Feijo, H. Martins and J. de Pina-Cabral (eds) Death in Portugal: Studies in Portuguese Anthropology and Modern History. Journal of the Anthropological Society in Oxford, Occasional Papers 2, 1–15. Oxford: Oxford University Press.

Gulyás, J. (2007) Álom és elbeszélés. In V. Ambrus and G. Schwarcz (eds) Változó folklór. Tanulmányok Verebélyi Kincső tiszteletére. Folcloristica 10: 211–224. Budapest: ELTE BTK Folklore Tanszék.

Järvinen, I-R. (1998) Wives, husbands and dreams. In S. Apo, A. Nenola and L. Stark-Arola (eds) Gender and Folklore. Perspectives on Finnish and Karelian Culture. Studia Fennica Folkloristica 4, 305–314. Helsinki: Finnish Literature Society.

Järvinen, I-R., Stark, L., Timonen, S. And Utriainen, T. (1996) Constructing the moral community: Women's dream narratives in a Russian-Orthodox Karelian village. In R. B. Pynsent (ed.) The Literature of Nationalism. Essays on East European Identity, 247–274. London: Macmillan Press.

Kaivola-Bregenhøj, A. (1998) Az álom mint folklór. In É. Pócs (ed.) Eksztázis, álom, Látomás. Vallásetnológiai Fogalmak Tudományközi Megközelítésben. Tanulmányok a Transzcendensről I, 351–365. Budapest: Balassi Kiadó/ Pécs: University Press.

Kenna, M. E. (1976) Houses, fields, and graves: Property and ritual obligation on a Greek island. *Ethnology* 15 (3): 21–34.

Körner, T. (1970) Mutatvány a készülő hiedelemmonda-katalógusból. A halál és a halottak. *Ethnographia* LXXXI: 35–96.

McLaughlin, M. (1994) *Consorting with Saints. Prayer for the Dead in Early Medieval France.* New York: Cornell University Press.

Møhl, P. (1997) *Village Voices. Coexistence and Communication in a Rural Community in Central France.* Copenhagen: Museum Tusculanum Press, University of Copenhagen.

Schmitt, J-C. (1998 [1994]) *Ghosts in the Middle Ages. The Living and the Dead in Medieval Society.* Chicago, IL: The University of Chicago Press.

Tedlock, B. (1987) Dreaming and dream research. In B. Tedlock (ed.) *Dreaming. Anthropological and Psychological Interpretations,* 1–31. Cambridge: Cambridge University Press.

Tüskés, G. and Knapp, É. (1998) *Egy dunántúli parasztasszony álomel- beszélései az 1980-as években.* In É. Pócs (ed.) *Eksztázis, álom, Látomás. Vallásetnológiai Fogalmak Tudományközi Megközelítésben. Tanulmányok a Transzcendensről* 1, 366–379. Budapest: Balassi Kiadó.

Virtanen, L. (1989) Dream-telling today. In A-L. Siikala (ed.) *Studies in Oral Narrative. Studia Fennica,* 33: 137–148.

Religious Legend as a Shaper of Identity: St Xenia in the Mental Universe of a Setu Woman

Merili Metsvahi*

Introduction

Words create reality. They not only refer to phenomena and events, it is through words that phenomena and events come to be. It is thanks to words uttered and recorded by humans that have made the world what it is today. The words that human beings have heard and said, read and written in the duration of their lives, have shaped these worlds and lives, and through this shaped the people themselves and made them what they are today.

The present article will analyse the words used by Ksenia Müürsepp (1911–2004) in creating her identity. In particular, the article will focus on the religious legends narrated by Ksenia and will analyse the religious legend she told twice to her interviewers, the protagonist of which is her name saint, and discuss the significance of the legend to Ksenia.

Ksenia Müürsepp was of Setu origin and spoke Setu dialect – a version of Estonian that has very many discrepancies from Estonian literary language. Ksenia was born in the village of Kuurakõsõ (in Russian it has had two names: Kosenki and Bresdelyevo) in Setumaa and spent the first part of her life there. Setumaa straddles the Estonian–Russian border, being partly in southeast Estonia and partly in northwest Russia. Between the two World Wars the area that is today part of the Russian Federation belonged to the Estonian Republic. Today very few Setus are left on the Russian side of Setumaa. Ksenia moved away from Russia in 1995. From her birth in 1911 until 1963 she lived in Kuurakõsõ village, not far from Pankjavitsa (in Russian Panikovitsi), and in 1963 she moved to the small town of Petchory (Petseri in Estonian), to the house of her daughter's family. In 1995

* Merili Metsvahi is a Research Fellow at the Department of Estonian and Comparative Folklore, University of Tartu, Estonia.

1. Borders of Setumaa according to Tartu Peace Treaty (1920)

2. Current border between Republic of Estonia and Russian Federation

3. Grey colour - area inhabited by the Setu in the 1930s

Setumaa is an Orthodox region on the border between south-eastern Estonia and Russia. For the location of Setumaa, see the map on p. 11.

she moved to Estonia and started to live with her granddaughter's family in Tartu. While Setus are Orthodox believers, Estonia is a predominately Lutheran country.

Between the years 2001 and 2003 I visited Ksenia on several occasions and recorded a number of stories of different genres narrated by her. Ksenia told the legend of St Xenia (Ksenia) to me and my colleague(s) on two occasions: 17 February 2001, when I visited Ksenia with Risto Järv and Kristina Veidenbaum, and on my last visit to her, on 4 November 2003, when I was accompanied by Andreas Kalkun.

What testify to the importance of the legend of St Xenia to Ksenia's mental world are the placement of the legend in the narrative situation and the name of the protagonist: Ksenia was born on 18 January and, as the Russian Orthodox Church celebrates St Xenia on that day, she was baptized with the name Ksenia. In the materials recorded in February 2001, the legend appears in the final section of the third minidisc recorded on that day, being the last story Ksenia told us on that occasion. That day Tatyana Kodas, Ksenia's grandchild, joined us for the final part of the interview. Ksenia had spoken at length and was clearly tired, and therefore, possibly to give her time to rest, Tatyana initiated a new topic concerning the funeral of her colleague's mother, which she had attended, and how she had later described the event to Ksenia. 'Buried like a dog', was Ksenia's response to the

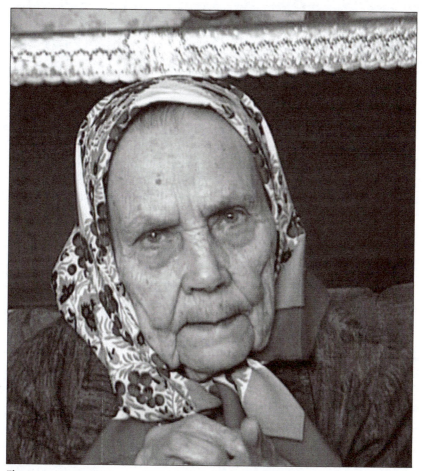

Figure 1: Ksenia Müürsepp (1911–2004) (photograph by Risto Järv).

Figure 2: Kuurakõsõ (Bresdelyevo) village in 2008 (photograph by Merili Metsvahi).

story. According to Tatyana, Ksenia did not like funerals that follow Estonian customs (which she compared to Setu funerals). Tatyana's words made Ksenia turn to topics associated with matters of mortality. She said that the priest from Pechory had recently asked Ksenia's daughter Manni whether Ksenia was still alive and sent his greetings to her. Ksenia proceeded to say that praying is not something done on somebody else's orders but of one's own free will. This thought was followed by the legend of St Barbara (Varvara) and Ksenia's version of the legend of St Xenia.

On another occasion, Ksenia's version of the legend of St Xenia also followed the legend of St Barbara. Then, Ksenia told the legend in the first part of the interview. Andreas Kalkun, who was visiting Ksenia for the second time, initiated a religious topic early in the interview. Turning to questions about saints, he enquired about St Nicholas (*Mikul*) and Praskeva Pyatnica (*Päätnitsä Praskeeva*). Ksenia did not know any stories about Praskeva Pyatnica; instead she started to talk about St Barbara. After that Andreas Kalkun stated that there was another church next to the one dedicated to St Barbara in Petchory. Ksenia immediately identified the church as *Sorokamuutsenika* church (the name is derived from the Russian name of the church, *Soroka*

Figure 3: Icon of Forty Martyrs above the entrance of the Church of Forty Martyrs in Pechory (photograph by Pille Niin).

mutchenitskii (Forty Martyrs)) and then told her version of the story of St Xenia.

The plot of the religious legend narrated by Ksenia is based on the legend of Forty Martyrs of Sebaste that originates from the fourth century. According to the legend crusaders perished in the icy waters of the lake in Sebaste, in Armenia Secunda (today's Sivas in Turkey), during the reign of Licinius (308–324) because they did not renounce Christianity. They were sent to ice-strewn water naked, while warm baths had been prepared on the shore for those who were ready to renounce their faith. When one of the 40 soldiers, indeed, renounced his faith, his place was taken by a guard who accepted Christianity, took off his clothes and stepped into the icy water with the 39 other men (Doyé 1930: 507; Farmer 1997: 189–190). The 40 martyrs were eulogized by Basil the Great, Gregory of Nyssa and Ephraem of Syria (Ferguson *et al.* 1999: 435).

Ksenia's version of the religious legend, told in 2001, goes as follows:

> Ah Sorokamuutsenika church, this thing is thus. One king drove his people towards the devil. But the people did not want that, they wanted God's faith. The king started to drown all men, drove them into the great sea. And drowned many. And then he gathered those who wanted to follow God and drove them away. There is a picture showing this on the church wall, there is the icon and the men in the water up to here. And then went one, a daughter of a father, Blessed Xenia (Zhenny Blazhennyi), took a big club and told the men: get out of the water and let us fight the king for he has drowned all of our men, not leaving any men behind. And then the men did get out and started to fight, there was a war. And then some men stayed alive, otherwise the king wanted to drown all men. That was the power of the king. Then it was so that what the king ordered, they did. (MD-0101-27)

The following is the transcription of the version of the same religious legend told on our last visit to Ksenia:

> Andreas: There is another church next to the one dedicated to St Barbara, right?
> Ksenia: That is Sorokamuut(s)enitski. That is … there was once a king's law. He did not want God's faith, it seems, he was of some other faith. But those who were of God's faith, those the king drove to the sea and drowned them. And it once was so that there went many people, most of them men, and all of them followed God. And the king started to drive them into the sea, to drown them there. But then took blessed Xenia (Ksenia Blazhennaya),[1] went from her father, she took a club and said: 'Why are you letting him drown you? Why is he drowning all the folks?' And well then a war started, they started to fight. And those who were … in this great war the Orthodox faith was born. Blessed Xenia. And in all churches there is a picture, she also goes, with a club, to the men and to fight. This is how those stories go. And this is how it was in ancient times. But now. Now there is no God and no devil. (MD-0110-12)

Most of what I know about Ksenia and her background I have learned from the narratives told by her. Narratives express thoughts and feelings that would remain otherwise inaccessible. Rosan A.

Jordan claims approximately the same: 'Narratives sometimes express ideas and feelings that would never emerge from a questionnaire or an interview, or they may express them more powerfully' (1971: 27). According to Bakhtin, the mastery of genres constitutes a sufficient prerequisite for the realization of a free expression of ideas in speech (1989: 278–279). As Ksenia had great mastery in different folk narrative genres, the stories evoke not only the social circumstances and world picture of the past but also Ksenia's personal world view and ideals, not only figures of speech once used in the Setu language but also the particular figures of speech that reflect Ksenia's personal preferences and character. Already the fact that Ksenia created an idiosyncratic story shows her good command of the rules of the genre and makes it possible to understand something about Ksenia herself from the text of the religious legend.

Suffering and Avoidance of Suffering

Ksenia connects the legend of the Forty Martyrs of Sebaste with the figure of a woman saint on whose initiative people go to war against a pagan king, and thus brings resolution to the story. In the canonical version of the legend, the story culminates when the Christian warriors sent to the icy water do not surrender despite their suffering, and resolution is reached with their canonization after their deaths. There is no great suffering or canonization in Ksenia's legend, as emphasizing suffering would conflict with Ksenia's generally optimistic attitude to life and canonization does not fit into the realistic and mundane discourse of popular Christianity.

However, torture and suffering were mentioned to an extent during our interviews with Ksenia. First, suffering is a key theme in the legend of St Barbara, which preceded the legend of St Xenia. On the first occasion the legend of St Barbara was told as follows:

Well … from where … those … about Barbara's church, well. In Estonian, Sorokamuutsinika church is in Russian but Barbara's church is in Estonian. And Barbara's icon is also there. Barbara was … he was a king or something, well, her father was a great man …. And Barbara converted to God's faith, the Russian faith. But the father did not want that, he was against it. And the father took and broke her legs, Barbara's, because she had gone … But it did not matter to her, she said: 'Yes, I believe in God and believe in Christ.' Then her arms were broken. 'I believe in Christ, I am on God's side.' Then her father cut her head off, his own daughter's. The father's name was Oskar, you see. And the daughter was called Barbara. But this is not a fairy tale, this has really been. But this has been after the birth of Christ. And there is also that icon of Barbara. It is called Barbara's church and there is Barbara's icon. (MD-0101-27)

The story tells of the conflict between Barbara and her father, caused by Barbara's conversion to Christianity. Despite her father's opposition and corporal punishment, she does not renounce her faith and thus her father cuts off her legs, arms and finally also her head. When Ksenia recounted the legend the second time, she seemed to place a greater emphasis on suffering than on the first occasion:

> There is Barbara's church in Pechory. I still do remember Barbara. Barbara was a … Her father was Oskar, but the daughter's name was Barbara. And Oskar did not believe in God, Oskar did not believe in God but Barbara did. And she, that Barbara, started to incline towards God. And her father did not … he took and broke her arms. 'Why do you believe in God?' She still believed, despite all. He then chopped her legs off, his own daughter's. And she still believed in God, 'God, help me. Jesus Christ, St Nicolas, help me!' And then he cut her head off, her own father. And there is a picture in Pechory, and the name is also Barbara's church. You see, her own father did it. (MD-0110-11)

Ksenia's use of more phrases reminiscent of prayer in this interview session could be attributed to the fact that her health was worse on this occasion than during any other of our visits and possibly also to the fact that Andreas Kalkun's questions concerned religious themes from the beginning of the interview.

Ksenia once talked about suffering when describing the daily life of the past. On 11 May 2002 Ksenia told Mari Sarv (who had come to the interview with her infant daughter Pihla) and I that in the past people lived with their parents regardless of whether that was comfortable or not. After this general statement Ksenia recalled that her mother's godmother, who was also like a godmother to them (probably her half-sister and half-brother), had said to them when they were children: 'Dear children, suffer! Two shall see the suffering. One has to suffer!' To my question: 'Who will see it?' Ksenia responded with an explanation in almost standard Estonian: 'Suffer! And two shall then see that you suffer. But who those two are, whether it is somebody from God or from among the people, I also do not know. That's how it was' (MD-0107-10). Although the instructions about suffering were uttered during the only visit when there was no male present, Ksenia probably did not directly associate suffering with women: her mother's godmother's saying had been directed to her as a child or human being, not as a girl or woman.

Although pain and suffering are associated with morality in Russian Orthodox culture (see Kalkun 2000), and, according to the Christian interpretation that started to spread in modern times it is women specifically who are born to suffer (Kroll 1995: 60; see also Nenola 1986: 133–135). Ksenia personally distanced herself from the glorification of suffering. Although Ksenia had had to endure considerable sorrow in her life – for example, of the six children she bore only two survived past infancy – she rarely talked about suffering and sorrow. Speaking about herself, Ksenya used the word sorrow only in connection with losing her husband (see MD-0106-28). Typically her attitude to life seemed to be different. On our last visit, when we had already switched off the minidisc recorder, Andreas asked Ksenia whether she also watched TV. Ksenia responded that she hardly ever did because her doctor had told her that she was the sort of a person who should not watch 'bad things' because they are bad for her health and there is very much fighting on TV. The doctor had also said that it would be better if Ksenia did not go to funerals (my notes, 4 November 2003). Thus, at least in the final period of her life, Ksenia did not adopt the ideal of suffering provided by Setu culture (worded to her by her mother's godmother). Because of her character, it was easier for her to adopt the idea generally accepted in our culture that suffering has to be avoided, an idea that has influenced Western culture from the period of the Enlightenment onward (Taylor 1989: 190, 394). Nevertheless, remaining a bearer of Setu culture, she could not generalize about the avoidance of suffering as something universal and thus she narrowed it to a principle that applied to her alone.

In addition to the fact that the theme of suffering is absent in the version of the legend of St Xenia told by Ksenia, another indication of how Ksenia's character seeks positive experiences can be found in her need to tell another story, one with a more positive ending, after recounting the legend of St Barbara.

The Religious Legend as a Genre

According to Hans-Peter Ecker, one of the leading European scholars working with religious legends, the religious legend is one of the most undetermined genres in our culture (1993: 145). He also argues that the definitions of the religious legend offered by different authors can be roughly summarized as follows: the religious legend is 'a narrative with religious content, believable within certain limits, presented in a simple, pious and serious manner, that talks about holy persons and miracles with the help of which a divine entity realises the plan of redemption of humankind' (Ecker 1993: 26). Irma-Riitta Järvinen, a scholar who has studied Karelian religious legends, states when speaking about Karelian religious legends that they talk about saints, their acts and influence and about miracles that take place through them (Järvinen 2004: 13).

Several scholars have attempted to define the religious legend in comparison with other folk narrative genres. One of the possible points of comparison is the legend. The legend and the religious legend can be successfully compared because of their truth value in the community in which they circulate: 'religious legends (Germ. *die Legende*) dedicated to the lives and acts of saints are as true stories to believers as legends (Germ. *die Sage*) are to the community in which they exist' (Rosenfeld 1972: 14). Legends and religious legends are also similar in their being associated with numinosity. But while the legend speaks about an event – the invasion of the numinous into the everyday sphere – the religious legend tends to focus on the character (Rosenfeld 1972: 17–18). The religious legend and the legend can also be contrasted through the characteristics of their psychological impact on the hearer: 'The saint's legend … invests everything with meaning. It relates everything to one and the same center, God. Whereas the legend confuses, amuses, frightens, and arouses humankind, the saint's legend clarifies and confirms. The legend poses questions; the saint's legend gives answers' (Lüthi 1986: 84).

In its explanatory function the religious legend can be compared to that of the myth. Meletinskij argues that it is difficult to draw a clear line between myths, religious legends and legends (1992: 127). For Ecker the myth is the genre that is the closest to the religious legend (1993: 50). According to him the fact that myths have found extensive treatment in Western academic discourse, starting from classical antiquity, could explain why the study of religious legends has been of secondary importance. Treatments of myths dedicate considerable attention to features that are also important for legends. Discussions of myths and legends have frequently reached the same conclusions, although the discussions have taken place within different disciplines (Ecker 1993: 50). However, representatives of more psychologically oriented approaches have ignored the religious legend as a genre. Carl Gustav Jung does not use the term in his in-depth psychological work *Bewusstes und Unbewusstes*, although his analysis also tackles religious legends: he attributes the content of religious legends to fairy tales or myths and treats them as representatives of those genres (Karlinger 1986: 28).

The central meaning and function of myths is the explanation of the phenomena in the world and the expression of a worldview (Segal 2005: 215). Researchers see an important connection between myths and rituals the performance of which, following sacred examples, prevents the descent of the world into chaos (Honko 1984: 49). It has been argued that the myth – which syncretically contains elements of what later developed into religion, philosophy, science and art – in the early development of humankind performed the role taken by history in later societies (Lévi-Strauss 1980: 49–50; Meletinskij 1992: 121). It has been assumed that the study of myths would enable us to find the universal characteristics of the human mind. Thus, according to Claude Lévi-Strauss, the anthropologist who has greatly influenced the academic study of myths, the study of myths is of enormous importance from the perspective of the self-perception of the human mind as the collective imagination expressed in myth is free from other areas of life and enables us to discover the anatomy of the human mind and human thought (Meletinskij 1992: 35). Gary H. Gossen, a folklorist who has dedicated himself to the in-depth study of one culture, criticizes anthropologists for focusing excessively on myths. On the basis of his observations of the ethnic genres of the Chamulas who live in south Mexico he reaches the conclusion that no genre takes precedence over others and that categories of the world (or knowledge about cosmology and social categories) are encoded both in myths and other genres (Gossen 1984: 82, 113). Dell Hymes has pointed out that the genre that has been called 'the myth' may vary greatly depending on the culture and therefore it is important to define it on every particular occasion, proceeding from the culture studied (Hymes 1971: 51).

On closer inspection, the religious legends told by Ksenia fall into four types. The first type includes stories the action of which is told from a spatial and temporal distance[2] and the characters of which are not ordinary people but saints and ancestors of today's people who can be perceived as mythical (legends of St George (*püha Jüri*) (e.g., MD-0100-12), St Xenia and St Barbara); these religious legends seem the closest to myths. The characters and the time of action of the religious legends of the second type can be characterized similarly to the first type, only in this case the action takes place in a specific location and this feature makes these stories similar to local legends (the story of sheltering Christ,[3] legend of St Nicholas as the founder of St Petersburg (MD-0102-14; MD-0107-26), legend of St Cornelius (*Karniil*) as the founder of a monastery (MD-0100-18; MD-0110-17)). The latter two, because of their aetiological final motif, also resemble aetiological legends. However, this should not be overemphasized as the aetiological final motif is a strategy also favoured by Ksenia outside the genre of the belief legend, possibly because of the sense of closure that the use of this motif creates. Of the two versions of the legend of St Xenia, one has an aetiological ending and its function is – as in the case of other religious legends – to give the religious legend the authority of a historical event.

The stories of the third and fourth type, which resemble legends or memorates, can be considered religious legends if we add background knowledge to their literal form, as they do not explicitly mention a saint. The fact that the person behind the action is actually a saint is revealed through intertextual associations. An example of a religious legend that resembles a memorate is a story about how Ksenia's husband and brother had made hay on St Elias' Day (*jakapäiv*, 2 August) and how, as a punishment for working on a holy day, lightning had struck the haystack in September (MD-0103-17). The connection with St Elias (*püha Ilja*) appears in the reference to lightning as St Elias has been associated with that natural phenomenon (according to Ksenia in the past lighting had been linked with the saint: 'St Elias is coming, there is thunder' (MD-0103-19)).

There is another religious legend that resembles a legend rather than a memorate. This tells of a rich man of foreign extraction ('a German or a person of some other nation') who blasted the great stone dedicated to St John (*jaanikivi*) at Meeksi and used the pieces to build a cattle shed. When cows started to die in the shed, he took the stones out of the corner of the shed and returned them to their original location (MD-0109-18). It can be concluded that we are dealing with revenge from St John (*püha Jaan*). Already at the beginning of the story Ksenia talked about how there were always large crowds at St John's stone and chapel (*tsässon*) in Meeksi on St John's Day and that a 'church service' was held there. In contrast to the legend of St Elias, John's name is explicitly mentioned here: 'Germans did not trust that John'.

These stories differ from the stories of the first type as they describe events that took place during Ksenia's lifetime (in Ksenia's words 'in my time') and in an environment familiar to her, and the characters include people close to Ksenia (in addition, in the case of the Meeksi story she mentions her relatives who had gone to the St John's Day service at Meeksi). Although the stories express and affirm the religious values and norms of a community, they do not do it by referring to the beginnings of time periods (Honko 1984: 49) but through specific examples which, at least while she was living in Setumaa, had not lost their relevance for Ksenia.

The stories of the fourth type resemble those of the third type but in this case Ksenia has internalized the relationship with the saint. The religious legends concern direct contact between Ksenia and a saint during a ritual encounter (Honko 1991: 110–113) and the outcome of the encounter is positive. I have called the best example of the stories of this type – a story that describes how Ksenia was ill and how, after she had gone to a service in Värska on St George's Day and touched the icon of St George, the doctor whom she went to see afterwards recognized the disease immediately and prescribed the right medication for her – a personal experience narrative in an earlier article (Metsvahi 2002a: 311). I preferred the term personal experience narrative, rather than memorate or (proto)legend because I attributed the greatest importance to the fact that the story describes events of Ksenia's own life. Deciding whether Ksenia's recovery should be attributed to the saint or to the doctor depends on one's worldview. As the intertextual associations reveal that in Ksenia's mind her recovery is directly linked to the saint, it is also possible to classify the story as a memorate or (proto)legend.

Textualization of the Religious Legend

The textualization strategies applied to the religious legends of the first and second type have been influenced by the fairy tale genre. Fairy tales served an important function in our interviews for several reasons. Ksenia's grandchild Tatyana Kodas, who acquainted us with Ksenia, mentioned that she was a good teller of fairy tales and initially Ksenia assumed that our aim was to record fairy tales specifically. Second, Ksenia was indisputably masterful in her narration of fairy tales. Third, the fairy tale was a genre of which the importance of our recording was more readily comprehensible to Ksenia than other genres. The aesthetic value of the fairy tale is perceptible because of the textual orientation of the genre: on the scale of contextual-textual genres fairy tale was the most textual of the genres narrated by Ksenia and thus most clearly distinguishable from the conversational context (Briggs 1988: 223). As in the case of the genres with a strong textual orientation, the narrator or the listeners do not sense the contextual aspects of the genre (Briggs 1988: 347). The decision to tell fairy tales was a safe bet, so to say, even in cases of a relatively unknown and unpredictable interlocutor, where the satisfaction of the need for recognition was guaranteed.

The religious legend is a more contextually oriented genre than the fairy tale, as saints participate in a religious person's life and reality. Therefore it was more difficult for Ksenia to verbalize or recontextualize religious legends than fairy tales to the interviewers who came from a different environment and had different worldviews (Bauman and Briggs 1990). The fact that the (de- and) re-contextualization of religious legends in an interview situation differs from their possible recontextualization in other circumstances, to a greater extent than the retextualization of fairy tales, can be seen in the considerable variation of Ksenia's religious legends on different occasions. Subconsciously doubting her choice of textualization strategies and believing that we had come to primarily record fairy tales, Ksenia used startegies more characteristic to fairy tales in narration of a religious legend on the first occasions and moved away from them on later occasions. Thus, telling the legend of St George on the first occasion, she used the dramatic present more than on later occasions. At our request, Ksenia told the legend on five different occasions, although on the last she stressed everything that made St George a saint: among other things the fact that George was unmarried. The inconsistent use of the aetiological ending probably signalled insecurity about the choice of textualization strategies.

The same reasons that created insecurity in the choice of strategies also directed Ksenia's thoughts in a particular direction (during interviews and in between interviews) and Ksenia worded the result of this contemplation as follows at the end of our final visit when finishing the legend of St Xenia: 'This is how the stories were. And this is how it was in the past. But now. Now there is no God and no devil.' With this utterance Ksenia distanced herself from the legends she had told, moving from what K. Young (1987) has called the taleworld, to the level of conversation, that is, the same level as the interviewers. Thus Ksenia attempted to be in as symmetrical a relationship with us, the interviewers, as possible and to understand us. The attempt to understand us was realized in the cited utterance and its idea that the world picture of today's people and the morals that derive from it are different from those of the past, but that such change is only natural.

The attempt to understand the interviewers was connected with contemplations about the changing world and one's place in it. A longer textualization of the thoughts took place in the final part of the interview during our last visit: 'Our people [the Setu who moved to Estonia from Russia after Estonia regained independence] went away, our people came to Estonia. In Estonia, here there was Lutheran faith, here there was another faith. But our people do not have Lutheran faith or our own faith, do not know who we are [smiling]. But in Russia there is still strong faith in God' (MD-0111-12). Then Ksenia said, in an interspersed narrative, that churches have been renovated and opened in Russia in recent times and that Russians go to pray there, but also that when already living in Tartu, she had gone to Pechory for Eucharist, when it was easier to cross the border. When I asked Ksenia where she got the information about Russia, she said that she had been told by a woman from Russia and that it had also been shown on television. After a pause Ksenia added that the people of the past had said that the world will survive as long as there are believers but 'when all people of faith are dead, the world will also perish' (MD-0111-12).

Ksenia's Name Saint

Their name is something people identify themselves with in the changing world throughout their lives. The act of naming – which is understood as a person's social birth in many cultures – determines an aspect of a person's identity. Theophoric names or personal names derived from the name of God were widespread in classical antiquity as well as many other cultures. Records of theophoric names from Egypt, dating from 3000–2600 BCE, are considered the oldest written sources that testify to people's religiosity. According to Herodotus, the Greeks borrowed the belief that there is an essential connection between the person and the god born on the same day from Egyptians (Mitterauer 1995: 45–55).

Ksenia was named after St Xenia. This name cannot be considered theophoric as in Russian Orthodox theology a saint is not a god but an intermediary between people and God, while also being the friend and helper of an individual believer (Diedrich 1989: 127). Russian Orthodox Setu believed that the name saint protected the person who bore his or her name. Therefore, in church the icons associated with the name saint or the name icon had a special significance for a person. In earlier times godparents gave name icons to their godchildren and at a wedding ceremony the name icons of the bride and bridegroom were carried above their heads (Saarlo 1996: 128; Bome 2003: 35).

Saints have been seen as persons whose help and intercession believers can seek, but they have from the beginning also served as examples to be followed (Synek 1994: 11). According to Jane Tibbetts Schulenburg who has studied the hagiographies of women saints, the life stories of saints as examples of holy behaviour strongly influenced the lives of religious women and men in medieval society. However, Schulenburg admits that the lives of women saints imparted different messages to women, the applications of which as religious symbols were flexible (Schulenburg 1998: 54). We are also dealing with flexible use of religious symbols in the case of Ksenia. The legend of Ksenia's name saint offered Ksenia the possibility to identify with the saint. It is interesting to note that Ksenia had actually created the legend herself, using different legends as sources of inspiration.

It is possible that Ksenia had heard the legend of St Olga (d. 969), on whom was conferred the title of *ravnoapostolna* ('equal with the Apostles', the title given to a saint who brought Christianity to his or her homeland) for initiating the Christianization of Russia, and whom a chronicle of the time named 'wiser than all men'. Although Olga tried to spread Christianity to Kiev Russia, the first ruler to accept the faith was her grandchild Vladimir. Vladimir, among other things, issued the order that the people of the country had to come to a mass baptism in the Dnieper River (Schulenburg 1998: 201–204). It is not impossible that the common motif – the ordering of a great number of people into a body of water – created an association in Ksenia's mind between the legend of Forty Martyrs of Sebaste and the Christianization of Kiev Russia. Probably aware of the fact that a female saint played a central role in the Christianization, Ksenia identified that saint as St Xenia, whose icon could be found in the church of

St Barbara (information from Manni Gulova, MD-0110-11) and who is represented on the icon bearing a cross in her hand.

According to a lexicon of saints, the cult of St Xenia, whose day is celebrated on 18 January, was widespread among the Greeks, although nothing is known about her but for the fact that she died a martyr's death in fire (Vollständiges ... 1975: 840). St Xenia of Rome (originally Eusebia, d. 450), whose day is celebrated on 24 January and who is frequently depicted on icons with a cross in her hand, fled with two of her servants on her wedding day in order not to marry and later founded a convent on the island of Kos or Malyssa.[4]

The day of Blessed Xenia of St Petersurg is also celebrated on 24 January. Saints like her are called *Yurodivy* or 'God's fools' in Russia. Ksenia Grigoryevna was married to a colonel whom she had loved with all her heart and considered the focal point of her life. However, widowed at the age of 26 when her husband died unexpectedly and without communion, she dedicated her life to God and started to pray for her husband's soul. She gave away her house and other property and started to live on the streets of St Petersburg, following the example of Jesus Christ, the great sufferer. Initially she wore the clothes of her deceased husband, Andrey Fyodorovitch, trying to persuade people that it was not her husband who had died but she, Ksenia Grigoryevna. When her husband's clothes decayed, she started to wear a red blouse and a green skirt or a green blouse and a red skirt, wearing light clothing regardless of the season. She is also said to have carried a staff and this is how she is depicted on icons. She died at the age of 71 and is buried at the Smolensk cemetery. Inhabitants of St Petersburg, especially women, visit the grave of Blessed Xenia even today to seek help in the case of health problems and other matters that make up a human life.[5] From the interviews made with Ksenia it transpires that during several summers she had communicated with visitors from St Petersburg, who had rented a room from the house of Ksenia's daughter and son-in-law in Petchory, where she lived from 1963 until 1995. It is possible that Ksenia heard about Blessed Xenia of St Petersburg from them.

Drawing connections between the war and a woman with a similar name to Xenia could have been made easier because of the possible image of the warrior princess Xena in Ksenia's mind. In the years when the interviews were made, the serial 'Xena: Warrior Princess' was shown on Estonian television. Although Ksenia herself denied watching television a lot, her daughter and granddaughter stated that she watched television very often, and was a devotee of serials (interview with Manni Gulova and Tatiana Kodas 15.04.2007).

The icon of Forty Martyrs in the lake that used to stand in the Church of Forty Martyrs in Pechory does not depict St Xenia, Blessed Xenia or any other woman. The fact that Ksenia claimed, when talking about Xenia, that 'in every church there is a picture, she goes with a club to men and to fight' indicates on the one hand that Ksenia uses the help of visual images that may have merged in her mind in recollecting narratives and, on the other hand, that for Ksenia icons served to testify to the veracity of the events that took place in the religious legend.

The religious legend of St Xenia told by Ksenia attracted my attention primarily because my idea of the gender stereotypes of a patriarchal society could not be reconciled with the image of a woman who takes a club and calls men to get out of the water and start fighting against the king. It does not make a difference that, as a result of genre conventions, the word war here does not refer to war in its historical or political sense. In the following section I will concentrate on the question of why the representation of the woman is unusual here, while the last two sections will be dedicated to why Ksenia has chosen to talk about the woman in the manner described.

Ksenia in the Patriarchal World

Ksenia lived in a patriarchal world where man was the owner of his wife and children and in which men exploited women (see for example Irigaray 1979: 148). There is ample evidence to demonstrate that in Setu society men considered women as symbolic commodities and the man who had taken a wife not only increased his symbolic capital (honour) (Bourdieu 2005: 62–63) but also became richer because of having gained the woman as a worker and the producer of children, in addition to her dowry. In 2004 a 68-year-old woman from the village of Küllatüvä in the former Obinitsa parish in Setumaa told folklorists that in the past men took a wife from where more was given as dowry. A cow was given on every occasion, often also some forest. A pretty girl was given less, an uglier or even crippled girl more dowry (MD-0345-05). Choosing a wife on the basis of the woman's ability to work – her health and physical strength – and the size of the dowry was also common in other peasant societies in Europe (for Germany see Sieder 1987: 60–61).

In the material recorded during interviews with Ksenia there is also ample evidence of men's dominant position in society. In the religious legend about St Xenia the practice of identifying a woman through her father or husband is reflected in the phrase that says that St Xenia went to the men 'from her father'. Another sign of the exclusion of women (specifically the girl's mother) from dealing with women as a commodity exchanged between men can be found in the practice of the time according to which, in the case of the death of the father of the girl who was being courted, the terms of marriage had to be settled by a brother of the father. When Ksenia was being courted for the first time, her father had died and thus her uncle had been summoned. We can also see evidence about behaviour that conforms to the norms of a patriarchal society in Ksenia's recollection about the Sunday after she had been courted for the first time. Ksenia sat proudly by the village lane, looked at other girls and thought: 'Ha, I will marry, but all of you will remain with your parents, nobody will take you!' (MD-0107-14, see also Metsvahi 2004: 142–145). The sentence that testifies to Ksenia having fully accepted the stereotypes and models of behaviour of the male-centred world is softened by what Ksenia added. When a relative had asked Ksenia whether she would be getting married now, Ksenia claimed to have answered: 'I can try of course! If it will be good, then I will do it, but if it will be bad, then I will come back home.' The latter, however, should not be interpreted as a sign of resistance to the norms of a patriarchal society but could merely serve as evidence of the foolishness of youth (the statement is accompanied by Ksenia's laughter). Ksenia herself emphasized that she was very young then and pointed out that she did not even know the meaning of the word 'in-laws' (Metsvahi 2004: 142). Emphasis on youth could suggest that her socialization into Setu society had not yet been completed.

The examples provided reflect the structures of domination characteristic of a patriarchal society that were not questioned by the members of the society. Ksenia also did not question them, as can be seen from the next two examples where Ksenia describes events that took place in the past without expressing her opinion about the relations of domination that are apparent in the narratives. Ksenia told us about a woman who had had a kind mother-in-law: when the woman, who had given birth a couple of days earlier, was lying in bed and the mother-in-law saw men approaching the house, she told her daughter-in-law that she should start moaning because otherwise men would send her to work. As a comment, Ksenia adds that in the past one could not argue with what one's father or husband said: what they ordered, one had to do (MD-0109-04). Ksenia also does not protest against her husband's behaviour in a narrative of personal experience about how she had been mowing hay while pregnant and how her husband had reproached her about not working properly. Obeying her husband, Ksenia started to mow more vigorously as a result of which the fetus turned in the womb and this made the childbirth very difficult (MD-0107-16; see also Metsvahi 2004: 138).

Gender stereotypes used in the socialization process, which reproduce structures of domination, are disseminated through models of behaviour as well as narratives. Although the Christian church played an important part in the distribution of gender stereotypes all over Estonia and Setumaa, its influence was different in different social strata and in different denominations, that is, among Lutheranism and Russian Orthodoxy. All Christians shared the belief that the woman was subordinated to the man and dependent on the man (Beinert 1989: 169), but the Bible was of greater importance in transmitting this knowledge among the higher social strata and among Lutheran peasants than among the Setu. The Setu, whose faith was more 'syncretistic', less verbal, more visual and placed more emphasis on emotions (and less on reason) than the Lutheran faith, mystified books as sources of wisdom. The church teaching distributed through books and the folk beliefs that spread only in the oral form were intertwined in people's consciousness and formed an organic whole.

In Genesis, the Bible explains the woman's subordinate position with the fact that Adam was made first and Eve second, of Adam's rib. It can be hypothesized that Ksenia had heard or read the creation story but she did not associate it with herself or her life to the extent that the story would have been recorded in her memory and/or seemed valuable enough to tell to us. However, our interviews demonstrated that Ksenia was familiar with the biblical story which explains man's moral superiority to woman. According to the Bible, after Eve had, tempted by the serpent, eaten the fruit of the tree of the knowledge of good and evil, God punished her for the transgression: 'Unto the woman he said, I will greatly multiply thy sorrow and thy conception; in sorrow thou shalt bring forth children; any thy desire shall be to thy husband, and he shall rule over thee' (Gen. 3:16). Ksenia's version of the story, or its short summary, was given as an answer to our question about whether and why one should kill snakes: Christ said to the serpent that people shall force you down and you shall bite their heels (MD-0100-11; MD-0111-08). This story reflects Ksenia's poor knowledge of the Bible (Christ can also participate in a story derived from the Old Testament) and the fact that the stories heard and read by Ksenia had already passed through a filter of individual attitudes before she had made the stories her own and was ready to pass them on. In Ksenia's retelling, this biblical story was never specifically associated with a woman in any way.

It can be argued that during our last visit in November 2003 Ksenya consciously tried to use words from the Bible for the explanation for two reasons: the words 'as has been said', uttered with an intonation that resembled that of a priest at the beginning of the utterance that contained the biblical story and the correction of wording in the sentence where Christ tells the snake that it shall bite the heel of Man: Ksenia replaces the word 'foot' which she had initially used, with the word 'heel', which is closer to the wording given in the Bible (Gen. 3:15). Telling the same story on 17 February 2001 Ksenia used the word heel but instead of referring to the Bible or to the priest she then stated that this was what the people of the past had said. This suggests that there does not seem to be a clear distinction in Ksenia's mind between what she had heard from older people and the teaching of the church. In addition to what she had heard in the church, she also assigned the stories that she had once read among what could be called the 'knowledge of the ancestors' (MD-0109-25).

The study of fairy tales, the genre probably studied most extensively from a gender studies perspective, has demonstrated that although the female characters of folk tales are somewhat more active than those of literary fairy tales, they also fit within the framework of the gender stereotypes of their culture. A good woman is, above all, humble and obedient, that is, in her case the features considered valuable sharply differ from those applied to male characters. The idea of women's moral superiority (even up to the belief that a woman can save a man),[6] which started to spread among the middle classes in late eighteenth and early nineteenth centuries, had no place in the worldview of tellers of fairy tales (Apo 1990: 25–26). The study of fairy tales, but also other genres of folklore, has led to the conclusions that in the Western folkloric sources the prevalent mode of representation of female characters and protagonists (or heroes) is as objects rather than active agents who were admired the more they suffered and the more difficulties they bore (Wienker-Piepho 1988: 156, 162).

What then are the genres that make women's voices more audible, make it possible to abandon stereotypical gender roles and offer alternatives? On the basis of the material collected from Ksenia, who had a good command of different genres, it can be argued that for her such a genre was a joke (see for example MD-0106-31), but that alternative gender roles could also be explicated via religious legends.

St Xenia as a Female Saint

Donald Weinstein and Rudolf Bell analysed 864 religious legends derived from written sources that represent the Western Christian tradition and found that only 17.5% of them are related to female saints (Weinstein and Bell: 1982). According to the analysis of Schulenburg based on materials concerning about 2,680 saints who died in the years 500–1200, less than 15% were women (1998: 63). In the interviews, Ksenia mentions female and male saints with an equal frequency. Ksenia's greater allusion to female saints is derived from the fact that Ksenia herself was a woman, but written religious legends and hagiographies have predominantly been recorded by men. Because of the feminization of the Russian Orthodox religion women saints were popular in Setumaa in the twentieth century in general (for the feminization of the Karelian Orthodox religion, see for example Keinänen 1999).

The stereotypes that were mentioned in the previous section were created by men. If we look at the work of women, we get a completely different picture. Caroline Walker Bynum, a scholar who has studied the hagiography of the Late Middle Ages, has argued that it was male authors who wrote about Mary as a model of womanhood in the Late Middle Ages, while female authors preferred to speak about Christ as a role model (Bynum 1986: 258–259). It is also exclusively male authors who claim that a woman's religious commitment involves becoming a man. While the association of men with spirituality and rationality, and women with carnality and irrationality (see for example Pissarek-Hudelist 1989: 32) was endemic in late Medieval literature (Bynum 1986: 261), female authors did not perceive the binary oppositions to be very strong and did not associate personal characteristics like authority, rationality or emotionality with only one gender. According to Bynum, female authors did not see women as a marked category but saw them primarily as human beings (1986: 261, 269–271). Thus, for example, the prophetess Hildegard (1098–1179) writes in her *Liber divinorum operum*: 'Man … signifies the divinity of the Son of God and woman his humanity' (Bynum 1986: 274). Bynum argues that female authors' self-perception was not associated with the sinful, the weak or the non-male but, rather, with the corporeal. Self-identification with the corporeal and the human explains why female authors liked to speak about following or imitating Christ (Bynum 1986: 274).

Regardless of the gender of the person who had recorded the lives of female saints, they spoke to women and helped them develop their self-image (Schulenburg 1998: 53). The scholars who have studied the lives of female saints have shown that women's roles as they appear in hagiography were very diverse (Synek 1994: 203). We can find evidence of the fact that gender stereotypes of woman as a wife and mother, or as a nun who leads a life of modesty, do not cover the roles of all female saints already extant, judging by the religious legends about St Olga and St Xenia mentioned above. Probably the lives of saints and religious legends, with the help of icons, conjured up a desirable higher reality, so to say, worthy of emulation in a similar way to how today's serials and popular films offer the viewer a visual representation of dreams and desirable models of behaviour and communication that the viewers seek to imitate.

Tales circulating among people as oral tradition, played a central role in shaping Ksenia's worldview and life, and the religious legends of the lives of saints did not constitute a great proportion of the narratives she had heard. However, religious legends, including the lives of saints, were stories the authority of which was great owing to their association with the church. Religious legends seemed to link 'the wisdom of the ancestors' to the teaching of the church, in addition to which icons that allowed considerable freedom of interpretation to the viewer acted as mnemonic devices that helped listeners remember stories (Messerli 1989). It is probable that Ksenia stored religious legends in her memory as imaginary pictures or a series of pictures rather than in a verbal form (see also Goldberg 1997: 230–231).

What is it that makes the legend of St Xenia, told by Ksenia, an exciting object of study? There is nothing special in the fact that Ksenia used the character and plot of the legend of St Xenia in a manner that does not allow us to classify the religious legend among the types of folk narratives generally accepted in folklore studies. Such idiosyncratic behaviour generally characterizes Ksenia as a creative narrator, regardless of the genre (a good example among religious legends is her idiosyncratic narrative of how St Nicholas founded St Petersburg, MD-0102-14; MD-0107-26). What makes the legend of St Xenia an exciting object of study is the reason why Ksenia associated the image derived from the icon of the Forty Martyrs of Sebaste with this decisively active saint whose name she bore and the victory of Christianity over paganism.

I hypothesize that in Ksenia's mind the legend of St Xenia was associated with the legend of St George. Their main topic is similar: in both religious legends an evil person (or somebody of a different faith) drowns people in the sea and plans to continue his activities, but the intervention of an armed hero ends the (chaos-creating) situation. What is different is the gender of those being drowned and that of the hero – in the legend of St George, girls are being drowned and they are saved by a man; in the legend of St Xenia, men are being drowned and they are saved by a woman. There is also a difference in the representation of evil. The snake of the legend of St George, reminiscent as it is of fairy tales, made Ksenia (also influenced by the contemplation initiated by the questions of the interviewers) doubt the veracity of the story and she backgrounded it in her mental world (see Metsvahi 2002a). A king who did not follow Christian ways, however, was a character whose historical accuracy did not raise any doubts in Ksenia. It is for this reason that the legend of St Xenia, rather than the legend of St George, manifested the tendency to improve over time. Ksenia, after all, wanted to tell us the truth and do it in as effective a manner as possible.

This tendency can be noted if we consider that on the second occasion of telling Ksenia's health was worse than ever before, as a result of which her performance in telling folk tales was not as effective as earlier. She commented on the situation by explaining that while her memory had been good the year before, the headache that had come with the illness she had just recovered from 'has wiped ... memory all clean' (MD-0111-12).

I suppose that in Ksenia's mind it was not only the plots of the legends of St Xenia and St George that were associated but also the protagonists of the two religious legends. What demonstrates the fact that the categories of masculine and feminine are not opposed to one another in Ksenia's mind is the self-evident manner in which she recounts how a woman takes up arms, and the utterance that St George makes in the legend of St George, in which he says that he should not be taken as a husband. Ksenia said the following about rejecting the men who had come to court her after her husband had died: 'I did not have the strength to set myself to [man's] liking, I did not go, I did not go to anybody, I did not want to!' (MD-0106-28). Her long life without a husband was probably one of the factors that made it possible for her to identify with the saint.

Conclusion

The fact that Ksenia did not interpret the categories feminine and masculine similarly to men in her society does not suggest that Ksenia was not involved in the society's structures of domination or that she had acknowledged to herself that she wanted to liberate herself from male domination. The legend of St Xenia allowed divergence from gender stereotypes because its plot was placed at a spatial and temporal distance. But the fact that the religious legend was for Ksenia a true story, the protagonist of which was a woman, made this subconscious identification possible here rather than in the case of other genres, for example the joke.

The image of St Xenia who incites men to fight, as created by Ksenia, depicts a woman who goes to fight for Christianity (in Ksenia's words: 'for the Orthodox faith' or 'God's faith'). The cross that St Xenia held on the icon – a symbol of Christ that, among other things, represents victory over the forces of evil in Russian Orthodox theology – had been replaced by a club in the hand of Xenia in the religious legend. The club as a weapon fits the plot better than the cross because of the logic of the narrative: a narrative should involve action. However, in Ksenia's mind there was probably also an association between the saint and the cross that marked St Xenia's belonging among the 'great believers'. Considering what Ksenia said about the antagonism between heathens and Christians in bygone times (something she did not seem to fully believe in, although she claimed that the stories were believed in the past) and especially her eschatological ideas (for example the world perishing when the last believer dies) which she had fully accepted into her worldview, the greatest possible hero in Ksenia's imagination was a person who fought for the well-being of the 'people of God's faith' (or Christians) and the survival of Christianity.

The fact that this hero was a woman certainly seemed more natural to Ksenia than to me. It is possible that during her period in Setumaa Ksenia had seen pictures of *Rodina mat* (Mother Homeland) popular in the Soviet Union, and during her life in Tartu moving images of Xena, warrior princess, the hero of a television series.

Such folkloric texts allowed women to relieve tensions created by the duty of submission to male power. Neither the tension nor the duty of submission have generally been acknowledged because we perceive 'society and its arbitrary divisions', in accordance with which we live from situation to situation, 'to be natural and self-evident' (Bourdieu 2005: 21–22). However, in some situations the woman's inability to use power and the need to suppress this experience may have created tensions. A woman who grabs a club and calls men to fight is the kind of a character with whom another woman could identify and, through that, relieve such tensions. This religious legend also demonstrates that women do not accept the male-centred worldview completely.

A man would certainly not have told us a legend of St Xenia in the way of the one told by Ksenia. Historically it has been men who have benefited from the differentiation of men and women and the opposition of the masculine and the feminine. Examples of how men tend to differentiate genders and women associate them can be found in many cultures and eras (this was mentioned above in connection with male and female authors from the Middle Ages). In Christian cultures the fact that both women and men are baptized serves an important unifying factor.[7] Regardless of what a woman was in the eyes of men, from her own perspective she as a Christian could not be less valuable than a man. Kushkova (2001: 122) cites a story in which a Russian woman says to her boasting husband, who calls her an animal, that she is baptized like her husband. Ksenia identified herself primarily as a Christian and only then as a woman. It is in between those two categories that we can situate her self-identification as a person close to St Xenia (Ksenia Blazhennaya).

Yet these are my words. We can no longer hear the words of Ksenia, which could have either confirmed or contradicted this.

Acknowledgement

The present article has been completed within the framework of Estonian Science Foundation research grant No. 7516. It was also supported by the European Union through the European Regional Development Fund (Center of Excellence, CECT). I am thankful also to DAAD for the possibility to work in Germany in the spring of 2006 and to use the libraries in Göttingen. Many thanks to Prof. Ülo Valk for the many valuable comments on the present article that helped me to improve the text. This article has been translated into English by Raili Põldsaar.

Notes

1. Both forms, 'Zhenny Blazhennyi' and 'Ksenya Blazhennaya', indicate that Ksenia had probably received all her information about St Xenia from Russian-language sources. The fact that Ksenya never uses the Estonian expression *Püha Ksenia* (Saint Xenia) probably suggests that this saint had a different place and role in her mind in comparison to other saints.

2. For example, to the question of whether the action of the legend of St George took place in Pechory or somewhere else, Ksenia responded that it did not take place in Pechory as there is no sea there, it took place somewhere else, the holy books state where exactly (for transcript see Metsvahi 2002b: 132). About the time of action Ksenia said that she did not know how many hundreds of years ago it had been (for transcript see Metsvahi 2002b: 127; 131). In the folk tales of the Chamula Indians the spatially distant events are also distanced temporally (Gossen 1984: 110). Ulf Palmenfelt has written about the equivalence of space and time in legends (Palmenfelt 1993: 155–156).

3. In its brevity it is a note rather than a religious legend. It tells of Mary sheltering Christ in underground caves in Pechory – a passage of which is supposed to run as far as Kiev – when he was pursued by the Jews (MD-0100-19).

4. www.glaubenszeugen.de/kalender/x/kalx003.htm [Accessed 26 December 2008].

5. http://www.roca.org/OA/43/43m.htm [accessed 13 August 2010].

6. The idea of women's moral superiority to men started to spread in Western Europe in the late eighteenth century, the time that is characterized by the feminization of religion. As increasing numbers of women came to churches, while the attendance of men declined, the Catholic church could not limit itself to the stereotype of a corporeal and sinful woman and thus, the woman as the daughter of Eve, tempter to sin, is increasingly balanced by the stereotype of a pious woman as the daughter of Mary. The claim of women's moral superiority was also associated with the Romanticist idea of the regrettable fragmentation of human existence into different spheres of social life and the possibility of unfragmented human existence only in the domestic sphere that was associated with women. These ideas also spread outside Catholicism (Schlögl 1995: 21–30).

7. The Bible also confirms that women and men are equal before God. Although both the Old and the New Testament generally hold that woman should submit to man, Paul's Epistle to the Galatians states: 'There is neither

Jew nor Greek, there neither bond nor free, there is neither male nor female: for ye are all one in Christ Jesus' (Gal. 3:28).

References

Published Sources

Apo, S. (1990) Kansansadut naisnäkökulmasta: suuren äidin palvontaa vai potkut Lumikille? In A. Nenola and S. Timonen (eds) *Louhen sanat. Kirjoituksia Kansanperinteen Naisista,* 24–35. Helsinki: Suomalaisen Kirjallisuuden Seura.

Bakhtin, M. (1987) *Valitud töid.* Tallinn: Eesti Raamat.

Bauman, R. and Briggs, C. L. (1990) Poetics and performance as critical perspectives on language and social life. *Annual Review of Anthropology* 19: 59–88.

Beinert, W. (1989) Die durstigen Töchter der Samariterin oder: Des Gottesvolkes langer Marsch zum Jakobsbrunnen. Die Antinomie des kirchlichen Frauenbildes. In H. Pissarek-Hudelist (ed.) *Die Frau in der Sicht der Anthropologie und Theologie,* 152–176. Düsseldorf: Patmos Verlag.

Bourdieu, Pierre (2005) *Meeste domineerimine.* Tallinn: Varrak.

Briggs, C. L. (1988) *Competence in Performance: the Creativity of Tradition in Mexicano Verbal Art.* Philadelphia, PA: University of Pennsylvania Press.

Bynum, C. W. (1986) '... And woman his humanity': Female imagery in the religious writing of the later middle ages. In C. W. Bynum, S. Harrell and P. Richman (eds.) *Gender and Religion: On the Complexity of Symbols,* 257–288. Boston, MA: Beacon Press.

Diedrich, Hans-Christian (ed.) (1989) *Das Glaubensleben der Ostkirche. Eine Einführung in Geschichte, Gottesdienst und Frömmigkeit der orthodoxen Kirche.* In collaboration with H. Goltz, L. Kratzsch, K.-E. Langerfeld, B. Lehmann, P. Lobers, H. G. Thümmel. München: Verlag C. H. Beck.

Doyé, F. von S. (1930) *Heilige und Selige der römisch-katolischen Kirche.* Zweiter Band. Leipzig: Vier Quellen Verlag.

Ecker, H-P. (1993) *Die Legende. Kulturanthropologische Annäherung an eine literarische Gattung.* Stuttgart: Verlag J. B. Metzler.

Farmer, D. (ed.) (1997) *Oxford Dictionary of Saints.* Oxford: Oxford University Press.

Ferguson E., McHugh M. P., Norris, F. W. (eds.) (1999) *Encyclopedia of Early Christianity* Vol. 1. Oxford: Taylor & Francis.

Goldberg, C. (1997) *The Tale of the Three Oranges. FF Communications No.* 263. Helsinki: Academia Scientiarum Fennica.

Gossen, G. H. (1984) Chamula genres of verbal behavior. In Richard Bauman (ed.) *Verbal Art as Performance,* 81–115, with supplementary essays by B. A. Babcock, G. H. Gossen, R. D. Abrahams and J. F. Sherzer. Prospect Height, IL: Waveland Press.

Honko, L. (1984) The problem of defining myth. In A. Dundes (ed.) *Sacred Narrative: Readings in the Theory of Myth*, 41–52. Berkeley, Los Angeles, CA and London: University of California Press.

Honko, L. (1991) *Geisterglaube in Ingermanland. FF Communications No. 185*. Helsinki: Academia Scientiarum Fennica.

Hymes, D. (1971) The 'wife' who 'goes out' like a man: Reinterpretation of a Clackamas Chinook myth. In P. Maranda and E. Köngäs Maranda (eds) *Structural Analysis of Oral Tradition*, 49–80. Philadelphia, PA: University of Pennsylvania Press.

Irigaray, L. (1979) *Das Geschlecht, das nicht eins ist*. Berlin: Merve-Verlag.

Jordan, R. A. (1971) The vaginal serpent and other themes from Mexican-American women's lore. In R. A. Jordan and S. J. Kalčik (eds) *Women's Folklore, Women's Culture*, 26–44. Philadelphia, PA: University of Pennsylvania Press.

Järvinen, I-R. (2004) *Karjalan pyhät kertomukset. Tutkimus livvinkielisen alueen legendaperinteestä ja kansanuskon muutoksista*. Suomalaisen Kirjallisuuden Seuran toimituksia 962. Helsinki: Suomalaisen Kirjallisuuden Seura.

Kalkun, A. (2000) Masohhism kui ideaal. 'Jeesuse surm' ja 'Neiu veri'. *Maa-alused. Pro Folkloristica* VII: 13–25. Tartu: Eesti Kirjandusmuuseum.

Karlinger, F. (1986) *Legendenforschung. Aufgaben und Ereignisse*. Darmstadt: Wissenschaftliche Buchgesellschaft.

Keinänen, M.-L. (1999) Some remarks on women's religious traditionalism in the rural Soviet Karelia. In Ü. Valk (ed.) *Studies in Folklore and Popular Religion* 2, 151–171. Tartu: University of Tartu.

Kroll, R. (1995) Von der Heerführerin zur Leidensheldin. Die Domestizierung der *Femme forte*. In B. Baumgärtel and S. Neysters (eds) *Die Galerie der Starken Frauen. Regentinnen, Amazonen, Salondamen*, 51–63. München: Klinkhardt & Biermann.

Kushkova, A. N. (2001) Konstruirovanie gendera v tekstakh o krest´yanskikh ssorakh vtoroĭ poloviny XIX. v. In K. A. Bogdanov and A. A. Panchenko (eds) *Mifologiya i povsednevnost´: gendernyĭ podkhod v antropologicheskikh distsiplinakh*, 116–149. St Peterburg: Aleteĭya.

Lévi-Strauss, C. (1980) *Mythos und Bedeutung. Fünf Radiovorträge. Geschpräche mit Claude Lévi-Strauss* (ed. R. Adelbert). Frankfurt am Main: Suhrkamp Verlag.

Lüthi, M. (1986) *The European Folktale: Form and Nature*. Bloomington and Indianapolis, IN: Indiana University Press.

Meletinskij, E. M. (1992) *Mythologie und Folklore im Werk von Claude Lévi-Strauss*. Hamburg: Reinhold Schletzer Verlag.

Messerli, A. (1989) Angst und Wunderzeichen in Einblattdrucken. Überlegungen zu einem Bild/Text-Medium aus der zweiten Hälfte des 16. Jahrhunderts. In R. W. Brednich and A. Hartmann (eds) *Populäre Bildmedien. Vorträge des 2. Symposiums für ethnologische Bildforschung in Reinhausen bei Göttingen 1986*, 131–150. Göttingen: Volker Schmerse.

Metsvahi, M. (2002a) On the position of the religious legend of St George in the mental universe of the Setu woman Ksenia Müürsepp. In E. Bartha and V. Anttonen (eds) *Mental Spaces and Ritual Traditions. An International Festschrift to Commemorate the 60th Birthday of Dr. Mihály Hoppál*, 307–339. Debrecen/Turku: University of Debrecen/Department of Ethnography.

Metsvahi, M. (2002b) Inimene ja narratiiv. Püha Jüri legendi näitel. *Lemmeleht. Pro Folkloristica* IX: 121–146. Tartu: Eesti Kirjandusmuuseum.

Metsvahi, M. (2004) Cultural differences of narrating life-stories. In A. Leete and Ü. Valk (eds) *Studies in Folk Culture* 2, 132–159. Tartu: Tartu University Press.

Mitterauer, M. (1995) Abdallah und Godelive. Zum Status von Frauen und Männern im Spiegel 'heiliger Namen'. In E. Saurer (ed.) *Die Religion der Geschlechter. Historische Aspekte religiöser Mentalitäten,* 45–72. Köln: Böhlau Verlag.

Moser-Rath, E. (1999) Frau. In *Enzyklopädie des Märchens* Band 5, 101–159. Berlin: Walter de Gruyter.

Nenola, A. (1986) *Miessydäminen nainen. Naisnäkökulmia kulttuuriin. Tietolipas* 102. Helsinki: Suomalaisen Kirjallisuuden Seura.

Palmenfelt, Ulf (1993) On the understanding of folk legends. In M. Chesnutt (ed.) *Telling Reality. Folklore Studies in Memory of Bengt Holbek*, 143–167. Copenhagen and Turku: Nordic Institute of Folklore.

Pissarek-Hudelist, H. (1989) *Die Frau in der Sicht der Anthropologie und Theologie.* Düsseldorf: Patmos-Verlag.

Rosenfeld, H. (1972) *Legende.* Stuttgart: J. B. Metzlersche Verlagsbuchhandlung.

Saarlo, L. (1996) Pühakutest ja mõnest muust ning mis nende ümber. In H. Valk and E-H. Västrik (eds) *Palve, vanapatt ja pihlakas. Setomaa 1994. a. kogumisretke tulemusi. Vanavaravedaja* 4, 92–132. Tartu: Tartu Ülikooli arheoloogia kabinet.

Schlögl, R. (1995) Sünderin, Heilige oder Hausfrau? Katholische Kirche und weibliche Frömmingkeit um 1800. In I. G. Olenhusen (ed.) *Wunderbare Erscheinungen. Frauen und katholische Frömmigkeit um 19. und 20. Jahrhundert,* 13–50. Padeborn: Ferdinand Schöningh.

Schulenburg, J. T. (1998) *Forgetful of Their Sex: Female Sanctity and Society ca. 500–1100.* Chicago, IL and London: The University of Chicago Press.

Segal, R. A. (2005) In defence of mythology: The history of modern theories of myth. In A. Dundes (ed.) *Folklore: Critical Concepts in Literary and Cultural Studies* III, 212–254. London: Routledge.

Sieder, R. (1987) *Sozialgeschichte der Familie.* Frankfurt am Main: Edition Suhrkamp.

Synek, E. M. (1994) *Heilige Frauen der frühen Christenheit. Zu den Frauenbildern in hagiographischen Texten des christlichen Ostens. Das östliche Christentum. Neue Folge, Band* 43. Würzburg: Augustinus-Verlag.

Taylor, C. (1989) *Sources of the Self: The Making of the Modern Identity*. Cambridge: Cambridge University Press.

Vollständiges ... (1975) *Vollständiges Heiligen-Lexikon* (Johann Evangelist Stadler, ed.). Band V. Hildesheim: Georg Olms Verlag (Reprint: Augsburg 1882).

Weinstein, D. and Bell, R. (1982) *Saints and Society: the Two Worlds of Western Christendom, 1000–1700*. Chicago, IL: University of Chicago Press.

Wienker-Piepho, S. (1988) *Frauen als Volkshelden. Geschichtlichkeit, Legendenbildung und Typologie*. Frankfurt am Main: Artes Populares (Studia Ethnographica et Folkloristica 16).

Young, K. G. (1987) *Taleworlds and Storyrealms: The Phenomenology of Narrative*. Dordrecht: Nijhoff.

Other Sources

Bome, H. (2003) *Püha Nikolause ikoonid Setu rahvapärimuses*. Master's thesis. Tallinn: Estonian Academy of Art. Manuscript at the Department of Estonian and Comparative Folklore, University of Tartu.

MD (minidisc digital recordings). Sound recordings archive, Estonian Folklore Archives in Tartu.

www.glaubenszeugen.de/kalender/x/kalx003.htm [retrieved 15-08-10].

www.piibel.net [retrieved 15-08-10].

PART III

Relationships between Humans and Others

Things Act: Casual Indigenous Statements about the Performance of Object-persons

Graham Harvey[*]

Eagles are quite common along Newfoundland's Conne River. They live among the forested rocky crags across the river from the Mi'kmaq town of Miawpukek (a First Nations reserve recognized by the Newfoundland and Canadian governments). They often take salmon or trout from the community's fishery in the nearby Bay d'Espoir. Local people see them every day. However, when the people of Miawpukek held their first traditional, non-competitive powwow in 1996 an eagle flew one perfect circle over the central drum group during the final 'honour song', and then flew back to its treetop eyrie across the river. Everyone, locals and visitors, noticed. Cries of '*kitpu*' or 'eagle' simultaneously greeted the eagle, expressed pleasure at its beauty and presence, and declared that its flight demonstrated approval for the event. The flight of this eagle, in this way, at this moment, was celebrated by many participants as an encouragement to the Mi'kmaq community to continue the process of (re-)gaining confidence in traditional knowledge and its relevance in the contemporary world. Several people told me that what was happening at Miawpukek was not a 'revitalization movement' because traditional worldviews and lifeways did not need revitalizing, the eagles and bears had always maintained them. Now that significant numbers of the indigenous human population of the area, and of the island more generally, were returning to participate in traditional ways of life and traditional understandings of the world, a representative of the eagles was honouring them for coming home and joining in. The eagle participated in the powwow because the humans were participating in local culture again.

This article reflects on a series of casual statements and acts that reveal the core of animist worldviews and lifeways and provoke me to

* Graham Harvey is Reader in Religious Studies, The Open University, UK.

re-think what religion (and not only indigenous religions) means. If the unusually precise but hardly supernatural flight of an eagle impresses itself on all witnesses as probably being a communicative act, there are other elements of indigenous worldviews (and indigenizing practices) that might require more effort to appreciate. A series of casual comments and acts at Conne River began to initiate me into a clearer understanding of local people's knowledge of a world in which not only humans and eagles, but also fires, rocks and buildings can be relational actors negotiating the joys and sorrows of being neighbours and even kin. Much of this article is about North American indigenous religious traditions (specifically those of Mi'kmaq and Ojibwe people). Much of it is also about human relationships with animals and birds, though rocks are important too. However, the final third of the article engages with a Maori diaspora community and a building that draws attention to the most radical elements of animist discourses: casual statements that human artefacts – things – act relationally.

The Conne River Powwow

Powwows are indigenous North American cultural festivals with a particular stress on dancing. Sometimes dancers compete for prizes (best costume, best dancer of a particular style), but at Conne River the powwow was not competitive. The drum groups and dancers were part of a recovery of pride in being indigenous or native, and a celebration of recovery (evidenced most obviously in a range of cultural and economic forms). The dances were not thought of as religious or sacred, except perhaps for the honour songs which paid respect to elders and veterans, and involved the use of eagle feathers and eagle bone whistles which *are* considered sacred by many native people in North America. Nor were the powwow dances traditional in the sense of having ever been performed in this particular place before, or by the ancestors of these particular people. At Conne River and across native North America, such dances are, however, significant aspects of the performance of contemporary indigeneity, being indigenous or native.

More than this, powwows are an element of contemporary movements in which people are indigenizing (Johnson 2005: 42). In both elite (deliberate) and vernacular (casual) modes, indigenizing contests the modernist insistence that indigenous identity is given or natural, a matter of blood quantum or genes. Simultaneously, it contests the assertion that indigeneity is a moribund simulation of antique, pre-colonial primitivism. Rather, indigeneity is cultivated and achieved in a process of effort and experiment. It resonates with the genuinely traditional encouragement of committed effort to become a respectful person (as expressed in locally meaningful ways in particular place-communities). Thus, in the ever-changing circumstances in which people find themselves, tradition is the current expression of abiding taught/learnt protocols and etiquette of respect towards others (co-participants in a pervasively relational world). Indigenization is the practised corporealization of local relational ontology as everyday behaviour, mediated by initiatory experiences and rituals. In other words, it is not enough to be native by birth, there is an inheritance to be achieved in collaboration with others. The expression of these efforts in casual statements and acts is the enactment of today's version of traditional worldviews and lifeways. Conne River's powwow was not only celebrating the indigenizing process, it was a significant part of that ongoing process. Nobody preached, hardly any explanation was given. People danced or watched dancing, drummed or listened to drummers. Some, at least, caught what was happening. The eagle's flight helped. As he walked past me shortly after the eagle's affirmative flight, a young man who I had never met before spontaneously volunteered, 'This is the first time that I've been proud to be native'.

Near the powwow dance grounds were a series of explicitly sacred places. A fire was kept alight throughout the three days of the powwow and was the focus of ceremonies each dawn. People would gather and smoke a pipe of tobacco together, always offering smoke to the six directions (east, south, west, north, above and below). They would also make small offerings to the fire. When they talked about this they would say that it was important to feed the fire not only with wood but also with gifts of sacred herbs and even with the first portion of the food prepared for all powwow participants. 'Feeding the fire' was not just a metaphor, the fire was understood to desire and even require food, and to be grateful to those who made offerings. As a relational being, fire's receipt of various kinds of food led to the reciprocal gift to humans of light and heat. As relational beings, humans' receipt of light and heat led to reciprocal gifts of wood, herbs and other foods for the fire. Both humans and fire gained from the presence of the other. These are not automatic processes but relational behaviours that require effort and practice. While the reciprocal gifts and the gifting processes and rhetorics attract attention, their casual, seemingly natural performance reveals (once it becomes visible) the deep reality of relational ontology.

On the same promontory on a bend in the river, the organizers had constructed four sweat lodges. These were temporary domed structures in which about a dozen people could sit around a central hole in the ground. Stones were heated up in a large fire between the four lodges, and at appropriate moments in a lengthy and purposeful ceremony were brought in and placed in the hole. Water poured on the hot stones immediately turned to steam and raised the temperature dramatically. The coverings on the lodges kept the heat in and the light out. The ceremony in the darkness and the heat was not undertaken for individual health (lodges are not like Scandinavian saunas) but in order to pray for the wellbeing of all living beings. Some people talk about 'stone people lodges' rather than sweat lodges. This indicates that what is most important about the ceremony is not the technology and techniques of sweating but the collaboration of relational beings (rocks and humans in particular). The rocks are addressed as grand-fathers, a term of respect and kinship, and are understood to be giving up their lives in the effort of praying for the well-being of the wider community. Ceremonial participation in the lodge does not normally entail explanatory lectures, sermons or even discussion. Stones, humans and other beings are addressed or spoken about in ways that casually express their personhood, relational connections and reciprocal mutuality.

One day during the powwow I was talking with the leader of one of the sweat-lodge ceremonies about everything that was happening that week. He started to talk about how Conne River was not only home to human people but to a wide range of 'other-than-human people' including the bears, eagles, fish, trees, rocks and the fire. He said that there were also people who are only seen in visions, people who might come to teach someone how to live a better life, or to give them some piece of knowledge that they could use to help others. He said that the craggy rock across the river was home to a community of 'little people'. But as soon as he said this, he stopped talking to me, walked to the river bank and seemed to speak to someone over the river. Later he told me that it was not appropriate to speak about such powerful people without their permission and without offering respect. He apologized but insisted that no more should be said about them. The important thing, he said, was to talk with them if they showed themselves to you, but otherwise to leave them in peace. Having been given similar advice in Ireland I suspect that, as in Ireland, Newfoundland's 'little people' are not little, rather this term is used in order to speak about powerful beings without distracting them from whatever they may be doing at the time. Other-than-human persons may be called on for help, but they do not exist primarily for human benefit. Casual expressions of careful, cautious respect (Black 1977) reveals that this is not an anthropocentric world or worldview.

These four short stories about my experiences at Miawpukek's first powwow (the eagle's flight, the fire being fed, the sweat lodge ceremonies, and the 'little people') illustrate facets of a way of living that can be called 'animism'. Since this word has been used as a technical term in two contrasting theories, I need to say more about it.

(Re-)defining Animism

In the monumental proto-anthropology of Edward Tylor (1871), animism is a synonym of religion defined as 'a belief in souls or spirits'. Tylor had considered labelling his theory 'spiritualism', but that was already strongly associated with a particular religious movement. Animism, however, carried associations with the souls and spirits that Tylor saw as central, definitive religious beliefs. It had been previously used by Georg Stahl (1708) in a failed attempt to define the difference between living bodies and dead matter as the presence of a physical, chemical element, *anima*. All that is left of this theory in Tylor's work is the implicit question, how do we distinguish living beings from dead matter? Or, more simply, is it alive? Religious people continue the 'primitive' error of interpreting dreams and hallucinations as evidence that souls and spirits animate living beings. Metaphysics (an error by definition in this rationalist discourse) posits these constituent parts of beings to distinguish them from inert matter. In accepting such beliefs, religious people make a category error of projecting life where it does not exist (e.g. in rocks) or human attributes (such as intentionality) on to non-human creatures (e.g. eagles). From the belief in souls and spirits they also extrapolate a further false belief that these make their possessors at least potentially immortal. From there, vast edifices of different religious cultures evolved a panoply of supernatural notions.

Tylor's evidence for this grand theory of the nature of religion was drawn from data gathered from colonial sources globally as well as at home in Victorian Britain. It has an explicit polemical purpose: the furtherance of rationalism against the mistakes of religious belief. Tylor's animism should not be mistaken for a categorization of a type of religion distinct from monotheism, or for the name of a particular religion distinct from Christianity. Tylor's animism *is* religion. He claims to be defining religion as distinct from science, politics, entertainment or any other human endeavour.

It can seem possible to encounter Tylor's animists because many people in many places do talk about spirits or souls, or use words that can be translated in this way. Some do talk as if the death of trees was as personally meaningful as the death of humans, or as if deceased relatives continued to communicate with their descendents. Alan Campbell illustrates this with reference to the Amazonian Wayapí, noting that their 'conversation shifts between' thinking 'that all sorts of things round them are simply alive' and 'that all these things have a soul or spirit in them that makes them alive' (Campbell 2003: 136–137). Nonetheless, Campbell objects to the use of animism as a 'religious tag' of the sort used by people who produce 'colour-coded maps of the world' indicating where particular religions predominate. Much of West Africa and Amazonia can be labelled animist where people are neither Christian nor Muslim (although this can depend on who is defining any of these religious complexes). In fact, Tylor intended the term to be a tag, not for a type of religion, but for religion as an allegedly *sui generis* phenomena. Campbell does not, as he suggests, contribute to the sharpening of Tylor's blunt signpost, but to the understanding of a different approach to animism.

The new animism is appropriately associated with the increasingly influential research of Irving Hallowell among from the Ojibwe of Beren's River in south central Canada (Hallowell 1960). The key question here is not, is it alive? but, how should we relate? The problem is not beliefs about something that might distinguish life and death, but learning appropriate ways of behaving. Animism is an ontology not (primarily) an epistemology. Among the Ojibwe, Hallowell learnt, animism is implicit in grammar and becomes explicit in casual and deliberate discourse and performance.

In the Ojibwe language a grammatical distinction is made between animate and inanimate genders but not between masculine and feminine genders. A suffix, -g, is added to nouns that refer to animate persons rather than inanimate objects. Verbs indicating the actions of animate persons differ from those referring to acts done to inanimate objects. For example, the plural form of the word *asin* (stone) is *asiniig*, identifying stones as grammatically animate (Nichols and Nyholm 1995: 14). Ojibwe speakers use the same personal pronoun (*wiin*) for masculine and feminine persons, grammatically making nothing of the difference between masculine and feminine. But they use animate gender terms for a wider range of beings than the English language officially recognizes. In practice some English speakers do talk about their ships, cars or computers as if they were animate beings rather than inanimate objects, giving them names and applying the personal pronouns he or she rather than the impersonal it. How far can this 'as if' discourse be taken? In the French language, tables are marked as grammatically feminine, *la table* rather than *le table*. Do French speakers treat 'female' tables as animate female persons? Perhaps they do so in poetry and children's stories, but what about in everyday reality? So, the question arises, do the Ojibwe treat grammatically animate stones as animate persons? Do they speak with stones or act in other ways that reveal intentions to build or maintain relationships?

Irving Hallowell asked an old Ojibwa man, 'Are *all* the stones we see about us here alive?' (1960: 24). Grammatically all stones everywhere are animate, but did the old man actually think that particular rocks around him were alive? Did he treat them in some way that showed them to be alive? The old man answered, 'No! but *some* are'. He had witnessed a particular stone following the leader of a shamanic ceremony around a tent as he sang. Another powerful leader is said to have had a large stone that would open when he tapped it three times, allowing him to remove a small bag of herbs when he needed it in ceremonies. Hallowell was told that when a white trader was digging his potato patch he found a stone that looked like it may be important. He called for the leader of another ceremony who knelt down to talk to the stone, asking if it had come from someone's ceremonial tent. The stone is said to have denied this. Movement, gift-giving and conversation are three indicators of the animate nature of relational beings, or persons.

Hallowell makes it clear that the key point in each account is not that stones do things of their own volition (however remarkable this claim might seem) but that they engage in relationships. For the Ojibwe the interesting question is not, how do we know stones are alive? but, what is the appropriate way for people, of any kind, to relate? This is as true for humans as it is for stones, trees, animals, birds, fish, and all other beings that might be recognized as persons. Persons are known to be persons when they relate to other persons in particular ways. They might act more or less intimately, willingly or respectfully. Since enmity is also a relationship, they might act aggressively. The category of person is only applicable *when* beings are relating with others. This is quite different to the understanding of ontology in most European derived cultures, in which personhood is an interior quality, a fact about an individual (human) who is self conscious. Hallowell recognized this by insisting that we are not talking here about different belief systems, epistemologies, but about different ontologies, different ways of being in the world. Indeed, we could say that the Ojibwe old man lived in a different world from Hallowell's until the latter learnt to see the world as his teacher showed it to be. Once he saw it, Hallowell had to find new ways to use the English language to write about what he had learnt. To talk of animism may have suggested a discussion of life (animation) versus death. To talk of persons may have implied notions about human interiority (belief, rationality or subjectivity). But the 'animate persons' we are discussing are relational beings, actors in a participatory world. Hallowell's question is phrased in a way that indicates he had already appreciated some, at least, of what it meant to live in the old man's world. He did not ask, are all rocks alive? but inquired about nearby rocks: he was already recognizing the importance of relationship and participation.

The World is a Community

Having learnt from his Ojibwe hosts, Hallowell coined the phrase 'other-than-human persons' to refer to the animate beings with whom humans share the world. He has been criticized for privileging humanity, as if he was saying that what makes something a person is their likeness to humans. In fact, he is clear that 'person' is not defined by human characteristics or behaviours. The term is a much larger umbrella than 'human'. All beings communicate intentionally and act towards others relationally: this makes them 'persons'. It is useful *for us* (humans) to speak about 'human-' and 'other-than-human' persons only because: (a) we are humans talking to humans (if we were bears we might speak of 'other-than-bear persons'); and (b) because English-speakers are preconditioned to hear the word person as a reference to other humans. The word persons should be enough, and would be if English-speakers had not learnt to privilege and separate out humanity from other beings. Animists live in a different world: a community of persons all of whom are capable of relationship, communication, agency and desire.

There is no mute or inert 'nature' but only the many competing conversations of a multi-species cultural community. Another of Hallowell's informants told him that he had been visiting an elderly couple during a thunderstorm. He said, 'There was one clap of thunder after another. Suddenly the old man turned to his wife and asked, "Did you hear what was said?" "No," she replied, "I didn't catch it."' Hallowell comments that the casualness of the remark and even the trivial character of the anecdote demonstrate the psychological depth of the 'social relations' with other-than-human beings that become explicit in the behaviour of the Ojibwe as a consequence of the cognitive 'set' induced by their culture (Hallowell 1960: 34).

After a lifetime living as animists this couple assumed that thunder is an act of communication. Acceptance of not having caught what was said indicates another assumption: that not all communication is about us (humans in general or the hearers specifically). The elderly couple could carry on talking with their visitor while the thunder engaged in a separate conversation nearby.

By referring to relational beings, 'persons' invites us to consider what 'good persons' might be. In Ojibwe culture (and many other indigenous cultures) goodness too is relational: people are encouraged to be good towards one another, and they are recognized as being good when they reciprocate respect rather than enmity. On a short visit to the Midwestern United States, I was invited to join a group of Ojibwe[1] and Lakota people who were going to pick sage. They use sage in their prayers throughout the year, burning some when they seek purification, and making up small bundles to offer as gifts to helpful other-than-human persons. We drove out of the Twin Cities to a location where sage grew plentifully. Before cutting any sage, or even entering the field, everyone took pinches of sage left over from the previous year and held it to their hearts while introducing themselves to the field of sage, and requesting permission to cut some sage for the following year. After a pause each person placed their sage on the ground. Once these gifts were given and one of the elders had indicated that permission was given, everyone gathered sage, being careful not to destroy entire plants and expressing gratitude each time they cut.

A similar experience was told to me by a British couple who cut holly, ivy and yew annually in order to decorate their home for their midwinter Yule festival. Their common practice had been to introduce themselves and their purpose at a spring in the heart of a wood near their home. They lit a candle and some incense by the spring while offering season's greetings to the wood and its inhabitants. Then they offered gifts to each tree from which they cut greenery, sometimes pouring libations of some drink at the roots of the trees, or tying strands of wool around a branch. One year, as they were leaving the wood, they saw a holly tree burdened with ripe berries. What they had cut until then held few berries and they thought that just a few sprigs with their red fruit would enhance their celebrations. In too much of a hurry, or thinking that they had already addressed the whole wood, they attempted to cut from a branch. Although there was no wind that day, the prickly tree swiped the couple. Chastened, they apologized and left, being careful in future visits to pay particular attention to that tree.

Totemism and Shamanism

In one of her excellent discussions of Aboriginal Australian relationships with their land and other-than-human neighbours, Debbie Rose writes that not only humans, but also 'other animals like kangaroos have their own rituals and law, and … they too take care of relationships of wellbeing' among all the inhabitants of an area or 'country'. All related beings share rights and responsibilities, and are expected to be committed to and concerned for each other's 'flourishing in the world' (Rose 1998: 7, 11). Rose uses the term 'totemism' to refer to these relationships and commitments that cross species boundaries, involving high degrees of mutual care. The word totem originated among the Ojibwe and refers to clans that include humans and particular animals and plants. It has been used by academics to theorize human-animal relationships. Claude Lévi-Strauss established the notion that totem animals are chosen not because they are 'good to eat' but because they are 'good to think' (Lévi-Strauss 1969: 89). Here, once again, a scholar constructs an alien epistemology. In Ojibwe and Aboriginal Australian totemism, animals are good to relate with. As Chris Knight says, 'totemism is about enacting kinship – concretely and precisely in sexual and dietary engagements and etiquette. Totemism is, therefore, embedded in animism as an aspect of sociality' (Knight 1996: 550).

The title of one of Debbie Rose's books points to the central importance of totemic relationships in making people what they are: *Dingo Makes Us Human* (Rose 1992). Rose is careful to point out that relationships are not always harmonious, they can lead to tension, conflict and competition. There is often a need for mediators or diplomats (elsewhere they may be labelled shamans) to intervene between groups and individuals to sort out problems. But in an inclusive, cross-species community that privileges respect and seeks cooperation there is likely to be a bias towards trying to resolve differences amicably rather than destructively. That is the job that clans are supposed to do within the wider relationships posited by animism.

Nurit Bird-David has published an important consideration of the new animism entitled '"Animism" Revisited: Personhood, Environment, and Relational Epistemology' (1999). I have just noted, albeit briefly, that totemism and shamanism can also now be revisited in the light of a better understanding of animism (see also Harvey 2005a). So far, I have tried to show that animists casually and deliberately make statements (verbally and performatively) that draw attention to a relational ontology in which the world is a community of persons, only some of whom are human. Treating animals and birds as agents is not too difficult – even thorough-going modernists can ask their pets or companion animals about food choices. Understanding how rocks can be treated as persons is more difficult, especially if this is not interpreted as symbolism or metaphor. The really radical move is to engage with human artefacts as persons.

Ngati Ranana and Hinemihi

Since the 1950s, Maori living in London, UK, for a shorter or longer period, have met together to practise traditional performing arts as one means of maintaining Maori culture and community. Ngati Ranana (translated on a t-shirt as 'London Maori Club' but also readable as 'London's Tribe') are like and unlike *kapa haka* groups in Aotearoa New Zealand. They perform at cultural events but have also become the heart of a fluid diaspora community with something of the flavour of a neo-tribe (Maffesoli 1991, 1996; Bauman 1993).

Once a year, Ngati Ranana's *Kohanga Reo* ('language nest' for the teaching and learning of Maori language) hosts an event that is a Maori-style picnic, with food cooked in pits in traditional style, and a celebration of the wider Maori and Pacific Islander diaspora community. It takes place in the presence of Hinemihi, a Maori meeting house brought to England in the mid-nineteenth century and reconstructed in the grounds of Clandon House near Guildford, home of Lord Onslow, the retiring Governor of New Zealand.

It is possible to say of Clandon House, like many other buildings, that 'she' is attractive and 'has character'. But this is, for the most part, a deliberately metaphorical way of talking, and projects human likeness on to human dwellings. It can be said as casually as a French speaker might assign feminine gender to *la table*, and with as little intention to insist that the attributed gender is precisely equivalent to that of human female persons. On the other hand, when Maori say that Hinemihi participates in ceremonies or that she welcomes guests, they mean something quite different.

Hinemihi o te Ao Tawhito (to use her full name) is an ancestor. She is pleased to see her descendants. She welcomes respectful visitors and works with Maori to turn respectful visitors into guests. Maori introduce others to Hinemihi in a personal way. They can point to Hinemihi's welcoming arms, visible as the bargeboards that descend from an apex where the ancestral face observes those who come to visit her. Inside, Hinemihi's ribs and spine are visible in rafters and the roof beam. It is possible to hear these statements as metaphors, or interpret them as meaning that rafters *symbolize* ribs. But something about the way Maori say these things, and something about the way they move towards and within Hinemihi, suggests they are saying something quite different. Familiarity confirms this (and familiarity is gained by participation in a protocol-rich, staged approach to the ancestor and her descendants).

Maori can talk about Hinemihi as a human artefact. Not only do the descendants of the builders and carvers visit sometimes, they have also participated in some of the restoration projects that have kept Hinemihi secure and attractive. Maori have plenty of ways of talking about buildings, construction, craft, decoration, labour and artefacts. These means of labelling materiality and its manipulation do not, however, exhaust Maori discourse about 'things' like Hinemihi. Te Pakaka Tawhai (1988) demonstrates that Maori storytelling is multilayered; skilled orators can draw from a single narrative episode a range of possible implications to make a point and contest points made by others. Similarly, it is possible to describe the construction and decoration of a meeting house like Hinemihi, to say that 'those boards are her arms', and to invite visitors to enter the ancestor's embrace. Multiple understandings and appreciations are regular features of Maori knowledge systems. Indeed, Hinemihi is constructed to play significant roles in these multiple discourses.

It is, then, possible to say that Hinemihi is an ancestor *and* a meeting house. The ancestor lived in the past in human form, and continues to exist in the same human but post-mortem form as other Maori ancestors. (Perhaps it is necessary to note that 'ancestor' in most indigenous contexts does not simply point to someone having died. An ancestor is a person who, though transformed in the processes of dying, is still actively involved in the community formed by her or his descendants.) The living face of the ancestor can be recognized in the form of descendants in each successive generation (Henare 2007: 57). At the same time, but in yet another form, an ancestor can exist in various other physical modes, one of which is as a meeting house like Hinemihi. She is a *whare tipuna*, not only an 'ancestral [style] house' but also a 'house ancestor'. However, this description remains static as long as it only points to the objective materiality of the house. What Amiria Henare says of genealogy, *whakapapa*, is relevant here: it is '[n]ot simply a static record of lineages, it is an inherently dynamic cosmological system for reckoning degrees of similarity and difference, determining appropriate behaviour, and manipulating existing and potential relationships to achieved desired effects' (Henare 2007: 57). Hinemihi and genealogy are implicated in performed practices that familiarize people with their ancestor and other people with their (potential) guesthood. Indeed, people become guests in the presence of, with the full participation of, and by becoming familiar with Hinemihi, the ancestor. Just as rocks are always grammatically animate in Ojibwe but require others with whom to relate to show that they are indeed persons, so Hinemihi is technically always an ancestor but requires an opportunity to greet descendants and guests to show what being an ancestor is all about. New verbal forms, 'personing' and 'ancestoring', might indicate something of the dynamic involved. In both cases, being a person and being an ancestor are about becoming (increasingly) familiar and personable towards and to others.

Conclusion: Religion and Things

When Maori casually say that Hinemihi *is* an ancestor, centuries of habituation to the polemics of the Protestant and Catholic Reformations seem to force speakers of most European languages to automatically translate it into symbolism. When Maori casually say that Hinemihi's bargeboards *are* her welcoming arms, the same ingrained habits insinuate the language of representation. Versions of this tendency are standard practice in relation to European interpretations of art, and to the category 'art'. Maori are well able to talk about artistic representations and religious symbolism. But their ancestral culture has inculcated a celebration of diversity and materiality. Maori casual references to Hinemihi as 'she' and 'ancestor' can be taken to mean exactly what they seem to say – Hinemihi is a female ancestor – while also indicating a range of additional means that are neither entirely equivalent to nor ever exhausted by European art historical conventions.

The phrase 'Hinemihi is an ancestor' is unlike the Christian liturgical phrase 'this [bread] is my body' in many respects. In both, 'is' is a complex word, but in Maori usage 'is' is allowed to bear its most obvious surface meaning of equivalence. It can mean additional things, but it is hard to say that there is anything deeper or more true than the equation, house = ancestor. In Christian contexts, various authorized interpretations exist, but straightforward equivalence is almost everywhere disallowed and disavowed: bread cannot equal body but must somehow symbolize, represent or be transmuted into it. The problem of 'is' may well be compounded by the problems of ritual and the role of the dead in European contexts. The Reformations have made ritual at best an ambiguous word and most often a derogatory term for acts that people repeat without the necessary understanding. The Protestant initiated insistence on each individual's faith has divided and destabilized relational communities by elevating the dead (saints) to a remote world. This stress on interior understanding and choice underlies Enlightenment rationalism which reworks earlier matter/spirit dualism into body/mind dualism. Indigenous and indigenizing discourse and practice contests these constructions of humanity and the world by insisting on relational definitions.

Alan Campbell says:

> It isn't so much the particular [shamanistic/animist] beliefs that are incomprehensible to us. It's not that they were 'animists' and we are

not. The difficulty is rather than we have, for ourselves, through the material conditions of our lives and the relation with the natural world that comes from that, make their kind of relation with the animals and the trees and the waters profoundly incomprehensible. (Campbell 1995: 208)

Perhaps he overstates his case. Bruno Latour (1993) rightly argues that 'we have never been modern'. The exhausting effort put into the effort to be fully 'modern' (rationalist and individualist, let alone consumerist) demonstrates that modernity is a project rather than a given. Campbell's 'material conditions of our lives and the relation with the natural world that comes from that' is a world we have been attempting to construct. We have first thought a 'natural world' into existence, imposing it on the world that animists consider to be a community of persons. Our effort to turn a thought experiment into a habitable world has required us to blind ourselves to the comprehensibility of the world. The fact that this effort has taken place during European and Euro-American colonialism has marginalized or silenced alternative voices and relations.

Recent academic interest in indigenous and vernacular discourse and practice has generally valued these more positively than our nineteenth-century ancestors did. What was once derided as primitive folly may now be recognized as the expression of alternative (to modernist) ontologies and epistemologies. Amiria Henare, Martin Holbraad and Sari Wastell brought together a team of ethnographers to engage in *Thinking Through Things* (2007) which radically re-theorizes artefacts and the roles they play in different communities. They hear statements that assert the agency and active participation of things and seek to allow the 'things' to generate theory. They propose an 'artefact-oriented anthropology' that is 'not about material culture' (Henare 2007: 1). Artefacts are not simply products of human labour that reveal (human) social dynamics. They make and offer meanings. Sometimes these meanings are of an other-than-human world. If the flight of an eagle can celebrate the participation of humans in a larger-than-human, non-anthropocentric community, artefacts like Hinemihi can speak to and against modernism.

Casual indigenous statements (especially when supported by habitual actions expressive of relationality) can reveal more than formal and elite claims. Attention to the casual may aid academics to learn what their hosts already know. In seeking to understand what aspects of human life, or what acts of human living, are identified by the word religion, we may be greatly aided by noticing what people casually do and say with and to the things around them. There is little new in the claim that indigenous religious traditions are not focused on the supernatural but include relational engagement with everyday things and even artefacts. Perhaps all religions are like this. Some encouragement to pay attention to simple acts and to hear the self-evident in indigenous equations ('this house is an ancestor', 'this rock is active'), may support a re-visioning of what other vernacular religious activities and discourses entail. Object persons and human persons, along with animal persons and a host of other other-than-human persons, casually make the world that all beings then have to negotiate living in as they continue their constructive, destructive and re-constructive work.

Sacred ceremonies almost always entail the presence of objects. What difference would it make if instead of this inviting us to consider 'material culture' we thought about the 'culture of things'? What if these objects are not simply present but actively participate? Religion is, perhaps, a necessarily cyborg (human-artefact hybrid) activity that Donna Haraway (1991) ought to have included in her consideration. If so, this is not only a statement about being human, but also reveals that an anthropocentric view of religions that mis-perceives object-agency cannot fully understand what religious people (human or otherwise) say and do.

Note

1. A variety of spellings and different names are used by the people: not only Ojibwa and Ojibwe but also Chippewa and Anishinaabeg (among others).

References

Bauman, Z. (1993) *Postmodern Ethics*. Oxford: Blackwell.

Bird-David, N. (1999) 'Animism' revisited: Personhood, environment, and relational epistemology. *Current Anthropology* 40 (S1): S67–S91. Reprinted in Graham Harvey (ed.) 2002: 73–105.

Black, M. B. (1977) Ojibwa power belief system. In R. D. Fogelson and R. N. Adams (eds) *The Anthropology of Power*, 141–151. New York: Academic.

Campbell, A. T. (1995) *Getting to Know Waiwai: An Amazonian Ethnography*, 185–210. London: Routledge. Reprinted in Graham Harvey (ed.) *Shamanism: A Reader*, 123–144. London: Routledge.

Hallowell, A. I. (1960) Ojibwa ontology, behavior, and world view. In S. Diamond (ed.) *Culture in History: Essays in Honor of Paul Radin,* 19–52. New York: Columbia University Press. Reprinted in G. Harvey (ed.) 2002, *Readings in Indigenous Religions,* 18–49. London: Continuum

Haraway, D. (1991) *Simians, Cyborgs, and Women: The Reinvention of Nature.* London: Free Association Books.

Harvey, G. (ed.) (2002) *Readings in Indigenous Religions.* London: Continuum.

Harvey, G. (2005a) *Animism: Respecting the Living World.* London: C. Hurst & Co.; New York: Columbia University Press; Adelaide: Wakefield Press.

Harvey, G. (2005b) Performing identity and entertaining guests: Maori diaspora in London. In G. Harvey and Ch. Thompson (eds) *Indigenous Diasporas and Dislocation,* 121–134. Aldershot: Ashgate.

Henare, A. (2007) Taonga Maori: Encompassing rights and property in New Zealand. In A. Henare, M. Holbraad and S. Wastell (eds) *Thinking Through Things: Theorising Artefacts Ethnographically,* 47–67. London: Routledge.

Johnson, P. C. (2005) Migrating bodies, circulating signs: Brazilian candomblé and the garifuna of the Caribbean and the category of indigenous religions. In G. Harvey and Ch. D. Thomson (eds) *Indigenous Diasporas and Dislocations,* 37–51. Aldershot: Ashgate.

Knight, C. (1996) Totemism. In A. Barnard and J. Spencer (eds) *Encyclopedia of Social and Cultural Anthropology,* 550–551. London: Routledge.

Latour, B. (1993) *We Have Never Been Modern.* New York: Harvester Wheatsheaf.

Lévi-Strauss, C. (1969) *Totemism.* Harmondsworth: Penguin.

Maffesoli, M. (1991) The ethic of aesthetics. *Theory, Culture and Society* 8 (1): 7–20.

Maffesoli, M. (1996) *The Time of the Tribes: The Decline of Individualism in Mass Society.* London: Sage.

Nichols, J. D. and Nyholm, E. (1995) *A Concise Dictionary of Minnesota Ojibwe.* Minneapolis, MN: University of Minnesota Press.

Rose, D. B. (1992) *Dingo Makes Us Human: Life and Land in an Australian Aboriginal Culture.* Cambridge: Cambridge University Press.

Rose, D. B. (1998) Totemism, regions, and co-management in Aboriginal Australia, draft paper for the Conference of the International Association for the Study of Common Property. Online http://www.indiana.edu/~iascp/Drafts/rose.pdf [accessed 18 January 2011].

Stahl, G. E. (1708) *Theoria medica vera.* Halle: Literis Orphanotrophei.

Tawhai, Te P. (1988) Maori Religion. In S. Sutherland and P. Clarke (eds) *The Study of Religion, Traditional and New Religion,* 96–105. London: Routledge. Reprinted in Harvey, G. (ed.) 2002: 237–249.

Tylor, E. (1913 [1871]) *Primitive Culture* 2 vols. London: John Murray.

Haunted Houses and Haunting Girls: Life and Death in Contemporary Argentinian Folk Narrative

María Inés Palleiro[*]

The way that ghosts and haunted houses have been recorded in folk archives, since the very beginning of Argentinian folklore documentation, reflects several aspects of the way in which the supernatural world is represented in folk narrative messages. Such representations express different ways of considering life and death in Argentinian culture, the distinctive feature of which is a heterogeneous blend of races, religions and worldviews.

As I have already discussed (Palleiro 2008), the representations of haunting ghosts, haunted houses, and the other manifestations of the supernatural in folk narrative archives, are connected with the different currents, trends and topics of Argentinian folkloristics. I use archive in its etymological meaning of *arkhé*, that is to say, as a principle of memory organization (Derrida 1997). That is how, in the first collections, tales about ghosts and haunted houses were not considered as main topics of Argentinean folk narrative. According to the folkloric paradigm of collectionism, these first archives were organized by anthological criteria, based on the general indices of types and motives. Such a way of filing narrative material tended to adjust the local archives to parameters of trans-national classification, with a privilege for the recollection of marvellous tales. At the same time, marked by the influence of contextualist paradigms of the new perspectives in folklore and performance studies, there has also been an opening both towards new topics like UFO narratives, new narrative species like cases, 'histories' and memorates, and new channels of discourse like the written and mediated registers. This was

* María Inés Palleiro is researcher in folk narrative at the Institute of Anthropology, Buenos Aires University and Professor of Methodology of Folk Research, National Institute of Folk Arts, Buenos Aires, Argentina.

the moment at which tales about ghosts and haunted houses began to appear in Argentinian folk narrative archives. In a counterpoint to the amplitude of the first general collections, the current trends in archive organization were oriented to give an updated look and to re-signify the past from the present. As I will discuss in this article, these new archives tend to consider folk narrative as a kind of message whose semantic content is linked to the expression of identities and social memories. It is also worth mentioning the beginning of the folklore paradigm associated with the 'oral and anonymous' production located within the rural ambit of the first archives towards urban ambits and towards the consideration of authorship and the style of folk narrators. These new trends highlighted the narrator's capacity to recreate in an aesthetic message the multiethnic and multicultural character of Argentina. The different features of this culture, reflected in the narrative archives, have to do with their radical heterogeneity, given by the plural convergence of contributions, both European, *créoles* and indigenous, strengthened by diasporic movements that revitalise the Argentinean cultural patrimony with their richness and diversity.

Ghosts and Haunted Houses: Trends and Topics in Argentinian Folk Narrative Archives

In the first general archive of Argentinian folk narrative, the 1921 collection of folk manuscripts, influenced by the historic-geographic method of the Finnish school, tales about ghosts and haunted houses were mixed with references to the supernatural, and thus classified as superstitions or folk beliefs. The classification is considered in that collection as a minor category, in opposition to the 'most important' categories: folktales and folk stories. Both the general folk narrative collections of Susana Chertudi (1960–1964) and Berta Elena Vidal de Battini (1980–1984) include several narratives dealing with haunting girls and haunted houses. Such narratives are classified as versions of Aarne-Thompson's tale type 332, Godfather Death (replaced by Godmother Death, in this collection: *La muerte por madrina*) and type 326, The Youth Who Wanted to Learn What Fear Is.

That is how, in Chertudi's first series of Argentinian folk tales, the tale filed with the number 35, entitled The Stingy Father (*El padre avaro*), refers to AT 326. In Vidal de Battini's collection, volume IV, which contains 'marvellous or magic tales', includes '13 versions and variants' (*sic*) of type 326, entitled 'The guy without fear' (*El muchacho sin miedo*), filed in numbers 904 to 916. It also includes '5 versions and variants' of AT 332, entitled Godmother Death (*La muerte por madrina*) filed in numbers 948 to 952. The titles of these versions are almost the Spanish translation of the English tale types. Such tales regarding Godmother Death refer to the personification of death, represented as an old woman who comes to fetch a person who tries to escape from her by changing his clothes or cutting off his hair. In both Chertudi and Vidal de Battini's collections, the point of the tales regarding 'the guy without fear' is the falling of the different parts of a corpse from the ceiling of an old house, without special references to any specific haunted house. This narrative structure corresponds to that of a canonic folktale, defined as a 'utopic and achronic' fictive action, happening at an indefinite time and in an indefinite space (Pinon 1965). As a curiosity, in Chertudi's collection, the narrator refers to the skeleton as that of 'a Christian' instead of 'a man'. The folktales of these collections reveal the influence of a Hispanic Catholic worldview in the symbolic representations of life and death. According to this worldview, narrators refer to Death as a personification of supernatural forces directly related to 'God the Father' and 'Jesus Christ'. In that way this personification works as a sort of allegory of a powerful divinity. The plot of these versions serves as a sort of *exemplum,* illustrating how good Catholics go to paradise and how sinners are seriously punished in the other world, according to the life they have led on Earth. The feeling of guilt and belief in the absolution of sins at the end of a person's life are also clearly expressed in these narratives.[1] The rhetorical composition of such tales is based on an antithetic static opposition between hell and heaven. In this way, the narrative action acts as a sort of argumentative resort used by the narrator to convince the audience about the status of reality and the onthological value of certain religious truths held by the Catholic institutional religion.

Since the coup that brought the last of Argentina's periodic military governments to power in 1976, and the first subsequent president under that regime, Jorge Rafael Videla, tales about ghosts and haunted houses gained a place in contemporary Argentinian folk consciousness, along with topics such as aliens, UFO narratives,[2] reincarnation and other esoteric topics like tales dealing with the possibility of communication with the dead and the transmission of spiritual energy.

When military president Galtieri was quickly replaced in 1983 with the last of the military presidents, Bignone, and he in turn gave way to a democratic government in the same year, stories dealing with aliens, New Age subjects and higher civilizations also began to appear in Argentinian folk narrative archives (see Palleiro in Arcaro 2004; Palleiro 2005).

Since these political changes, New Age culture began to gain attention in the mid- and late 1980s, when other perspectives appeared on the Argentinian cultural horizon in addition to the Hispanic Catholic worldview. In this period, in which the idea of Argentina as a multicultural country began to be accepted, these new perspective in folklore began to change the interest in Folklore studies from collectionism to a communicative approach to folk texts, which began to be considered as aesthetic messages oriented towards an audience. In this way both haunted houses and ghosts can be considered as symbolic expressions of new trends in Argentinian folk narrative collections.

Haunted Houses in Argentinean Narrative: From Rural Ranches to Urban Palaces

From 1985 to 1994, I collected a corpus of Argentinean folk narrative in rural areas of La Rioja dealing with haunted houses. One of these narratives dealt with 'A *gaucho* (horseman) who has been fighting with the Devil, there, in La Maravilla'. I collected this tale, whose title belongs to the narrator himself, in 1986. This narrative has several thematic features similar to Aarne-Thompson type 326: The Youth Who Wanted to Learn What Fear Is. The narrator, Cesar Soria, aged 16 when I registered the narrative, classified this tale as a 'case' that had actually happened in that place. This 'case' concerned a *gaucho* who entered a haunted ranch in La Maravilla where a big treasure was hidden. He arrived at this ranch by chance, on his way somewhere else, and once inside decided to remain there for the night. At midnight some parts of a corpse began to fall from the ceiling, one by one, until all the pieces were shaped into a 'devilish body'. As soon as this happened, the *gaucho* was compelled to fight with this personification of the devil. The point of the narrative plot (Labov and Waletzky 1967) is focused on the fight, as can be seen in the following quotation from the story:

So the *gaucho* and the Devil kept on fighting there, in that small ranch of La Maravilla and at last the *gaucho* stabbed a knife here to the Devil [The narrator puts the right hand on his chest] ... As soon as he had done this, the devilish body vanished, and then the *gaucho* went mad ...

It is said that the Aguirre family [who owned the ranch] made a deal with the devil. A treasure has been hidden for years and years in that ranch and a sort of curse was made against anyone who dared to enter, that he was supposed to fight with the devil for a whole night ...

And thus it is said that, from that moment on, people who dare to enter that ranch are scared by such devilish being, and that is why there are 'scares' there, at the Aguirre's, there, in La Maravilla.

This text shows the blending process of a folktale matrix with a local event. In fact, the characters of the narrative are people, such as the members of the Aguirre family, who once lived in the small Argentinian town of La Maravilla. The tale also expresses different aspects of collective belief regarding the supernatural. In fact the narrator includes allusions to group belief in ghostly apparitions. These ghostly apparitions are also metaphoric representations of devilish forces. Such a metaphoric condensation of human beings and supernatural forces can be connected with the animistic beliefs of the La Rioja rural, and even urban, communities, represented in local rituals such as The Salamanca. The Salamanca is actually a local rite regarding a deal with the devil, as another narrator, Marino Cordoba, explains in another text:

the Salamanca is a deal with the Devil, a rite, and also the name of the cave in which this ritual ceremony takes place. The Devil appears in the form of a pig, or a dog, or any other ugly animal, even in human form. The Major Devil appears with the head of a goat the tail of a lion the body of a pig and two arms and two legs, like the limbs of a human being, and the man or the woman makes a deal with the Devil in order to become rich or young, but first, both he and she are supposed to perform some difficult tasks, to fight with devilish beings. (Palleiro 1992)

According to this explanation, such devilish beings, personified in the form of the Major Devil, are connected not only to the Hispanic Catholic religion but also to animistic beliefs in the metaphoric combinations of animal and human beings, along with supernatural forces. These personifications make it possible to perform the ceremony of making a deal with the devil. Such deals are considered terrible sins and are seriously punished by Catholic institutional religion. It is worth mentioning that the Catholic sense of guilt and punishment in the post-mortem life is not even mentioned in these narratives. On the contrary, punishment is suffered in the earthly life by those who dare to enter haunted houses, such as the one mentioned by Cesar Soria, where hidden treasures are protected by devilish forces. In fact, 'the scares' are presented in Soria's narrative not only as ghosts but also as concrete beings who have undergone a sort of animation process.

In his analysis of the dead in Estonian folklore, Valk (2006) documents the relationship between ghostly possession and ownership of land in contemporary Estonian folk narratives. In a similar way, in Argentinean narratives, the aforesaid devilish forces seem to protect local people's possessions from foreign visitors. That is how the hidden treasures of the Aguirres come to be protected from the *gaucho* by a devilish being. Such treasures can be interpreted not only as material possessions but also as symbolic representations of local culture. One of these representations deals with this animistic worldview in which the supernatural dimension is related both to the human and the animal worlds, symbolized by the metonymic figure of the Major Devil, formed by the combination of human arms and legs, animal head and tail, and devilish supernatural forces. Such a worldview shares some features of other aboriginal cultures, along with some New Age elements such as belief in aliens and higher civilizations. Argentinian narratives manifest the generic traits of legend in that narrators tend to add references to reliable witnesses and other verifiable specifics in order to convince a sceptical audience that spirits are real. That is why the Aguirres are widely mentioned along with other witnesses, and also why the narrator adds modal clauses as argumentative resources to convince the audience of the tale's veracity: 'This is absolutely true. Such a strange event did happen in that small ranch, at the Aguirre's...'. The 'truths' emphasized by such modal clauses not only refer to the empirical validation of the event but also to the set of cultural values and beliefs of this rural community. In this way, the narrative message is presented to the audience as an expression of a social identity, the veracity of which is supported by group consensus. In this way the community's voice, introduced in the clause 'it is said in La Maravilla', operates as a source of testimonial authority. Such a clause, reinforced by deictic particles related to the local context, confirms the message's social dimension.[3]

These oral narratives about haunted houses, registered in the rural areas of La Rioja, can also be heard in the urban context of Buenos

Aires. An oral version that I collected in Buenos Aires in 1995 from the narrator, Claudia Ricigliano, aged 31, connects the same narrative pattern to the untimely death of a newly married couple in a tragic accident:

> In Devoto,[4] near the railway station, there is still a large house, almost a palace, with columns and balconies, very well furnished, with a royal atmosphere …
>
> Once, there, there was a wedding party. A young female who lived there married a young guy and the marriage was celebrated in that place. I mean the wedding party. And after the wedding, near midnight, the young female and the guy went out of the house in a car[5] and when they were crossing the railway the train suddenly came across and the car crashed and both of them died immediately …
>
> And from that night on, people say that voices can be heard late at night. Since that moment the house has been abandoned. Time passed, and everything remained there in the house as it was when the young couple was still alive …and it is said to be a haunted house …
>
> Once, a beggar entered the house at night, looking for a place to sleep, and it is said that he saw some human bones falling down from the ceiling, and heard a voice speaking, the soft voice of a young man and then a female voice, and then both of them speaking in a very low voice, and then the bones still falling. So the beggar went away. He didn't dare to take anything. Everything was covered with dust …
>
> And it is said that although the house has been offered both for sale and for rent over many years, no one wants to rent it, nor to buy it, although the price is very low because it is said to be a haunted house since the death of the young couple, in that car accident.

In this narrative, the motif of the corpse dropping in pieces from the ceiling (Thompson H 1411.1) is associated with the untimely death of a young couple in a car accident on the night of their wedding, and is set in the urban context of a luxurious wedding party. The construction of this text's rhetoric combines the synechdotic resource of the corpse's disintegration into different parts with the antithetical dynamics between erotic and thanatic forces. Such opposition can also be observed in the series of narratives referring to the female ghost in the ballroom. Such synechdotic disintegration of the corpse reflects the disorder caused by the tragic accident. As with the series of stories about the female ghost in the ballroom, this narrative about an urban haunted house also contains an allusion to haunting by a woman, the female member of the couple who was also at the ball with her new husband. The difference with the female ghost narrative is that on this occasion the female character was still alive during the ball, and died as soon as she left the ballroom. In spite of these differences, the antithesis between life and death remains the same in both narratives.

Argentinian and Estonian narratives of ghostly possession (Valk 2006) are similar in the respect that in both the ownership of material objects, such as the furniture and the house, remained 'protected' by a ghostly presence in the same way that hidden treasures are protected in the rural narratives. For this reason the beggar didn't dare to take anything away from the haunted house, in the same way that the *gaucho* couldn't find hidden treasure in the ranch at La Maravilla. Ghostly apparitions are in fact connected with chaotic change and social insecurity. Thus, when the young couple dies without the possibility of enjoying life in their large, beautiful house, they become ghosts who continue ownership of the haunted space in the supernatural dimension. A similar thing happens with the Aguirres, who make a deal with the devil in order to protect their human possessions when they are threatened by foreign invasions. In this way, supernatural beings such as the devil, as well as the ghost couple, serve the function of protecting spatial ownership. It is worth mentioning that Argentinian rural narratives about hidden treasure began to appear in the early times of the Spanish invasion, in the fifteenth and sixteenth centuries, when the land where aboriginal groups lived was violently occupied. It is said that the Quechuas, Mapuches and other aboriginal communities managed to hide their treasures before being conquered by the Spanish. In contemporary times, such narratives tended to appear in urban contexts in the 1980s, just after the fall of the last military government; a time in which properties belonging to those who were imprisoned or murdered – most of them young people and even young couples – were taken away from their owners.[6] That is how, in such narratives, supernatural beings like the devil and ghosts served the function of protecting ownership within the context of chaotic social change.

Something similar happened with the narratives about ghosts that began to appear in Argentinian folk archives during the same period.

The Haunting Lady (Female Ghost) in the Ballroom: Rural and Urban Narratives

During the period from 1985 to 1992, I collected stories in both Argentinean urban and rural areas, in total nearly 20 versions of the haunting female narrative pattern, classified alternatively by the narrators as a story, a legend or as a real case. I registered these versions in a folk narrative archive (Palleiro 2004). I considered this narrative pattern, identified by means of the intertextual comparison of different versions, as a matrix. I characterized the folk narrative matrix as a combination of thematic, compositional and stylistic features common to different narratives produced in specific contexts. Regarding the matrix of the female ghost, I reconstructed the following sequences, by means of an intertextual comparison of the aforesaid versions: (1) the meeting of a young female and a young man in a ballroom (or on a road, or in a pub) where they dance, have a drink and talk; (2) the separation of the two near a graveyard when they leave the ballroom; (3) the young man's quest for the young female; (4) the encounter of her grave; and (5) the recognition of the young female as a dead creature, by means of some identification signs in her clothes (a dress or a military coat, an evening gown or even a pair of shoes with a wine or coffee stain). This compositional structure has some thematic features common to Thompson's motif E 322.3.3.1, The Vanishing Hitchhiker. Along with these thematic and compositional similarities, the versions I collected also share some stylistic features, such as the enumerative accumulation of details that serve as signs of recognition (such as the coat, the stain and so on), and the metaphoric identification of the young female with death personified as a feminine character. The antithetical dynamic between life and death is the point of this narrative type, in which the erotic force of love, identified through a tender encounter with a young female in a ballroom, turns out to be an encounter with death in the loneliness of a graveyard.

The female ghost in the rural graveyard

In a rural version that I collected in 1987, the narrator of which was Marta Torres, a middle aged woman from La Rioja, the action was located in a ballroom called La Tierrita (the little dust), ten blocks away from the local graveyard. The precise title of the narrative was La Tierrita Ballroom and the name of the dead young woman was

Amelia. The action was presented as a real case. The narrative's veracity was reinforced by means of an enumerative accumulation of contextual details referred to the local cemetery ('… It has actually happened there, near the graveyard, just ten blocks away from La Tierrita …'). The narrator Marta Torres used such modal clauses as argumentative strategies to persuade the audience of the authenticity of this case, which 'actually happened'. She also added an evaluative clause at the end of the narrative, referring to it as an instrument of regulation of social behaviour. Such regulation has the aim or warning young people about the danger of approaching unknown young women at a dance.[7] Marta Torres also connects the narrative to local beliefs in ghostly apparitions that scare people at night ('… it is said: be careful, avoid going to dances late at night because late at night, near the graveyard, Amelia's soul may appear!'). It is worth noting that, in these narratives, the word soul doesn't refer only to an immaterial spirit in the sense of the Spanish Catholic religion, but as a kind of materialization of spirits in a ghostly shape, associated with local rites, linked to deathly events that may occur in the sexually charged atmosphere of a ballroom.[8] One of these local narratives connected with ritual performances is that of la Telesita. La Telesita is the name of a female character who is said to have been a pretty young woman who also went to a ballroom where she danced until she dropped dead. This type of narrative is linked to a sort of ritual dance performed by different members of the group who act as dancers and musicians. This ritual dance in honour of the young female dancer is called the Telesiada. The performers of this rite keep singing and dancing throughout the night in order to gain the favour of la Telesita, who is considered to be a sort of popular saint capable of performing miracles. In the narrative told by Marta Torres, the sign of recognition of the young female as a dead woman is a wine stain made by a young man, who spilled wine on the female's dress when pouring some onto the earth in La Tierrita ballroom, so called because of the earthly soil of this place. The action of pouring wine onto the earth is connected with a ritual performance that consists of offering a libation to the earthly divinity of the Pachamama, a female goddess who belongs to the sacral universe of Quechua culture.[9] Such ritual action, called the *corpachada*, consists of 'opening' the soil by pouring a libation.

This brief analysis points to the folk narrative pattern's tendency to serve the function of a pre-text, to be transformed by different narrators in different contexts. In this way, each narrator can express the different identity of their own culture by changing contextual details.[10] In this case, the narrator introduces some variations in the general pattern in order to incorporate local beliefs in the narrative text. Such variations can alter the text to the extent of changing the meaning of the whole narrative in order that it fit within the context of the local worldview. In this way, the folk narrative message proves to be an excellent instrument with which to express differential identities of social groups. In fact, the way in which the narrator Marta Torres recreates this narrative pattern – associated with local beliefs that deal with materializations of spirits in a ghostly shape, and other ritual performances well known to members of this specific community, such as libations and sacred dances – expresses different aspects of the culture of this group. In fact, the same narrative pattern is recreated by other narrators in other contexts. By changing some apparently irrelevant details, which can be considered metaphoric signs of the narrator's own culture, such as the ones analysed here in Torres's version, each narrator can express relevant aspects of their own culture.

The female ghost in an urban context

The same female ghost narrative pattern appears in urban legends, such as that related to Rufina Cambacéres. History and fiction are mixed in the case of this narrative, the main character of which is a young woman who lived in the nineteenth century. Rufina was the young daughter of a famous Argentinean writer, Eugene Cambaceres, who died in 1902. According to some accounts she was buried alive after suffering a catalepsy attack. Other versions say that she died of a heart attack when she heard that her fiancée was also her mother's lover. The historic facts are that she died very young, at the age of 19, and was buried in the luxurious Recoleta urban cemetery, in Buenos Aires. The lovely statue placed in front of her tomb, made by the German sculptor Richard Aigner, represents a young female,

> in the attitude of opening the door as if she were about to go out, as she would have needed to that tragic night when she was buried alive, and as she actually does late at night … in the shape of a female ghost, in the luxurious night of Recoleta pubs in Buenos Aires, where her haunting presence can be seen from time to time. (version of Sandra Gómez, student, aged 21, 1996)

Around the historic event of her tragic death, an urban legend sprang up, based on the narrative pattern of The Female Ghost in the Ballroom. Thus it is said in Buenos Aires that some people have seen Rufina as a female ghost dancing at night in the pubs of Recoleta district close to the graveyard, and even returning 'home' to the graveyard before the first light of day appears in the sky. Others state that they have felt and even seen her haunting presence rushing across the intersection of the Vicente López and Azcuénaga streets, past the wall of the graveyard as if she were in a hurry to enter.

Another version of this urban legend is that related by student Santiago Bonacina, aged 24, which I collected in Buenos Aires in 1996:

> And in Recoleta graveyard, there is a legend, the one of Clementina Cambacéres, so this is the name of the dead woman. In a grave there is a statue of a very young girl in an attitude of opening a door. And there was also a young guy, I don't know, they had gone to the ballroom and once they arrived, they kept on dancing for the whole night, he and a girl in a pink silk dress. So, when they were dancing, she stained her dress with some liquid, wine, I think or perhaps coffee, I don't remember. So, then she returns home and he begins the quest, her quest, and he notices that she enters a house near the cemetery, or just there, perhaps. And the day after, he comes across her parent's home and her parents say: 'Our daughter has died, too young, and all.' And the dress was hung just there, in her parent's house, the stained dress. This legend is about a real human being, it is told by the graveyard's guardians of Recoleta cemetery in Buenos Aires, and the statue is a funeral memorial of a young girl who actually died very young, belonging to a traditional family of Buenos Aires. They [the guardians] actually show the grave, the tomb, and the guardians just say: 'here she is, the living dead young lady!'

In this version, Bonacina adds a metanarrative initial clause in which he classifies the narrative as a legend told by the graveyard guardians and connected to the statue at Rufina's grave, the statue representing a young woman 'in an attitude of opening a door'. As I have pointed out, this statue does exist in Recoleta cemetery. Thus, the folk narrative pattern of The Female Ghost in the Ballroom is mixed up with the historic event of the burial of a young female, in the same graveyard in which the folk narrative action takes place. In fact, this female is said to be a living dead woman, buried alive after a catalepsy attack. As mentioned, the real name of this woman was Rufina and not Clementina Cambaceres, as the narrator says. The substitution of such details can be considered an index of the folklorization process within Rufina's history. It is worth mentioning that Mukařovský (1977) in his article 'Detail as the basic semantic unit in folk art', stresses that apparently irrelevant changes in details must be considered the basis of the folkloric construction process. In fact, the substitution of one detail for another is a measure of the contextualization processes of folk patterns. The substitution, as well as the addition of details, acts as a discursive strategy tending to guarantee the dynamic process of contextual transformations. It is by means of the contextual transformations of details that the folk message differentiates the identity of a social group (Palleiro 2004). In this text, the substitution of Rufina with Clementina generates an association with another folkloric character, Clementine, who also died in a tragic way when she was a child, as portrayed in the English ballad in which she first appears and which refers to the events of Clementine's untimely death in poetic stanzas. Rhythm and repetition are the main rhetorical resources of this composition: ('In a cavern, in a canyon/excavating from a mine/ dwelt a miner, forty-niner/and his daughter Clementine/Oh, my darling; oh, my darling; oh my darling Clementine/thou are lost and gone for ever/dreadful sorry, Clementine. Drove she ducklings to the water/every morning, just at nine/hit her foot against the splinter/fell into the foaming brine').

It is important to note that the version given by Bonacina, circulating in Buenos Aires among young students of the Universitary Institute of Folk Arts in 2002, is a tragic version of what was originally a comic ballad. This version suppresses the light hearted references to 'herring boxes without topses' that were 'sandals' for the young girl, as well as all references to the 'kisses' given by the narrator to the 'little sister' instead of Clementine, and focuses attention instead on the tragic end of young Clementine.

Such substitution can be considered a result of the folklorization process. In fact, this detail of the changing name reveals the narrator's association of this tragic event with a folk narrative matrix textualized in a well-known ballad contextualized in an English town, whose protagonist is another young female character, the daughter of a miner. It is worth noting that the urban Argentinean narrator is also a student of Folk art who surely knows this ballad. Thus, he is very likely to associate, in his memory, the historic event of Rufina's tragic death in the urban context of Buenos Aires city with this folk song, relating to the fatal accident of the untimely death of another female character. This substitution is a clear example of the life in variants of oral tradition (Menéndez Pidal 1975). In this way a folk matrix serves as a narrative pattern to recreate a historic event in a poetic way.

The final clause of Bonacina's narrative, referring to the 'living dead' woman, contains a reference to the rhetorical construction of this narrative, based on the opposition between life and death. The sudden disappearance of a young woman, whose life ends at an age when she should be getting married, has a significant impact on the most diverse audiences from widely differing cultures and contexts, both rural and urban. Such opposition between the forces of love and death can be observed in the organization of living space in La Rioja's rural zones, as well as in the architecture of Buenos Aires, where ballrooms, pubs and cafés are situated near the main graveyards. This also happens in other Argentinean burial places such as La Loma graveyard in Mar del Plata city, where tales about the female ghost circulate widely. In Buenos Aires's Recoleta zone there are a particularly large number of places to seek amusement, such as fancy restaurants, pubs and luxurious ballrooms, surrounding the graveyard in a sort of continuum between life and death. And, as Valk (2006) points out referring to Estonian narratives, ghost lore functions as an identity marker for those members of a social group who share certain knowledge concerning the supernatural. The same thing happens in Argentinean narratives like those I have collected in La Rioja, in which both devilish beings and female ghosts seem to protect local ranches and graveyards from 'invasion' by foreigners. That is why Marta Torres includes, in her version, a final clause warning foreigners against approaching graveyards on lonely nights. In the same way, Cesar Soria says that small ranches where hidden treasures could potentially be found are protected against newcomers by 'scares'. Following this pattern, in an urban version of the narrative, a member of the audience adds an interpretative clause concerning the contextual meaning of this narrative as an instrument regulating social behaviour. Such regulation deals with the habit of returning late at night from, for example, balls or pubs. Regulation that is seen to apply especially to young people ('My sister [said] to me: be careful, you might meet the dead woman! Do not return too late from the ball! Be careful, do not go to dance late at night!') In this way, the constructive process of the urban version of the narrative turns out to be that of an aetiological legend, that is to say, a narrative that gives an explanation about causes and effects. The specific version I have discussed refers to the cause of the form, and position, of the funeral memorial of a young female depicted opening a door, which has been placed in the urban cemetery in Recoleta. History and fiction are mixed up in the poetic reconstruction of the tragedy of a living woman buried in that grave. In a larger study (Palleiro 2004) I identified the same folk narrative pattern in daily news regarding other young Argentinean women who were murdered after having gone dancing, such as Valeria Servadio and Maria Soledad Morales.[11] These narratives are constructed around folk patterns within the fictionalization process in which ghosts and haunted houses undergo traumatic conflicts with the living, mirroring historic tragedies like untimely deaths.

Conclusion

These narratives can be thought of as symbolic representations of the supernatural in a society in which the relationship with the dead acts as a metaphoric expression of Argentinean culture. Narratives about haunted houses refer both to the intimate experiences of supernatural contacts with the dead, and to the collective experiences of different aspects of social life, such as the threat foreign invasion poses to the local sense of ownership of vital space. This aspect seems to be a common feature of Estonian narratives (see Valk 2006). Such narratives also express the tension between erotic and deathly forces, symbolized in haunting girls and female ghosts who act as metaphoric illustrations of this paradox. These fictional characters are associated with real people who lived and have a historic dimension. This blending of history and fiction is related to the problem of the poetics of history (White 1973). Folk narrative patterns function both as fictionalization devices for historic narratives, and as devices that connect the fictional world with social context.

The analysis of different versions of the same narrative pattern, or matrix, collected in different contexts, both urban and rural, shows the permeability of each pattern. Thanks to this permeability, these patterns serve as narrative devices that can express identity within heterogeneous Argentinean culture, the distinctive feature of which is a blend of different worldviews. In this way the rural versions from La Rioja, about female ghosts and haunted houses, express the mixture of Hispanic Catholic tradition and indigenous Quechua culture, while at the same time illustrating other manifestations of the supernatural drawn from the contemporary New Age worldview, such as contacts with higher civilizations. They also reflect historic conflicts over earthly ownership and material possessions that are protected by haunted, devilish, places or by female ghosts. Urban versions of the narrative from Buenos Aires show both similarities with, and differences from, rural versions, and these changes are related to the changing processes of narrative patterns within local and global contexts.

The way of collecting these narratives in Argentinean folk narrative archives is also affected by different trends within Folkloristics. In fact, in the first general archives, influenced by the historic-geographic method of the Finnish school, topics such as haunting female ghosts and haunted houses were not considered serious; in these collections only the *Märchen* was considered a main narrative genre.[12] The proposal of a communicative approach to folk narrative, present in *Toward New Perspectives in Folklore* (Paredes and Bauman 1972), encouraged contemporary Argentinean folklorists to include new topics in their archives, such as female ghosts and haunted houses, along with UFO narratives and tales of contact with higher civilizations, as well as other manifestations of the supernatural. In addition, folk narratives began to be collected not only in rural but also in urban contexts, where female ghosts seem to be seen rather frequently, walking in the streets, dancing in ballrooms or drinking wine, beer or coffee in city pubs (near graveyards). In these contexts there are also haunted houses, most of them larger than those of the rural areas where the devil protects hidden treasures. Urban ghosts are perhaps more polite than those of the rural ranches.

Finally, Argentinean folk narrative's attention to ghosts and haunted houses tells us something not only about death, but also about Argentina's heterogeneous, living, culture.

Notes

1. Such feelings of guilt, documented in Estonian legends (Valk 1999) in connection with a Lutheran mentality, can also be found in Argentinean tales connected to the Hispanic Catholic conception of the supernatural world.

2. Such narratives about contact with higher civilizations, UFO topics, aliens and other esoteric subjects, recently documented by Parente in fieldwork in Argentinean rural areas of San Juan, can often be found in a sort of heterogeneous narrative mixture with folklore patterns such as the 'deal with the Devil' (Palleiro in Fischman and Hartmann 2007; Palleiro 2008).

3. As Oring (2008: 127) points out, legend employs and extensive rhetoric in establishing its credibility. He considered that the genre of legend has

been long defined in relation to truth and belief. Revisiting the analysis of legend scholars, he provides a comprehensive description of the tropes of this rhetoric, based on Aristotle's categories of persuasion. As a result of this analysis, he wisely proposes the abandonment of the truth and belief criteria of analysis in favour of a performance of truth realized with this rhetoric. In fact, the rhetorical construction of oral versions of the haunted house and the female ghost is based on a 'performance of truth' oriented towards persuading the audience of each tale's credibility.

4. Devoto is a district of Buenos Aires.

5. In Argentinean wedding celebrations it is rather usual for the newly married couple to disappear in the middle of the party, while all the guests keep on dancing until dawn.

6. It is worth remembering that one of the main slogans of the electoral campaign of President Alfonsín, who replaced the last military president Reynaldo Bignone, was 'we are the life', an implicit opposition to the 'deathly' period of the military governments.

7. Other versions, such as a urban version that I collected in 1992 in Buenos Aires from Laura Azcurra, aged 17, reinforce the warnings that are given about getting in touch with unknown women by referring to the young female as a foreigner ('a Brazilian young woman, a *garota*, She was not from here, nobody knew her, the boy approached her anyway …').

8. In the same sense, other narrators refer to 'scares' as if they were almost living creatures, or at least metonymic materializations of the result provoked by the agent that caused fear.

9. In Quechua, *Pachamama* means 'Mother earth'.

10. Mukařovský (1977), in his work *Detail as the Basic Semantic Unit in Folk Art*, points out the extent to which the changing of a single detail can give a new sense to a folklore text.

11. The tragic history of Maria Soledad Morales was also fictionalized in a film entitled *The Maria Soledad Case*. In another article (Palleiro 1998) I identified the folk pattern of The Female Ghost in the constructive process of this film, as well as in the daily news.

12. These collections are the 1921 folkloric survey and the first and second series of *Argentinean Folktales* by Susana Chertudi, published in the 1960s. The third of these general collections, that of Vidal de Battini, was the first to include only two volumes of legends in a nine-volume collection, devoted mainly to rural folk narrative expressions. In this collection, the topics dealt with in this paper do appear, although they are not considered as relevant in this archive, in which the *Märchen*, along with animal tales, are the most important texts.

References

Aarne, A. and Thompson, S. (1961) *The Types of the Folktale: A Classification and Bibliography*. *FF Communications No. 184*. Helsinki: Academia Scientiarum Fennica.

Arcaro, M. d. C. (ed.) (2004) *Contar y bailar. Recreaciones literarias y trasposiciones coreográficas a partir de la narrativa tradicional*. Buenos Aires: Dunken.

Bauman, R. (1972) Differential identity and the social base of folklore. In A. Paredes and R. Bauman (eds) *Toward New Perspectives in Folklore*, 31–41. Austin, TX and London: The University of Texas Press.

Bauman, R. (1975) Verbal art as performance. *American Anthropologist* 77 (2): 290–311.

Chertudi, S. (1960) *Cuentos Folklóricos de la Argentina. Primera Serie*. Buenos Aires: Ediciones del Instituto Nacional de Filología y Folklore.

Chertudi, S. (1964) *Cuentos Folklóricos de la Argentina. Segunda Serie*. Buenos Aires: Ediciones del Instituto Nacional de Antropología.

Colección de Folklore. Encuesta Folklórica del Consejo Nacional de Educación a los Maestros de las Escuelas Ley Láinez (1921) Buenos Aires: Hemeroteca del Instituto Nacional de Antropología y Pensamiento Latinoamericano.

Derrida, J. (1997) *Mal de Archivo. Una Impresión Freudiana*. Madrid: Trotta.

Jakobson, R. (1964) Closing statement: linguistics and poetics. In T. A. Sebeok (ed.) *Style in Language*, 350–377. Cambridge, MA: MIT Press.

Labov, W. and Waletzky, J. (1967) Narrative analysis: Oral versions of personal experience. In J. Helms (ed.) *Essays on the Verbal and Visual Art*. Seattle, WA and London: University of Washington Press.

Menéndez Pidal, R. (1975) *Poesía juglaresca y juglares*. Madrid: Espasa-Calpe.

Mukařovský, J. (1977) Detail as the basic semantic unit in folk art. In J. Burbank and P. Steiner (eds and trans) *The Word and Verbal Art. Selected Essays by Jan Mukařovský*, 180–204. New Haven, CT and London: Yale University Press.

Oring, Elliott (2008) Legendry and the rhetoric of truth. *Journal of American Folklore* 121 (480): 127–166.

Palleiro, M. I. (1992) La Salamanca en una situación particular de entrevista. *Revista de Investigaciones Folklóricas* 7: 52–62.

Palleiro, M. I. (1993) La dinámica de la variación en el relato oral tradicional riojano. Procedimientos discursivos de construcción referencial de la narrativa folklórica. Síntesis de los planteos principales de la Tesis de Doctorado. *Formes Textuelles et Matériau Discursif: Rites, Mythes et Folklore, Sociocriticism* IX, 2, 18: 177–182. Montpellier.

Palleiro, M. I. (1998) 'El caso María Soledad': genética, historia y folklore. Hacia un estudio genético de las transformaciones de una matriz folklórica en un texto fílmico. In *Actas del II Congreso Latinoamericano de Folklore del Mercosur y VI Jornadas Nacionales de Folklore,* 27–39. Buenos Aires: Editorial Agustina.

Palleiro, M. I. (2000) Death in the ballroom: Orality and hypertexts in Argentinean folk narrative. *Fabula* 41 (3): 257–268.

Palleiro, M. I. (2004) *Fue una historia real. Itinerarios de un archivo.* Buenos Aires: Ediciones del Instituto de Filología y Literaturas Hispánicas 'Amado Alonso' de la Universidad de Buenos Aires.

Palleiro, M. I. (2005) Narrativa: identidades y memorias. In M. I. Palleiro (ed.) *Colección Narrativa, identidad y memoria* 3: 280. Buenos Aires: Dunken ediciones.

Palleiro, M. I. (2008) Archives of Argentinean folk narrative: Trends, topics and history of Argentinean folkloristics. *ISFNR Newsletter* 3: 20–28.

Palleiro, M. I. (2007) La Salamanca en representaciones icónicas: *performance* narrativa y discurso visual. In F. Fischman and L. Hartmann (eds) *Donos da Palabra: autoria, performance e experiencia em narrativas orais da América do Sul,* 157–189. Brasil: Editora da Universidade Federal de Santa María.

Palleiro, M. I. (2008) *Yo creo. Vos sabés? Retóricas del creer en los discursos sociales.* Buenos Aires: Facultad de Filosofía y Letras de la Universidad de Buenos Aires.

Paredes, A. and Bauman, R. (1972) *Toward New Perspectives in Folklore.* Austin, TX and London: University of Texas Press.

Parente, P. (2005) Géneros discursivos y creencia: OVNIs, abducciones y divulgación científica. In M. I. Palleiro (ed.) *Narrativa: Identidades y Memorias,* 237–254. Buenos Aires: Dunken.

Pinon, R. (1965 [1961]) *El cuento foklórico como tema de estudio.* Buenos Aires: EUDEBA.

Propp, V. (1972) *Morfología del cuento.* Buenos Aires: Akal.

Thompson, S. (1993) *Motif-Index of Folk Literature. New Enlarged and Revised Edition.* Copenhagen and Bloomington, IN (CDRom): Indiana University Press/InteLex Corporation.

Valk, Ü (1999) Traditional legends in contemporary Estonian Folklore. In M. R. MacDonald (ed.) *Traditional Storytelling Today: An International Sourcebook,* 207–211. Chicago, IL and London: Fitzroy Dearborn.

Valk, Ü (2006) Ghostly possession and real estate: The dead in contemporary Estonian folklore. *Journal of Folklore Research* 43 (1): 31–51.

Vidal de Battini, B. E. (1980–1984) *Cuentos y leyendas populares de la Argentina.* Buenos Aires: Ediciones Culturales Argentinas.

Watson, S. M. and Herrera, N. A. (1996) *De duendes, ánimas y otras historias.* Córdoba: Narvaja Editor.

White, H. (1973) The poetics of history. In H. White, *Metahistory,* 81–130. Baltimore, MD and London: The Johns Hopkins University Press.

Angels in Norway: Religious Border-crossers and Border-markers

Ingvild Sælid Gilhus*

Introduction

On 25 July 2007, one of the BBC news headlines on the Internet was 'Norway princess "talks to angels"'. The day before, the story had made the front pages of all the Norwegian national newspapers. In the BBC version it read as follows:

> Norway's Princess Märtha Louise says she has psychic powers and can teach people to communicate with angels. The 35-year-old daughter of King Harald and Queen Sonja made the announcement on a website promoting her plans for a new alternative therapy centre. She says she realised as a child that she could read people's inner feelings, while her experiences with horses had helped her make contact with angels. Princess Martha Louise is fourth in line to the Norwegian throne. The royal palace says it has no official link to the princess' planned alternative therapy centre, the AFP news agency reports. The princess, who trained as a physical therapist, says on the website for her Astarte Education centre that she has 'always been interested in alternative forms of treatment'. Students at her centre, she says, will learn how to 'create miracles' in their lives and harness the powers of their angels, which she describes as 'forces that surround us and who are a resource and help in all aspects of our lives'. 'It was while I was taking care of the horses that I got in contact with the angels,' she says. 'I have lately understood the value of this important gift and I wish to share it with other people, maybe with you.' A three-year programme at her centre costs 24,000 Norwegian crowns ($4,150; 3,000 Euros; £2,000) per year.

For several weeks during the summer of 2007 the media in Norway feasted on the princess and her business partner's planned therapy centre. National know-alls, scholars and religious people from

* Ingvild Sælid Gilhus is Professor of Religion at the University of Bergen, Norway.

various backgrounds were asked for their opinions. In the autumn, the alternative therapy centre started as planned and in the main the debate faded out. However, for the time being and for different reasons angels have been revitalized in Norway, not only in Astarte Education and various spiritual movements and therapy centres, but in the Norwegian Church as well.

This chapter will focus on the meaning of angels in contemporary religious discourse in Norway, and especially on their function as religious border-crossers (Ahn 2006) and border-markers. The source material is varied, encompassing circular letters from the Norwegian Church, research based on interviews about belief in angels among employees of the Norwegian Church and among 'ordinary' people, books, and media (especially newspaper) debates. The material dates mainly from the 1990s and later, following the impact since that time of what has been called the 'religion of angels' (Gardella 2007: 93) on popular religiosity, widely perceived as the result of American influence. The approach is a cultural analysis with stress on a discourse perspective.

At the heart of the chapter are the negotiations that are taking place between 'official' and 'popular religion' in relation to angels, as well as the flexibility of angels and their fluctuation between metaphor and reality in contemporary Norwegian discourse.

Norway – a secular society?

In Norway, 83% of the population are members of The Norwegian Church *(Den norske kirke)*, which professes the Lutheran branch of Christianity. A 2005 Gallup Institute survey of 65 countries found that Norway was the least religious among the Western countries surveyed. Only 36% of the population considered themselves religious, while 46% considered themselves neither religious nor atheists. However, even if only 3% attend church services or other religious meetings more than once a month, 73.5% of all infants were baptized in the Church in 2007, 44% of weddings took place there, and 93% of the funerals. It is not only characteristic for Nordic people to 'belong without believing', but also to believe in belonging (Anders Bäckström quoted in Davie 2007: 33, note 8). As Davie comments:

> Nordic populations, for the most part, remain members of their Lutheran churches; they use them extensively for the occasional offices (including in this case baptism and marriage) and regard membership as

part of national just as much as religious identity. More pertinently for the churches themselves, Nordic people continue to pay appreciable amounts of tax to their churches – resulting, among other things, in large numbers of religious professionals (not least musicians) and beautifully maintained buildings in even the tiniest village. The cultural aspects of religion are well cared for. That does not mean, of course, that Nordic populations attend their churches with any frequency or necessarily believe in the tenets of Lutheranism. Indeed, they appear on every comparative scale to be among the least believing and least practising populations in the world. (Davie 2007: 25)

So even if Norway, together with the other Scandinavian countries, is usually counted as one of the most secular societies in the world, the importance of the sense of belonging to the Church should not be underestimated.

At the same time there has been a growth in alternative spiritual beliefs. One out of four Norwegians has been in contact with New Age related activities. If one categorizes as New Agers those who believe in the majority of such ideas as astrology, reincarnation, Karma, fortune telling and spiritism, approximately 15% of the Norwegian population belong to this category. In comparison, people who both believe in a personal god and see Jesus Christ as their saviour – the church religious – consist of approximately 20% of the population (Botvar 2006: 2). As in other countries in the Western world, there has been in Norway in recent years a significant turn within the New Age in the direction of therapies and alternative medicine.

Angels and the Norwegian Church

Angels were introduced into Norway with the Christianization of the country about one thousand years ago. The worship of the archangel Michael especially had much support in the middle ages and 28 churches were consecrated to him, most of them near Oslo (Luthen 1999). Neither the introduction of Lutheran Protestantism in 1537 nor the age of reason nor the breakthrough of science did the angels much good. Dean J. L. Quisling published a book about angels in 1889 with the title, *Om Aanderne eller Englene efter Den hellige Skrifts Lære* (About the Spirits or the Angels According to the Teaching of the Holy Writ). According to Quisling, 'we most certainly must assume that these entities exist' (Quisling 1889: 71). The author creates a peculiar image of a nightly landscape, dimly lit, and claims that it is only in this twilight that angels may now be seen. They belong to the 'night side of life', no longer to the light of the sun (Quisling 1889: 36–37). These beings, traditionally seen as beings of light, metaphorically speaking and rather paradoxically, had been forced into darkness.

In the twentieth century angels were in the main restricted to the sphere of childhood, to Sunday schools and Christmas celebrations in which the religious, the popular and the childlike met. Since the 1990s angels have experienced a renaissance in Norway. Angels are part of popular belief as well as being promoted by the state church. There is, however, a tension between the belief in angels nourished by popular religion and the efforts made by representatives of the Church to bring the belief in angels under control. It appears that these intermediate beings are currently employed to mark the boundaries between Lutheran Protestantism and popular religion.

There is, as far as I know, no special teaching about angels in the main theological faculties in Norway,[1] and their roles are seldom part of the preaching in the Norwegian Church.[2] That does not mean that the Church is indifferent towards angels. On the contrary, in recent years there has been a new interest in them. One of the testimonies of this new concern is a book, *Engelen ved din side* (The Angel at Your Side), written by Øystein Bjørdal and Olav Skjevesland in 1994, both then at the Norwegian School of Theology in Oslo. Bjørdal is now a dean, while Skjevesland is one of the 11 bishops of the Church. According to them, the angels live 'at the outskirts of our theology and on the edge of the divine service' (Bjørdal and Skjevesland 1994: 26). The authors warn against New Age and that it may capture the interest in angels, declaring that angels should be kept 'as a real Christian concern' (Bjørdal and Skjevesland 1994: 23). Bjørdal and Skjevesland signal a clear wish to define religious borderlines in the shape of correct and incorrect views of angels.

The Norwegian Church followed up the wish to maintain angels as a 'real Christian concern' when it reintroduced Michaelmas (29 September) as a trial project in 1999, its celebration having been discontinued with the Struensee reform in Denmark-Norway in 1770. According to tradition, not only did Michael defend Christians against pagans and act as a protector of knights and soldiers, but in the sixteenth and seventeenth centuries he was also cast as the special guardian angel of exorcists and witch hunters (Luthen 1999: 64). Michael was for these reasons an obvious choice when the Church wanted supernatural aid against what it regards as the new superstitions. The liturgical committee (*Nemd for gudstjenesteliv*) said: 'In a time which is strongly preoccupied with the invisible part of reality and the supernatural, it is important that the church does not neglect its own strong biblical tradition and leave the field to speculations characterised by New Age and superstition' (Garlid 2005: 39). The counsellor for liturgical questions in the Norwegian Church says, referring to the biblical material, that 'in our close to post-Christian time we are in a similar situation. The same spiritual battle (*åndskamp*) comes to a head. The character of Michael can be useful as a figurative condensation of central motives in this battle.'[3] In a circular letter from the Church Council (*Kirkerådet*), the themes that were particularly stressed in relation to the churchly celebration of Michaelmas – which includes not only Michael, but all the angels – strike a balance between the conception of angels as cosmic fighters, and as God's servants who help humans. The eight themes that were stressed in the circular letter were the cosmic fight between good and evil; the Christological roots of the fight against and victory over evil; the archangel Michael and his role; the angels' hymn of praise before the throne of God; angels as God's servants who help humans; guardian angels; prayer for their help; and thanksgiving to God who has made the angels and sent them to help humans (Circular letter No. 5, 1999).

The guidelines for Michaelmas can also be regarded as guidelines for the angelology of the Norwegian Church, a point that has been stressed by the historian of religions Line Sæther Garlid (Garlid 2005). She interviewed 16 people: eight priests and eight people who were employed in different ways in Lutheran congregations in Bergen and Stavanger. The theme of her thesis was their conception of angels. According to Garlid's findings, 11 informants believed in angels. There was a general belief that good and evil forces fought against each other in the world and that angels were protectors in this battle. It was unclear whether the informants believed that angels acted as messengers today, but they believed that humans may act as angels. The most common stories about angels were that they watched over people and prevented accidents. The informants did not pray to angels, but one of them thought that it was possible. They agreed that there was a close relationship between angels and children and referred to the teaching in Sunday schools. Punitive angels were not important for any of the informants. Garlid's conclusion was that 'the Norwegian Church has no defined angelology and the theme of angels is to a very small degree taught in the theological education of the Norwegian Church. The result is that one finds different conceptions and attitudes towards angels in the Norwegian Church' (Garlid 2005: 113).

Garlid is obviously right. These interviews also show that it is now legitimate to speak about angels. In a series by the main channel of the Norwegian broadcasting system (NRK 1) broadcast over four Sundays in Advent 2007, Paul Erik Wirgenes, who is responsible for religious education in the Lutheran Church, interviewed four people about their experiences with angels (*Vårt Land* 14.12.2007). One catechist told him about her four-year-old daughter who had been woken up in the middle of the night by an angel: 'He looked like a man, but had no feathers!' The visit of the angel hindered a fire in the house. A missionary and member of the Pentecostal movement recounted an experience from his childhood, when he had been out on thin ice, and an angel had rescued him. A special adviser for peace in a church help organization (*Kirkens nødhjelp*), talked about his experience with an angel in Ecuador. The Indians waylaid his car, but a shining angel appeared at its bonnet and frightened the Indians into not attacking the car. A theologian talked about an experience in a theological seminar in Dublin where a stranger came in, sat for a while and then disappeared. The stranger had threadbare clothes, there were no lights or wings, although he represented a turning point at the seminar and was seen as a special messenger from God – an angel.

In these cases, angels are present in situations of acute danger or in relation to a special challenge. They still belong to the children's sphere, at least two of them do, but two of the angels appeared in other settings. One revealed himself in a situation which can easily be interpreted as a conflict between civilization (Christians) and wilderness (Indians); the other appeared in a theological seminar and the interpretation of the event does not reveal if the participants thought that a superhuman being really was present or if the man who appeared in the seminar was seen as a human being who functioned as an angel. Whether angels are 'real' or a way of interpreting turning points often remains deliberately vague. In the last case they are usually more than a turn of phrase, but less than a superhuman agent (see below). These four stories keep the angels within the limits of what the Church allows angels to be and do.

The book by Skjevesland and Bjørdal, the introduction of Michaelmas and the interviews about angels on prime-time television reflect the fact that representatives of the Norwegian Church use angels rather consciously to promote faith, show God's presence in the world and at the same time try to keep these supernatural entities at a safe distance from New Age mischief. According to the Church angels are the messengers of God, fight on God's side against evil, give protection, but are not independent spiritual beings and should not be prayed to. The conceptions of angels should, according to the Church, be kept within these limits.

In several ways the angels who are promoted and controlled by the Church are similar to what Hermann Usener, a German specialist on Roman religions, defined as *Augenblicksgötter* (1896) – 'momentary gods'. These entities exist only for a certain purpose, and only then and there. According to Usener, *Funktionsgötter* later replaced *Augenblicksgötter*. If we leave out the evolutionary framework, Usener's categories can be applied to contemporary angels. The angels conceived by representatives of the Church are only available at the moment they are present, and their further existence is not accessible. They are momentary gods. The archangels Rafael, Gabriel and Michael, are more like *Funktionsgötter* in the Usenerian terminology – Michael, as we have already seen, has some well-defined functions.

Vernacular Religion and Spirituality

The stories about angels referred to above are in line with the angelology of the Norwegian Church. There is, however, a huge field of conceptions and experiences of angels where the division between Church religiosity, popular beliefs and New Age/alternative spirituality is not easy to draw. New Age/alternative spirituality is often seen as the contemporary version of popular religion, at the same time as its continuity with Church religion can be stressed (Sutcliffe 2006). If the concept 'popular religion' designates the religiosity of ordinary people, who do not belong to an intellectual or religious elite, we may say that popular religion today gets strong impulses from Christianity on the one hand as well as from spokespersons for new religious movements/New Age/alternative spirituality on the other. The result is religious popular conceptions that contain both traditional Christian ideas (Lutheran and other) and ideas with non-Christian origins.

Folklorist Hege Kristin Arnesen wrote a Master's thesis about contemporary beliefs in angels (Arnesen 2007) in which she employed a comparative historical perspective. She did not, however, compare the contemporary belief in angels with earlier belief in angels, but with nature spirits in old Norwegian farming society, such as ghosts of the sea (*draug*), nixes (*nøkk* – water spirits) and wood nymphs (*hulder*), because these were then more prominent in folk belief than angels.

Arnesen interviewed 18 people with different beliefs and views of life. The point of the analysis was to present a variety of experiences of angels, independent of the religious belonging of the informants. The result was personal stories about situations in which the informants had experienced angels, the function of their experiences, and how these experiences had affected them.

The nature spirits were collective and traditional, connected with nature and farming society. They controlled and established borders. Humans made contact with them by means of rituals and formulae. They had functions in relation to individuals and society and were seen as both good and evil. Contemporary angels in popular belief are to a higher degree than nature spirits personal beings that humans contact by means of prayer and meditation (Arnesen 2007: 14). Angels also contact humans to help and save them in dangerous situations, which nature spirits did not. Angels are conceived as kind and as personal helpers, and they are based on personal experiences. And, we may add, they are momentary gods rather than intermediate beings and messengers. Unlike nature spirits, they are not concerned with maintaining borders.

Some of the conceptions of angels can more directly be related to New Age/spirituality, because they appear explicitly in this context. A mediator of New Age/spirituality in Norway is the organization *Alternativt nettverk* (Alternative Network), established in 1992.[4] The founder of *Alternativt nettverk* is Øyvind Solum. Solum combines a belief in the variety within the alternative movement with a belief in the existence of common ideas that unify the field. Solum believes in angels. In an interview with the Christian newspaper *Vårt Land* (25.08.07), Solum says that he met angels in the form of light beings when he was a child. He was then a Christian, but after having lived through an atheistic phase, he now belongs to the alternative movement. He still sees angels – they come to him in situations when he needs extra support. After a friend of his committed suicide by jumping from a roof, Solum saw angels come and take the dead man's soul away. According to Solum angels are spirits that make contact with humans, so that they shall experience God. In other words, they act in a traditional role as intermediate beings. Encounters with angels are, according to him, basic human experiences.

One important example of a new religious movement that has developed a systematic angelology is Anthroposophy. Except for Switzerland, Norway is probably the society in the world where Anthroposophy has been most significant. In Norway, the Anthroposophical Society nursed a belief in angels long before this belief was revitalized in the Church. The anthroposophists have developed a well-defined angelology and kept the belief in angels alive and kicking since the organization was founded. This belief seems to have received a boost during recent years. The Anthroposophical journal, *Libra*, had an edition about angels in 2002, and several of Rudolf Steiner's lectures about angels have been published in Norwegian recently (Steiner 1998, 2000). According to these lectures, angels and spiritual hierarchies participate in the lives of individuals and in the development of humanity and the cosmos. Every human being has a guardian angel, with whom one can get in touch through dreams and meditation. Guardian angels are present in childhood, but gradually recede so that the conscious ego shall continue the work of the angels. The idea of a connection between children and angels is important and is transmitted in the Steiner schools. These schools may have had some influence on the general conception of angels – ca. 2% of the population in Norway (pupils, parents, teachers) have been affected by Steiner educational science.[5]

Both Solum and the anthroposophists take Christian mythology as their point of departure. At the same time their conceptions of angels include more than the Norwegian Church does. In New Age/spirituality there are further synonymizations of angels with intermediate beings in other religions, such as gods, devas or fairies. Such synonymizations and syncretisms are also at work in Astarte Education.

Astarte Education and the Princess's Angels

The alternative therapy centre, Astarte Education, started in the autumn 2007 with the motto: 'Use angels and your own power to create miracles in your life' (http://www.astarte-education.com/eng/ (visited 10.08.10)). In the first year of the three-year course, the students learn about readings, in the second about healings and in the third about hands-on treatment. Angels are called upon to contribute to all these subjects. The name of the school refers to an old

Middle-Eastern fertility goddess, Astarte, who according to the Internet presentation of the school, is closely identified with Middle-Eastern, Mediterranean and Old Norse goddesses. There is clearly a syncretistic and universalistic aspect to the school. The princess, a trained physio-therapist and a Rosen Method Practitioner (a method established by Marion Rosen in California, according to which tension is regarded as old memories), and her business partner Elisabeth Samnøy, who has qualifications in Reiki, have both studied at the Holistic Academy in Oslo (an institution which no longer exists). According to the school's Internet presentation, there are angels, or light-beings, in all religions. They represent energies that always surround us, and are a resource and a source of help in all aspects of life:

> We at ASTARTE EDUCATION can give you tools to communicate with your angels and utilise them in your daily life. In our courses you will have the possibility to learn how to discover your inner source of truth and renew the natural contact you have with the angels and the divine Universe. The result will depend on your own approach and openness.

The focus on the self, the belief in spiritual helpers, the therapeutic approach to the individual and a universalistic approach to religion characterize the school. In Norway, people have not been much accustomed to private enterprises in the religious field. Religious services are paid through the tax bill. When the princess sells angel education, she gives the education credibility both by claiming that she is able to communicate with angels (and horses) and because of her social position. One could also argue that the Norwegian king's position as the head of the Church and the royal family's support of the Church, contribute to give credibility to Märtha's angels.

Several of the alternative therapists who were interviewed in the newspapers in the wake of the exposure of Astarte Education were happy to talk about flowering businesses in the wake of the angel school (Kraft 2008). When the book *Seeing Angels*, written by Emma Heathcote-James, was translated into Norwegian in 2007, the publishers gave it the title *Märthas engler* (Märtha's Angels) and put a picture of the princess on the cover. The princess took the publishing company to court. The company had to remove the picture, but was allowed to keep the title. The book was on the bestselling lists in Norway in December 2007 (Kraft 2008: 125).

Commercialization usually does something to a product. When religion is sold, some things are more marketable than others (Mikaelsson 2001). In the Jewish/Christian tradition angels were organized into hierarchies and could be quite scary. In Genesis, cherubim hid the access to Paradise with flaming swords. In the Revelation of John, angels punish humans in terrible ways. Contemporary angels, unlike the old ones, tend to be personal, close to humans, safe and helpful, even in small things. This type of 'user friendly' angel is obviously more saleable than biblical cherubs and punishing angels, or at least this is the case in some media. When angels are reinterpreted in literature, other traits can be stressed. The terrible side of cherubim comes to the fore in, for instance, the Norwegian author Karl O. Knausgaard's novel, *A Time to Every Purpose Under Heaven* (2008), which is a novel about the nature of angels and the ways of men.

The media exposure of Astarte Education was followed by a huge media debate. During this debate, the contemporary religious landscape in Norway appeared both as rather confused and as undergoing changes. The historian of religions Siv Ellen Kraft sorted the debaters roughly into three groups: (1) Supporters of a critical and secular discourse; (2) Christian critics; (3) Representatives of New Age/popular religion (Kraft 2008: 128–30). The secularists, those who believe in enlightenment, rationality and science, offered similar arguments against Astarte Education to those that have been offered against new religions since antiquity: They are new, dangerous, expensive, morally suspect and ridiculous. The Christian critics, especially low church ones, varied from encouraging people to pray for the princess, to claiming that she should resign her membership in the Church, or alternatively give up her royal title. Some characterized the princess as naïve and stupid, others condemned her to hell. The bishops were more careful, one invited her to dialogue, another warned against using angels for self-development. Representatives of New Age/popular religion spoke in support of the princess. They believed in angels, some had communicated with them and had supernatural experiences of them. The debate about the princess's angels was used both to mark the borders between the Church and popular religion, as well as between the secular elite and the credulity of ordinary people. One of the most peculiar things with the media debate was, in the words of Kraft: 'The journalists' angel coverage started with an idea of New Age as extremely special and almost peculiar or strange and ended with the headlines "half of Norway supports Märtha"' (Kraft 2008: 133). According to one of the main Norwegian tabloids, VG, four out of ten Norwegians believe in angels.[6] The princess's angels are typical of how such superhuman beings are conceived of in popular religion in Norway today.

Angels, Language and Religion

In popular belief in angels, the Western idea of the one god who can communicate with human beings by means of superhuman messengers is mixed with an idea of the human self as divine, and spiritual helpers are called upon to aid people in their self-development. Angels have come closer to humans, become more like humans and are part of a religious universe that is less determined by religious authorities and more by ordinary people and their religious needs. This universe represents a sort of democratization of religion. It may reflect a movement away from church religion and a hierarchy of people and beliefs, towards a subjectivization of religion (Heelas and Woodhead 2005). Perhaps because monotheism is connected to strong religious institutions, when these institutions are weakened, a more polytheistic worldview will occur, similar to what is happening in Norway today. The Lutheran Church, which has not been good at upholding contact with popular religious beliefs, is today, due to a lapse in authority, forced to take such beliefs more seriously than it has done, and to a certain degree more actively incorporate them in its religious language and belief system. In this process both an opening up and a maintenance of borders are visible.

The Norwegian Church talks rather poetically about 'The Church and the religious yearning in our time' (Laugerud 1999), which was the title of a report sent to the Church meeting in 1999. The Church sees this religious yearning as a challenge. It wants among other things to develop a more inclusive language to cater for some of the religious experiences and thoughts that people have, but at the same time draw a firm line against New Age beliefs.

Angels are part of contemporary religious language. They vary from being a phrase, a way of speaking, to being conceived of as physical or mental realities. Angels live their lives in language, which raises the question of how the references of this language ought to be interpreted. One puzzling expression is 'angel watch' (*englevakt*), which must be distinguished from guardian angel (*skytsengel*). Angel watch is, I think, a more vague expression than guardian angel.

Norwegian newspapers use the term regularly to describe and partly explain accidents in which the victims have narrow escapes. In December 2007 the expression was used about 14 different accidents, mainly road accidents: 'had angel watch when was hit by a car/bus/ train'. The expression stresses that the rescue was conceived of as somewhat miraculous. It is uncertain whether the journalists or the victim really believed that winged creatures were involved. However, the expression leaves open the possibility that a divine providence exists, without specifying what this implies (cf. Alver 1999: 185).

A similar ambiguity is at work when death notices for babies in the newspapers sometimes state: 'A small angel to us came, smiled gently and turned around.' It is unclear if the angel is a metaphor for the baby or if the reference should be taken literally, with the implication that babies who have died really become angels. The Church, however, does not support a literal interpretation of such expressions. According to its theology, people do not become angels.

Conclusion

Religious language is demanding. Angels fluctuate between reality and metaphor, and are not theologically well defined. In addition, angels may challenge the Christian version of monotheism, at least if they start to act on their own. Monotheism, however, is not only a theological affair it has been a broader modern concern as well. It is a way of defining Western religious tradition in contrast to non-Western, and binding secularized people to a common 'civil religion' (Smith 2001: 11). The term god is religious as well as secular and easy to refer to, even if there is no belief in the superhuman entity to which it refers. Norway has an ideal of being an egalitarian society in which there is a certain accord in the public discourse about significant subjects, secular as well as religious. The polarized discussion about angels in the media revealed that to talk about them in the way that Märtha and others did is not generally accepted.

The angels and the quarrel over them illustrate the relationship and the confrontation between traditional religion and a broader spiritualization and individualization of religion. Astarte Education is a symptom of the contemporary religious situation in Norway. Märtha Louise's marriage and baptism of her two children took place within the Church. At the same time she promotes New Age beliefs such as holism, alternative therapies, female goddesses, energies and belief in angels. Because she is difficult to place in terms of her religious affiliations, she epitomizes the religiosity of a large proportion of people in Norway today and reflects blurred lines between liberal Christianity and New Age (cf. Kraft 2008: 125).

From a wider perspective, the debate about Astarte Education reflects religious processes in which religious globalization of a New Age/spirituality type encircles and confronts Lutheranism and national churches. In this situation the Norwegian Church has employed angels to cater for lay people's renewed interest in intermediate superhuman beings, and thus renew its contact with popular religious beliefs. At the same time it has made angels, and especially Michael, spiritual guardians against the angel craze of New Age and popular religion.

Notes

1. Professor Halvor Moxnes (University of Oslo) and professor Jan-Olav Henriksen (The Norwegian School of Theology) have kindly given me this information.

2. Åge Haavik. The Church Council's adviser in liturgical questions (http://www.kirken.no/?event=doLink&famID=2028 (visited 10 August 2010)).

3. Åge Haavik. The Church Council's adviser in liturgical questions (http://www.kirken.no/?event=doLink&famID=2028 (visited 10 August 2010)).

4. In addition to publishing the magazine *Visjon*, the *Alternativt nettverk* organization also arranges alternative fairs – *Alternativmesser*.

5. The first Steiner school in Norway was opened in 1926. Today there are 34 Steiner schools and 35 kindergartens, which makes the Norwegian Steiner school movement the biggest in the world, based on population density. The schools have 5,000 pupils and 750 teachers, which implies that more than 100,000 people – pupils, parents and teachers – are acquainted with Steiner pedagogics (Bergesen 2000: 53). The schools are private, but have 85% state funding, and a turn over of 250 million Norwegian crowns each year. Until recently the Steiner schools were the main private alternative to the public school system in Norway, which may explain part of their success.

6. If we compare the Norwegian figures with Gallup surveys in Denmark and the US, we find that according to a survey made by Zapera (Gallup institute) and referred to by the newspaper *Kristligt Dagblad*, 43% of the population in Denmark believe in angels – 15% were certain, while 28% said perhaps. In the US, Gallup polls show that 79% believe in them.

Bibliography

Ahn, G. (2006) Angel. In K. von Stuckrad (ed.), *The Brill Dictionary of Religion*, vol. 1, 63–65. Leiden: Brill.

Alver, B. G. (1999) Fra englevagt til englevinger. Den mirakuløse hverdag og det hverdagslige mirakel. In B. G. Alver, I. S. Gilhus, L. Mikaelsson and T. Selberg *Myte, magi og mirakel i møte med det moderne*, 183–199. Oslo: Pax.

Arnesen, H. K. (2007) *Engler: guddommelige skapninger eller folketro*, Master's thesis, Universitetet i Oslo.

Bergesen, H. O. (2000) Steiners etterfølgere – subkultur eller motkultur? In P. N. Waage and C. Schiøtz (eds) *Fascinasjon & Forargelse. Rudolf Steiner og antroposofien sett utenfra*, 51–58. Oslo: Pax.

Bjørdal, Ø. and Skjevesland, O. (1994) *Engelen ved din side*. Oslo: Verbum.

Botvar, P. K. (2006) The 'spiritual revolution' in Norway: Why New Age spirituality will not oust Christianity. Paper to the 18th Nordic Conference in Sociology of Religion, University of Aarhus, Aarhus.

Davie, G. (2007) Vicarious religion: A methodological challenge. In N. T. Ammerman (ed.) *Everyday Religion. Observing Modern Religious Lives*, 21–35. Oxford: Oxford University Press.

Gardella, P. (2007) *American Angels. Useful Spirits in the Material World*. Lawrence, KS: University Press of Kansas.

Garlid, L. S. (2005) *Engleforestillinger i Den norske kirke*. Master thesis, Universitetet i Bergen.

Heelas, P. and Woodhead, L. (2005) *The Spiritual Revolution: Why Religion is Giving Way to Spirituality*. Oxford: Blackwell Publishing.

Heathcote-James, E. (2007) *'Märthas engler': Om folk som har møtt engler* (orig. *Seeing Angels*), Horten: Publicom.

Kraft, S. E. (2008) Märthas engler. En analyse av den norske mediedebatten. *Nytt Norsk Tidsskrift* 25: 123–134.

Laugerud, T. (1999) *Kirken i møte med den åndelige lengsel i vår tid: betenkning til Kirkemøtet 1999*. Oslo: Kirkerådet.

Libra (2002) 1–2, Særnummer om engler ('Special issue about angels').

Luthen, E. (1999) *Tusenårsengelen Mikael*. Oslo: Genesis.

Mikaelsson, L. (2001) *Homo Accumulans* and the spiritualization of money. In M. Rothstein (ed.) *New Age and Globalization*, 94–112. Aarhus: Aarhus University Press.

Quisling, J. L. (1889) *Om Aanderne eller Englene efter Den hellige Skrifts Lære*. Kristiania: Alb. Cammermeyer.

Scheid, J. (2002) Hierarchy and structure in Roman polytheism: Roman methods of conceiving action. In C. Ando (ed.) *Roman Religion*, 164–189. Edinburgh: Edinburgh University Press.

Smith, M. S. (2001) *The Origins of Biblical Monotheism. Israel's Polytheistic Background and the Ugaritic Texts*. Oxford: Oxford University Press.

Steiner, R. (2000 [1991]) *Engler: Vesen og virke: ti foredrag 1912–1924* (selected and edited by Wolf-Ulrich Klünker, translated by Arne Møller). Oslo: Antropos.

Steiner, R. (1998 [1956]) *Erkeenglenes virke i årsløpet: fire kosmiske imaginasjoner*. Oslo: Vidarforlaget.

Sutcliffe, S. J. (2006) Re-thinking 'New Age' as a popular religious *habitus*: A review of Paul Heelas and Linda Woodhead's *The Spiritual Revolution. Method and Theory in the Study of Religion* 18 (3): 294–314.

Usener, H. (1896) *Götternamen. Versuch einer Lehre von der religiösen Begriffsbildung*. Bonn: Verlag von Friedrich Cohen.

'We, Too, Have Seen a Great Miracle': Conversations and Narratives on the Supernatural Among Hungarian-speaking Catholics in a Romanian Village

Éva Pócs[*]

Since 2002 I have been carrying out fieldwork in the village of Gyimesközéplok in Romania, on the border between Hungarian speaking Székelyföld and Moldova (mainly inhabited by Orthodox Romanians). Gyimesközéplok (Lunca de Jos in Romanian), one of the three villages of the Gyimes region, is located in Harghita county, Romania, among the mountains of the Eastern Carpathians. It has around 4,000 Roman Catholic inhabitants who live by animal husbandry and dairy farming.[1]

The research project I have been carrying out in Gyimesközéplok has, as one of its aims, an examination of the role of the deities and saints of Christian mythology, the devil, and the figures of the demon world in the local religion and belief system. I am also interested in finding out what kind of role religion and beliefs (in this case in saints and demons) play in the life of contemporary society. In this chapter I approach the question from the angle of narratives, exploring which aspects of local religion and belief are reflected in different types of narratives, and in what ways. I also look at the ways in which we can draw inferences about religion and belief systems from these manifestations.

My investigations seem to show that in recent times the most persistent elements of this narrative tradition have been the figures of Christian mythology (the Virgin Mary, the devil), as well as a few demon figures from traditional folk belief that have been legitimized by 'official' religion (ghosts, revenants, witches and the *lidérc*). Religion

* Éva Pócs is Professor Emerita of the Department of European Ethnology and Cultural Anthropology, University of Pécs, Hungary.

is (still) a very important normative system covering numerous spheres of everyday life and worldview, and what has survived of traditional belief and belief narratives is that portion which was either integrated into the existing religious system or was repeatedly confirmed through the practice of religious faith, clerical dogma or religious rite. The portion of belief legend that is not supported by religion has become detached from the wealth of texts used within the religious function to become 'stories that cannot be credited'. These stories now live on as folklore texts, the survival of which depends greatly on the activity of collectors (although I certainly do not mean to deny, by this, the informative or entertaining category that has always existed within religious narratives).

In the light of Hungarian folklore collections it appears that in the past (that is, at the time of collection, or alternatively, in the past as construed by the collectors) narratives of the supernatural were usually told on traditional narrative occasions when it was the custom to tell stories. Folklore collections seem to suggest that narratives related on communal occasions were the only objects of oral transmission. Whether this was true or not in the past, today the people of the Gyimes region no longer really 'narrate' (except for the sake of the folklore researcher), but rather chat about (and read about) the mythical figures of the Christian religion and the non-Christian demon world both to the researcher and among themselves. The great majority of the narratives that are told today are embedded in conversations with the collector or with other small groups (family, visitors, friends, neighbours). They may be jointly shaped by participants in these conversations, or included among the news and gossip exchanged by neighbours, visitors or friends when they meet. At the same time, narratives about saints and demons are related almost exclusively in situations of folklore collection. The repertoire of good storytellers is kept alive by repeated waves of collecting and even by the narrators themselves reading publications containing similar texts.

In Gyimes today, the most important categories of religious narratives range from myths and legends through taboo legends and parables to dream and vision narratives. Narrative categories include family histories, life histories, educative stories, news, gossip, explanations, declarations of faith and discourses voicing belief/doubt/disbelief, as well funny stories and negative legends. Of the categories that have become canonized only in recent research (by Linda Dégh, Andrew Vázsonyi and others) it is also important to mention narratives of visions and miracles, stories narrated independently or integrated into conversations, as well as what Linda Dégh calls 'polyphonic narratives'[1] (see Dégh 2001: chapter 2, 97–103, 400–406; Dégh and Vázsonyi 1976).

It seems that from the point of view of our contextual research the various categories of narrative genres, which merge easily into each other, are of little significance. Similarly, our narrative stock seems to show no organic connection to the scholarly systems used in various collections of legends. Rather, contextual examination allows us to highlight certain functional focal points: various phenomena of the religious and belief worlds are arranged along the paradigmatic axes of the textual representations of saints and demons. In the following sections I describe some of these functional groups as examples. The totality of the narratives represent a very heterogeneous body of texts in which the individual formal categories do not range along the axis from faith value to text value. Envisaging such gradations appears to be no more than a scholarly construct that has not profited from the conclusions that may be drawn from field work. Even the first users of these categories, including Lauri Honko, were careful to point out that members of the same textual category, and indeed two instances of a text which are verbatim identical, can appear as a 'believed-in' story or merely as an 'interesting' story (an entertaining narrative) when related by different narrators (Honko 1962: 135).[2] It is clear that one story may fulfil different communicational functions at the same time, and can have divergent meanings in various speech situations (cf. Dégh 1995). We have to judge from the context, from the process through which the text becomes constructed, from the manner of the performance and the accompanying discourse, whether in that particular case we are talking of a religious instance, a living belief held by the speaker, or of something that is 'merely a text'. Texts about Christian or non-Christian mythical beings reflect, to varying degrees, the function that these beings fulfil in the religion and worldview of the people to whom the texts belong. From this perspective we can distinguish two categories within my textual corpus, categories which are not, however, very sharply delineated: (1) a tradition with an objective, informative, primarily cognitive, communicational function: teachings, parables, confessions about a rite, myth, idea, belief or mythical being; and (2) texts with an emotional function made relevant by faith and/or a religious experience characterized by the presence of sacred communication.

Texts of both types live on or may exist as simply informative or entertaining texts with no more than a merely 'textual' value. In this respect religious texts behave differently from those featuring the beings of folk belief. Stories about the central figures of the official religion are kept alive by religious faith, while those about the figures of folk belief tend to die out if they lack the support of (religious) faith; or they live on only in particular circumstances. Primary among these circumstances are situations of folklore research, in which stories are presented to the collector as merely entertaining stories.

Accordingly, I will outline a few tendencies based on the conclusions that may be drawn from the hundreds of textual units and narrative situations collected to date. In doing so I present the results of a partially completed survey, which feeds into a future comprehensive summary of religious narratives in Gyimes. (The present article's frame of reference does not allow the presentation of such crucial topics as, for example, the traditions of the otherworld, of revenants and witches nor of natural demons such as the 'wild girl' and the dragon. This is despite the fact that without these, neither the functional system – the *paradigmatics* – nor the textual system – the *syntagmatics* – of these narratives can be considered complete.) I take my illustrative examples from the world of deities, saints and demons. I offer at least one phenomenon for each of the important functions of the local religion, and through these examples present the mythical beings that play a central part in this worldview. I also make room, at least by way of examples, for some important non-Christian demonic beings.

Deities and Saints: Their Lives and the Miracles They Perform

This subject area offers an extensive, varied, easy-to-collect stock of texts: biblical and apocryphal stories about the life of Jesus (his birth, childhood, suffering, death and resurrection), apocryphal stories about Mary and also the lives, miracles and suffering of those saints who enjoy a local cult.

The textual corpus appears to be largely book-based. My informers claim to have heard the stories they tell in sermons, but more frequently they were heard during lay occasions of worship (prayer sessions, the Stations of the Cross) after which they passed them on within their families. Communicational channels other than speech also play an important part in transmitting such narratives. One of these is reading (prayer books, hymn books, chap legends, calendars, private notebooks for prayers, publications for religious festivals), and the other is writing (it is common practice to copy prayers, songs, saints legends, spells, etc. between notebooks, chapbooks, etc.). Often instead of narrating a story my informers chose to read something out to the collector. There is also some importance attached to looking at pictures (pictures of the saints, illustrations in prayer books), commenting on them or telling stories about the pictures. Another important phenomenon observed in the case of all narrative types is the creative use of written sources. Speakers tend to expand on the canonical texts with motifs alien to the canon, from oral traditions (for example, from the stock of apocryphal legends), or relate them in individual variants.

As far as miracle stories are concerned, this group of narratives was probably part of a tradition with more of a cognitive function, offering information and education using the apocryphal miracle stories about the baby Jesus, the Virgin Mary, St Peter, Christ and St Peter together, St Anthony, St Elisabeth and St Elijah, etc. These stories can be considered repertoire pieces for those informers known to be good storytellers. Today they are generally revived in collecting situations (people are particularly fond of stories of St Elijah's miracle of multiplying flour and oil at a time of starvation).

The other main thematic group within our corpus of texts, and indeed a central paradigmatic point, is related to the sufferings and death of Jesus Christ. (These stories are also prominent because of their sheer number compared to any other subject area.) As far as it is possible to discern from the collection situations, this textual stock played an emotional rather than a cognitive role when compared to the previous group. In terms of themes this group includes stories about the massacre of the infants by Herod and the flight of the holy family, presaging Christ's later life. Several of the informers tied the sufferings of the child Christ in with those of the adult Jesus Christ (or more precisely, with the torments suffered by Mary as mother), as is shown by the passage below.

The presence of miracle motifs is also a common characteristic in this group. This is how we encounter the miracle of the holy family being rescued by a flood, or the miracle of the Virgin Mary giving rise to a spring of healing water in a story which, although apocryphal with a canonical base, follows the life of Jesus from Herod's slaughter of the innocents to the crucifixion.

Figure 1: Wooden cross with Crucifix (photograph by Éva Pócs, 2003).

Mary's life was great, great suffering. The little baby Jesus was always persecuted from his birth until he was crucified when he was thirty three, he was always hunted and chased, so at that time they fled through forests and over the wall and the Almighty God ordered it so that when they were all but caught he sent such a great flood that their pursuers could not catch them, it brought down the wall and they could not follow them any further. And so they wandered on and on through the hills until it grew dark and they came upon a thieves' shelter. The thieves were away but their wives were at home with a nest full of children. And so they gave shelter to Mary, St Joseph and the little baby Jesus. They slept for the night and were not hurt. Then as Mary was leaving, her hair kind of touched a rock and from that place a spring came forth, a spring of water. She asked for a dish so she could bath the baby Jesus. She bathed him and said to the woman: why don't you now bath that crippled baby. The woman bathed it and that way [the thief's palsied child was restored to health]. ... The thieves came home and wondered and marvelled who these people were. The thief who was the baby's father – for there were two thieves – said to them not to worry, because they had had to escape, they should wander on so they do not get caught because Herod's soldiers want to kill the little baby Jesus at any cost. They had killed forty four thousand little saints and the little Jesus must have been among those, they had thought. And then the thief said he would go along and guide them and show them the way, so the father of the child they had cured showed them the way and accompanied them. [It was in gratitude that Jesus forgave one of the thieves at the time of the crucifixion as he was crucified next to him.] (Woman aged 75)

In this group of narratives about saints, the integrated miracle motifs often echo the canonical miracles (e.g. the resurrection or the virgin birth of Mary), offering, as it were, a more human, 'personal' parallel to the more doctrinal canonical miracles. This is the function of, for example, the story of the resurrection of the roast cockerel, the miraculous escape of Jesus by hiding among the corn, or the miracles quoted above in the context of the history of Christ's birth. Further non-canonical elements from the stories about Christ are motifs-of-origin myths or origin legends. Narratives of his birth, suffering, death and resurrection all include elements of this kind (for example, the origin of the red Easter egg is the dripping blood of Christ on the cross; the prohibition on harming redbreast robins is because they extricated the crown of thorns from Jesus' flesh). Passion narratives can also include the traditional origins of festivities relating to the cult of Christ; thus the 'origin' of Lent is reportedly related to the death of Jesus on Good Friday.

In addition to cognitive function, i.e. the instructional quality of myths, the emotions related to religious faith also shape texts. In cases like this in which the narrator 'lives' the story, their emotions, faith, sympathy, fear, or their appeals for help, turn the text into a communication with these beings. (This usually happens when people talk of deities or saints who have a cult, are addressed in prayer and who receive appeals for protection.) Emotional identification implies encounter with the saints, what would be in grammatical terms the vocative: 'my sweet Mary!', 'sweet Jesus!' The most noticeable feature in this respect is that speakers identify Jesus, Mary and the saints as people who suffer. The emotional charge related to the aspect of suffering is typical of the passion story as related by women. The passion of Jesus is augmented by the pain suffered by Mary: women identify with Mary and look on the suffering Jesus as that suffered by a child they have emotionally adopted.

she suffered a lot as she saw the sufferings of the Lord Jesus and she carried him when he was being persecuted, when Herod persecuted the baby Jesus. And then the Virgin Mary had to flee with Saint Joseph and the baby Jesus. [...] Forty days the Virgin Mother spent in the humble stable with the baby Jesus and by this time Herod was after

Jesus. And then, because of the baby Jesus, forty-four-thousand little martyrs had to die. Did you know that? Because what Herod wanted was: he thought that the baby Jesus would be there among those little ones. (Woman aged 72)

Half crying, a woman of 74 related to me the sufferings of Jesus in an emotional tone from her prayer book and from pictures of the Stations of the Cross during Lent. (She also integrated in a spontaneous way the origin myth of the robin redbreast which was not included in her book.) She accompanied her narrative with comments such as 'look, there they are taking him already, with his hands tied behind him ... he wouldn't hurt a fly and still, how much he had to suffer'. Faith based on sympathy humanizes the figures of the mythology and brings the story away from the mythological past and closer to the present, approximating a memorate describing an encounter with the supernatural. Pictorial representations help narrators or readers attain sacred communication through emotions. (This is the function of glancing at the pictures of the saints in the prayer book or on the wall during prayer.)

Religion is an extremely powerful supporting factor in the lives of these stories. The normative role of the narratives, and their mission to influence mentality and regulate behaviour, are still extremely important, particularly among older women. This role is continually reinforced by new influences from outside: from the stories, often used as parables, which people hear or read in church or in the media. Informers are also keen to offer these stories in the shape of parables, or to capture events within the stories they read or hear that can serve as parables (for example, the instance of Christ and St Peter asking for shelter or the poor man who became rich).

We might suspect that these narratives played an important normative part in transmitting tradition and in providing education within the family. Even in the situation of ethnographic collection work, the informers are using the texts to educate: they interrupt or finish the stories with morals, declarations of faith or faith-doubt discourse aimed at persuading the collector. The message they suggest is that God will help you if you are in trouble, he performs miracles. 'Do not doubt, for God is very powerful', as was said by one informer during and after relating the miracles of St Anthony.

Deities and Saints: The Miracles that Happen to People

The most widespread versions of the miracle story are narratives concerning the personal miracle. The central message of these texts is that in difficult situations or unexpected trouble God, the Virgin Mary or one of the saints will help. These are instances when an ordinary everyday event is interpreted as supernatural and appears as part of raw life experience with hardly any effort made to render them stereotypical. This is essentially adding a religious touch to individual life events. The emergence of this highly emotional class of narratives with a high faith value owes a great deal to miracle narratives, which are read as parts of the legends of the saints or are heard in church sermons. The logic seems to be that whatever happened to the Biblical or legendary archetypes can help us to experience events in our own lives as miracles.

The actors who perform the miracles in these personal stories are figures with an active cult in whom the narrator believes, prays to regularly and indeed expects to perform miracles. The most prominent among such persons is St Anthony of Padua. His life and stories are well known from readings. Many people say a prayer every Tuesday that starts, 'ye who wish to see miracles/oh come to St Anthony', addressing this to the saint, who is believed to offer protection from thieves and to help people find lost belongings.[3] When going to church for mass, the number of people performing some extra piety in front of the statue of St Anthony is higher even than those praying in front of the Virgin Mary's likeness. We may fairly assume that they are making individual requests for everyday miracles. A woman of 73 tells the story of her lost wristwatch as a miracle performed by St Anthony. 'I even woke up at night and said, St Anthony of Padua, please show me a miracle, oh please order that lost watch, lost part, lost property to come back' (at this point she was integrating, almost verbatim, one part of the prayer to St Anthony, mentioned above). Then, in the morning, after St Anthony had, so to say, revealed to her the whereabouts of the watch, she told her husband where exactly he would have to go and look for the object, which was on the bank of the river Tatros. The same woman considers that her pig's recovery from illness is another miracle performed by St Anthony. This is not uncommon as many people pray to St Anthony to cure animal diseases. Men of the older generation often hold a fast for the

Figure 2: A 79 year old woman telling miraculous stories (photograph by Éva Pócs, 2003).

sake of their animals' health on each of the nine Tuesdays before St Anthony's day. The pig's recovery took place after medication was administered by the vet. In other words a highly ordinary situation was subsequently interpreted and related by the old lady as a miracle attributed to St Anthony.

St Anthony also helped a woman of 45. Because of this she and her daughter are agreed that if the daughter should have another son they will call him Anthony. The lady in question also pledged she would fast on St Anthony's day all of her life. Thus the profound belief in this saint apparent in the community allows us to glimpse not only the role of faith and cult in creating miracle narratives, but also the reverse: it allows us to observe the way in which narratives support and strengthen faith and cult.

In other everyday situations it is the Virgin Mary or God himself who intervenes in the earthly course of events, this intervention allowing for a religious interpretation of narratives that deal with escaping misfortune. A woman of 73 had a memorable 'miraculous' experience when she was younger. She and her husband were making a journey to get salt when their baby, who they had taken with them, fell out of the cart. The wheels drove over the baby and yet it remained unhurt.

We, too, have seen a great miracle. So many miracles happened to me, indeed to one of us … Well I had to cry so much that God had given us this great miracle that my little baby's feeble little bones were not crushed.

The vivid nature of these stories gives us a clear perception of the degree of everyday religiosity and the role that faith plays in the everyday lives of these people. There are many stories of this kind still alive in the community of Gyimesközéplok. Most of my informants related the miracles that had happened to them in an entirely spontaneous way, in the course of conversations about St Anthony and the Virgin Mary. The normative role of narrative may be discerned in the narration even when the collector is offered these stories as evidences of faith or as parables.

This group of the miracles from everyday life represents the type of sacred communication in which the sacred almost penetrates everyday life. Another type of miracle narrative talks about instances in which people visit saints or sacred places in order to experience miracles. The nearby shrine of Csíksomlyó received regular visits from the people of Gyimes, generally on the occasion of the great pilgrimage of Whitsun, but also at other times if the need arose. They usually prayed to the statue of the Virgin Mary for a healing miracle. Miraculous recoveries experienced at this place are frequently the subject of spontaneous conversations, or are related in the accounts of the pilgrimages. They still consider it a miraculous recovery if the improvement actually takes place in the sick person's home, as long as the person's clothes were taken to the shrine and had touched the statue of Mary, or their body was stroked with cloth that had brushed against the sacred statue.

The shrine at Szőkefalva,[4] which gained popularity about 15 years ago, was visited regularly over a 6–7 year period by a group of inhabitants from Gyimes on the previously advertised days of Mary's appearance. Here they could witness the miracle of the apparition directly through the seer's dialogue with the Virgin Mary. Miraculous recoveries were reported, mainly by touching the woman seer or using the shrine's healing water. The narrative mechanisms previously described are also at work in the stories of recovery at Szőkefalva, leading ordinary everyday events to be interpreted as miracles. This is no surprise, given that the enthusiastic, highly religious group from Gyimes used to go to Szőkefalva specifically to 'see the miracles'.

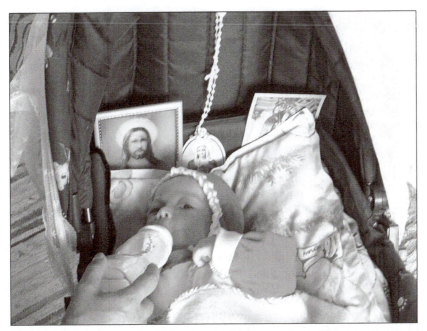

Figure 3: Holy cards and rosary in pram of a baby protecting her from the devil, one day after her baptism (photograph by Eszter Csonka-Takács, 2005).

> Here was a little child or a little girl I don't know, it had some trouble with one or both of its kidneys and the parents and grandparents all went there and the little girl recovered. They just took her there and there she recovered, you see. (Woman aged 36)

The ways in which the miracles of the various shrines are experienced and related are also influenced by the international miracle stories that are transmitted by the media. Many people in the Gyimes region have some written material on the apparitions of Mary at Szőkefalva, such as home-made copies of Mary's Messages, newspapers, pictures, brochures. We can also find, as reading material or home decoration, accounts, pictures and sculptural representations of the miracles of Medjugorje, Lourdes or Fatima as well as sacred pictures and sculptures of Mary. The shrines that the church has approved have serious value as models:

> Well, even the priest talks about the magic spring and that Mary appeared to Bernadette; that was where the thing about the spring happened, there were all those people lining up and the priest often mentions this even in his sermons. And also the story of the child at

Fatima, he has been known to talk about that, too. Then if anyone likes reading and gets hold of one of these books, they can find out all about these matters in more detail. If they read the whole book ... I once read an example about an apparition at Lourdes, where they took the child in a kind of tub from its parents, took the sick child on the train and then bathed it, had it bathed in that tub [...] and then it recovered there and came back healthy. (Man aged 55)

These stories are then confirmed by informers' own histories of recovery:

This happened to my father. Yes. What happened to him, may God grant him to rest in peace, he had a hernia, in his loins [...] he kept meaning to have the operation but never dared to in the end. [...] And then once the news was heard that the Virgin Mother, that somewhere the Virgin Mother had appeared. Then my father knelt down and raised his hands and asked the Virgin Mother, saying he cannot go to her because he is not able [...] that the Virgin Mother should come and take pity on him. (Woman aged 72)

These miracle narratives are often told to the collector, but also to friends and family, with the aim of confirming faith in the Virgin Mary's ability to perform miracles (and to justify the rites connected with visiting shrines). The function here described seems to be rather old; it was probably the original base for relating these stories in the small community. In a similar way to miraculous recoveries, narratives of Mary's miraculous appearances are told as declarations of faith. The informer who related the above history of recovery at Szőkefalva concluded his narrative with the following words: 'So it was faith, strong faith. You have to believe and hope; God is good.'

On the other hand, as far as the (so far unofficial) Szőkefalva shrine is concerned, the church tends to confirm the doubts that surface spontaneously in the community. It interferes with the faith-doubt discourses that I had the occasion to witness on a number of occasions by voicing its own dilemmas concerning the reality of the 'alleged' apparition of Mary at Szőkefalva. Several people have quoted the opinion of the parish priest, according to which the Virgin Mary is already with us here, consequently there is no need to make the pilgrimage all the way to Szőkefalva. Such an official opinion is bound to increase the number of sceptics, among them a 70-year-old informer of mine, who does not believe in the apparition at Szőkefalva (as a miracle). She thinks there must be a trick involved. Otherwise why did God not also perform a miracle in order to restore healthy eyesight to the blind seer of Szőkefalva?

Deities and Saints: Taboo and Punishment

The normative role played by Christian mythical beings becomes most evident at times when they appear to warn or sanction people who transgress the norms. In stories about warnings and sanctions, delineated within the research work as taboo legends, dreams or vision narratives, Christ or the Virgin Mary appear to those communicating with them: they deal out punishment and speak their words of admonition or guidance. Certain parts of these narratives refer only indirectly to the sanctioning figure. For example they talk about punishment for breaking the prohibition of work during Christian festivities simply as divine punishment without one or other of the higher Christian personalities appearing in the narratives. And yet, through conversations about prohibitions and sanctions, we may glimpse the image of a fair and just God who deals out blessing and punishment evenly.

As far as sanctions are concerned, it is believed that breaking the prohibition of work during festivals, as well as the breach of taboos relating to women being unclean during menstruation, or 'unchurched' mothers in childbed, will bring about natural disasters: storms, hail, floods, or water will dry up or become worm infested. More generally, as a result of these sanctions the natural order, previously bought under control by human work, now breaks down and reverts to a pre-cultural state. People who spoil the holidays, i.e. those who do hay work or hoe potatoes on days when work is prohibited (e.g. the days of the patron saint's festival, or the days of Our Lady, St Peter, Peter and Paul, Mary Magdalene, etc.) will also be punished by storms and hail. The same punishment comes to those who harness their animals on a festival day. Prohibitions against weaving and washing (mangling) are associated primarily with the days that commemorate the suffering, resurrection and ascent of Jesus Christ (Good Week and Holy Thursday).

Some of the narratives collected are stereotypical texts about 'other people'. Thus, for instance, parables about festival breakers are often relocated so that they occur in the neighbouring Romanian community, or in the Hungarian villages of the neighbouring county.

This confirms and generalizes the value of the text as parable. For example:

> over there, by the chapel [...] people were hoeing, Romanians of some sort. They were hoeing in a place where the fields were all scattered, a long field here another one over there, just like here, you see. They were not hoeing all in one place. And we were at mass and my relatives said to me, look how they are hoeing away, when it is St Peter's day, a holiday, and look at them, hoeing. Then later we went in to have lunch. And all of a sudden it looked as if it was going to rain, it grew all dark in the sky, just like now. And we looked out and just the spot where they had been hoeing, in that strip over there, professor. Not a hand's span this way, not a meter that way, the hail beat it all away. (Woman aged 72)

The normative role of being god-fearing, in other words the willingness to adapt to the religious norm, is still easily sensed today. In conversations with each other or the collector, people make frequent allusions to the figures who apply divine sanctions as powers dispensing justice. According to a woman of 40, the storm that punishes the Sabbath breakers is 'a sign', 'God speaking through the disaster'.

At other times, and this is on the majority of occasions, we come across highly personalized narratives. Topical misfortunes are accompanied by this kind of improvized reasoning, which reveals that the system of norms and sanctions is consciously born in mind. In response to a single question by the collector, several people related a series of taboo legends about people being punished for haymaking, for harnessing animals or hoeing their potatoes, as parables to prove their point to the collector. The frameworks of these 'parables' usually also include personal stories of taboo transgressions. I asked a man of 71 about work taboos during festivals. As a parable to illustrate his answer he told me that on one occasion his family were haymaking on St Anthony's day and that this led to a cloudburst and a flood. In the same family a male relative lost his eyesight by a branch hitting his eyes after he had herded his cows into the forest on Good Friday.

In the context of female fertility, the most numerous group of narratives relates to abortion, threatening or warning about the possible sanctions of such an act. In these stories we see Christ or the Virgin Mary within the framework of dream and vision narratives, acting as guardians of norms on birth control. The stories about the religious figures in whom people believe and surround with cults almost automatically merge into sacred communication. The narratives themselves are highly personal reports of encounters with these figures in dreams or visions; encounters which are usually frightening and always carry a great emotional charge. In terms of content, the most frequent version deals with a pregnant mother who has aborted or is about to abort her baby but meets a figure who warns or sanctions her. The following reminiscences come from a woman of 73:

My mother-in-law, may she rest in peace, had eleven children. She was such a dear, clever woman, such a good woman [...] and she said she had seen the Lord Jesus with her own eyes as he came in through the door and, you know, she said she even saw the little crown that was on his head ... She was feeding, breastfeeding her baby and she was supporting herself on one elbow and she was already pregnant with the next one. She brought eleven children into this world. So she was thinking to herself [...] that she was either feeding or carrying, because they came one after the other like that, there was never a time when she wasn't either feeding or carrying [...]. And then she said she looked in the direction of the door and there she saw a beautiful little child in a white gown, like a child of five or six and she could even see that thing that they usually draw round the head of saints, and with its fingers raised [showing the waving motion of the two fingers] it said, quite sharply, 'Woman, what is it you want?' [Eventually she gave birth to her baby].

According to the reminiscences of other female narrators, it is the Virgin Mary who, appearing in a dream, warns the woman who is thinking about abortion, while in a third story type, the mothers or their relatives see the baby about to be born in a dream of admonition. For instance, the father of a pregnant woman saw a young girl in his dream who said 'grandfather, why do you want to kill me?' (Subsequently the girl was allowed to be born.) Finally, the fourth version of these narratives dwells on the awful hellish torments suffered by the women who committed abortion, as well as the family members who had encouraged the killing of the foetus. The aunt of a pregnant woman saw the Virgin Mary in a dream. Mary was seen to lead the woman by the hand to heaven where she was shown the terrible punishment awaiting women who had aborted their babies: they had to eat the foetuses. Going through the ornamented gate of heaven, to the left they saw these mothers, while to the right there were women of a pious life, wearing white clothes and holding rosaries.

In the case of these narratives we have to emphasize the joint role of the cognitive and the emotional functions. Knowing and passing on the norms, communication about norms and adherence to them are based on emotion, which in turn relies on a person's faith in these sanctioning figures. Behind this phenomenon we find the simple fear of punishment. The textual tradition outlined above is still very much alive and the participation of these narratives in the communication processes of the small communities in the study area is noticeable even today. The stories crop up in everyday conversations within the family (for instance at the table after dinner) as improvized parables that point out the correct path in life within the context of topical everyday problems (the weather, hay work) or family events.

It appears from the situations in which they were collected that these narrative types (and the prohibitions they represent) played a very important normative role in regulating the rhythm of work through religion, in guaranteeing that the Christian festivities are celebrated with the due attention. The same is also true of family life, where the religious morality they impart played a role in regulating female fertility. While these norms strengthen everyday religiosity, we may also observe the reverse: the church plays an important role in sustaining the stories and conversations about the breaking of taboos. When a feast day is approaching, the priest warns people not to do any hay work on the holy day and gives advice regarding solutions that may represent a compromise. The prohibition of abortion is also a recurring motif in sermons.

Deities and Saints: Dream and Vision

The boundaries are blurred between the last group – dreams of taboo and punishment – and the narratives discussed under the present heading, as in the present case, too, we are talking about sacred figures appearing in dreams and visions. However, in these communicational situations Christ, the saints and the Virgin Mary appear not as deities dispensing justice but as figures expressing religion's function of protection. Here we witness the spontaneous, 'self-seeking' communication with the sacred that is generated by the conscious or unconscious striving for mystical experience, or for direct encounter with the beings who protect, support, grant mercy, bless or advise.

Stories about this kind of experience are told, at least to the present collector, almost exclusively by women (old and young alike). The original narration situation was probably the same, in other words a small circle of family and friends. The stories are highly personal and strong emotions are shown, even in the collecting situation, especially when these emotions are signs of devout love for Jesus or Mary. It is precisely because of this subjectivity and intimacy that it is considered unlikely that these stories were told to a wider public very often; their emotional value means they are not 'entertainment' stories, which have a higher text value.

The sacred figures generally appear in situations of crisis or illness, bringing comfort to those who ask help from them. A woman of 70 told the following story in response to my question, 'has the Virgin Mary appeared to anybody?'

> Do you know what I've got to tell you and I am not lying, I was so sick with typhoid that the doctor said he had many patients with typhoid but none of them as bad as me […] I was so terribly ill and I was staying at my father and mother's house. And I became so bad I lost all sense of myself and once when I came round, there was a little candle, it was alight, burning on the table and I saw Mary. Only, she was not facing me but with her back turned towards me, but she was so beautiful and after I had seen her, every day I just got better and better all the time and this is how I came to be healthy again. Well, Mary, the mother … you should know that God and Mary and Jesus [pointing at the devotional pictures on the wall], see what guests I have in my house! I love them so much; I always sleep alone and I am alone. I am alone. So, that's how it goes by the dear good Lord!

The informer's commentary, which ties vision in with pictures of the saints on the wall, is no accident. It is necessary, once more, to point out the parallel role of visual communication: the images of the saints may play as important a role in the emergence of these visions and vision narratives as texts.

I have collected several similar narratives about seeing the Virgin Mary or Christ as helpers: Jesus comforts the ailing person in a dream, predicts the outcome of the illness, cures people in their sleep. When the vision is experienced in the loneliness of the night, with the person waiting for a comforting Mary to arrive, then these could be described as instances of spontaneous visions, as defined by Honko (*kasuale Begegnung*) (Honko 1962: 110–113). The conditions in which a person 'sees' (e.g. fear of death alone at night) along with traditional knowledge (e.g. about sanctions in hell) jointly form the basis of the experience of encountering these spirits.

It would appear that similarities in lifestyle and emotional and religious life should produce similarities in the experience and narration of sacred communication. However, these individual, subjective accounts of dreams and visions are highly varied. It would be hard to say that a speaker followed any stereotypical pattern. Let us see another account of a dream encounter, reported by a woman of 50:

> Yes, yes, yes. I remember it clearly. It was a dream but I was really afraid that the soil … as if there was a slide and I hid underneath it. It was on the side of a road. As if something was coming to run me over. Well … heavier traffic or something, I don't know, I hardly remember this dream at all. I was so frightened, I kind of hid under the ground as best I could so that if something should fall from above then with my back I could … I could feel warm breath or something on my face. And I had this odd feeling, I said, good Lord, who is it who is with me now, what is happening. But it was just such a, well, just such a lovely feeling, I could sense a point of support. And then from all of this I … I kind of imagined that Jesus was standing by my side and he was protecting me from this … so I wouldn't get into trouble. And then I started singing 'Jesus I love you, I seek you in heaven and on earth …' But it was as if he was protecting me from behind and I could feel that warm breath on my face as if he was breathing over me, but I can hardly remember this, it was such a long time ago.

Faith founded upon emotions plays a strong role in the emergence of these visions (as does emotion grounded on faith). For this reason there are also voices of scepticism, naturally, from those people who have not had a vision experience. Throughout our collecting work we frequently heard commentaries accompanying the narratives, such as explanations given to the collector, denials, faith-doubt discourses with the collector or other people present. A woman of 70 declared that she did not believe in visions. In order to illustrate her case, she quoted an instance from her own life. When she was a little girl she had an illness with a high temperature and then saw Mary, but she believes that this was only brought on by the fever. (As previously mentioned, hallucinations experienced while in a similarly fevered state are considered 'real' visions by others.) People who believe in visions, on the other hand, use the fact of the visions as demonstrations of faith. A woman of 71, for instance, told the story of her brother-in-law's vision of God, which brought about the man's religious conversion. (This story was not told in response to a question but as a kind of creed offered for the benefit of the collector.) The fact that, even among the deeply religious, many people do not believe in the possibility of visions is not a gauge of faith. It is partially due to the doubts voiced by the church (particularly in connection with the visiting of the new shrines). As far as the church is concerned, this is a 'peripheral phenomenon' and is only partially recognized. Thus, in their sermons priests do not encourage the people of Gyimes to see visions. If they do, it is clearly part of religion at the personal level only, extending to a limited number of people even among the religious.

Even this highly subjective and emotional group of narratives has its more objective, informative, correlatives, which play a mainly cognitive role independent of sacred communication. These are the stories of the 'transportation' of one or other of the saints, found in the recognized hagiographies. Even people who seriously doubt the possibility of themselves having visions show no difficulty in fully embracing the visions of the saints. This is partly because it appears probable to them that in the past, in the mythical times before the reality of our everyday lives, things of this nature could happen; and partly also because whatever is written in the holy books, even if it is apocryphal, is authorized by the church and the priesthood. These offer a form of cognitive support that helps the act of seeing visions to become a credible replacement for absent emotions. Even people who believe in visions benefit from these hagiographic accounts because they confirm the reality of personal visions and in this way help to formulate a person's own experiences.

The Devil: His Nature and Temptations

The crucial normative role of the Catholic religion is confirmed by contemporary belief in the devil. Conversations about the devil are continually rehearsed, and not only for the collector. For most people in Gyimesközéplok Satan is a perpetually present power tempting people to do evil and threatening to harm body and soul alike. It is particularly in the thinking of the older generation that the dualistic concept of the divine and the satanic, the juxtaposition of these two ideas and the constant fight between the godly world and an ever ready Satan, becomes distinctly apparent. In response to questions about knowledge of the devil ('What do you know about the devil? Who is the devil?') only a small number of informers offer narratives on the mythological level, and these are generally the people who

Figure 4: Pictures of the Virgin Mary and Jesus on a kitchen wall (together with family photos) (photograph Éva Pócs, 2003).

already have experience of ethnographic collection situations. These stories mainly have a cognitive function and play an educational role, e.g. about the original sin or the falling of the angels. Several members of the older generation also tell variations of the frequently read and much liked legend of the fight between St Michael and the devils.

It is far more common for narratives about the devil to be accompanied by a clearly perceivable, strong, active faith giving an awareness of the devil's permanent presence. People fear the devil because he aims to procure souls. At the moment of death the devil tries to snatch the souls of the dying and carry them off into damnation. Even the most widely known and frequently read stories are filled with emotion when recounted by my informers. It is usually in this context that the two most favoured and most frequently related strands of the devil narrative are told: the devil tempting a person to suicide, and the fight between the angels and the devil over the soul of a dying person. The histories of both of these highly stereotypical legends go back at least as far as the Middle Ages and have become widespread since then, both in written, pictorial and verbal forms.[5] However, I have managed to collect a large number of surprisingly personal, life-like variants of both, particularly the former. The suicide rate is very high in the study community. It is a widely held view that by committing suicide people give their souls to the devil, and that in fact it is the devil who tempts them to suicide. This is what many people believe to be the most evil temptation of Satan. They often tell stories based on the personal experiences of their family or friends. According to the story of a woman of 75, at one time a male relative suddenly started shouting:

> Oh, God, oh God, I feel so terrible, oh dear, someone is pressing on me, he says, oh dear, they are throwing the rope over my neck. So the people next door just grabbed him real quick and oh dear, let's take him home, hay, Pityu what's come over you? And even as they were walking he just kept saying, oh, they are putting the rope over me, they are skinning me, oh, please, don't let me, they are skinning me ...' [His wife quickly sprinkled holy water over him and images of the Virgin Mother and the Lord Jesus were placed next to him, along with a rosary and a prayer book.] We were so scared, even the next day we were quite beside ourselves after seeing what that filthy devil was doing to a poor little man.

People in Gyimes also tell many variants of the old church legend about the deathbed struggle between angels and the devil. Besides written sources, many of these stories also rely on pictorial representations in chapbooks, prayer books and in some cases even on pictures hung on the wall. The latter is an Orthodox tradition and continues the rich medieval iconography on the subject. It would seem that visual images have also influenced local narratives. A woman of 77 told the following story in response to my question:

> *I have heard that over the deathbed the devil and the angel ...*

> Well, what happened, you see, is that once I saw a picture like that ... the devil was there and the angel was also there, and they were fighting it out to see which one would win, you see. And they said, they said that there were people with a lot of money, people all filled with money and that people like that were ruled by the devil. And that the angel was there, too. And I once heard a story, I have just remembered this, one of my aunts told me, may she rest in peace, that it was said that when the devil manages to capture somebody's soul, the angel is all a'crying when it goes away. Yes, it really cries so hard to see that the devil has the power, so that's how it is.

Throughout the course of human life, the devil never ceases to try to tempt people into drunkenness, blasphemy, or into neglecting mass, prayers or fasting. Educational stories or parables about personally experienced temptations play a powerful normative role and are an important fixture in family conversation and the religious education of children. Those who succumb to the devil's temptations get into trouble, those who laugh in church or speak ill of others will be taken, or possessed, by the devil. My informers talk of someone who behaved badly in church and was then tormented by apparitions of the devil all the way home. Embedding the story of the most recent suicides in the framework of such stories serves to feed the fear of damnation – and vice versa. It is no accident that such stories are often told as parables, rich with declarations of faith, both to the collector and within the community.

Telling stories of the deathbed struggle between the devil and the angels in the context of other people's deaths has the effect, when used as parable, of a *memento mori* in the preparation for death. Those who flirt with evil will be visited at the time of their death by the devil who will try to snatch their soul. This is what happened to a money-minded woman who was infatuated with the cantor and grinned at him even in church, even though she was married. When she was dying, 'the evil ones' came. 'For she had not cared about the Good Lord. Only money, and possession, and all that, … about wealth' (Woman aged 74).

It is common, when these narratives are delivered orally, for the speaker to apply the temptations of the devil to situations within daily life and to draw a conclusion from them. Often one can also sense that the effect of these parable-like stories come from people's own reading and from the sermons they hear. Several women have reported that they suffered temptations. They complained, for instance, that they fail to fast as they should and explain that the devil seems to be calling them to eat. At other times the devil tempts them to defame other people.

The various types of parable about the devil are frequently included in faith-doubt discourses regarding the existence of the devil and his power to do harm, and even more frequently in declarations of faith. Sometimes the expressions used in these parables are borrowed from the Bible or from sermons. For instance, they tell the story of someone who did not believe in the devil until one day he was visited by a group of devils making rattling noises and throwing things about. From that time the person believed 'that the Devil exists and so does God'. Another story talks about the punishment suffered by a sinner. The informer's comment ran as follows: 'the devil is forever going round, looking, like a roaring lion, whom to swallow. So those who have a strong faith can resist'.

The main factor in the normative role of these stories is the fear of damnation and the punishments of the other world. The strength of the emotional factors, such as fear and faith, is shown by the fact that an entire defence system has been set up with the aim of thwarting the devil. This system consists of prayers, sacramentals and gestures. Because of the permanent presence of the tempter, these are permanent elements of all types of conversations or narratives about the devil. When speaking about the devil people spit or cross themselves and ward off evil with a hand movement or by reciting a spell or prayer, something that is particularly true of older women. The conversation quoted below is a good example:

> *And what do they say about the devil, what is he like or what harm does he do?*
> That's evil, too, really evil. He is always doing wrong.
> *And what sort of evil does he do?*
> Well, everything; you see how many people there are who destroy themselves and take their own lives. Only this summer look how many people had hung themselves, and even young people and young women at that.
> *And that's the devil?*
> Well, they say the soul goes to the devil. God save us, my dear Good Lord, may he go away from us, my dear sweet Mary save us. (Woman aged 72)

Non-Christian Demons: The *lidérc* and the *szépasszony*

While it is not possible to discuss these in detail here, I must mention briefly two figures highly prominent in Gyimes traditional belief: the *lidérc* and the *szépasszony* ('beautiful lady'). Both play a significant part in the narrative culture and, by inference, belief world of this community, as well as in its religious life

In Gyimes, *szépasszonys* are demonic beings supposedly of a fairy-like appearance who ride on the backs of hemp breakers. They pick up and scatter the hay that has been collected like a whirlwind; confuse horses, attack and ride them to death; change babies; while in the shape of incubus demons they press mothers in childbed; and snatch men and 'give them a ride'. *Lidérc* are malevolent demons who carry out assaults. They are perceived as a fiery phenomenon flying through the sky. When a *lidérc* lands, it usually appears to men as a woman or to women as the alter ego of a man who is away from home. This alter ego may be invoked, it is believed, by a powerful yearning for the original man. As a sexual partner (always with the feet of a goose or horse) a *lidérc* transports, possesses, sickens and wastes its victim.

In response to the collector's question many people are ready to recollect stories about these figures, in particular the more 'practised', and relatively older, informers who have been trained through several instances of folklore collection. In relating these narratives they make a marked effort to produce complete, rounded stories, something in which they display a self-conscious skill.

The characteristics of these two demonic beings are more clearly outlined in narratives with a pronounced text value and which play a cognitive or educational role. By contrast, in the accounts of personal experience inspired by demon assaults, which have mainly an emotional function, the two figures merge more easily into one, and also into the other demons (such as malevolent dead persons or the devil) that show a similar proclivity to attack humans.

In the experience of the contemporary collector, the most frequently encountered narratives relating to *lidérc* and *szépasszony* demons are those in which natural phenomena such as lights and sounds (for example moving lights, shooting stars) are perceived as *lidércs*; or where stormy winds, winds that pick up and carry hay, whirlwinds, or in some cases knocking noises, are interpreted as a *szépasszony*. Therefore informative, educational narratives distinguish the *szépasszony* and *lidérc* from each other. They also separate them from other demonic figures and show them as beings which provide explanations for natural phenomena. In response to questions such as 'what is a *szépasszony*?', most informers offer explanations of symptoms or of phenomena, such as:

> As for szépasszony – *what can one know about them?*
> Well I don't know, we just heard about them, and when they go about in the summer they stir [stir up the dust] in the evening and people say, look, the *szépasszony*, see how they dance. But then whether really they are beautiful or ugly, no one has seen. (Woman of 74)

Others speak of light phenomena in the sky as *lidérc*: 'I have seen a *lidérc* move across the sky and it was scattering stars all over the place, shooting fire wherever it went' (Woman aged 65).

Even from the collection situation it is possible to infer that narratives and conversations of this kind must have had an old community tradition. The situations that made them relevant were the concrete occurrences of the natural phenomenon in question. Statements of this kind often act as cues to longer, legend-like narratives about *lidércs* and *szépasszony*. These describe how demons which appear as natural or light phenomena attack humans. Stories of *lidérc* and *szépasszony* formed a part of the local educational/normative tradition serving to regulate behaviour. By relating stories of personal experience and hearing the experiences that happened to other people and drawing conclusions from these, people could learn the interpretation of certain environmental phenomena. They learnt about emergency situations when demonic disasters might be expected, as well as about the methods for averting them. The following discussion is about how a father taught his child all that needs to be known about *lidérc*, embedded in the usual framework of 'nature explanation'.

> My father and I were out hauling, we had two large oxen, there was moonlight and we were out hauling. Then we saw this thing moving ahead in front and it was like a fire and I said, 'Father, what is that? What sort of thing is that?' And he said that was a *lidérc*. And I said to him, 'do I need to be afraid of that?' 'You may,' he says, 'but you must pray,' so we cross ourselves, may the Good Lord aid us and take that thing away somewhere else. This is how my father said it when I was a young girl.
> *Yes, yes, and what was that a* lidérc?
> Well, it was a *lidérc*, the devil. That was how my father said it. The *lidérc* goes round in the shape of the devil and if it manages to push someone into despair or doubt it will be released from the sin under which it is. (Woman aged 90)

Each of the narrative topics associated with the *lidérc* and the *szépasszony* can also become embodied in other, simply entertaining, stories and serve a purely cognitive/informative function, including accounts of assaults by the devil. When the informers relate these stories in a neutral, tête-à-tête collection situation in response to the collector's question, they, in effect, reconstruct the passing on of the educational tradition. These dyadic conversations, however, give us no hint about the original narrative situation in which these stories lived, and the supposed entertaining role they must have played in the past. In this respect all we can do is register the extinction of their entertainment function within the community.

Informative/entertaining stories about being snatched by the *szépasszony* never refer to the experience of the speaker or a close acquaintance, but rather are always about unnamed others, or 'someones'. Informative accounts of the *lidérc* pass on traditional knowledge of this figure attacking or assaulting man, while at the same time often describing the ways in which the protagonists rid themselves of the demon. Stories about the *szépasszony* are usually humorous in their tone and lack the emotions engendered by powerful faith. Also lacking is the fear of assault by demons which is otherwise so characteristic in this context. These stories often have a witty punch line. It is also common for the storyteller to insert into these stories motifs from migratory international legends or fairy tales. These are alien to local belief and experience and thus create the impression of an 'incredible' fairy story. (One such example is when people who think of holy things or utter holy words while being 'given a ride' fall back to earth.)

Entertaining stories of the *lidérc* and *szépasszony* offered to the collector are usually accompanied by commentaries, apologies or denials, with reference to other people or the past. This is common with all elements that the speakers consider superstition, particularly of the fairy story-like elements of *szépasszony* beliefs mentioned above. Other people may believe in them in other places: 'in Csík county' or 'in Moldova', or they were believed a long time ago, 'when I was a child', or 'the old people of bygone times' believed in them, and so on. Denials of this kind may well be sincere expressions of doubt and reflect an earnest stance of rejection, however, to a certain extent at least, they are clearly addressed to the collector.

Texts stemming from personal experience, i.e. texts proceeding from the basic premise, 'I have seen it, therefore it is', form part of the faith-doubt discourse that the informer maintains either with himself/ herself or with the collector. Explanations that rationalize belief, or its rejection, also feed into this overall discourse. A woman of 75 explained, for example, that the *lidérc* had 'ruined' a woman; she became nervous and 'it affected her mind'. According to my informer this is what is called 'melancholy' today.

Within the framework of faith-doubt discourse we encounter a special textual category: the negative legend. This text type turns the supernatural into the rational, dispelling certain beliefs and, at least on the surface, manifesting disbelief and doubt through the use of evidence. Yet we cannot regard the negative legend as merely the wish to be rational. One inevitably detects compensation for the fear of the supernatural; in other words the attempt to suppress an existing belief in these beings. Some of the belief legends collected in Gyimes fall into this category. The jocular tone of these narratives must be interpreted as wavering between faith and doubt.

In the meantime we must bear in mind that merging a narrative into an entertaining story, or applying other forms of distancing which turn the narrative into a purely informative text devoid of emotions, are not necessarily expressions of the informer's faith or doubt, and indeed several parallel incidents of data collection confirm this. They should be taken as describing the degree of faith sustained by the wider community to an even smaller degree. It would also be a mistake to see in this merging any symptoms of the extinction of beliefs or religious views. Remarks of denial take on a different meaning when, in another context, the same informer sheds his or her doubts and shows profound faith by relating a personal demon experience. I have noted several cases of this nature.

Demons Assaulting Humans: The *szépasszony*, the *lidérc* and the Devil

It seems that remnants of the supernatural world of non-Christian belief-figures are called to life most intensely by the emergencies of everyday life, such as the dangerous period around childbirth, the terrors suffered at night by lonely women or deep-rooted night fears about demons and the dead. Narratives about intimidating phenomena at night (unusual noises, lights, bad dreams) are based on a faith that is rooted in emotions related to fear. Despite the frequent expressions of doubt, certain physical symptoms and natural phenomena are still, persistently, interpreted as demonic assault. These are talked of in the relevant discourses as lived evidences, meaning dreams, visions or apparitions. This allows emotions, fear and faith to flood into the narratives, together with motifs of sacred communication between people and demons.

Among the *lidérc* and *szépasszony* narratives are individual accounts reflecting genuine faith. These were either based on experience or became relevant in situations of crisis. They speak of assault by demons, the symptoms of the assault (pressure, possession, snatching, being carried away, being changed, etc.), and have stories about the assaults of the Christian devil mingling in with the narrative. The devil who snatches people or assaults them as one of the demons of the night can hardly be separated from the demons of folk belief. Tempting people (through thought) and carrying them off to damnation are characteristic only of the Christian devil. When, however, people speak of assaults in the form of apparitions from the nightly demon world, which are projections of fears of the night, the devil becomes intertwined with the demons of these folk beliefs.

In line with the medieval duality of God and the devil, figures such as the *lidérc*, the *szépasszony* and the ghosts of the dead without status (e.g. the ghosts of unbaptized souls) have become enlisted on the side of the devil. Consequently, the church also includes them in its fight against Satan and through this channel these beings have gained religious legitimacy. In Orthodox areas (and in the territories bordering them) this quasi-medieval attitude persists even today, in turn contributing to the survival of narratives about non-Christian demon figures. Within their stories my informers often identify the devil, excluded souls (malevolent dead persons), the *lidérc* and even the *szépasszony*, and mould them into a vaguely defined notion of 'evil'.

We cannot ascertain on what occasions the people of Gyimes used to talk about their personal experiences of the devil's assaults before folklore scholars appeared. What is clear is that even in collecting situations we can witness cognitive narratives merging, in certain speech situations, into a more personal account. The narratives receive an emotional charge and begin to reflect fears of the night, a psychological and physical fear of these aggressive demons. Situations of this kind may emerge if a group of acquaintances gather together and start reminiscing about specific local instances, or talk about them as interesting news or gossip. It is often possible to witness situations of this kind even in tête-à-tête discussions with the collector. In this way the crisis situations or assaults that people experience, or hear from others, keep faith in these powers alive, something proven by the rich stock of relevant narratives. On the other hand, interpreting the natural phenomena mentioned above as *lidérc* or *szépasszony* must have repeatedly confirmed their survival as assaulting demons. Again, the approach employed here was probably along the lines of, 'I see it, I perceive it, therefore it is.' At one point my informers and I had been talking about revenants, and from this topic the two women moved on to the *lidérc*.

> a: No one actually came back from the cemetery, no one could say that. No one came here from the other world either, but that is what they say according to the books and that is what people say all over the place. People used to be very superstitious round here in the old times, they kept everything, but today … They used to say that the womenfolk were visited by *lidércs*.
> b: I saw one once!
> a: I, too, have seen a *lidérc*, moving along the sky!
> *Well, and what was it like?*
> b: It was just shitting out the stars like that … it was like the rod that lies over the hay on top of the wagon. And bright, and the stars were just like that at the back …
> a: At times like that we used to go up on St John's day at the back, past Béla Kondor's house and then it just rose up from over the cemetery, rose up high like a big coil and moved on over the cemetery like a long fiery thing.
> b: But my father and mother used to say when we were little girls that one of their relatives there started to have the *lidérc* visit her. For she had had a lover and then he left her and she grieved so hard that the lad started coming to her in the image of a *lidérc*, but a *lidérc* is what it was. And it used to come at night, but a *lidérc* has one proper foot and one goose's foot, that is how you recognize them. And then they said that it tortured the girl so much, it would visit her every night and lie down there and it would take all sorts of things to her, and then in the morning it would say that all it had given her had been […], had been horseshit, that's what they are like, all of them. This is what they said. The *lidérc* visited the girl so often, it was killing her. (Women aged 82 and 73)

Snatching People

The above mentioned entertainment narratives of snatching also have their serious, demonic counterparts. These mainly talk about encountering *szépasszony* who appear in a whirlwind, or they talk about being frightened of these or of personal experiences of being snatched. These are the least frightening narrative variants of the demonic assault story. I did not hear many of these stories and even these seem to merge easily into entertainment narratives, and vice versa. The following sample is a demonic version of the adventure of the man who was snatched away by accident. The story was related by Éva, a woman of 70, in response to the question 'what is a *szépasszony*?'. An interesting feature of the story is that the experience of being snatched is described here as a vision. The vision was provoked by the ritual method of looking in a mirror. (After the account is finished, the other woman present, Marika aged 82, adds a brief summary of an amusing variant of this legend.)

> a: … My mother told me that she had seen them, too, whispering.
> *And did the* szépasszony *snatch anyone?*
> a: They sure did, […], they did.
> *Well, and how was that?*
> a: She said, the old man had said they should look in the dark mirror if they dare. Who dares? I'll dare he said, if only everyone goes out of the house first. So they went out and there was such thundering in the house that it knocked everything over. When the others eventually managed to get back in through the door, everywhere was cinders and ashes and the man was nowhere to be seen. He said later, they gave me such a ride, they took me to the top of every hill, and all over the place. I broke off the tops of the trees but when eventually they let me down I almost died. But never again, he said, never again will he look into the mirror or talk about these women.
> *And do people talk about anybody else being snatched by the* szépasszony?
> a: Yes, Géza Jakab was. Aunty Marika knows it.
> b: Well, little Éva, even if I did know it I have forgotten.
> *So how was that?*
> a: They sat him in a washtub and carried him away and gave him such a ride that when eventually they dropped him, that almost killed him. And then one said to the other one, we snatched the wrong man, we made a mistake. So they threw him down so hard he almost died.
> (Women aged 82 and 70)

Night fears, bouts of ill health, pressure (sometimes even the 'changing' of the newborn baby) are often attributed to the devil, the *lidérc*, the *szépasszony* or to a vague composite figure of evil consisting of the 'evil dead' and the devil. These beliefs are manifest in widely known, fear based narratives with a powerful emotional charge. The collector's questions on this subject provoke answers from almost any member of the community, although I have also heard accounts of these experiences, clearly believed by those present, at gatherings of friends and family members.

The *lidérc* and the *szépasszony*, like the devil, are spoken of in terms of fear. When speaking of them people use gestures and spells aimed at warding them off, or at least distancing them. Protection by the use of sacred objects is also a sign that these demons are identified with the Christian devil, and that therefore these figures are legitimate in religion. The same is true of purifying rites used against the *lidérc* that visit or possess people. Purifying the house and the person with holy water, as a quasi-exorcistic rite, is something that a Roman Catholic priest would also do on request, according to the recollections of my informers.

As far as the non-Christian demon world is concerned, it is often impossible to separate the symptoms of those possessed by *lidérc* from those possessed by the devil. Some of the narratives about *lidérc* assaults show the figure of an alter ego *lidérc*, for example when women see the alter ego of their husbands in an apparition/vision/dream/daydream. The belief is that by yearning, 'grieving', for your partner, you can conjure up the likeness of a person who is far away, and 'a *lidérc* starts going about as their image'. Contrary to the objective/informative account type mentioned previously, the first reports of assaults by *lidérc* have a positive outcome. They describe the appearance of the *lidérc* and then the way in which the person dispelled them. The experience, which had come about through fear or has itself given rise to fear, is now a thing of the past. Yet these narratives have not lost their latent emotional charge. They still reflect the powerful belief of the informer in the demonic *lidérc*.

A great many narratives similar to those on *szépasszony* assaults are told about the devil snatching people or 'grabbing' them, making these stories a folk version of possession by the devil (Pócs 2005: 109–115). This is usually perceived as one of the devil's temptations, an activity through which he lures people into damnation and which is therefore often accompanied by declarations of faith. Narratives about the devil snatching people from their deathbeds have, as a more profane correlative, narratives about people who were snatched while still alive.

Conclusion

In the course of my research at Gyimesközéplok I aim to map out religious life and the world of beliefs in the community, with a specific focus on saints, deities and demons. I have presented here a brief preliminary survey of the textual world surrounding these mythical beings. The question now arises as to what conclusions we can draw at this stage regarding the supernatural world and its role in local society as reflected in these narratives and conversations. Some of the narratives on Christian and non-Christian mythical beings are now essentially extinct, or can only be recaptured in a collection situation as the repertoire pieces of the 'good' informers. These stories may be considered no more than textual folklore detached from living belief, a merely entertaining narrative tradition. It may be assumed, however, that in the recent past this textual stock was still part of a narrative tradition sustained by this small community and fulfilling primarily a narrative function. On the other hand (particularly as regards narratives containing events from the lives of Jesus, Mary and the saints, and the miracles of distant shrines) they played an important normative and educational role and had a function in the raising of children within the family.

Parallel to this extensive category of narratives, is another group of texts connected to saints, deities and demons (surrounded by religious faith/fear). This category, which plays a mainly emotional role, even today sometimes forms the subject of spontaneous conversations without intervention from the collector. From these accounts of personal experience, based on living faith, we can draw inferences regarding the role played by the deities, saints and demons in the local religion. Conversations about visions, miracles and temptation by the devil testify to the protection and assistance that religion offers; while taboo stories and accounts of demonic assault illustrate the important normative function of religion as it regulates everyday life. This is also shown by lively faith-doubt discourse and the declarations of faith that surround conversations on the subject. One important source for the relevance and survival of this textual world is the living faith in the devil, which is supported by the teachings of the official church and its sacred scriptures. In fact it is to this that the rich wealth of narratives on demonic assaults owes its survival. Religious legitimacy also plays an important role in sustaining both the Christian and the non-Christian demon world and the narratives that describe them.

It has been revealed, with respect to each of the areas explored, that the boundaries between two large textual categories, those with a cognitive and those with an emotional function, are not rigid. We are essentially witnessing the appearance of narratives of similar subject matter, taking on different communicational functions in different speech situations. There are several examples of informative stories with a plain cognitive function shifting, under certain conditions, to become personal to the speaker. The narrator shifts from the objectivity of the mythological level, to identifying with the suffering of the mythological figure and thus into communication with the sacred. More generally, there is a clear sense of an ambition to transpose the narratives that deal with the credible creatures of religion, from a mythological distance to a more human, personal plane. These efforts break the purely informative framework using emotional factors such as belief, identification, compassion or fear. The story is then rebuilt using personal encounter experience, which sometimes causes the narrative to approach sacred communication.

The way in which one or other of these two approaches is provoked probably has much to do with the speech situation. Variations in the degree of text value and faith value seem to depend on the momentary disposition of narrator and audience. Faith and doubt, information or cognition, as against emotion, faith value and textual value, are certainly not indicators of the faith or extinction of faith in the individual or community.

I was cautious not to generalize my observations due to the currently incomplete state of the research. In harmony with my intention to survey the present situation as accurately as possible, I drew hardly any conclusions as to the history of these beliefs, their more extensive presence in the past, their extinctions or transformations. I have endeavoured only to identify some very obvious tendencies. To give a more detailed and precise description of these tendencies, and to draw further important conclusions, are tasks for the future, tasks that must be founded on the most extensive examination possible of the rites, gestures and texts of the local religion and beliefs. To what extent, and in what proportion, all of this is valid for various members of the community must be explored, as must the general and individual characteristics of the local religion.

Notes

1. For the map of the region see the article by Ágnes Hesz in this volume, p. 142.

2. For further information on these categories and grades, and also scepticism about them, see for example Honko (1968: 60), Hultkrantz (1968: 78, Pentikäinen (1968), Honko (1989), Dégh (1996), Dégh (2001: 98–203).

3. Called 'the prayer of St Bonaventura'.

4. Szőkefalva (Rom: Seuca, Mureş County) is a Transylvanian village. The emergence of the Szőkefalva shrine started with visions delivered by blind gypsy woman Rózsika Marián in 1994.

5. For international examples of legends in which the devil tempts humans to suicide see Tubach (1969: 22, 251, 394); for the struggle of the angels and the devil over the deathbed see Tubach (1969: 24–25, 122).

References

Dégh, L. (1995) *Narratives in Society: A Performer-Centered Study of Narration. FF Communications* No. 255. Helsinki: Academia Scientiarum Fennica.

Dégh, L. (1996) What is a belief legend? *Folklore* 107: 33–46.

Dégh, L. (2001) *Legend and Belief: Dialectics of a Folklore Genre.* Bloomington and Indianapolis, IN: Indiana University Press.

Dégh, L. and Vázsonyi, A. (1976) Legend and belief. In D. Ben-Amos (ed.) *Folklore Genres,* 93–123. Austin, TX and London: University of Texas Press.

Honko, L. (1962) *Geisterglaube in Ingermanland. FF Communications No.* 185. Helsinki: Academia Scientiarum Fennica.

Honko, L. (1968) Genre analysis in folkloristics and comparative religion. *Temenos* 3: 48–66.

Honko, L. (1989) Memorates and the study of folk belief. In R. Kvideland and H. K. Sehmsdorf (eds) *Nordic Folklore: Recent Studies,* 100–109. Bloomington, IN: Indiana University Press.

Hultkrantz, Å. (1968) Miscellaneous beliefs: Some points of view concerning the informal religious sayings. *Temenos* 3: 67–82.

Pentikäinen, J. (1968) Grenzprobleme zwischen Memorat und Sage. *Temenos* 3: 136–167.

Pócs, É. (2005) Possession phenomena, possession-systems: Some East-Central European examples. In G. Klaniczay and E. Pócs (eds) *Communicating with the Spirits: Demons, Spirits, Witches 1,* 84–154. Budapest and New York: CEU Press.

Tubach, F. C. (1969) *Index Exemplorum: a Handbook of Medieval Religious Tales. FF Communications No.* 204. Helsinki: Academia Scientiarum Fennica.

PART IV

Creation and Maintenance of Community and Identity

Komi Hunter Narratives

Art Leete[*] and Vladimir Lipin

The Komi people live near the Ural Mountains in the northeastern part of European Russia. According to the official census of 2010, the total number of Komis (the Komi-Zyryans) was 228,000. The total size of the Komi Republic is 416,800 km². Forests cover three-quarters of the Komi Republic's territory, both swamps and tundra occupy 10% and only 1% is cultivated agricultural land.

Our main fieldwork region has been Kulymdin district on the upper course of Ezhva River in the southeastern part of the Komi Republic. The Komis of Upper Ezhva River (*Vylysezhvasayas* in Komi) are relatively active in hunting practices.

The Komis are traditionally followers of the Russian Orthodox Church. The hunter's worldview is generally considered as apart from the official Orthodox faith. Even today, certain elements of pre-Christian belief can be detected in the Komi hunters' narratives and practices.

The religious domain enables us to characterize male and female roles in Komi culture. During the Soviet period, old ladies obtained a special role in religious life in the villages. As the priests were absent, old ladies carried out religious ceremonies and were recognized keepers of local religiosity in general (Sharapov 2001; Chuvyurov and Smirnova 2003: 170; Vlasova 2003; Mitrokhin 2006: 45). Today the existence of these ladies with special religious authority gives a distinct aura to their local community. In addition, the faith of the other villagers becomes more 'real' because of a feeling of religious continuity (Koosa 2010).

Although folk religiosity in the Komi villages is constituted mainly by women, they are almost totally denied any authority in the hunters' spiritual domain. Women are excluded from all hunting related issues. Komi women have some secondary knowledge about hunting affairs and can also tell relevant stories.

[*] Art Leete is Professor of Ethnology at the University of Tartu, Estonia.
Vladimir Lipin is Research Fellow at the Department of Ethnography at the National Museum of Komi Republic, Syktyvkar, Russia.

During our joint fieldwork among the Komis (annually from 1996 to 2009) we have recorded many hours of hunting stories and discussed hunting rules. These stories reveal different aspects of the Komi hunters' worldview and behavioural rules, and tell us something about methods of narration among the Komis. We have worked with approximately ten hunters. Their ages varied from 15 to 70 although most of these hunters were middle-aged men (in their 30s and 40s). Most of our data originates from conversations with three hunters who have practised hunting from their childhood. Two of them have a hunting ground for autumn seasonal trapping of hazel grouse. In addition they make a couple of one- or two-week trips to remote hunting areas every year. Our principal informant is a full-time hunter who earns his income by selling hunting products and organizing hunting trips for tourists.

According to Dan Ben-Amos, narrating can be treated as a form of cultural negotiation that might alleviate the tension between norms and actual practices in a given society, with narratives as specific programmes for such negotiation. Scientific research should aim at empirically explaining the emergence of narratives as processes of cultural negotiation (Ben-Amos 2005; Leete and Seljamaa 2005: 309–310). Ben-Amos has also analysed ethnic genres as 'cultural modes of communication', 'relative divisions in the totality of an oral tradition', 'folk-taxonomic systems which are culture-bound and vary according to the speakers' cognitive systems', 'structures of local tradition' and 'part of an ethnic system of folkloric communication' (Ben-Amos 1981: 215–216, 221). People's manipulation using folk genres can be treated as a key to cultural discourse on a local or even an individual level.

We focus on the very local and personal level of cultural discourse among the Komis, more specifically on hunting dialogues. In this context, it is appropriate to apply a functional approach that can be seen as 'focused upon the relationships between forms of verbal art and existing cultural, psychological, and social needs' (Ben-Amos 1981: 223). The functional approach allows us to analyse Komi hunting narratives as a blended genre and to concentrate on the usage of these stories without attempting to categorize local hunting narrations according to any strict principles.

During our stay in the Upper Ezhva region of the Komi Republic in 2004, Art Leete wrote in his field diary some situational thoughts about Komi hunter narratives:

Sometimes Volodya [Vladimir Lipin] repeats his hunting stories. That is very human, we all repeat stories that we are used to telling. Our life is just one big narration.

And, of course, Volodya started telling his hunting stories during our smoking break on the balcony and I did not have an MD recorder prepared for recording. And it is impossible to write with your cigarette on the wall ... If I would run to get my recorder, for sure, he would interrupt his narration. And, anyway, that was a kind of a half-story. This means that it was not told with full feeling but just as it appeared in his head. I just think that it was in a way a fragile story that cannot be interrupted but you must listen and try to remember, even if you have some doubts about the issue – is it any story at all? However, I try to write down every bit of the story about hunting, every situational, unpredicted piece.

No matter whether they tell a hunting joke, describe some old action or even something completely new, it is told in a stereotypical way. There is always some intrigue, pieces of advice or humour in them. If I started thinking this way, it would be possible to interrupt somebody who was talking, tell them to wait for a moment and bring a recorder, and he could continue from the same point (or even from the beginning). This is because the feeling of the story is always present in some form. There is a certain stereotype, even in the case of new stories. (TAP 939: 11)

In this paper, we will attempt to make a broad categorization of the functions of Komi hunter narratives. As it is also possible to distinguish several factors influencing the 'truth', 'character' or the hybrid nature of the genre of Komi hunting narratives, we will also make a short analysis of the categories distinguished.

Situations of Storytelling

Most of the interviews conducted during the field trips were unstructured. As a general rule, we do not ask questions to initiate narration but rather try to catch the moments when hunters start telling stories by themselves. Fieldwork experience says (unsurprisingly) that narrations concerning hunting is a situation-specific activity. Often hunters start describing hunting episodes when we reached a point in the forest where something remarkable had happened to them. The same situation can also arise when staying in a hunting cabin, or beside the fire in the forest. Situations that somehow resemble hunting actions, cause predictable associations. Storytelling may also start in forced passive roles (during a long train trip, or when passing time in a town apartment or village house).

There is also a kind of reverse law that applies to documenting narratives – people start telling stories in unpredictable situations when you are unprepared. Narrating is initiated by people in situations that exclude the possibility to grab a recording device (for example, if we moved noisily through deep bushes).

Hunting Magic

The Komi people traditionally believe that hunting life is framed by specific forest laws, constituted by the forest spirits. The forest spirits '… were the guarantors of all norms and rules of behaviour in the forest that were to be observed. It was especially important in order to keep good morale within the hunting group. Since hunting morality also involved ethno-ecological norms, the belief in forest master-spirits ensured a careful attitude to the vegetable and animal kingdoms' (Konakov 2003: 342).

The Komi hunters consider that every violation of behavioural rules in the forest provokes the anger of the forest spirits, and can bring severe punishment, even for seemingly insignificant faults (Konakov 2001: 197, 203–205; 2004: 136). This belief has been documented several times at the beginning of the twentieth century. As a traditional understanding of a dialogue between forest spirits and hunters, this view is reflected in the Komi volume of the *Encyclopaedia of Uralic Mythologies*:

> Three brothers who were tired during a hunt lay down to sleep but did not light a fire and did not throw a crumb of bread into it (i.e., did not feed the fire, as was customary). At night a whole herd of evil spirits came. They killed one of the brothers, the second one went crazy, and the third brother lit a fire but thrust his feet into it instead of bread, and burnt them. (Konakov 2003: 344)

Beliefs in forest spirits are relevant among contemporary Komi hunters as well. On numerous occasions we have documented the cautious attitude of the Komi towards the supernatural inhabitants of the forest. Stories about the forest spirits have been told by the hunters themselves, and also by women who do not have any experience in hunting:

> Men believe in the Spirits of the Hunting Cabin … For example, just recently, one or two weeks ago, a hunter arrived to a hunting cabin

Figure 1: *Gazha kerka* ('beautiful cabin' in Komi) and storehouse in Komi hunter Yevgeni Chalanov's hunting grounds (photograph by Art Leete, 2003).

> late in the night. He didn't knock, didn't ask. He ate, heated the stove and fell asleep. When he woke up, he was outside. He entered the hunting cabin for a second time, fell asleep and [woke up] outside, again. And that's it. He didn't enter for a third time. As people say, the Spirit of the Hunting Cabin threw him out … I had a chat with a hunter, an elderly man just a week ago. He said that, you see, what happened … You see what our hunters believe. (FM 2006, F 45)

One of the general magical rules is that you cannot tell the whole truth about your hunting activities. For example, you should never pride yourself on a good catch, so as not to lose the hunter's luck. According to hunters' beliefs, a boastful hunter will be unsuccessful in the future. When someone has caught a marten, for example, he says he has caught a squirrel. The take is considered to be fatal, depending basically on the will of the forest spirits who provide the catch for the hunters (Konakov 2001: 205).[1]

Hunting may also be stopped if everything goes wrong from the very beginning, as Vladimir Lipin relates:

> Once we went hunting with S. We were skiing when all of a sudden S said he had forgotten to switch off his kettle. So we had to go back. I asked why we went all the way back. There was half a kilometre to go until we got home, could he not just see if any smoke was coming

out of the roof. If not, it was OK. But no, he demanded that we should return home. We did. The kettle was switched off. Yet we did not go hunting again. When it goes wrong at the beginning, you would not go hunting at all. (FM 1999)

If, during the hunt, you hit a twig on the ground, S will ask: which leg? If you hit the twig with the left leg, there will be no hunting luck, but if you hit it with the right, you'll be successful. (FM 2005)

These magical stories are definitely not taken as seriously today. Komi hunters almost always make jokes, even about superstitions that they otherwise accept. However, sometimes they also appear serious. For example, in order to avoid the loss of hunter's luck, a person is not allowed to use swear words when hunting. Even in a state of excitement, as Vladimir Lipin relates:

When I was a child, I ran to the take. There was the swamp and pine woods across it. And I saw a black grouse sitting there. I shot it, but it was still alive. 'Damn!' I screamed and ran to it. But the bird got lost in the middle of the swamp. One should not speak like that. (FM 1999)

This case has historical parallels in traditional Komi hunting beliefs. Komi hunters always believed that if a hunter looses his path in the forest, it may be the result of a curse sent by a hunter-witch (Sidorov [1928] 1997: 44–45).

There are quite a number of occasions when Komi hunting narratives include magic, and there is a common factor binding these together. It seems apparent that Komi hunting narrative as a whole is at least slightly influenced by a feeling of possible supernatural impact on further hunting.

Social Problems: Officials, Poachers and Customary Law

The real Komi hunter is always in some kind of confrontation with the authorities. Over the centuries, Komi hunters always thought of the forests, lakes and rivers as belonging to neighbouring communities, and that local customary law dictated the main principles of behaviour in these territories (Konakov 2004: 132–136). Hunters felt that they might get into trouble if they told hunting inspectors or the local police exactly what they did in the woods. The general attitude of the hunters in the Komi territories is that a 'real hunter' is not obliged to ask the permission of the authorities to hunt. Rather, Komi hunters buy licences ('tickets') to hunt a small number of elk or other game. However, they kill many more and give as their reason the fact that the inspectors, who also set the quotas, do not – as the Komi see it – know the real situation in the forest: how much game there is, the limit of over-hunting, etc. The hunters, particularly in Komi areas, consider the forests to be their own according to customary law, rather than public property. Yet, unfortunately, officials consider these hunters, who have more 'traditional attitudes', to be poachers. So the Komi feel it is sometimes better not to tell officials the whole truth about what they do.

In general, narratives describe different social relationships (within the local community and beyond). By using narratives, hunters also transmit knowledge concerning some of the options available to them, e.g. how to get customary permission to occupy a hunting ground or how to treat intruders, as Vladimir Lipin says:

> When I was in the army, someone made a hunting track near mine. I left him a warning: he did not react, but kept on hunting. Then I vandalised his traps. Then he vandalised my traps. I do not know who he was. This happened a number of times. We vandalised each other's traps. Then finally he stopped it: he did not vandalise my traps or hunt. Perhaps he realised that I had more rights than him. Someone told him it was my ground. I had picked berries there for many years and saw that for 10 years no one had tracked there. Then I occupied this track and marked it with my signs. (Leete and Lipin 2000: 79)

The Individual Characteristics of Hunters and Questions about Hunter Identity

Our research shows that Komi hunters break the social sub-group of hunter into several further categories. These so-called hunter types are: real hunter, average hunter, neophyte hunter and fool hunter.

Real hunter

In earlier scholarly works we find descriptions of Komi hunters with extraordinary, even supernatural, skills. For example, Alexei Sidorov ([1928] 1997: 50–51) writes (in the context of the Komi in the early twentieth century) that some characteristics reminiscent of an epic may be given to a hunter (even to one still living) by the community. For example, some hunters were so well known for their magic skills that other people were afraid to come close to their hunting ground (Sidorov [1928] 1997: 61).

In modern times it is less easy to find clear descriptions of the real Komi hunters in narratives. Yet people are differentiated by their hunting skills. For example during our trip to the Komi hunters in the autumn of 2005, VL said that, 'K is a real hunter because he tells lies all the time' (FM 2005).

Prohibitions on truthful talk were, and still are, widespread among hunting peoples. But what is 'the truth' in a cultural situation where you are supposed to lie in order to be 'real'? In fact it is clear that the only way a man can be thought of as a real hunter is when his peers consider him to be so. And as a general rule a man who is considered to be a real hunter by his peers does not talk about himself as such. Sometimes they may describe their hunting skills, proving the amount of game they are able to catch.

> YCh (38): I graduated from school and started to work. During the Soviet time there was always a plan, and plan obligations. In the first year, I got the first place among the hunters of the Komi Republic in fur hunting. I caught one thousand two hundred squirrels. And you must take off and prepare their furs.
>
> Art Leete: That was one season's catch?
>
> YCh: Yes, that was for the fall season only. I got so many squirrels. There were plenty of cones in the forest during that season and so the squirrels were also numerous … I caught squirrels and pine martens and minks. I caught so many fur-animals, twice as many as the hunter who got second place in the Republic.
>
> AL: What was the award?
>
> YCh: The award … various things: they gave you a rifle and a ticket for a trip to VDNH[2] every year. In principle, the awards were insignificant. And, maybe, sometimes they gave you some money. (FM 2005)

But the status of real hunter may be lost in time if the hunter ceases to hunt so intensively, as hunter P says: 'I have abandoned hunting, almost … I mean, that, of course, I hunt but not as much as before. You can say that I have already put hunting aside' (FM 2005). And: 'You see, how was the everyday life of hunters, hanging around with a back-bag? And nobody told us to do so, we did it on our own initiative. I lived this way for 25 years, but 5 years ago I abandoned it' (FM 2005).

There are many descriptions like these in our field notes. Reports on the characteristics of the real hunter among the Komi may sometimes be contradictory but it is evident that people admit the existence of more skilful hunters. These real hunters catch a lot of game and are good at telling lies (or, at least, are ambiguous in their statements) and are honoured by their fellow hunters and community members. The existence of this category of hunters in the narratives constitutes an important feature of many hunting stories.

Average hunter

The average hunter is almost the same kind of man as the real hunter. Usually he follows the hunting rules and can partially support his family with his catch. However, the main difference between him and the real hunter is that he is not as fully dedicated to hunting. He does not catch as much game as a real hunter. And the main point to raise here is that in narratives he does not appear as the complete equal of the real hunter. Descriptions of the hunter's general feelings characterizes the essential attitude of all hunters towards hunting, but is expressed more by the average hunter:

> VL: I returned from the hunting trip last year and I couldn't work a whole week. I was just high. It was so good. What's a bloody job after that – nothing! [Laughing.] You feel like a completely different person … I don't like the peasant's job. You are supposed to work so hard. I prefer to hang around somewhere with my rifle … I don't like that [peasant's] job.
> VSh (41): That's because you, all the Komi hunters, are just too lazy!
> VL: No. That's not the point! Why lazy? Sometimes you must clear the hunting path. Nowadays it is easy, you go with a chainsaw. But [the old hunters] managed the same thing with an axe in early times. That's really a hard job. I just don't feel any attraction towards agriculture, towards that peasants' work. [Laughing.] (FM 2005)

Average hunters tend to make a clear difference between themselves and real hunters. Compared to the latter, they often do not consider themselves to be hunters at all. For a researcher, the concept of 'hunter' may be wider, although in fieldwork situations it is hard to argue against the self-evaluation of the hunters themselves.

Neophyte hunter

The neophyte hunter may be a young boy who has just started his hunting career. He learns hunting skills and sometimes even has some special training in elements of hunting. For example, P, who is 'the real hunter', is very skilful in passing over narrow tree trunks that were laid down as improvized bridges over swamps and small rivers. P explained his extraordinary skills by the fact that in childhood, he used to run on the fences around his family house (FM 2005).

The second sub-category among the neophytes is constituted of adults who try to become hunters. They are trained by more skilful hunters who provide some areas that are not owned or actively used by any other hunters. And ethnographers may be distinguished here as the third group. If you work with hunters, you need to obtain at least a few hunting skills. And you also become a distinctive character in Komi hunters' stories.

At the beginning of our first trip to the forest in 1996, Vladimir Lipin and YCh put a piece of wood on a road and asked Art Leete to shoot it using a rifle. AL hit the wood. Then they asked AL to shoot a cigarette box and he hit this as well. The Komi asked: 'Have you had a rifle in your hands before?' AL replied that, in fact, he is a former Estonian shooting champion. The Komi: 'That is not fair! Why did not you tell us about that?' AL: 'But you planned to tease me!' VL and YCh: 'Yes, that was our plan but it is not fair, anyway!' The Komi have recalled this incident several times over the following years.

Figure 2: Komi hunter Yevgeni Chalanov having dinner in a hunting cabin (photograph by Art Leete 2003).

Of course it is normal for ethnographers to relates stories of field initiations as reflexive success stories, while hunters' stories about their own deeds are usually quite heroic.

Hunter fool

Among the Komi there are some hunters who tend to overestimate their take. One of them, VCh, was taught the following lesson by his father. VCh's father crossed his hunting track and saw there a hazel grouse in the boaster's trap. Then father took another grouse out of his bag and put it into the same snare. When VCh went home he told everyone the story about two birds in the same trap with tears in his eyes. Everybody laughed and could not believe it. Vch thought, however, still thought he had encountered the first true hunting miracle in his life[3] (Leete and Lipin 2000: 83–84).

However, hunting jokes that demonstrate insufficient skills can also be told about an average or even a real hunter. So it appears that everybody can be a fool in particular situations, or can be treated as such, as Vladimir Lipin says:

> Near the river Lov pua bears were as numerous as cows. Bear tracks were everywhere. I told my brother: 'give me some bullets … I mean cartridges with bullets'. And he gave some … I asked: 'when did you prepare these cartridges? How many years ago?' He said: 'approximately five years.' [Laughing.] And he continued: 'but don't worry – from a short distance it will kill a bear.' [Laughing.] 'Don't worry – from five or six metres it may kill, perhaps.' (FM 2005)

This kind of story demonstrates in addition to some hunters being considered full-time fools, it can be said that at times everyone makes some funny mistakes and so can be temporarily 'downgraded' to the status of fool. In addition hunters like to talk about their own failures and can be very self-critical, although these narratives often contain an element of humour.

It seems that the boundaries between different categories of hunters are treated as being fluid and it can be unclear into which category certain hunters fall.

Differences in Criteria Defining Truth and Certainty as They Apply to a Researcher and to a Hunter

As it has been noted above, telling lies is a characteristic feature of a real hunter, although in this respect average hunters and hunter fools can compete quite successfully. A Komi man can be even proud of the fact that he always tells lies. But how can a researcher be sure that hunters are not lying when confessing to this continual falsehood of their statements?

Let us try to analyse the Komi hunter's plans as a manifestation of the truth of uncertainty. During the autumn of 2005 (September and October), AL participated in two hunting trips (one lasting two days and the other ten days) with the Komi hunters. We had already planned a longer trip in July, although this did not mean that anything was clearly settled by the anticipated start date, nor even during the course of the trip. However, as AL had some previous experience of dealing with 'the forest men', he tried not to be surprised by anything. In the following part of this paper, we will provide some extracts from AL's field diary:

> September 14th, Syktyvkar
> In general, it looks uncertain whether we will go on the hunting trip or not.
> September 18th, Kulymdin (Katydpom)
> The bad news is that P, with whom we are supposed to go hunting, has a fever. We do not know what will happen next.
> September 19th, Katydpom
> P's Plans (as told to me by VL): Today P and I will go to Parma for a week, and after that to the Kuk-yu River for two weeks ... The initial plan that I heard in July, and which I used to prepare my own travel arrangements – to go to the Kuk-yu on the 20th – is not in force, of course.
> September 20th, hunting cabin on the Churk-yu River
> P said that VL called him in July and demanded that he should take me to the Kuk-yu ... According to what VL said, the hunting trip was P's own plan. The hunters are such men that you cannot hear a certain word from them.
> September 21st, Katydpom
> P and I are waiting for VL who should arrive from Syktyvkar over the weekend. After that we'll all go together to the road.

September 25th, Katydpom
VL did not turn up today. Perhaps he'll arrive tomorrow. This means that we cannot depart to the forest before the day after tomorrow ... This is a typical way of planning a hunting trip ... Let's see what will happen. The best I can do is just wait and observe the situation. Sitting in the village may be a good way to relax before the hunting trip. I hope that the trip will take place anyway ...
September 26th, Katydpom
VL called and said that he will arrive tomorrow. It's really interesting: these big hunters invited me on a hunting trip that was supposed to start on the 20th ... But nobody recognises the 'copyright' of the idea of a hunting trip that was supposed to start exactly on that day ... All this looks very traditional: hunter ethics prescribe uncertainty in the discourse concerning the beginning of a hunting trip.
September 27th, Katydpom
VL promised to arrive tomorrow ... And M told that the engine of the P's UAZ [small truck] has a problem and at best we could start our hunting trip the day after tomorrow. You just cannot plan anything.
October 1st, hunting cabin at the mouth of the Kuk-vozh Creek
Don't ever believe, what a hunter tells you ... But this continuous tactical planning seems to be an essential part of hunting. P's 'plan' for the following days: tomorrow he will go downstream to catch a boat and will then arrive after a couple of days. After that he and I will go fishing ... Today we will go to a longer hunting path. Tomorrow I will go to the shorter one. The day after tomorrow we will have some rest, and the day after that I will check the traps on the longer path. The next day we will fish. On the 7th I must check the traps on the shorter path and on the 8th the longer path again. On the 9th we will return to the first hunting cabin, The Pretty Cabin (*Gazha Kerka*). On the 10th we must arrive in Kulymdin ... Later P decided that it would be better to check the longer path on the 7th and the shorter path on the 8th.
October 5th, hunting cabin at the mouth of Kuk-vozh Creek
It's not hard to guess: our plans have changed again. Today P and VL will go fishing and I must check the shorter hunting path to the north. Tomorrow I will check the longer path and the day after tomorrow we will leave for The Pretty Cabin. P said: 'Without rowan berries we have nothing to do here.' (FM 2005)

In summary, hunting plans for our fieldwork period were made 14 times over three months. Strategic plans concerning the start of the longer hunting trip were changed nine times (in some cases, these changes had a circumstantial nature and did not depend only on our personal decisions). It is even impossible to figure out who was really the initiator of the hunting trip as both VL and P distanced themselves from that role. The logistical plans concerning everyday activities during the hunting trip were changed five times. Ultimately everything ran smoothly.[4]

A considerable amount of time was dedicated, on an almost daily basis, to discussing further hunting plans (despite previous plans remaining in place for at least a week). I think that this kind of conversational or narrative uncertainty is a characteristic feature of the Komi hunters' identity. You must be flexible and able to change your hunting tactics continually in order to be as successful as possible. However, I did not feel that these planning changes were of any direct practical value. It seemed that plans were changed every day without any clear or good reason.

We cannot be sure whether all the events described by the hunters have really happened or not. Perhaps a kind of narrative truth is always present, even if it is given in a humorous form. There must be some uncertainty in hunting stories. It is not good for a listener to know exactly what really happen with a hunter in the forest. Perhaps hunting magic, as mentioned above, also has some influence. The Komi hunters' narratives are not pure lies, but rather continuously uncertain stories in which the listener can never decide whether they are hearing a fabrication, or the truth (in a positivistic sense).

Discussion

Our aim was not to make clear sense of Komi hunters' narrative genres or practices. These narrations are hard to classify. We attempted to provide an overview of the ways in which narrations help to build up the Komi hunter self-image, and of how hunting stories function in the local cultural discourse.

Hunting reflects very clearly a construction of male-female identities in Komi culture. Women (just as priests) are considered to have a distinctive potential to harm hunters' luck. This causes the exclusion of women from the hunting domain and cuts them off from corresponding knowledge. As they are members of the same narrative community, women also know hunting stories. Women's random stories about hunting are not derived from direct experience and they interpret hunting differently from the hunters themselves, basically as a strange male hobby that is related to peculiar beliefs, distanced from the Orthodox faith.

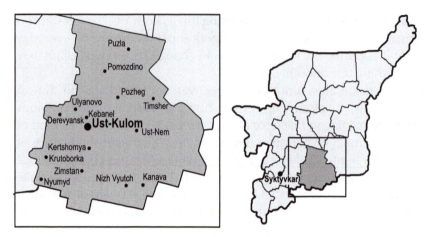

The Komis are a Finno-Ugric people in Russian Federation. For the location of Republic of Komi, see the map in the introduction.

Storytelling is a loosely structured phenomenon. In many cases it is not clear how to distinguish genres, facts from fiction, and the limits of the narrator's creativity. Narratives that scholars can record are sometimes the results of a certain provocation or professional demand, yet sometimes narrating starts spontaneously. So the circumstances of particular storytelling situations also have a certain influence on the material collected. The narrators' general cultural background and their individual characteristics also have a certain impact on their storytelling.

Pasi Enges has drawn attention to the complex relationship between fact and imagination in the genres of belief:

> Skilful narrators may creatively mix up traditional narrative motifs and motifs invented by themselves, report true as well as made-up events, and quite freely expand the boundaries of the realistic world. Thus, in narrating and listening to stories about encountering the supernatural, there is often an interplay going on between fact and fiction. (Enges 2005: 101)

Yet we are not supposed to work only with skilled narrators, and there is no reason to underestimate the role of the less skilled story-tellers in any culture. Even if somebody can be categorized as a skilful narrator, creating close contact with him or her and encouraging them to narrate can be tricky. In particular situations, a person's mood on a certain day or the amount of free time they have may also play an important role in the work of the researcher. The data that scholars can collect, and their impression of someone as a good narrator or otherwise, depends on factors such as these.

According to Pasi Enges, (2005: 101) narrating memorates has several functions among the River Sámi people. Narration may be carried out to pass the time, or from a pedagogical or humorous point of view, or a narrator can test listeners' gullibility, comment on social relations, display his creative skills. Memories are also told to prove the existence of the supernatural world, although this purpose is not necessarily primary. In principal there is an infinite number of possibilities when making scholarly distinctions between the functions of the folk narrative. Unlike Enges we didn't follow the generic paradigm, but rather attempted to analyse stories as functionally related to certain aspect of the Komi way of life. However, from Enges' approach, we can derive a few issues that are also worth discussing in the Komi hunters' case.

Komi hunters' lives are linked to supernatural issues in many ways. Telling stories in a forest has traditionally been related to hunting luck: 'A popular belief existed that the forest spirits liked stories, and so the Komi told stories in the evening in order to have success in hunting on the following day' (Konakov 2003: 343).

Storytelling is related to proper behaviour in the forest. Nowadays, the Komi hunters touch supernatural topics randomly in their stories. And a possible addressing of stories to spirits is not indicated in contemporary data.

At the same time, it is obvious that hunters like to talk about hunting in the forest and not in a village. Narrating is mostly situational (as impressions of hunting are still fresh in the forest, several hunters spend much time together and during dark evenings there is little else to do in a hunting cabin) and functional (enabling the sharing of operative experience and knowledge during a hunting trip). The similarity of storytelling practices has been preserved through different Komi hunters' generations across a long time period.

Problem of truth in the Komi hunting narratives must be stressed again. On one hand hunting rules prohibit hunters from telling the truth about hunting. As one hunter told us: 'Let's drink a tea and I'll tell you few lies.' On the other hand, another Komi hunter made a reflexive statement during our fieldwork: 'I don't want to say anything about hunting because I'm afraid that nobody believes me.' So, it appears that the Komi hunters know that nobody believes them and this makes it difficult for them to report anything, as tradition-conscious narrative community somehow denies their discourse. However, these statements also indicate that the Komi hunters have different individual strategies concerning the treatment of the truth. Some hunters enjoy the status of liar and some do not.

We can see certain functional diversity in Komi hunting stories. There is no dominant purpose for telling these narratives, and in many cases the genre of the stories is not easily identifiable. The motivation of each narrator, and the situations that prompt storytelling, may be very different, although we can observe some general rules that mean the exchanging of messages must be, 'mutually comprehensive to be effective' (Ben-Amos 1981: 230).

In this paper we analysed some of the different features that characterize narration among Komi hunters. We identified patterns within the stories. Elements like hunting magic, the description of social threats Komi hunters should consider, as well as highlighting the importance of individual hunter characteristics, the circumstances and locations of storytelling and differences in criteria governing the relative truths of the researcher and the hunter.

Acknowledgements

The article was written with the support of the Estonian Science Foundation (project no 8335) and of the European Union through the European Regional Development Fund (Centre of Excellence, CECT). Photographs are from the Collection of the Estonian National Museum in Tartu: ENM Fk 2914: 166; ENM Fk 2914: 237.

Notes

1. Prohibitions concerning talk about the catch are common among the hunting peoples of Siberia and the Russian north (see, for example, Alekseenko 1967: 174; Vasilevich 1969: 69; Lukina 1986: 133; Potapov 2001: 125; 133–134; Lar 2003; Oshchepkov and Povod 2003: 51).

2. VDNH – Выставка достижении народного хозяйства СССР 'Exhibition of the Achievements of the National Economy of USSR' (in Russian). A huge permanent exhibition of national achievements in the fields of heavy industry, building enterprises, agriculture, transportation, culture and medicine, displayed in Moscow since 1959.

3. The same family owned a Russian hunting journal containing quite a similar story: 'But one hunter told me that he caught two hazel grouse, both

by the head, in one trap. Perhaps they ran towards each other and went into the same trap' (Frolov 1999: 40).

4. Continuous plan-making is also a characteristic feature of contemporary Finnish hunting management (see Hacker 1977: 44–45).

Sources

Collection of Photographs of the Estonian National Museum in Tartu: Illus. No 1: ENM Fk 2914: 166; illus. No. 2: ENM Fk 2914: 237.

EA – Ethnographical Archives of Estonian National Museum: 239 = Komi materials 1996, 209-241.

FM – Fieldwork materials of the authors, 1996–2009.

TAP – Topographical Archives of Estonian National Museum: 939 = 6. Siberi lugemised Kunstkameras (MAE RAN) Peterburis, välitööd Komi Vabariigis ja esinemine Euroopa Ülikoolis Peterburis Etnoloogia teaduskonna seminaris. Art Leete päevik 27. oktoober – 19. november 2004.

References

Alekseenko E. A. (1967) *Ketȳ: Istoriko-etnograficheskie ocherki.* Leningrad: Nauka.

Ben-Amos, Dan (1981) Analytical categories and ethnic genres. In D. Ben-Amos (ed.) *Folklore Genres.* Austin, TX: University of Texas Press.

Ben-Amos, Dan (2005) Narratives: What are they good for and why do we keep telling them. In *Folk Narrative Theories and Contemporary Practices. Abstracts. 14th Congress of the International Society for Folk Narrative Research (ISFNR),* 77–78. Held in Tartu, Estonia. Tartu: Estonian Literary Museum and University of Tartu.

Chuvyurov, A. and Smirnova, O. (2003) Confessional factors in the ethno-cultural processes of the Upper-Vychegda Komi. *Pro Ethnologia* 15: 169–196.

Enges, P. (2005) Memorate: A uniform genre? Examples from River Sámi tradition. In *Folk Narrative Theories and Contemporary Practices. Abstracts. 14th Congress of the International Society for Folk Narrative Research (ISFNR) Held in Tartu, Estonia,* 100–101. Tartu: Estonian Literary Museum and University of Tartu.

Frolov, V. (1999) Dorogaya redaktsiya! In *Okhota i okhotnich'e hozyaĭstvo,* 12: 40.

Hacker, R. (1977) The Finnish hunting system: A case study. *Ethnologia Fennica* 6 (1–2): 40–48.

Konakov, N. D. (2001) Religioznoe mirovozzrenie promȳslovogo naseleniya naroda komi. In N. D. Konakov (ed.) *Khristianstvo i yazȳchestvo naroda komi,* 196–228. Sȳktȳvkar: Komi knizhnoe izdatel'stvo.

Konakov, N. D. (2003) versa. In A.-L. Siikala, V. Napolskikh and M. Hoppál (eds.) *Komi Mythology,* 340–345. Budapest: Akadémiai Kiadó, Helsinki: Finnish Literature Society.

Konakov, N. D. (2004) Traditsionnaya sistema prirodopol'zovaniya i khoziaistvennȳe zanyatiya komi. In N. D. Konakov (ed.) *Zȳryanskiĭ mir: Ocherki o traditsionnoĭ kul'ture komi naroda,* 65–181. Sȳktȳvkar: Komi knizhnoe izdatel'stvo.

Koosa, Piret (2010) Naiste rollist külakomide usuelus. In *Eesti Rahva Muuseumi aastaraamat,* LIII, 82–150. Tartu: Eesti Rahva Muuseum.

Lar, L. A., Oshchepkov, K. A. and Povod, N. A. (2003) Dukhovnaya kul'tura nentsev. In A. N. Bagashev (ed.) *Etnografiya i antropologiya Yamala,* 50–112 Novosibirsk: Nauka.

Leete, A. and Lipin, V. (2000) Komi hunter ethics at the end of the 20th century. In A. Leete (ed.) *Cultural Identity of Arctic Peoples. Arctic Studies 4. Pro Ethnologia* 10, 77–85. Tartu: Estonian National Museum.

Leete, A. and Seljamaa, E.-H. (2005) The 14th Congress of the International Society for Folk Narrative Research. *Asian Folklore Studies* 64: 308–312.

Lukina, N. V. (1986) Kul'turnȳe traditsii v khozyastvennoĭ deyatel'nosti khantov. In C. M. Taksami (ed.) *Kul'turnȳe traditsii narodov Sibiri,* 121–138. Leningrad: Nauka.

Mitrokhin, N. (2006) *Russkaya pravoslavnaya tserkov: sovremennoe sostoyanie i aktual'nȳe problemȳ.* Moskva: Novoe literaturnoe obozrenie.

Potapov, L. P. (2001) *Okhotnichiĭ promȳsel altaĭtsev. (Otrazhenie drevnetyurkskoĭ kul'turȳ v traditsionnom okhotnich'em promȳsle altaĭtsev).* St Petersburg: MAE RAN.

Sharapov, V. E. (2001) Zhivaya traditsiya: zavetnȳe i khramovȳe prazdniki u sovremennȳkh komi. In N. D. Konakov (ed.) *Khristianstvo i yazȳchestvo naroda Komi,* 148–168. Sȳktȳvkar: Komi knizhnoe izdatel'stvo.

Sidorov, A. S. (1997) [1928] *Znakharstvo, koldovstvo i porcha u naroda komi. Materialȳ po psikhologii koldovstva.* St Petersburg: Aleteĭya.

Vasilevich, G. M. (1969) *Evenki. Istoriko-etnograficheskie ocherki (XVIII – nachalo XX v.).* Leningrad: Nauka.

Vlasova, V. V. (2003) Predstavleniya o krestnȳkh u komi (zȳryan). In *Studia Juvenalia. Sbornik rabot molodȳkh uchenȳkh Instituta yazȳka, literaturȳ i istorii Komi NTS UrO RAN,* 110–119. Sȳktȳvkar: Izdatel'stvo Komi nauchnogo centra.

Stories of Santiago Pilgrims: Tradition through Creativity

Tiina Sepp[*]

I saw him when I was about to go out of the Cathedral of Santiago de Compostela. Bearded and shaggy, carrying a backpack and a staff, this recently arrived young pilgrim was standing in the middle of the entrance and talking to the people who were going out of the church. Self-contentment was oozing from each of his cells ... When I got closer, I heard him ask 'the ladies to let the tired pilgrim get in'. The women backed off respectfully, and he walked in as a hero. Somebody asked where he had started the pilgrimage, and the man said with a voice full of pride: 'France'. At that moment I recalled that on my own first arrival in Santiago I also felt that I had accomplished something extraordinary and felt superior to the 'common people' and tourists crowding the cathedral. What might bring one back down to earth is the fact that every year almost 100,000 *compostelas* are issued to people who have completed the Santiago pilgrimage. (Extract from my fieldwork diary, November 2007)

Introduction

This chapter is based on my fieldwork in Spain during the years 2003–2008. I have walked the Camino de Santiago four times: in June–July 2003, November–December 2004, May 2005 and April 2008. In October 2008, I spent two weeks working as a *hospitalera* (voluntary hostess) in a pilgrims' refuge in Granyon, Spain. The languages I used for talking to pilgrims or interviewing them were Spanish, English and Estonian.

Camino de Santiago, also known as the Way of St James, is one of the most important modern pilgrimage routes in the Western world. The Camino is actually a network of routes that have been used since

* Tiina Sepp is a Doctoral Student of Folklore at the University of Tartu. Her research areas include Catholic and contemporary pilgrimage and vernacular religion. Since 2003, she has been researching various aspects of the Santiago de Compostela pilgrimage and has published two books on that subject.

the eleventh century to reach Santiago de Compostela, a city in the north-west of Spain that is the reported burial place of the apostle Saint James the Greater. Although the Santiago pilgrimage has a religious foundation based in Catholic doctrine, nowadays it is not walked for religious motives only. The most popular route is called the *camino francés* (The French Way) and it covers about 750 kilometres. The route is marked with yellow arrows and scallop shells. Pilgrims carry a *credencial,* the so-called pilgrim's passport, which is stamped daily at authorized places and gives the right to stay in the hostel-like refuges provided by the state, confraternities or parishes (which ask for a donation or make a small charge). On presenting the *credencial* at Santiago Cathedral's office of reception, the pilgrims receive the *compostela,* a document certifying the completion of the pilgrimage. In 1985 UNESCO named Santiago de Compostela a World Heritage City, and in 1987 the pilgrimage route became the Council of Europe's first Cultural Itinerary.

My main interest lies in the belief narratives told by pilgrims. In this chapter I write about several people, although the main focus is on the stories told by Roger, a Belgian pilgrim I met in Burgos in April

Figure 1: Pilgrims on the Camino de Santiago. Navarre, April 2008 (photograph by Tiina Sepp).

2008. He first caught my attention with his looks – his unusual hat and recumbent bike decorated with multicoloured flags reminded me of a circus artist rather than a pilgrim. Thirty-eight-year-old Roger, who works as a lawyer in Brussels, started the pilgrimage in order to pay for his sins. He started from his home in Brussels and, unlike the majority of pilgrims whose goal is to reach Santiago de Compostela, Roger's aim was to cycle to Finisterre (an alternative destination for the Santiago pilgrimage situated on the Atlantic coast) and back. He had started twice on foot but both times had to turn back home because of knee problems. In the evening we went out for dinner with a group of pilgrims, and Roger told us two stories that he called 'Camino legends'. In addition to its use as an analytical folkloristic term, 'legend' has a wide vernacular usage. Since Roger called his stories Camino legends, I will use the same word, even though it does not correspond to the folkloristic definition.

From the day we met until the day he arrived home more than a month later, Roger sent me text messages from his mobile phone, and also various emails and postcards. I have saved all of them and with his kind permission I have used them in writing this article. After reaching home from his pilgrimage, Roger travelled to Estonia to tell me some more stories, all of which I have recorded.

In the first section of the article I observe how a pilgrim's identity can be constructed through the telling of stories. The second section is about the pilgrims' accounts of their encounters with the supernatural, and the third looks at some aspects of Roger's storytelling.

Constructing a Pilgrim's Identity: Who is an 'Authentic' Pilgrim?

Roger Abrahams argues that for many psychiatrists, sociologists and also folklorists, identity emerges from the stories one tells of oneself or one's community. However, researchers often approach their informants with stereotypes (Abrahams 2003: 201). During my field trip to the Camino in April 2008 I experienced it myself. I met an elderly Dutch pilgrim who had started walking from his home. When he heard that I was writing my dissertation about pilgrims he found it very interesting and wanted to know what I had found out about 'us'. I told him about some conclusions I had reached and that I had defined a pilgrim as someone who experiences communitas[1] as opposed to a tourist who simply enjoys the Camino, goes sightseeing, etc. The Dutch pilgrim did not agree with me, and he said: 'For me there is no communitas on the Camino. What matters to me is that I can walk alone, I am free of duties, I feel well and peaceful.' He suggested that I just liked the idea of communitas and I saw it because I wanted to see it. 'You are creating the communitas. Without you it does not exist.' In the middle of our conversation I had to leave the room for a while, and on returning I saw that the Dutch pilgrim had left some grapes on the bunks of our roommates and myself. When I thanked him, he said: 'I am sure you would call it communitas. But it is not. I just wanted to give you some grapes.'

So, according to him, I create the communitas, describe it and put it in a theoretical framework. The researcher's personality certainly influences his or her work. For example, if I were more introverted, I might have defined a pilgrim in a different way.

Identity is a very popular subject for scholars as well as for 'ordinary people'. We can do several things with our identity: we can lose it, search for it, achieve it. Today it is very easy to lose one's identity. Roger Abrahams has said that personal choice is the main factor in achieving one's identity. 'Having an identity and using it as a way of creating a sense of self-worth becomes an obligation' (Abrahams 2003: 211). The pilgrimage to Santiago offers many people a good opportunity to acquire a pilgrim's identity, at least temporarily. Many Santiago pilgrims hope to escape from the twenty-first-century city scene into the idyllic medieval countryside. Referring to Benedict Anderson (1983), American anthropologist Nancy Frey has pointed out that pilgrims often feel part of an 'imagined community' and this imagined community links them 'through their bodily actions and geography of pilgrimage routes, to past, present, and future travellers of the way' (Frey 1998: 207).

Present-day pilgrims to Santiago are not always religious, so they may need to think of some other ways of identifying themselves as pilgrims. Being a pilgrim is what the Camino is mainly about, no matter how the word pilgrim may be defined. People going to Santiago sometimes search for the 'other', hoping that this might help create and strengthen their own pilgrim's identity.

As soon as I started my first Camino in 2003, I noticed that people going to Santiago are sometimes called tourists and sometimes pilgrims, even though they seemed to be doing the same thing: walking or cycling to Santiago, carrying their backpack and staying in refuges. Researchers of tourism offer several examples of the traveller who

Figure 2: Pilgrims relaxing after dinner in a pilgrims' refuge. Belorado (Burgos), November 2004 (photograph by Tiina Sepp).

tries to distinguish himself from the tourist, unable to see that they are involved in the same activity (Bendix: 2002). Tourists tend to be looked down on, they are considered inferior.

The people going to Santiago often talk about the 'authentic' pilgrim. The opposite of an authentic pilgrim is apparently a tourist, who is considered demanding, complaining and superficial and who is accused of using the Camino infrastructures for cheap holidaymaking. In Spanish the word *turigrino* is formed from two words, *turista* (tourist) and *peregrino* (pilgrim). This word is considered rather offensive.

On my second Camino in November 2004, I interviewed my walking companions on the distinction between a pilgrim and tourist. The answers I got ranged from 'everybody who goes to Santiago is a pilgrim', to 'everybody who goes to Santiago is a tourist'. I also asked my companions if they identified themselves as pilgrims and what the qualities of an authentic pilgrim were. Most of the people I interviewed considered themselves pilgrims even though they often added they were not religious or 'churchy'. Some said that they started the Camino as a tourist and arrived in Santiago as a pilgrim. Their reasons for calling someone a pilgrim varied widely. For example, a Czech pilgrim Pavel told me that people called him a real pilgrim because he had started the Camino from his home in Prague and was sleeping under the stars. However, on seeing his mobile phone, the same people changed their mind and said that he was not a real pilgrim. Similarly, Gintars from Lithuania was considered by many a pilgrim *par excellence* because he had been on a pilgrimage for five years, he had also walked to Rome and Jerusalem. But even he lost a considerable part of his halo the moment he reached for his mobile phone. The time of the year may also play the role in whether or not one is considered a pilgrim. In Spanish there is a saying: *En verano hay mucha gente y pocos peregrinos, en invierno hay poca gente y muchos peregrinos* (In summer there are a lot of people but few pilgrims, in winter there are few people and many pilgrims). Those who start walking alone are also taken more seriously than those who go with a group. And *bicigrinos* (a colloquial term for those who go on a bike) are often looked down on.

It must be said that participants in the modern Camino have rather differing views on what makes a pilgrim authentic. Nancy Frey (1998) has suggested that in the modern pilgrimage one can be an authentic pilgrim without being religious; the metaphoric pilgrim seeks an inner way, or alternatives to modern society or the alienation of daily life.

I have walked the Camino as a tourist as well as a pilgrim. In winter 2004 I felt I was in a state of liminality as described by Victor Turner

Figure 3: Pilgrims leaving the refuge in the morning. Atapuerca (Burgos), November 2004 (photograph by Tiina Sepp).

(1979: 94–95). I lived in a time of enchantment when anything seemed possible. I experienced communitas, I felt an intense sense of intimacy with my fellow pilgrims. We gave each other courage and support, and I am still in touch with all of them. Then, in May 2005, I went with a friend and I felt as if I was enjoying a picnic that lasted for a couple of weeks.

Pilgrim's Identity through Camino Legends

Even though several scholars agree that authenticity is an emotional category that cannot be measured using scientific methods, people still try to do so. I have also tried to find out what is behind the concept of the authentic pilgrim: how pilgrims identify themselves and who they consider to be an authentic pilgrim. After completing my MA thesis, called *Pilgrims and Tourists on the Way to Santiago de Compostela*, I was certain that I had exhausted the issue of the authentic pilgrim and I had no intention to take it up again. However, while reading Roger's messages and listening to his stories, I realized that as this subject was of utmost importance to him, I could not possibly leave it aside. In his text messages and emails he was constantly emphasizing his identity as a pilgrim. I will quote his first text message: 'Last night a man said I was radiating something he called chivalrous and Christ-like. But I am just a simple pilgrim, nothing more, and a few stories are all I have … May your day be blessed.'

On the day we met, he said: 'Yes, I have time. I don't have common sense or money but I have lots of time.' The fact that he more than once pointed out that he was 'just a poor pilgrim', may have had something to do with his not-so-humble job as a civil servant in Brussels. He obviously wanted to distance himself from that role.

The fact that his identity as a true pilgrim was very important to Roger was also revealed in the stories that he told me. Identity is formed through opposing oneself to the other. For pilgrims the other can be either local people or fake pilgrims (*turigrinos*). Roger said that he sometimes met people who asked him to pray for them and light a candle for them in a chapel along the Camino; in Belgium a woman had stopped her car and given him 20 euros without saying a word; a priest had embraced Roger's legs and told him that pilgrims pray with their feet. Roger often told local people that it was thanks to them that he could do his pilgrimage. 'If everybody went on a pilgrimage, who would be working in the shops?' At the same time he is convinced that if someone refuses to receive a pilgrim, he is committing a sin. When Roger told me about a priest in France who had refused to host him in the monastery (claiming that there was no spare room), his eyes filled with tears and he said: 'If there had not been all these people around, I would have punched him out.' What most upset Roger was that somebody who represented the church, had refused to receive a pilgrim. He added that hopefully God would give that priest 'what he deserves'.

On the first day we met, Roger told me and a few other pilgrims two stories that he called Camino legends. One of them was about a greedy woman who refused to give bread to a passing pilgrim.

The story of the bread of St James

It's a kind of an urban legend in ancient days, it's a story pilgrims told each other to give each other hope in ... when they had it difficult. It's also a story, I think, that pilgrims used to tell to encourage people to be helpful to them because pilgrims were not always that very welcome in all times. And the story goes that St James has heard complaints about people not being very hospitable to pilgrims on the way. And he decides to go out and check it out for himself. He puts on his robe, he picks up his pack and ... light pack of course because in those days they used to travel light, nobody knows when those days are but it's always somewhere in the past, in the good old days I'd say, and St James passes by a farm, and he smells bread. Well, there was the farmer's wife who had been baking bread and she had this oven outside, this oven where all the bread had been baked. She had gotten out the loaves from the oven, and laid them on the, what you call it, the thing under the window, the window sill, to let the bread cool down. And St James well he passed by, and smelled the freshly baked bread and said: 'This is as good a moment as any other to try out the hospitality of people, especially since this lady has been baking bread.' And he goes up to the house, and there's a dog barking wow wow wow, and the lady of the house, the farmer's wife comes outside and she sees St James and she says: 'What do you want, man?' St James, very nice as he is, says: 'Oh my fair lady, I'm a pilgrim, and I'm kind of hungry. Would you have something for me to eat?', 'Pilgrim, I have nothing for you. If you want water, there's a stream a couple of miles down the road, drink there.' And St James, he says: 'Well my lady, I think I smell bread somewhere. And those I see, are those not freshly baked loaves?' The woman says: 'Pilgrim, you must be sick, for I don't see anything. What you see there, well, they are not loaves, they are stones'. And St James says: 'Woman', he does not address her as my lady because she's lying to him and he knows it because he can smell the bread, he can basically see them there. And St James says: 'Woman, are you sure?' 'Yes', says the woman, 'I'm sure, pilgrim, those are stones you see'. And St James says: 'So be it, woman'. And he turns around and waves with his hand, ok, I understood. And he just goes on. And then the woman who says well it's been long enough now, the bread has cooled down. She goes to the window sill to fetch the bread, and what does she see? That all the bread has turned into stone. Just as he said it would. They were not loaves, they were stones. And ever since then, that woman was always very hospitable to any pilgrim that came by.

Roger did not invent the plot of this story; bread that has not been shared turning to stone (or blood, worms, etc.) is a common motif in religious tales (Tubach 1969: 758–759; ATU 751G; Uther 2004). Roger adapted the plot to the context of the Camino because, as he put it: 'If you are on the Camino, you have your story take place on the Camino.'

Roger has already decided that on his tombstone there will be the following line: 'He is moving on to the other side of the world.' By the other side of the world he means Finisterre, the destination of his pilgrimage.

In the Middle Ages it was easy to recognize pilgrims by their clothes. Sometimes criminals dressed up as pilgrims in order to get the benefits meant for the latter, to rob them, or for other evil reasons. Pilgrims really had to watch out for them. Today the main villains in pilgrims' eyes seem to be tourists who take advantage of the Camino's cheap accommodation. I have heard numerous stories about exhausted pilgrims who reach the refuge after a hard day's walk to discover that the last bunks had been given to 'pilgrims' who had allegedly got there by car. The tourists have often been seen to park their car at some distance from the refuge and tramp their feet in the mud or dust to get the look of somebody who has walked a long distance. We can almost talk about the demonization of the tourist. The way a Santiago pilgrim feels about a tourist may vary widely. It may just mean looking down on the 'poor uninitiated beings' but it can also extend to hatred because they unfairly take something that is not theirs, thus depriving pilgrims of certain things, most often accommodation.

To show his contempt for tourists, Roger has made up a host of longer and shorter stories. For example, he told me a joke: 'The main cause of death for *turigrinos* is being run over by the bus they just got off. Because they are so anxious to get to the *albergue*.' He added: 'pilgrims often tell jokes about *turigrinos*'.

The story about Saint James punishing a *turigrino* by miraculously deleting all the stamps from his *credencial* also has a similar moral to it.

The story of the turigrino *who was converted to a* peregrino

If you come to the pilgrims' office in Compostela, you'll see that they have a small museum there, they have this cupboard with all sorts of things that pilgrims have given them, or brought, and one of the things they have is this *credencial* with only one stamp in it somewhere in the middle of the booklet, and they keep it there as a souvenir from a *peregrino*. And the name isn't visible, so nobody actually knows who it belongs to. And there is a nice story ... nice, no it's a truth how it got there. There once was a *peregrino* who left in Saint-Jean-Pied-de-Port and was quite determined to go on foot to Compostela. But on the first day it was raining when he woke up and he decided to take a bus to Roncesvalles. He got on a bus, checked in the refuge ... washed his clothes, did the things that pilgrims do in the refuge. And the next morning he got up at 6 o'clock like pilgrims do, he was feeling very tired, and decided to take the bus again to the next refuge 25 km away. He went to the refuge, got a stamp like all other *peregrinos* ... the next day he had another excuse for taking the bus, on the 3rd, 4th, 5th day ... always had a good excuse. But one day he found out that there was no bus to the village he wanted to go to. So he started to walk, it was a hot day, he got blisters, had it difficult. And he was complaining a lot about all this, and St James heard it and decided to go and check it out. He decided to teach him a lesson. He got himself a car, disguised himself and drove in the same direction as the *peregrino*. He stopped his car and asked the *peregrino* if he wanted a lift. 'No no, I'm a real *peregrino*, I walk. Thanks.' The next day the pilgrim was so tired after having walked and took the bus again, and the next day ... And on arriving in Santiago his *credencial* was filled with stamps as if he had really walked it on foot. He went to the pilgrims office to get his compostela. And St James who had been watching him, said to himself: 'Now is the payback time.' And as the *peregrino* handed in his *credencial*, St James clicked his fingers and all the stamps in the *credencial* disappeared. Just leaving one stamp from the day when the *peregrino* had walked. And the *peregrino* was refused a compostela, the man was shocked when he saw his empty *credencial*, and when he recognised the one stamp. He went out, he was so shocked that he became converted, and he became very deeply religious. He rushed to the cathedral to confess to the priest what he had done. After that he went back home, to leave once again and this time he walked every mile, no complaining whatsoever, and when he came to Compostela the second time, he explained in the office what had happened. And since then his first *credencial* has been kept there as a warning to other *turigrinos*, as a sign of the saint being active today. People have asked who is this pilgrim. They refuse to show the name. The *peregrino* became a priest, and is the present bishop of Santiago.

The protagonist does something that an authentic pilgrim would probably call a mortal sin – instead of walking the Camino he gets on a bus. In this story the opposition between a real pilgrim and fake pilgrim (tourist, *turigrino*) is plain and clear. The *turigrino* is too lazy to walk, so he takes a bus instead, and on arriving in Santiago he has the impudence to go to the Pilgrim's Office to apply for the *compostela* as if he had walked the Camino. After converting to become a pilgrim, he decides to do the Camino again, this time in the right way: 'He walks every mile, no complaining whatsoever ...'

Roger told me that he made this story up in the Pilgrims' Office in Santiago when he saw '*compostelas* being handed out to *turigrinos*'. While in real life *turigrinos* often get away with cheating, in Roger's story St James interferes and punishes the protagonist.

The story has the structure of a folktale: (a) the protagonist ignores the ban; (b) he is punished for this; and (c) he is converted and his empty *credencial* goes on display as a warning for others.

Being a pilgrim is obviously something extremely important and valuable for Roger. When I told him about Indian folklorist Jawaharlal Handoo's suggestion of applying Propp's fairy tale structure to a pilgrimage – the hero sets out, meets obstacles on his way and finally achieves his aim – Roger did not like the idea and said: 'The fairy tale has a happy end, the pilgrimage does not. When you get back home, everything is the same as before.' Instead, he suggested comparing pilgrimage to hagiography. Roger has also told me that he sees a parallel between Moses on Mount Sinai and himself on the Col de Somport (on this mountain he met God). He added that on top of a mountain man comes to great things.

Stories about Miracles and Supernatural Encounters on the Camino

Col de Somport – Roger's Encounter with God

I first heard about of this very special event when I met Roger in Burgos, on the Camino. He did not elaborate on it, just mentioned that some days ago he had seen God who had helped him ride up the Col de Somport. When we met again, I asked Roger to tell me more about it, and I recorded his story. Here are some excerpts.

I saw the Pyrenees and got scared. You see the mountain in the distance, the clouds in the sky, and you could still see snow on the slopes. I got scared. You have to get over them. Will I be able to make it? You've been climbing for a lot of kilometres … The last part, 8 km uphill, is quite hard. I was sort of talking to God. 'You'll have to help me.' Then you come to a mountain stream. I was so worn out that I decided to eat and rest to get power to do the next part. I just didn't have the power to get up. No cramps, no feeling sick, but just a feeling of not being able to do it. I couldn't move on. My legs hurt but not of physical things … I just couldn't get up. I had to stop again because I couldn't do it. I sort of gave up. It was 2 kilometres to go, I had ridden 100 metres. I stopped once again, lay my head on the handlebars, I was so tired I wanted to cry. I would have stayed there all night. I remember thinking, 'I can't do it'.

The next thing I remember was this light movement of feeling I was not there. Ultimate second of not being there. I didn't realise it first. 'God, if you want me to get going, you have to do it because I can't do it any more.' I put my feet on pedals, switched gears, why didn't I do it before? My legs moved by themselves. They didn't really hurt anymore. I went on, saw the ski station, wanted to stop there. My legs did not stop moving. I wanted to stop moving but couldn't. I saw San Miguel [Spanish beer], I thought this must be Spain now, why else are they selling Spanish beer.

God drove up these last few kilometres with me … It was not a personal god who cares whether you go to church or cares about you. It was ultimate potential power. If you get in touch with it correctly, with this power, it doesn't matter if you use this power for good or bad. It was not about good or evil. Like electricity in your room, you can use it for good or for bad. It's neutral. Then I knew I was going to make it. I figured I was forgiven. Not that he would have cared. If I had sinned, if he had cared, he would not have helped me. He didn't seem to be caring about good or bad. From that on I knew I was going to make it. That the rest would be easier. To find out that God might not care is first relief but then it raises a lot of questions. I don't go to church anymore. Why are church doors closed?

Roger said that his experience differs from the revelations approved by the Catholic Church, and he is even afraid to tell his priest about it because it may sound too heretical. 'In the Middle Ages they would have burnt me for that.'

The encounter with God changed Roger's attitude towards the church. He does not believe in the confession any more. He does not believe that the God he saw would need any dogmas. I could not help noticing a certain contradiction here. On the one hand, Roger said that the God who had helped him was beyond good and evil, beyond any dogmas. On the other hand, the fact that God helped him up the hill, showed him that his sins had been forgiven. 'He was riding with me', Roger said and added that at that moment he felt that he had been forgiven for all his sins. Moreover, he also felt that maybe he even did not have to pay for any sins at all.

Roger's miraculous experience fits very well into the context of the Camino miracles.

Pilgrims' Stories About their Encounters with the Supernatural on the Camino

Victor Turner reminds us that all sites of pilgrimage are believed to be places where miracles 'once happened, still happen and may happen again'. Miracles or the revivification of faith are regarded as rewards for undertaking long and often perilous journeys (Turner 1978: 6).

While walking the Camino, one is constantly aware of St James. There are many churches and chapels dedicated to the saint, and many statues depicting him. You will hear about him at mass and read about him in pilgrim guides.

Many legends have been created about St James and his pilgrims. One that appears in most pilgrim guides is the following: James the Apostle came to evangelize the northern part of the Iberian peninsula. After returning to Jerusalem, he was beheaded by King Herod, who then wanted to give his dead body to be eaten by dogs. James's two disciples stole his body and placed it in a stone boat, which miraculously sailed to the Galician coast. The saint's body was buried there, and everything about it was forgotten until the year 813 when a hermit called Pelayo discovered the tomb thanks to guidance from a bright star. In the Cathedral of San Salvador in Santo Domingo de la Calzada, a live cock and hen are kept in a cage to commemorate one of the many miracles associated with St James' protection of his pilgrims. A hen that had been roasted, returned to life to prove the innocence of a pilgrim wrongly accused of theft.

There are many accounts of the inexplicable strength that an exhausted pilgrim feels when he is least expecting it (Frey 1998). At the moment when all resources seem to be exhausted, the pilgrim experiences a mysterious force that carries him forward. The idea that St James comes in many, often unexpected, forms leads pilgrims to attribute a seemingly miraculous encounter to the saint even if they do not consider themselves religious (Frey 1998: 106). Some believe that he appears in the guise of a fellow pilgrim or local person. I have heard people talk of angels in the guise of pilgrims. Jane, a 33-year-old Estonian pilgrim, told me she called some of her fellow pilgrims angels because she met them on her first day on the Camino and to this day she cannot imagine how she could have made it without them. When I asked her to elaborate on this, she said: 'Angels as beings exist, and often they live on earth in the form of humans, helping other people. Usually they don't call themselves angels.'

When an atheist sees an angel or hears a voice talking to him in a snowstorm, he may start questioning his sanity. A Dutch pilgrim who said he was an atheist, told me a story about his miraculous salvation. He told me his story after I had told him about a fellow pilgrim of mine who, despite being non-religious, felt that he had protection while walking the Camino. He could not specify who or what it was that protected him, though. The Dutch pilgrim said that there is nothing unusual about this feeling, and told me his story. We stayed in touch, and after returning home, I emailed him and asked him to tell me about that incident once again. Here is an excerpt from his email.

> I was lost on the Puy du Montoncel, a mountain with a lot of snow. I already tried several times to go down but I was always stopped by either a brook, half hidden under the snow, or some piles of snow. I panicked because I was not able to find a way down. Because of all the attempts to go down through the snow I was getting exhausted. When I was convinced that I had to stay on top of the mountain during the night and that it would become very cold, I heard a voice in my head saying to me 'Don't panic, don't be afraid. You will get off the mountain. Be calm, don't get exhausted and think about a way to get down. Then you will get off the mountain.' It did not come from outside, I heard it inside my head. It was in Dutch.

I am still convinced it was St James speaking to me to help me. I don't think I was hallucinating because I was exhausted. When you are exhausted you do not spontaneously stop to think about the situation. The voice gave me the mental rest to consider the situation.

So I realised that I had to stop all needless efforts and to consider other possibilities to get down. I realised that trying to go down directly was impossible. I also realised that I was alone since the skiing season ended a few days before; so it was very unlikely that I would meet somebody to help me. I had to find an old path. So I climbed up the slope until I found a trail going around. It was hardly visible but I recognised some traces of skiing. I followed it and after an hour (or two hours, I didn't pay much attention to the time I spent) I found an old trail going down.

Therefore I have added to all my emails *Solo dios es el Senyor del dia de manyana* (only God knows what will happen tomorrow) to remind me that I can plan a lot of things but that there is no guarantee that it will happen as planned.

That pilgrim had started walking from his home in Holland, and he said that in the refuges in France one often comes across the sentence 'Saint James looks after his pilgrims'. On hearing this I could not help thinking that this sentence, which had etched in his memory, may have saved his life at that critical moment.

We can see a certain paradox here. A man who calls himself and atheist, hears the voice of the Saint in the snowstorm and is miraculously saved. Elliott Oring has written about different verification strategies used by narrators to increase the credibility of their stories. The narrator sometimes presents himself as a reluctant interpreter of what he has witnessed, and within this reluctance is much of his rhetoric of truth (2008: 136–137).

An English pilgrim, Phil, felt that God came to help him as well, though in a less dramatic way. Here is the story that he told me in a pilgrims' refuge. This event had taken place on his previous pilgrimage. He had started with his father and his uncle, Brian. His father became so ill that he had to return to England, but Brian and Phil continued the journey. As the journey progressed, Brian became worried because he was afraid that he was running out of time, and also because of family problems back home. Before starting, Phil had set himself an aim of walking 300 miles. Now, because of Brian, they had to take the bus to get to Santiago earlier, and doing so they lost about ten days of walking. He was thinking of still walking the miles that were missing from his target. He returned to Roncesvalles (one of the most popular starting-points of the Camino), went to the pilgrims' mass, and went to take the bread. He described his experience with the following words:

I took the piece of bread from the priest, and I turned away from the altar with the bread in my hand ... started to put the bread in my mouth ... when from an inch and a half from my right ear, I heard an audible voice saying: 'it is time to go home'. There was no one standing near enough to me ... The words were very distinctive, they were very clear. I believe it was the voice of God saying to me that it was time to go home and that my journey was complete. I believe that there are places on the Camino where the barrier between heaven and earth becomes extremely thin. There are many such places in the world, I believe, where people are much more capable of being spiritually aware of themselves, of other people ... because they are in a place that is sacred and holy. In England we talk about the theology of place, and we also talk about holy place. This is where people from the past have encountered God, this is where people are encountering God ... The experience I had in Roncesvalles is not something I had had before; it is not something I have had since.

Estonian pilgrim Annemalle told me about her fellow pilgrim, a 60-year-old German woman.

She had been married for 40 years, and it had been a long and meaningless marriage that almost ruined her health. She had been living an empty life. The woman had always wanted to go on the Camino, and finally she got a chance to do so. When she left for the Camino, she was ready for either life or death. She was gravely ill, and in her own words 'she went to the Camino to die but came back to life again'. During the first days she was moving on very wearily, but then she suddenly felt as if her legs had got wings. Her health problems – diarrhoea, pains – disappeared and she was feeling really good. But the miracles – wings on her legs – don't last forever. The woman was too hard on herself and got tendonitis.

Walking the Camino is quite a big physical as well as emotional exertion, and affects people in different ways. Jane said: 'Getting closer to Santiago I felt my sensitivity growing – at times I would get very emotional, I would suddenly feel like crying, and then in less than 15 minutes I would pass a monument to a pilgrim who had died on the Camino.' She explained it in the following way: 'Every event, action, thought and emotion leaves a mark on the surroundings. The stronger the event, the stronger the mark it leaves. In certain conditions it is possible to perceive these marks. I think I was in such an open-to-everything mental-emotional state that I just perceived these places.' She added that in general, the experiences, events and people were more pronounced and clearer than in everyday life.

Because walking the Camino can be such a challenge physically as well as emotionally, people often doubt that they are going to make it. Who or what may be behind the force that the exhausted pilgrims experience? Roger was certain that he was helped by God. 'God was riding with me.' The Dutchman who heard the voice on the snow-covered mountain was sure that it was St James who saved his life. I have also heard people talk about guardian angels who take the form of pilgrims and help them. Annemalle's fellow pilgrim, a middle-aged woman, met three young men whom she called her guardian angels. 'One made a bandage for my foot, the other helped me with my backpack, the third was supporting me.'

In November 2004, I met José Maria from Barcelona, who asked a friend and I to join him for lunch because he felt it was sad to eat alone. When I asked José Maria why he had started the Camino, he told me: 'I started in order to hear one word from Jesus, but I have heard so many words. He usually talks to me while I'm cooking.'

Belief in reincarnation has been spreading in Europe as part of the New Age worldview (Heelas 1996: 108). It seems to be rather wide-spread among the Santiago pilgrims, as well. While walking the Camino, people sometimes get vivid flashbacks from their former lives. Interestingly, most reincarnation stories I have heard from fellow pilgrims, are related to war. A 25-year-old Italian pilgrim told me that one day after having climbed up a mountain he suddenly recognized the place and was certain that in his former life he had fought in a battle there. He even remembered all the details of that medieval battle. One Estonian pilgrim had a similar experience. Going up a mountain, she looked at her fellow pilgrim and noticed that the man was wearing an old-fashioned soldier's uniform. She then looked at her own clothes and saw that these too had changed. She believes that in her former life she had walked at the same place with the same companion.

As a comment on the miraculous stories about feeling the presence of a superior being, I would like to say that those of my informants (Roger, Phil and José Maria) who heard God speaking to them or felt his help, were Christians. The Dutch pilgrim who heard the voice of St James in the snowstorm, was an atheist. This is certainly too small a number to make any generalizations, but I am still tempted to suggest that it may be easier for an atheist to attribute the mysterious voice to the patron saint of the pilgrims rather than to God.

Writers and Scholars as Creators of the Religious Tradition of the Camino de Santiago

I think it is very important to consider the influence of Camino literature on the pilgrims' experiences and on their repertoires. It may be similar to what folklorist Anu Korb has experienced in her fieldwork in Estonian settlements in Siberia. She writes: 'When my Siberian books reached the Siberians themselves, I made an astonishing discovery – some Siberians regarded the book as a textbook, and started to seriously use the spells, wisdom of folk medicine, advice on farming, etc. from that book' (Korb 2005: 122).

I have noticed that Nancy Frey's book *Pilgrim Stories* (1998) is very popular with former as well as prospective pilgrims. The stories she has collected are going back to the pilgrims themselves. I have sometimes told my fellow pilgrims a moving story about the 'dog pilgrim', which I read in that book. 'A Portuguese man recounted that on his first journey to Santiago in 1995 he was joined one afternoon outside Logronyo by a large, white, female dog to whom he had given something to eat. He was convinced that the dog would not make it to Santiago, but each day she rose and set off with him and his companions. On the day they reached Santiago he said he sensed that she too knew the story had ended; after having visited the cathedral they all went to a local park, and there she lay down and died' (Frey 1998: 108). It is believed by many pilgrims that the dogs that start following pilgrims, were in their former lives pilgrims who could not make it to Santiago. On my winter pilgrimage I met a little white dog in one village, who started to follow me and kept doing it for a couple of days. A Spanish fellow pilgrim said that in his former life that dog had most probably been a pilgrim who had died on the way and so could not make it to Santiago.

In addition to being a source for academic research, the Camino has been an inspiration for several works of fiction, as well. The most famous books would probably be Shirley MacLaine's *The Camino* (2000) and Paulo Coelho's *Pilgrimage: The Diary of a Magician* (1987). Several pilgrims I talked to had read MacLaine's book; almost all pilgrims had at least heard of Coelho's novel. These two, and no doubt several other books, have helped create the image of the Camino as an esoteric, mysterious journey that goes along enigmatic energy fields and where supernatural events often occur.

I have heard several Santiago pilgrims say that the reason why they started the Camino was that it had called to them mysteriously, and the seed was often Paulo Coelho`s novel. Paulo Coelho is a Brazilian author whose other best-selling novel is *The Alchemist*. *Pilgrimage* is written in the form of a diary, and it describes the author's journey of esoteric initiation. It depicts the Camino de Santiago as a magical journey full of supernatural events such as encounters with demons. The protagonist sets out with the task of finding his sword, hidden at some place on the Camino. In Cebreiro he finds this sword, which will convert him into a magician. At the same time he finds spiritual enlightenment.

This novel reflects the popularity of esoteric or individualized religious practices characteristic of New Age movements and contemporary spirituality. Several people believe that the Camino contains a certain kind of energy. It may be thought of as the energy of all the people who have ever walked it. The Camino de Santiago is also called the Road of the Stars, because it is believed to go directly under the Milky Way. Some pilgrims and *hospitaleros* claim to be modern-day Templars, knights of the order of the Temple of Jerusalem formed in 1118 to protect pilgrims on the way to the Holy Land. To this day Templars are shrouded in mystery and said to be the holders of esoteric knowledge. One of the most colourful refuges on the Camino is run by Tomas, who calls himself Ultimo Templario, the last Templar. Every day he performs a special religious service that contains some elements from the Catholic mass. A distinctive feature of the ceremony is the use of swords.

People who set out for the Camino after reading Coelho's book are sometimes disappointed because of the discrepancies between the novel and the real Camino. They seem to regard the novel as a reference book.

One of the frequent questions that is asked by would-be pilgrims in internet forums dealing with the Camino is about the 'mad dogs'. Dogs have been seen as a threat to pilgrims from the early days of the Santiago pilgrimage, and folklore abounds with stories about demonic dogs. Victor Turner has pointed out, referring to Georgiana Goddard King's *The Way of St James* (1920), that many European folk tales tell of penitent souls journeying to St James's shrine at Compostela in the far northwest of Spain (Turner 1978: 113).

Some people take Coelho's book as a true diary and fear that they too may be attacked by the supernatural dogs described in the novel. Coelho's protagonist has to fight with some dogs, and he has to kill one of them in order to get his sword. This has probably been one of the sources to the beliefs about the legendary dogs on the Camino.

Analysing Roger's Stories

When Roger told us his two Camino legends in Burgos, he started his stories with the words 'I heard this story from a pilgrim ...' and 'this story was told me by a pilgrim when I was complaining about a trivial matter'. It was obviously important for him to connect his stories to the Camino tradition. He was not telling us just any stories, but the stories that he had heard from another pilgrim, thus pointing to his narratives as being passed on.

We may ask what makes up the Camino tradition, apart from 'traditional' Christian legends about St James. Are Roger's Camino legends part of that tradition? Most of his stories are either Christian legends adapted from literature and transferred into the context of the Camino, or stories made up by himself. Creating a tradition is a natural part of the process of folklore. Anna-Leena Siikala has pointed out that when a narrative is lifted from one culture or community to another, its surface semantics – its references – change: 'Folklorists have observed that the legends migrating from one nation to another are localised by placing the events in a familiar setting, by describing the characters using familiar features or by transferring some familiar character to the role of hero' (Siikala 1990: 29).

Roger told me two kinds of stories: first those that he called Camino legends, and second his own memorates – events that had happened to him on the Camino. He was obviously enjoying himself while telling his legends; whereas while talking about his encounter with God his voice broke and he was keeping back tears.

According to Linda Dégh, traditional *Märchen* tellers conscious of their craft are careful to distinguish legends from tales. She writes:

> The legends they tell appear to be marginal in their repertoire, as first-hand learned true events that may be part of their life history. They know that their audience appreciates high-flying fantasy in the formulation of tales but that the audience would not tolerate artistic embroidery of the truth they believe in. It is one thing to tell a Märchen,

to enjoy the liberty of creating a fictitious story, and another thing to tell a legend and reproduce reality. (Dégh 1995: 82)

None of Dégh's informants included their own legends in their repertoires; these legends were more autobiographical, not for public storytelling.

Why did Roger choose to tell his stories to me? Without my asking, he told me that at home no one would understand him. He seemed to have a need to 'talk himself empty' and he believed that I understood him better than his friends and family back home. A quote from his email:

I've changed since I left on this pilgrimage and that is what I want to share with people, not just all sorts of details they would be asking about. It is such an overwhelming experience and little do they know back home, and answering questions would not do it justice.

Why did Roger decide to tell one story or another? For entertainment – allegedly an important function of folklore – to pass the time, or maybe because he knew I was collecting stories? I have also tried to observe what the trigger for a story is. For example, the Dutch pilgrim who had heard St James's voice in the snowstorm, told me his story after I had told him about my friend Pavel who felt he had protection on the Camino, even though he too was not a believer.

Yet another function may be telling a story in exchange for something. Folklorists have pointed out that the ability to tell good stories has fostered interpersonal relations, facilitated finding overnight accommodation or getting a job, it has helped beggars make a living, etc. (Viidalepp 2004: 155). I got a similar reply from Roger when I asked him to whom and in what situations he had told his stories. Sometimes he told the person who had put him up a story as a thank you. He also told his host a story when he could not think of anything else to say. By telling stories he did not have to talk too much about his own life. Here is an extract from an interview:

TS: I really enjoyed listening to that story in Burgos. Did you often tell people stories on the Camino?
R: Sometimes, yes.
T: On what occasions?
R: When asked, and when there were a few people, not that much on the Camino, mostly in France when I was housed by people for the night. And when people are so kind to take you to their house, and sometimes people are not that talkative, they just take you in but they

are not that sociable … the best way to give something to the people … the next day I always asked how much I owed them, they never wanted any money … what I do, I think you give me a place to sleep, I'll tell you a nice story about what happens to pilgrims and to people along the Camino. As a way to repay having me for lunch, for dinner, for having me sleep over. And with some pilgrims on the Camino … what do you say … you don't have that much in common to talk about … and … some remarks about things in your personal life … I told a story. Without any special reason but just to say something. … what do you do … there's not that much happening. I'm not that sociable, so sometimes it's easier to tell a story than have a conversation.

In addition, Roger's stories seem to serve the purpose of legitimizing norms of behaviour and belief. Marisa Rey-Henningsen argues that folklore's function of legitimizing prevalent norms of behaviour, beliefs and rituals is second only to the entertainment function of folklore in the Spanish cultural tradition (Rey-Henningsen 1994: 21). In his stories Roger makes it perfectly clear what kind of behaviour is expected from Santiago pilgrims and also from other people connected with the Camino. For example, pilgrims should never get on a bus, and one should never refuse hospitality to a pilgrim.

Last but not least, and following on from the previous point I would like to include the function of 'getting even'. The story about the inhospitable woman's bread turning to stone may be seen as a tribute to the priest who had refused to host him and who he wished would 'get what he deserved'. Likewise, the story about the lazy pilgrim whose stamps disappeared from his *credencial*, came to Roger when he saw 'compostelas being handed to *turigrinos* in Santiago'.

How do Roger's stories fit into the context of the Camino? He is certainly very different from the other pilgrim storytellers I have met. Whereas the others tell of events that have really happened to them, most of Roger's stories are Christian legends that he has moved to the context of the Camino.

To a certain extent this peculiarity may be explained by the difference between spontaneous conversation and the interview situation. All the other pilgrims told me their stories on the road and I did not have the possibility to record them; Roger was interviewed thoroughly and the interviews were recorded, and this may have disposed him to a more artistic performance.

Finnish folklorist Annikki Kaivola-Bregenhøj has observed the difference between two situational contexts: the interview situation and spontaneous telling. She writes:

> In an interview situation the researcher gives his undivided attention to the narrator, while in a spontaneous telling context the narrator must succeed in holding his listeners' interest. The interaction between the narrator and the interviewer, the narrator and the other listeners, and the various reactions expressed by the listeners are very important to the shaping of the telling and the comments framing it. (Kaivola-Bregenhøj 1996: 52)

Only once did I hear Roger perform spontaneously. This happened in Burgos when we went out for dinner together with four other pilgrims and Roger told us two of his Camino legends. I was the only one who listened to the stories until the end; the rest of the group soon started to talk about other things. While telling his Camino legends, Roger did bear some resemblance to a preacher. Except that instead of a pulpit there was a dinner table covered with beer glasses, which felt a little like a conflict of roles.

I have also noticed the difference between the content of Roger's and other pilgrims' narratives. Roger's stories seem to have sprung from a collection of the legends about St James, compiled and published by the Catholic church. In my opinion his stories bear certain similarities to medieval exempla. Most of the other pilgrims talked more about the mysterious energy and other phenomena that are more connected to a New Age worldview.

Conclusion

I believe that the Camino de Santiago is a narrated journey. It is being continuously created by the narratives people read and write, hear and talk of concerning this pilgrimage route. What you read or hear about it beforehand is going to influence your experience. If you are walking it with a conviction that St James will look after his pilgrims, you are quite likely to encounter the Saint, as did the Dutch pilgrim who heard the Saint's voice helping him find the right way in the snowstorm. Likewise, those who get inspiration from Paulo Coelho or Shirley MacLaine's books, will probably start the journey with different expectations from those who have not read these books. The former may be more aware of the 'magic of the Camino' and the energy fields, and therefore experience flashbacks from former lives.

Roger Abrahams has pointed out that our identity emerges from the stories we tell about ourselves (Abrahams 2003: 201). One way to emphasize and strengthen one's identity as a pilgrim is to tell Camino legends. I saw in Roger a pilgrim whose identity is expressed through the stories he tells. He was a very creative storyteller.

Even though Roger did not present his Camino legends as true stories, it was important for him to emphasize their belonging to the Camino tradition. 'This story was told to me by a pilgrim', was one of his favourite openings, even though he admitted he made the stories up. By using this kind of opening, he tried to present his narratives as old and traditional. He wanted his stories to be part of the Camino heritage, something that pilgrims have been passing on, not just stories he made up on the spot. At the same time he admitted adapting the stories: 'If you are on the Camino, you have your story take place on the Camino.'

Each of Roger's stories has a clear message, usually in the form of a warning. If a command is not obeyed or a prohibition is ignored, punishment follows. For example, you must not cheat on the Camino by taking the bus instead of walking, if you do, St James will punish you; you must treat everybody with equal hospitality, because you never know which of them is St James in disguise. Elliott Oring reminds us that 'wickedness punished, righteousness rewarded' is the formula that underlies the religious legend (Oring 2008: 158).

One should also bear in mind that after the Reformation the popularity of the Santiago pilgrimage decreased considerably. It was rediscovered in the twentieth century, and in the 1980s it began to be newly waymarked by scallop shells and yellow arrows. There obviously was an interruption in pilgrims' traditions, and this may have led to the necessity to create new traditions, for example inventing new Camino legends.

Listening to Roger, one may get the impression that pilgrims often tell each other stories about St James coming to the aid of his pilgrims. And they do, except that the stories they tell are usually memorates, not Christian legends. The story that the Dutch atheist pilgrim told me about his miraculous salvation on the snowy mountain is by no means exceptional. And stories like that would make everybody, pilgrim or not, prick up their ears.

I would like to conclude with an idea about conscious and unconscious creation of the Camino tradition. All my informants were contributing to the Camino tradition by telling their memorates,

Camino legends and jokes. The difference between Roger and my other informants was that by trying to make his legends seem a natural part of Camino heritage, Roger was consciously creating the Camino tradition. The others were telling stories about what had happened to them or their fellow pilgrims. What might have been the reasons for Roger's invention of the Camino tradition? I would like to give some speculations.

First, people walking the Camino have their ups and downs. The refuge you expected to be open may have closed down, or it may be full of *turigrinos* so that you will need to keep walking even though it is getting late. A priest may refuse to give you shelter even though his abbey is on the list of Santiago pilgrims' refuges. After the initial indignation is over, a pilgrim may feel like sublimating his frustration into Camino legend, in which St James invariably intervenes whenever he sees his pilgrims being treated unfairly.

Second, Roger may have felt that there was something missing from his image as a true pilgrim. He was riding a bicycle instead of walking, and for many people this is not the right way to do the pilgrimage. Telling Camino legends may have made him feel more authentic.

Last but not least, we should bear in mind that the number of people walking the Camino for non-religious reasons is increasing. Being a devout Catholic, Roger was not at all happy to discover that the Camino was full of 'fake pilgrims'. By telling his stories Roger may have wanted to recreate the past – a time when there were real pilgrims on the road to Santiago. Could we see Roger as a preacher whose task is to remind us that the Camino de Santiago is, above all, a pilgrimage to venerate the remains of a Christian saint?

Acknowledgement

The present article has been completed within the framework of Estonian Science Foundation research grant No. 7516. It was also supported by the European Union through the European Regional Development Fund (Centre of Excellence, CECT).

Notes

1. A term introduced by Victor Turner (1979; 1989) referring to modality of social interrelatedness, true fellowship; relationships among people who are jointly undergoing ritual transition through which they experience an intense sense of intimacy and equality.

References

Abrahams, R. (2003) Identity. In B. Feintuch (ed.) *Eight Words for the Study of Expressive Culture*, 198–223. Urbana and Chicago, IL: University of Illinois Press.

Bendix, R. (2002) Capitalizing on memories past, present, and future: Observations of the intertwining of tourism and narration. *Anthropological Theory* 2 (4): 469–487.

Bendix, R. (1997) *In Search of Authenticity: The Formation of Folklore Studies.* Madison, WI and London: University of Wisconsin Press.

Coelho, P. (2002) *Palverännak: Maagi päevik.* Tallinn: Philos.

Dégh, L. (1995) *Narratives in Society: A Performer-Centered Study of Narration. FF Communications* No. 255. Helsinki: Academia Scientiarum Fennica.

Frey, N. L. (1998) *Pilgrim Stories: On and Off the Road to Santiago.* Berkeley, CA: University of California Press.

Heelas, P. (1996) *The New Age Movement: The Celebration of the Self and the Sacralization of Modernity.* Oxford: Blackwell Publishers.

Kaivola-Bregenhøj, A. (1996) *Narrative and Narrating: Variation in Juha Oksanen's Storytelling. FF Communications* No. 261. Helsinki: Academia Scientiarum Fennica.

Korb, A. (2005) *Venemaal rahvuskaaslasi küsitlemas: Folkloristliku välitöö metoodilisi aspekte. Studia Ethnologica et Folkloristica Tartuensia* No. 9. Tartu: Tartu Ülikooli Kirjastus.

MacLaine, S. (2000) *The Camino: A Journey of the Spirit.* New York: Pocket Books.

Oring, E. (2008) Legendry and the rhetoric of truth. *Journal of American Folklore* 121 (480): 127–166.

Rey-Henningsen, M. (1994) *The World of the Ploughwoman: Folklore and Reality in Matriarchal Northwest Spain. FF Communications* No. 254. Helsinki: Academia Scientiarum Fennica.

Siikala, A.-L. (1990) *Interpreting Oral Narrative. FF Communications* No. 245. Helsinki: Academia Scientiarum Fennica.

Tubach, F. (1969) *Index Exemplorum. A Handbook of Medieval Religious Tales. FF Communications* No. 204. Helsinki: Academia Scientiarum Fennica.

Turner, V. (1979) *Process, Performance and Pilgrimage: A Study in Comparative Symbology. Ranchi Anthropology Series-1.* New Delhi: Concept Publishing Company.

Turner, V. (1989) *The Ritual Process: Structure and Antistructure.* Ithaca, NY: Cornell University Press.

Turner, V. and Turner, E. (1978) *Image and Pilgrimage in Christian Culture.* New York: Columbia University Press.

Uther, H.-J. (2004) *The Types of International Folktales. A Classification and Bibliography. Based on the System of Antti Aarne and Stith Thompson.*

Part I: Animal Tales, Tales of Magic, Religious Tales, and Realistic Tales, with an Introduction. FF Communications No. 284. Helsinki: Academia Scientiarum Fennica.

Viidalepp, R. (2004) Eesti rahvajuttude laadist, funktsioonist ja jutustajatest. *SATOR* 4. Tartu: Eesti Kirjandusmuuseum.

Restoring/Restorying Arthur and Bridget: Vernacular Religion and Contemporary Spirituality in Glastonbury

Marion Bowman[*]

Introduction

In this chapter I shall examine some of the ways in which expressions of belief concerning two significant figures connected with Celtic myth, Arthur and Bridget, have been revived, recycled and manipulated in the contested context of contemporary spirituality in Glastonbury, a small but highly significant town in the south-west of England.[1] In order to understand this context, I shall briefly introduce Glastonbury (where I have been conducting fieldwork since the early 1990s),[2] its status as a multivalent sacred site, and the varied ways in which Celtic spirituality has taken shape there. Thereafter, I shall explore some of the trends and shifts in emphases that have taken place within contemporary spirituality in Glastonbury over recent years with specific reference to Arthur and Bridget.[3]

The narratives, rituals, events and ideas surrounding Arthur and Bridget reported here are presented as a study in vernacular religion, stressing the importance of the geographical and cultural context in which belief and praxis occur – the 'bidirectional influences of environments upon individuals and of individuals upon environments in the process of believing' (Primiano 1995: 44) – and paying 'special attention to the process of religious belief, the verbal, behavioral, and material expressions of religious belief, and the ultimate object of religious belief' (Primiano 1995: 44).

In looking at Arthur and Bridget in Glastonbury, we will not be examining the minutiae of Celtic Studies scholarship around these two characters, but how they have been and are being envisaged and used

* Marion Bowman is Head of the Department of Religious Studies and Senior Lecturer, The Open University, UK.

there. Contemporary Celtic spirituality owes much to romanticism, primitivism and late twentieth/early twenty-first-century religious trends, and academic investigation of this phenomenon tends to involve what Leerssen has described as 'Celticism':

> not the study of the Celts and their history, but rather the study of their reputation and of the meanings and connotations ascribed to the term 'Celtic'. (Leerssen 1996: 3)

In Glastonbury, the interaction of myth, belief story, vernacular religion and contemporary spirituality provides a constantly evolving means whereby varied groups of people interact with the past, the landscape and whatever they perceive as their spiritual goals. Beliefs are not simply narrated but expressed through ritual, the creation of custom and material culture. Through such expressions of belief Arthur and Bridget have been revived, restored and 'restoried' in Glastonbury.

The Glastonbury Context

Glastonbury occupies a unique position in the spiritual and spatial imagination of a range of religious believers. Superficially, Glastonbury is simply a small town (pop. c. 9,000) in rural Somerset, but myriad claims are made for it (Prince and Riches 2000; Ivakhiv 2001; Bowman 2005). Many regard Glastonbury as a major prehistoric centre of Goddess worship, while for others Glastonbury's significance lies in the claim that it was the site of a great Druidic university, a centre of learning to which people flocked from all over Europe and beyond. For many Christians, past and present, Glastonbury's status has rested on the legend that St Joseph of Arimathea established the first Christian church in the British Isles there. On arriving at Glastonbury, Joseph is said to have thrust his staff in to the ground at Wearyall Hill, and according to local tradition this became the Holy Thorn that blossoms twice a year, in spring and around Christmas (see Bowman 2006). Joseph reputedly brought with him the Grail, that mysterious artefact regarded variously as the chalice used at the Last Supper, the blood of Jesus in some form, or phials containing the blood and sweat of Jesus (for a good summary of this legend and related literature, see Carley 1996: 87–94). Furthermore, some believe that Jesus was the nephew of St Joseph, and that he may have accompanied his uncle on trading trips before his ministry began, visiting Glastonbury and perhaps even spending some time living there. One attraction for Christian pilgrims coming to Glastonbury is that they might literally be walking in the footsteps of Jesus.

Glastonbury is visible for miles on account of its Tor, a distinctively contoured hill rising from the Somerset Levels. Originally accessible by water before the Levels were drained, Glastonbury has also been identified with the Isle of Avalon, the place where, according to legend, King Arthur was taken for healing after his last battle (Ashe 1957). The association between Arthur, Glastonbury and Avalon seemed to be confirmed when in 1191 the bodies of Arthur and Guinevere were allegedly 'discovered' by monks in the grounds of Glastonbury Abbey. In 1278 the bodies were re-buried in a magnificent tomb in the Abbey chancel in the presence of King Edward I and Queen Eleanor (for a summary of literature relating to this see Carley 1996: 154–166). Nevertheless, the popular tradition persisted that Arthur merely lies sleeping in Avalon, waiting to return at some time of great national emergency.

By the middle ages Glastonbury Abbey, allegedly built of the site of Joseph's original church, was a major pilgrimage centre and site of Marian devotion, boasting a huge collection of relics and a fine library, but it was brutally suppressed at the time of the Reformation.

Figure 1: Mists of Avalon? View of Somerset levels and Glastonbury Tor on a misty day (photograph by Lisa Isted, © 2010).

The library and relics were dispersed or destroyed, Arthur's tomb and remains disappeared, and the Abbey was left to fall into ruins. Nevertheless, many aspects of vernacular myth and religiosity survived, and in the course of the twentieth century Glastonbury again rose to spiritual prominence in the wake of religious experimentation and speculation inspired by such diverse influences as Christianity, Theosophy, the Celtic Revival, assorted New Religious Movements, Paganisms and New Age (see Hexham 1983; Benham 1993; Ivakhiv 2001; Bowman 2005). Now perceived by many as the 'heart chakra' of planet earth, Glastonbury is also regarded as a centre of earth energies, a node where leylines converge and generate powerful forces for healing and personal transformation. Many people on varied 'spiritual paths' narrate how they feel 'drawn' to Glastonbury (Bowman 1993; 2008).

Celtic Spirituality in Glastonbury

Many of the spiritual seekers Glastonbury has attracted since the early twentieth century have been involved in some form of 'Celtic spirituality'. The term 'Celtic spirituality' in contemporary parlance in Glastonbury and elsewhere covers a huge variety of belief and praxis. It is used broadly to describe pre-Christian Celtic religion, the Celtic Church and contemporary religiosity inspired by the 'Celtic spirit', and is often predicated upon the image of the 'spiritual Celt', inherently spiritual and intuitive, in touch with nature and the hidden realms, epitomizing in many ways that which is lost but longed for in contemporary society (see Bowman 2002). Many people in Britain and beyond regard Celtic spirituality as their ancestral, pre-Christian 'native' religion and current Celtic Pagan spirituality is often influenced by the assumption that Celtic religion was and is akin to that of contemporary indigenous or tribal groups. Thus, while Celtic myth, art and literature are utilized by some to 'reconstruct' Celtic religion, there is also copying and 'Celticizing' of contemporary native peoples' practices, such as 'Celtic Shamanism' and Druidic sweat lodges. In what is regarded as the revival or continuance of ancient Celtic tradition, offerings are frequently left at archaeological sites and natural features such as springs and trees. Many Celtic spirituality practitioners observe the so-called 'Celtic' or 'eight-fold' calendar of Samhain (Hallowe'en), Imbolc (Candlemas), Beltane (May Day), Lughnasadh or Lammas (Harvest), summer and winter solstices, and spring and autumn equinoxes, with the 'Celtic year' starting on 1 November. Customs have been 'revived' or invented in relation to this calendar and rituals are frequently performed at what are regarded as Celtic sacred sites (such as Stonehenge, Avebury and Glastonbury). Reincarnation is widely regarded as a Celtic belief in Pagan, New Age, Druidic and even some Celtic Christian circles. Some find echoes of Hinduism and Buddhism in Celtic spirituality, and vice versa.

In contemporary Celtic spirituality, the Celtic Church (however, whenever and wherever conceived) is generally characterized as gentle, tolerant, 'green', meditative, egalitarian and holistic, an early 'pure' form of Christianity that came directly to the Celtic lands. Some view the transition from the Celtic 'old religion' to Celtic Christianity as essentially smooth and harmonious,[4] believing that the allegedly unique nature of Celtic Christianity owed much to its preservation of a body of esoteric Druidic wisdom unknown to other branches of Christianity. (Contemporary Druidry includes Christian as well as Pagan Druids.) Numerous mainstream Christian denominations currently aspire to or express 'Celticity' visually in Celtic knots and crosses, verbally in 'Celtic' prayers and blessings, and physically in pilgrimage to places like Iona, Lindisfarne and Croagh Patrick (see Meek 2000).

Part of Glastonbury's appeal and status rests upon it being considered a Celtic location. Pagans who come to celebrate 'the wheel of the year' in Glastonbury regard it an ancient site of 'indigenous' religion, and traditions such as tree and well dressing have been 'revived' and 'reclaimed' there at various times. Druidry flourishes in a variety of forms: the Glastonbury Order of Druids (GODs) see themselves as perpetuating and practising Druidry in a significant ancient Druidic centre; OBOD (the Order of Bards, Ovates and Druids) has a Glastonbury grove, and other Druids gather in Glastonbury for celebrations of the eight-fold calendar. The Bardic Chair of Ynys Witrin (considered a 'Celtic' name for Glastonbury, the Isle of Glass) was 'restored' in 2005. The Isle of Avalon Foundation is seen by some as a successor to, or in the tradition of, the Druidic University, offering a wide range of 'spiritual education', including a certificated course in Druidry.

There are those who regard Glastonbury as a bastion of Celtic Christianity, traditional connections between Glastonbury and Celtic saints such as David, Patrick and Bridget (Carley 1996: 99–112) reinforcing this image. It is suggested that here flourished a more nature-oriented, egalitarian, 'purer' form of Christianity than the

Roman version later 'imposed' on Britain. Some claim this was in part because of insights and esoteric knowledge incorporated from Druids who became Christians there. The myths of Joseph and Jesus in Glastonbury are also important in relation to Glastonbury's Celtic credentials; some claim that Joseph and Jesus would naturally have been attracted to Glastonbury on account of the great Druidic centre of learning there, others reason that if an early, pure form of Christianity flourished in 'Celtic' Glastonbury, that Christianity was Celtic Christianity.

Knott claims that 'The particularity of a place arises from the complexity of its social relations and the sum of the stories told about it' (Knott 2005: 33). In the case of Glastonbury, much of the complexity of its social relations arises from the sheer quantity and variety of the stories told about and within it, and the key to understanding the 'ongoing interpretations and negotiations of religion' (Primiano 1995: 51) there lies in how Glastonbury is narrated by the various groups and individuals for whom the place is special. Notwithstanding Bascom's definition of myth as prose narratives 'considered to be truthful accounts of what happened in the remote past' (Bascom 1984: 9), the Religious Studies usage of myth as 'significant story', regardless of issues of truth or proof (Smart 1977: 18–19), tends to be better appreciated and articulated in Glastonbury, for example when people refer not to the town's history but its 'mythtory' or consciously create 'new myths'. Also helpful in understanding contemporary spirituality in Glastonbury is the multifunctional 'belief story', characterized by Bennett as an informal story which enunciates and validates the current beliefs and experiences of a given community (1989: 291), for different stories are told by and have resonance for the varied groups of spiritual seekers there.

The manipulations and manifestations of religiosity in relation to two significant characters in Celtic myth, Arthur and Bridget, demonstrate the complexity, creativity and contested nature of Celtic spirituality, the power and pervasiveness of myth, and the importance of vernacular religion in twentieth- and twenty-first-century Glastonbury.

Restoring and 'Restorying' Arthur in Avalon

Arthur has always been something of a 'shape shifter', so it is perhaps no surprise that in the heightened atmosphere of spiritual speculations in twentieth-century Glastonbury, Arthur was again remythologized and reinterpreted.

The connection of Arthur, Avalon and Glastonbury had been made specific by the Church with the 'discovery' of Arthur's body in the twelfth century, and for the next few centuries Arthur's grave and tomb were major attractions. Since 1907 Glastonbury Abbey has been in the ownership of a charitable trust and is run as an historic site, although annual Anglican and Catholic pilgrimages are held there. The Arthurian connection is still emphasized, with the Abbey shop selling considerable quantities of 'Arthuriana', including posters, books, cards and T-shirts relating to Arthur and the Knights of the Round Table. In 2006 as a 'special summer attraction' the Abbey had 'King Arthur Tours':

> Meet Sir Edwyn the Unpredictable, one of King Arthur's most loyal followers and a knight of The Round Table. He will take you on a tour around the grounds of Glastonbury Abbey and let you hear the legends of The Sword in The Stone, The Lady in the Lake, Excalibur and the adventures of The Knights of The Round Table. (Publicity leaflet)

Thus, conventional (if popularized) versions of Arthurian legend and Arthur's connections with Glastonbury Abbey are perpetuated.

However, in the wake of the eighteenth century and late nineteenth/early twentieth-century Celtic revivals, there was renewed interest in and reappraisal of Arthur. Some argued that the 'Christianized' Arthur had been conflated with a pagan Celtic hero or god, whose Grail was originally the Celtic cauldron of wisdom and inspiration. Others, influenced by the search for survivals characteristic of early folklore studies, regarded Arthur as a solar deity. Arthur's links with the 'old religion' through his mentor Merlin, often identified as a Druid, were also used to reinforce the idea of a connection between Glastonbury and Druidry.

Arthur was again reappraised in the latter part of the twentieth century. This was a time of growing awareness of ecological issues and interest in sacred places, plus some political discontent in relation to road building, restricted access to sacred sites and concerns about the erosion of civil rights in Britain. Arthur Uther Pendragon – the man formerly known as John Timothy Rothwell – now sees himself as the reincarnation of Arthur as ancient Celtic chieftain, who has returned at a time of great national emergency. Although the return was traditionally interpreted in relation to 'the nation' in a political sense,

Arthur/Rothwell claims that in fact what was meant was the nation in the sense of 'the land' – and this is considered a time of *spiritual* emergency when the land, and in particular sacred sites, are under threat. His Loyal Arthurian Warband has undertaken to fight for the ancient virtues of truth, honour and justice (see Pendragon and Stone 2003), and this has found expression in ritual activity, in supporting road protest and in challenging what they consider unjust laws (such as those relating to access to Stonehenge for ritual purposes). Arthur was declared the 'Pendragon' of the Glastonbury Order of Druids, and some considered Rollo Maughfling, former chief of the GODs, a reincarnation of Merlin.

In terms of the 'bidirectional influences of environments upon individuals and of individuals upon environments in the process of believing' (Primiano 1995: 44) one of the most significant developments has been the reappraisal of the Arthurian Round Table in relation to the landscape in and around Glastonbury. In the 1920s Theosophist, sculptor and artist Katherine Maltwood, while working on the illustrations for an edition of the *High History of the Holy Grail*, discerned in the landscape in and around Glastonbury a huge planisphere, The Glastonbury Zodiac (Maltwood 1964 [1929]). She described this as a pre-Christian 'Round Table of the Grail', arguing that the events described in the Grail stories had in fact taken place in the Glastonbury Zodiac area, the different characters, creatures and challenges encountered simply reflecting movement through the year. This new connection between Arthur and Glastonbury, with the Round Table literally rooted in the soil of Glastonbury and the surrounding area, has been immensely influential, giving rise to new interpretations of Arthurian legend and presenting the opportunity for people to actually participate in it. Chris Trwoga's *Grail Quest in the Vales of Avalon* (2001), for example, lays out seven journeys in the Glastonbury area, allowing the individual to 'literally follow in the footsteps of the knights of Britain's Heroic Age as they searched for the greatest treasure of all – the Sangreal – the fulfilment of all we have ever yearned for' (publicity leaflet).

Typically for Glastonbury, various versions of the Zodiac have appeared, with further interpretations of its structure, function and origins.[5] Some people reason that the Glastonbury Zodiac/Round Table could only have been constructed with the aid of those who could see the whole structure *from above*, thus confirming a long term interest in Glastonbury in extraterrestrials, whose presence has been inferred through the UFO sightings commonly reported in the Glastonbury area from the 1970s onwards and later from crop circles. This raises the possibility of Arthur as neither solar deity nor pagan hero, but extraterrestrial.

On Maltwood's Glastonbury Zodiac some of the signs are somewhat unusual, with Aquarius represented by a phoenix dipping her beak into Chalice Well. This connection between Glastonbury and Aquarius, and by extension the 'Age of Aquarius', seemed significant to those who regarded humanity as being on the brink of a New Age, a paradigm shift to a more holistic, spiritually informed and aware era, when ancient mysteries and esoteric traditions would be explained, earth's relationship with extra-terrestrials, other planets and life forms would be revealed, and a new universalistic spirituality would emerge. With the growing emphasis from the 1970s onwards on people taking responsibility for their own spiritual lives, finding what 'spiritual tools' worked for them, Arthur came to be regarded as the epitome of the New Age warrior, the quester after spiritual truth. As one Glastonbury resident and self-styled 'New Ager' told me:

> the whole idea that he lies here sleeping and will rise again, some people interpret that as meaning he'll rise again to lead us into a New Age, a new cycle, a new beginning, a new phase in world evolution.

This phase of Celtic New Age and Arthur's role in it was in many ways epitomized by the opening of the shop Pendragon in 1990 in The Glastonbury Experience. (An important landmark for spiritual materialism in Glastonbury, The Glastonbury Experience is a complex off the High Street including shops, galleries, the Library of Avalon and the Isle of Avalon Foundation. The site was purchased in 1977 by Dutch visionaries and philanthropists Helene and Willem Koppejan, who were initially drawn to Glastonbury on account of its connection with Joseph of Arimathea and Jesus.) According to its proprietors, Pendragon

> grew out of a deep association with Glastonbury over the years and a desire to see the resurgence of the Celtic spirit, which to us means living in harmony with the Earth, following a path of the spiritual warrior, and bringing again the artist/craftsperson''s importance into the community. (*Glastonbury Times:* 33)

The venture was commercial, but it also had a mission – 'to help people start on their own inner journey'. The shop interior aimed not only to display the crafts, but to create an atmosphere of beauty and harmony, the integration of the male and female principle. Amid striking colours, crystals and astrological information there was a painted Round Table (in fact their former dining table) showing the layout of the Glastonbury Zodiac. Above it hung a sword, symbol of the spiritual warrior, and on the wall were heraldic shields relating to Arthurian knights. If some forms of Christianity can be described as 'muscular Christianity', by analogy this was 'muscular New Age'. Arthur was seen as a valuable jumping off point and role model, the Grail quest being a good way of expressing the inner search. As a notice in the shop declared:

> Words and images you see in the shop are not about academic accuracy, clever deduction or historic fact. They are a language that speaks to the heart; a long forgotten language that the Earth needs to hear, and that each person discovers in their personal quest for the grail.

Arthur, it seemed, had done it again – a Celt for all seasons, he could be a Christian hero, a pagan hero, *and* a New Age hero.

However, on 1 June 2001, Pendragon became Birth of Venus. Owner Bahli Mans-Morris explained that they felt they had 'worked through' the Pendragon energy, which was a very male energy, and were now working with 'a softer, more feminine energy'. The stock became more focused on colour, colour therapy, and aromatherapy, though there were still cards, pictures and jewellery inspired by Celtic art. In 2002, the transition apparently complete, the shop simply became Venus.

While there is still a considerable variety of Arthur-related myth, belief stories and spiritual searching in Glastonbury (and replica Excaliburs to be purchased in Man, Myth and Magick), the movement from Pendragon to Venus reflected significant shifts in emphasis and the public face of spirituality in Glastonbury towards the feminine and specifically towards the Goddess. Against this backdrop, we see the (re-)emergence of Bridget and a number of expressions of belief in relation to her.

The Coming of Bride

St Bridget and other Celtic saints reputedly visited Glastonbury. The Irish St Bridget (458–523) is said to have been the daughter of a chieftain (sometimes described as a pagan or Druid) and his bondswoman, a Christian. Bridget established an abbey c. 480 on the

Hill of Kildare (Cill Dara – Cell or Church of the Oak), where she was Abbess of a double monastery for men and women. Some claim that her foundation may have evolved from a sanctuary of Druid priestesses who converted to Christianity. At Kildare 'Bridget's Fire', a perpetual flame, was kept alive by Bridget and her nuns, possibly until the time of the reformation; again, some claim this was a continuation of a pre-Christian tradition on that site. It has long been accepted that legends of the St Bridget of Kildare became conflated with those of an older deity of the same name, and Henken (1987: 161) suggests that further conflation may have occurred with another Irish saint of the same name, a St Brigid of North Wales, and the Swedish St Brigid.

It is said that St Bridget visited Glastonbury in 488 and spent time at Beckery or Bride's Mound, an area on the edge of Glastonbury where there seems to have been a chapel dedicated to St Mary Magdalene. This chapel is identified in local legend as the site where Arthur had a vision of the Virgin in which he was presented with a crystal cross. After this, Arthur reputedly changed his arms to green with a silver cross, with the Virgin and Child in one quarter – the arms later adopted by Glastonbury Abbey (Carley 1996: 110). A chapel on the site of the Magdalene chapel was later rededicated to St Bride, and reputedly relics of the saint, including a bell and a necklace, were displayed there. There was also a nearby spring known as Bride's Well, which some claim was known for its powers of healing and fertility. An image of St Bride with a cow appears on the tower of St Michael's chapel on the Tor. Thus, while there was undoubtedly long standing interest in Arthur, there was also a well established tradition of Bridget being connected with Glastonbury.

Among the extraordinary visionaries and spiritual seekers to settle in Glastonbury early in the twentieth century was Alice Buckton, an educationalist, poet and dramatist who was keen to promote sacred drama. In 1920, at a ceremony for the laying of the foundation stone of a theatre in the grounds of Chalice Well, Buckton described her theatre as 'another Round Table':

> Arthur had a round table at which knights only sat. The women were apart. Today we are able to build a table at which women and men and all the rhythmic powers of Life shall sit represented. (Cutting 2004: 63)

Already in 1914 a pageant play written by Buckton called 'The Coming of Bride' had been performed in Glastonbury (see Cutting

2004: 63–67). In summary, the play starts with Bride spending seven years on Iona learning from friendly Druids their herbal lore and other wisdom. The scene then shifts to Ireland, where Bride, after tending her cattle, falls asleep and has a dream in which she takes in weary travellers who turn out to be Mary and Joseph and the child Jesus. Bride then comes to Glastonbury with an entourage of maidens, where she is welcomed and consecrated by St Patrick, and goes to Beckery to live with her companions. The play seems to reflect plans with which Buckton was involved to bring about the spiritual renewal of Britain by reactivating sacred sites in Iona, Ireland and Glastonbury through pilgrimage (Cutting 2004: 99–101), but more significantly points to a conscious attempt to revive awareness of Bride.

Attention to Bride revived then accelerated in the latter part of the twentieth century. Helena Koppejan was very interested in Bridget, and when The Glastonbury Experience healing space was opened in 1982 it was called the Bridget Healing Centre. Also in The Glastonbury Experience complex is a fourteenth century building which in the 1980s and 1990s was known as Bridget's Chapel – this was non-aligned, deliberately kept free from all iconography and decoration other than flowers and candles, and was considered by many to be special to women, both Christian and non-Christian. In 1995, the Friends of Bride's Mound group was formed to protect the area from inappropriate development, and an annual pilgrimage has been instituted on 1 February, St Bridget's day and Imbolc on the eight-fold calendar. The Friends' vision is to plant the area with flowering herbs, re-instate Bride's Well and maintain a perpetual fire there, as well as opening the area to people of all faiths for leisure or ceremonial use (Bang 2005: 12).

While Glastonbury is immensely spiritually diverse, for many people now Glastonbury is above all a centre of Goddess spirituality, and a significant, ancient, sacred site of Goddess worship. In the late nineteenth century John Arthur Goodchild claimed that there had been in Glastonbury the survival of an ancient Irish cult venerating the female aspect of the deity which became attached to the figure of St Bride (Benham 1993). Kathy Jones, Glastonbury resident, author and priestess, claims 'Where we find St Bridget we *know* that the goddess Bridie was once honoured' (2000: 16). Jones also contests Maltwood's reading of the sign of Aquarius on the Glastonbury Zodiac. Instead of a phoenix, she sees in the landscape a huge swan ('the swan being one of Bride's totem creatures'), Wearyall Hill forming the swan's head and neck, with the rest of her body and wings encompassing all of Glastonbury's hill and vales (Jones 2000: 14–15).

Although rituals are framed around the eight fold or Celtic calendar, the Glastonbury 'wheel of the year' adopted by the Goddess movement there is also influenced by Native American tradition, typical of the integrative nature and global awareness of contemporary spirituality. It is referred to as Britannia's wheel or Bridget Anna's wheel, the British Isles being thought of as originally Bridget's Isles. Rather than the more common threefold 'maiden, mother, crone' form, the Glastonbury goddess is envisaged as fourfold: maiden (whose colours are green and white); lover (red); mother (yellow and gold); Crone (black and purple).

The first Glastonbury Goddess Conference was held in 1996, co-organized by Kathy Jones and by Tyna Redpath of The Goddess and the Green Man shop, which opened originally in 1991 in The Glastonbury Experience. The Conference, now considered by many to be a Glastonbury institution, is always held to coincide with Lammas. Vernacular Irish Catholic traditions such as making 'Bridie Crosses' and baking Lammas bread have been 'reclaimed' to honour the Goddess, but the most obvious tradition connected with the Glastonbury Goddess Conference is the Goddess Procession. This procession through the streets of Glastonbury, which frequently takes in sites such as Chalice Well and the Tor, originally featured a large effigy of the Goddess pulled in a cart, although lighter wicker figures tend to be used now, carried by volunteers. Each year in rotation, an image of the Goddess as maiden, lover, mother or crone usually presides over the conference, is decorated during the event, and carried in the procession. Jones told me that she sees the procession as 'claiming space' in Glastonbury, as a way of saying that 'this belongs to Her'. In 2000 the Goddess Procession started to go 'sunwise', leaving from the Town Hall (beside the entrance to the Abbey), up the High Street 'circumambulating the Abbey', to the Tor becoming, in effect, a mirror image of the Christian Pilgrimage processions. (See Bowman 2004 for more detailed comparison between the Christian and Goddess processions.)

In addition to 'reclaiming' Bridget from Christianity, Avalon (so long Arthur's preserve) has also been re-narrated for some. Marion Bradley's novel *Mists of Avalon* (1982) created and sustains great interest in a female, goddess-based interpretation of Arthurian legend in Glastonbury. Jones has described Avalon as 'the Otherworldly

Figure 2: 2004 Goddess Conference procession on Wearyall Hill carrying image of Bride to Bride's Mound, with Glastonbury Tor in the background (photograph by Marion Bowman, 2004).

counterpart of the small country town of Glastonbury in Somerset, England. It is a magical land where the Goddess has lived from time immemorial and still lives today' (Jones 2001). In 2003 the Goddess Conference focus was celebrating the 'Nine Morgens'. The programme for this event explained:

> In legend the Nine Morgens are Nine Sisters, Faeries, Fates, Goddesses, Ladies, Crones or Crows, who rule the Isle of Avalon. The most famous is Morgen La Fey – Morgen the Faery or Morgen the Fate, who in Arthurian legend was Morgana, the maligned half-sister to King Arthur.

However She is so much more than this, and She has eight Sisters of whom little is known. During the Conference we will be exploring the true nature of the Nine Morgens as Goddesses of transformation, as Sisters working in circle, as Healers, Muses and Guardians of Avalon. Our purpose is to bring them forth from the mists of our forgetting, so that we can recognise and honour these ancient Goddesses of Avalon once again. (2003 Goddess Conference programme)

In the course of the event conventional Arthurian legend was to some extent challenged, reinterpreted and 'reclaimed'. Nine wicker Morgens were constructed and taken in the procession on the last day of the conference, then subsequently installed in the Goddess Temple.

In 2004 the Conference theme was 'Celebrating Bridie and the Maiden Goddess', and embedded in the conference were events that exemplify the flexibility of contemporary Celtic spirituality, as well as the most public 'restoration' of Bridget to Glastonbury. For the first time, procession activity was staged on Thursday rather than Sunday, and was much longer than ever, with the image of Bridie being taken during the course of the afternoon and evening to four 'sacred sites' (Chalice Hill, the Tor, Chalice Well and Bushey Coombe).

On Friday the entire day was devoted to 'Honouring Bridie'. The guests of honour were two Irish Catholic nuns, Sister Mary Minehan and Sister Rita Minehan, Brigidine Sisters based in Kildare. Sister Mary was one of two Brigidine nuns who, in 1992, established a small centre for Celtic Spirituality in Kildare, Sloas Bhride (Brigid's Light). In 1993 the leader of the Brigidine Sisters relit 'Brigid's Fire' in the Market Square of Kildare at the opening of a justice and peace conference, since when the Sisters became keepers of the flame at Solas Bhride (Minehan 1999: 14-15). Sisters Mary and Rita ceremonially brought the sacred flame of Kildare to Glastonbury, and relit it in a ceremony at the conference venue on Friday morning. At this ceremony both Sisters spoke, talking of the cult of Brigid, revered and worshipped in ancient Ireland, associated with poetry, healing and smithcraft, nurture, fertility and fire, and of how Christianity took root slowly in Ireland, assimilating features of older beliefs and practices. At this time of transition Brigid of Kildare was born, Brigid the saint inheriting much of the folklore associated with the goddess Brigid. Sister Rita concluded:

It may be an exercise in futility to try separating the historical Christian Brigid from the goddess since, clearly, the two are so interwoven.

St Brigid stands at the meeting of two worlds. Neither the boundaries of Christianity nor the older beliefs can contain her exclusively. (See Minehan 1999: 12, from which this seems to have been quoted.)

Such sentiments were prefigured in a striking painting of Bridget created for the 2004 conference by artist Wendy Andrews, depicting her in Glastonbury, positioned both physically and metaphysically between Bride's Mound with its chapel on one side, and the Tor

Figure 3: Wendy Andrew's painting 'Brigid' on display at the White Spring, Glastonbury (photograph by Marion Bowman, 2006)

on the other, symbolizing her relationship to both Christianity and paganism.

There then followed a session in which Bridget crosses were made, to be carried in another procession. On Friday afternoon, the image of Bridie was taken out again, the route this time taking the procession past the Catholic Church, and up and over Wearyall Hill, where some stopped to decorate the Holy Thorn. The destination of this procession was Bride's Mound, which had been beautifully decorated by the Friends of Bride's Mound for the occasion. The highlight of the ceremony was the bringing of the Kildare flame by Sisters Mary and Rita, to be rekindled on Bride's Mound. It was felt by many there that Bride had truly come home to Glastonbury.

Conclusion

The restoring and 'restorying' of Arthur and Bridget in Glastonbury exemplify certain characteristics of both contemporary spirituality and vernacular religion. Both can apparently ride the tide of any number of changes in spiritual focus and ethos. Both occasion great creativity in 'the verbal, behavioral, and material expressions of religious belief' (Primiano 1995: 44), as we see, for example, in the creation of goddess images, the 'revival' of Bridget crosses, the sale of replica Excaliburs, the development of rituals and spiritual journeying focused on particular sacred sites. Both seem happy to incorporate and embrace elements from a variety of sources. Above all, myth plays a crucial, inspirational role in vernacular religion and contemporary spirituality, and myth-making is a dynamic process in each.

Glastonbury has clearly been a 'storied' location for many centuries. The twentieth and twenty-first century flurry of myth-making involves in many cases simply the recycling or reworking of the myths upon which Glastonbury's vernacular Christianity was built. However, the rediscovery and reappraisal of myth that took place in the twentieth century, fed by such influences as the study of folklore and the works of Joseph Campbell and Carl Jung, has led to the perception of myth as far more than narrative; in various forms of contemporary spirituality it is assumed to be therapeutic, participative and empowering. Myth is seen as constantly evolving and emerging as new insights give a different lens through which to view old myths, or new myths are created around contemporary experiences and phenomena. The belief stories of different groups both confirm their vision of

Glastonbury's past and reflect their visions for the present and the future. Glastonbury could be seen in Lane's terms as an example *par excellence* of 'the storied nature of place' (Lane 1988: 20), with significance and sacredness being read into – and indeed read in – the landscape itself. Both Arthur and Bridget have been subjects of conflation, Christianization, manipulation, contestation and inspiration for many centuries; that their stories are now pressed into service for a variety of contemporary spiritual seekers is merely the latest chapter. The people who now follow their own grail quest on the Glastonbury Zodiac, those who feel they have located Avalon, those who 'restore' or 'perpetuate' Goddess worship or Druid ritual in Glastonbury are not simply story tellers but 'story dwellers'.[6]

To conclude, a European postscript must be added to this chapter (see Bowman 2009). The 2004 Goddess Conference was attended by a Hungarian woman who had studied English at university and had been fascinated by Arthurian myth; she had read and loved *Mists of Avalon*, but 'didn't think there could be such a place now'. Already involved in Budapest's burgeoning alternative scene, she found out through the Internet about the Glastonbury Goddess conference. Inspired by her Glastonbury experience, she started to train as a Priestess of Avalon, and in 2006 both organized her first Goddess Conference and opened a Goddess Temple in Budapest. The programme for the 2008 Hungarian Goddess Conference reveals both continuity and change, as we see features of the Glastonbury conference being replicated but re-negotiated in their new physical, cultural and (pre)historical environment:

> Brigit, Bride, Brighdie, Bridie, Saint Brigit … Her name once meant Goddess. Once She was the Great Goddess, Maiden, Lover, Mother, Crone and Lady of the four elements. She still is the healing Goddess whose presence we feel in the healing springs and in the fire of our hearts. In Hungary, the name of the very first Roman settlement in Pannonia, established on the land of the Celtic Azalus tribe, Brigetio, bears witness to the honour that was paid to Brigit in those days. (http://www.goddessbudapest.com/ accessed 5 June 2009)

Elements of the Glastonbury Goddess movement, a highly localized, landscape-rooted form of contemporary spirituality developed in a much mythologized, contested site of pilgrimage in England, and beliefs about Bridget have transplanted (thanks to the Internet) to a new context with quite different topography, history, mythology, and cultural traditions to draw upon in the creation of new expressions of belief.

Notes

1. A version of this paper appeared as Arthur and Bridget in Avalon: Celtic Myth, Vernacular Religion and Contemporary Spirituality in Glastonbury *Fabula, Journal of Folktale Studies*, 48 (1/2) 2007: 1–17.

2. When no specific reference is given for a quotation, it comes from fieldwork tapes or notes. I am grateful to all who have given me the benefit of their time, knowledge, experiences, insights and company.

3. The spelling of Bridget is varied, appearing as Brigit, Brigid, Bridie and Bride. Here for the sake of consistency I use Bridget and Bride, the most commonly adopted forms in Glastonbury, unless quoting others.

4. This is not a new idea. Eighteenth century antiquarian and Anglican cleric William Stukeley envisaged the Druids coming to England with the Phoenicians, 'during the life of Abraham, or very soon after', with a religion 'so extremely like Christianity, that in effect it differ'd from it only in this; they believed in a Messiah who was to come, as we believe in him that is come.' (Quoted in Stuart Piggott's *Ancient Britons and the Antiquarian Imagination*, London: Thames and Hudson 1989: 145.)

5. Artist Forrester Roberts, for example, produced a print entitled 'The Challenges', which presented the Glastonbury Zodiac as a symbolic 'Life Wheel', influenced by the mandala. The text below the picture explained that the problems encountered by each knight as he moves through the different signs are illustrative of the challenges we meet along the way in life, and in each sign a different lesson should be learned. When the knights come full circle, either they can, like Galahad, leave the Wheel forever or, like Lancelot, fall short and have to start the whole journey again.

6. I have borrowed this phrase from Gershon Gorenberg (2000: 247) as it is so apposite for Glastonbury.

References

Ashe, G. (1957) *King Arthur's Avalon: The Story of Glastonbury*. London: Collins.

Bang, L. (2005) Bride's Mound revisited. *The Chalice* 12: 12.

Bascom, W. (1984) The forms of folkore: Prose narratives. In A. Dundes (ed.) *Sacred Narrative: Readings in the Theory of Myth*, 5–29. Berkeley, Los Angeles, CA and London: University of California Press.

Benham, P. (1993) *The Avalonians*. Glastonbury: Gothic Image Publications.

Bennett, G. (1989): Belief stories: The forgotten genre. *Western Folklore* 48 (4): 289–311.

Bowman, M. (1993) Drawn to Glastonbury. In I. Reader and T. Walter (eds) *Pilgrimage in Popular Culture,* 29–62. Basingstoke and London: Macmillan.

Bowman, M. (2002) Contemporary Celtic spirituality. In J. Pearson (ed.) *Belief Beyond Boundaries: Wicca, Celtic Spirituality and the New Age,* 55–101. London: Ashgate.

Bowman, M. (2004) Procession and possession in Glastonbury: Continuity, change and the manipulation of tradition. *Folklore* 115 (3): 273–285.

Bowman, M. (2005) Ancient Avalon, New Jerusalem, Heart Chakra of Planet Earth: Localisation and globalisation in Glastonbury. *Numen* 52 (2): 157–190.

Bowman, M. (2006) The Holy Thorn ceremony: Revival, rivalry and civil religion in Glastonbury. *Folklore* 117 (2): 123–140.

Bowman, M. (2008) Going with the flow: Contemporary pilgrimage in Glastonbury. In P. J. Margy (ed.), *Shrines and Pilgrimage in the Modern World: New Itineraries into the Sacred,* 241–280. Amsterdam: Amsterdam University Press.

Bowman, M. (2009) From Glastonbury to Hungary: Contemporary Integrative Spirituality and Vernacular Religion in Context. In G. Vargyas (ed.), *Passageways. From Hungarian Ethnography to European Ethnology and Sociocultural Anthropology,* 195–221. Budapest: L'Harmattan Publishing House.

Bradley, M. Z. (1986) *Mists of Avalon.* London: Sphere Books.

Carley, J. P. (1996) *Glastonbury Abbey: The Holy House at the Head of the Moors Adventurous.* Glastonbury: Gothic Image Publications.

Cutting, T. (2004) *Beneath the Silent Tor: The Life and Work of Alice Buckton* Glastonbury: Appleseed Press.

Gorenberg, G. (2000) *The End of Days: Fundamentalism and the Struggle for the Temple Mount.* New York: The Free Press.

Henken, E. R. (1987) *Traditions of the Welsh Saints.* Cambridge: D. S. Brewer.

Hexham, I. (1983) The 'Freaks' of Glastonbury: Conversion and consolidation in an English country town. *Update* 7 (1): 3–12.

Ivakhiv, A. J. (2001) *Claiming Sacred Ground: Pilgrims and Politics at Glastonbury and Sedona.* Bloomington and Indianapolis, IN: Indiana University Press.

Jones, K. (2000) *In the Nature of Avalon: Goddess Pilgrimages in Glastonbury's Sacred Landscape.* Glastonbury: Ariadne Publications.

Jones, K. (2001) www.kathyjones.co.uk/local/h-pages/kathyj/gdstemple-newsJuly2001.html accessed 10 February 2003.

Knott, K. (2005) *The Location of Religion: A Spatial Analysis.* London and Oakville: Equinox.

Lane, B. C. (1988) *Landscapes of the Sacred: Geography and Narrative in American Spirituality.* New York: Paulist Press.

Leerssen, J. (1996) 'Celticism' In T. Brown (ed.) *Celticism, Studia Imagologica: (Amsterdam Studies on Cultural Identity) 8,* 1–16.

Maltwood, K. E. (1964 [1929]) *A Guide to Glastonbury's Temple of the Stars: Their Giant Effigies Described from Air Views, Maps, and from 'The High History of the Holy Grail',* 16th edn. London: James Clarke and Co.

Meek, D. E. (2000) *The Quest for Celtic Christianity.* Edinburgh: The Handsel Press Ltd.

Minehan, R. (1999) *Rekindling the Flame: A Pilgrimage in the Footsteps of Brigid of Kildare.* Kildare: Solas Bhride Community.

Pendragon, A. and Stone, C. J. (2003) *The Trials of Arthur: The Life and Times of Modern Day King.* London: Thorsons.

Primiano, L. N. (1995) Vernacular religion and the search for method in religious folklife. *Western Folklore (Reflexivity and the Study of Belief)* 54 (1): 37–56.

Prince, R. and Riches, D. (2000) *The New Age in Glastonbury: The Construction of Religious Movements.* New York and Oxford: Berghahn Books.

Smart, N. (1977 [1969]) *The Religious Experience of Mankind.* Glasgow: Collins Fount Paperbacks.

Trwoga, C. (2001) *Grail Quest In the Vales of Avalon.* Glastonbury: Speaking Tree.

PART V

Theoretical Reflections and Manifestations of the Vernacular

Belief as Generic Practice and Vernacular Theory in Contemporary Estonia

Ülo Valk*

The contemporary mentality of Estonians seems to be materialistic and rational. The diverse world of folk demonology and beliefs about devils, revenants, spirits, ghosts, fairies and other supernatural entities started to vanish together with the modernization of society soon after the boom in folklore collection in the late nineteenth century. At the same time the Lutheran church and educational system supported enlightened rationalism and the persistent fight against 'ignorant' superstitions, preparing the ground for the spread of the scientific worldview. In the course of the Second World War the country was annexed by the Soviet Union, whose far-reaching social experiments to eradicate religion and belief in the supernatural had a strong effect on the majority of the people, who distanced themselves from the church. The New Age movement has nowadays invigorated vernacular religion in Estonia, although it is difficult to judge how many people believe in supernatural powers outside the fictitious genres of art, film, literature and the cyberworld. UFOs, haunted houses, healers and psychics sometimes reach the front pages of Estonian tabloid newspapers, although these articles are flooded with ironic and mocking comments in the digital media. However, the dominant rhetoric of disbelief in the public sphere does not mean that super-natural beliefs are waning in Estonia. On the contrary, expressions of scepticism and scientific rationalism form a part of the versatile and vital discursive web that surrounds and generates supernatural beliefs. This article explores how beliefs are maintained and constructed in a seemingly secular and rationally oriented society within the context of the Internet as a 'contested terrain, a battleground of discourses' (Warf and Grimes 1997: 270).

* Ülo Valk is Professor of the Department of Estonian and Comparative Folklore, University of Tartu, Estonia.

Belief as Generic Practice

Belief is a vernacular category, used in everyday communication to refer to the act of attributing veracity and validity to something, having a conviction, accepting a truth or expressing a firm opinion about how things are. Belief is also used as an analytic category in different academic discourses, such as anthropology, folkloristics, psychology and philosophy. Beliefs have been studied as cognitive entities, elements of worldviews and mental states, although today the focus of research has shifted towards believers, the social formation of beliefs and their discursive construction as actions performed through language (Ferreira Barcelos and Kalaja 2006; Kramsch 2006). Lisa Bortolotti has noted that belief has three dimensions: (1) it relates to the subject's other beliefs and other intentional states; (2) it is sensitive to the evidence available to the subject; and (3) it is manifested in the subject's behaviour (Bortolotti 2009: 12). Bortolotti's psychological and philosophical characterization of belief is supported by research in folkloristics and religious studies about the associative webs and constellations of beliefs, known as belief systems, that are closely tied to social and physical reality and function as programmes of behaviour and ritualized action (Hoppál 2000). Folklorists have studied beliefs in their multiple expressive forms and usually conceptualized them as vernacular genres that address the supernatural, spiritual and magical. However, the genre boundaries have been left open, because belief overlaps with other categories, such as superstition, custom, ritual, legend, memorate, charm, omen, divination, folk religion and faith healing (Mullen 2000: 119–120). Many beliefs are unstable and inconsistent, their contents cannot always be univocally fixed and their articulations take multiple forms, therefore approaching them through the paradigm of genre offers effective conceptual tools with which to see unity in their seemingly endless variation.

Thinking about beliefs as generic practices relies on the observance that verbal expressions of vernacular creativity follow certain patterns, devised by a multitude of earlier communicative acts and perfor-mances. Some of these expressive forms have been crystallized into definite artistic genres, such as myths, folk tales, proverbs, riddles or ballads, with clear compositional or stylistic features and traditional contents. Others can be better characterized as individual concrete utterances, relevant to particular spheres of communication (Bakhtin 1986). There is a multitude of communicative forms in society and many of them could be described as families of genres or genre hybrids whose *genus* remains unclear (Bergmann and Luckmann 1995: 300–301). Genre is thus not so much a neat category for classification but rather an 'orienting framework for the production and reception of discourse' (Bauman 2004: 3).

For our current discussion the fairly definite genre of legend is of great importance. There are multiple definitions of legends but generally they have been characterized as belief narratives: stories that present arguments about the supernatural (Bennett 1988; Dégh 2001; Oring 2008). Legends mix reality with the world of fiction; they shape social life, as they demonize others by drawing borders between ethnic and social groups and by confronting these groups (Tangherlini 2007; Valk 2008). Legends usually address issues, beliefs and places that are familiar to the audience, who often know the protagonists as fellow members of their community. These stories concentrate on single episodes and tend to follow the structural pattern of personal experience narratives (Nicolaisen 1987). Such generic features constrain and mould the performances of legends, setting the limits of what can be said and how it can be said. However, performers cannot finalize genres as the listeners are equally involved in generic practices. Edgar Slotkin has argued that 'genre is not fixed to content but a function of the performance situation, especially the narrator's relationship to his or her audience' (Slotkin 1988: 108). For the listeners, genres are interpretative perspectives that evoke certain expectations and attitudes, such as humour, irony, scepticism, numinous awe, fear and other reactions. In order to identify genres, it is crucial to make a distinction between a hoax and a piece of true information, between innocent kidding and rude insult, between fabulated joke and personal witness story, between fiction and truth. Some narratives carry certain clues to mark the generic intentions of their performers, such as 'once upon a time' to open up the poetic world of a fairytale, or 'let me tell you a true story' to introduce an anecdote with claims to veracity. However, the audience or readers often remain clueless if extraordinary stories do not fit their worldviews and constitute challenges for them to find proper interpretations. Attentive listening or reading is always interpretative, while the performance is analysed to find its generic markers. If clear traits are missing and the intention of the story-teller is not clear, the audience faces a challenging task to interpret something incomprehensible, such as in the following example.

Some years ago I met my previous fellow students in a guest house in the north Estonian countryside, as 20 years had passed since we received our diplomas. Jokingly the meeting was called a congress, where everybody had to briefly relate one's life story since completing studies at the university. We heard 26 improvized narratives and in spite of differences, it was possible to observe the formation of an *ad hoc* expressive genre with its thematic limits, register, appropriate length and the scope of listeners' responses.

A language teacher told us about her difficult career choice, when she had to decide whether to continue working at the University of Tartu or become a sixth-form college teacher. Under mental stress strange things started to happen. First, a small mirror on the wall of her home suddenly fell down and broke into pieces. A couple of days later she heard a crash and found pieces of glass on the floor, because the big mirror had mysteriously broken. Soon the storyteller visited a friend, another former fellow student of ours. While having coffee they heard a loud bang and crash in the other room and found a broken mirror on the floor. After these events, the storyteller made up her mind to become a sixth-form college teacher. The strange events stopped.

The story evoked some gales of laughter and a puzzled silence after it was finished, as its mysterious content had broken the chain of other stories, mainly told as anecdotes in a humorous mode. Then light hearted questions were asked: how many mirrors were finally broken, and did the storyteller compensate the damage that she had caused to others? However, as the 'congress' had to move on, the audience did not have time for discussion and the formation of interpretations in order to finalize the story. When I later asked the storyteller whether she had something to add, keen to find out whether the story had any supernatural implications for her, she confirmed that this was her personal witness story but she had nothing to add as she could not explain the experiences. Thus, possible interpretations were left for the listeners, including me and a few other folklorists who had recognized the patterns of traditional storytelling, such as tripartial composition, the gradation of tension, and some elements of legend, told as a personal experience narrative. However, if this is a legend, it should rely on some supernatural beliefs – but which beliefs, and beliefs in what? Can we extract from the story some particular belief statements, such as 'if people are under stress mirrors break' or 'broken mirrors signal the need to make life changes'? Most probably not, although there seems to be a link with the traditional belief that breaking a mirror brings bad luck, which adds to the disquieting atmosphere of the story. Here we are dealing with belief as a certain modality, attitude, uncanny feeling towards something incomprehensible, as a tacit acknowledgement of supernatural powers.

Without knowing the life world of the storyteller, her beliefs, values and psychology, the meaning of this personal narrative cannot be properly judged. The unclear generic intention of the narrator and limited reactions of the audience left a certain vacuum around her story, although it had good legendary potential for evoking a variety of interpretations. Web portals and newspapers often publish legends and offer excellent opportunities to study their ability to trigger disagreement and discussion, and to evoke other narratives. One such interactive website in Estonia is the Delfi portal, which was launched in 2000 (Runnel 2008: 581). Its main attraction is entertainment together with local and international news and the possibility to write anonymous comments without moderation. On 25 January 2005 at 16.07 Delfi published an article about ghostly haunting in the regions of Thailand that had been devastated by the tsunami. The text starts as follows:

> People who survived the tsunami, which claimed 280,000 victims, have to face different kind of hardships, such as those caused by ghosts. Local taxi driver Lek told a true story about seven tourists who took seats in his car and asked him to drive to Kata beach. The travellers vanished half way, leaving the driver alone on the road and paralysed with fear, the BBC reports. Lek says that during the trip he suddenly felt his body become numb and when he turned around, he saw nobody in the car. The man is so frightened that he is afraid to drive taxi at night and is planning to find another job. A whole mass of such stories have happened in Thailand recently. There is a story about a white woman, who screams raucously in the ruins of a hotel. At least one security guard had to quit his job because of the shouting. In Khao Lak there is a certain family, whose phone keeps ringing every day and night. If one picks up the phone, one can hear the cries of friends and relatives who beg that they should be saved from the cremation fire.

In contrast to the first example, this is a hybrid media text, containing a cycle of three legends, compressed into brief renderings of their basic plots. It starts with a version of the Vanishing Hitchhiker (Brunvand 1983), told as a personal experience narrative and attributed to a local taxi driver. Other compressed belief narratives about the restless dead follow. The emotional article conveys folkloric aftershocks to the global catastrophe from its very centre, far from Estonia but generating a discussion that is typical to legends. The first response appeared more than an hour after the article was published as a reaction to the stunning silence and was followed by 37 more commentaries:

¤¤¤¤¤,5.01.2005 17:11
There are no comments, indeed…

Terri, 25.01.2005 17:21
Believers believe and non-believers do not believe in spirits and haunting. There is not much to comment here…

Ha, 25.01.2005 17:52
Ha. Folk are speechless. I have once seen a spirit too. She was sitting on the edge of my bed and had a serious talk with me. Her face was so beautiful and shining, but not because of a smile. She had unnaturally high cheeks; however, she radiated such goodness that I was not afraid of her. Instead, I felt extremely good in the company of that person. She was a woman as I am. However, I have forgotten what we talked about.

Pöörduge tagasi, [return] 25.01.2005 18:26
Return to the traditional wisdom. Clergymen of all ancient religions can help. One has to begin with death prayers to secure peace to all those who perished suddenly.

Mennu, miffi.maffi@muffi.ee, 25.01.2005 19:43
Help, how frightening, I would not go there even if I would be paid one million kroons… Awful, cold shivers come over me…☻

A web of such diverse responses reinforces the legendary traits of the article, obviously read by most commenters as a proof of the existence of supernatural powers and otherworldly beings. The article could also be read as an entertaining report of exotic Thai folk beliefs, irrelevant to the spiritual quests of Estonians, although instead the commentaries opened up a spontaneous chain of vernacular beliefs and legends. It is no wonder that folklore can cross language borders and spread so speedily thanks to the Internet as an ideal channel for transmission (Blank 2009). However, it is somewhat surprising that beliefs that have been ascribed to the Thai people were internalized so easily by Estonians, who expressed these beliefs in the form of multiple emotional comments. (Needless to say, most Estonians have no knowledge about Thai culture, folklore and religion and its repre-sentations in the Estonian media are scarce.) We can note that webs of belief are formed across language and cultural borders, therefore labelling beliefs as an ethnic heritage of a certain people is problematic. We also see that beliefs do not have textual and generic forms only, but they cause psychological reactions and bodily expressions, such as the cold shivers caused by fear or discomfort. Beliefs also tend to appear in narrative form and to generate new stories – such as the above memorate of seeing the spirit – and other verbal evidence.

Comments, interpretations, emotional reactions and other responses that narratives generate, link them with the broader web of vernacular ideas. These intertextual rejoinders express the subjective perspectives of the members of the audience, whose generic reading and listening finalize the genre. Each narrative may be interpreted from multiple points of view, which may, but need not be, expressed in verbal responses that function as the framework that determines the generic features of the narrative.

Let us now explore another media text expressing a variety of contemporary Estonian beliefs and the concomitant vernacular theories.

The Poltergeist of Risti Street and Vernacular Theories of Belief

According to Linda Dégh many legends are born and thrive through the media, which carries more elaborate and diverse versions than those appearing in oral forms (Dégh 2001: 84). Television is both a conduit and a constraint to the transmission of narratives about personal supernatural experiences because it offers brief, intense, forms of communication as sustained, lengthy recitation of narratives is not possible (Primiano 2001: 48). The short format of narratives and beliefs is also suitable for communication in the Internet, which has become a major medium for the generation and spread of folklore due to its interactive, instrumental qualities. These qualities differentiate it from television and radio, both of which divide people between broadcasters and audience (Bronner 2009: 25).

On 1 September 2004 – on the evening of the first school-day when families are at home and many watch TV – Estonian Television's popular broadcast *Pealtnägija* ('eyewitness') surprised its audience with sensational news from an apartment in Tallinn, allegedly troubled by a poltergeist. Next morning the tabloid newspaper *SL Õhtuleht* published a huge front-page headline: 'Incredible: for three months

Figure 1: Front page of the newspaper *SL Õhtuleht* (2 September 2004): 'Incredible: for three months a poltergeist riots in an apartment. A flat in Tallinn is destroyed by a mysterious spirit.' Evi demonstrates a torn up shirt.

a poltergeist riots in an apartment. A flat in Tallinn is destroyed by a mysterious spirit' (Paas 2004). The newspaper cover was illustrated with a photo of a distressed elderly lady who demonstrates a torn shirt. The article, which was advertised on the front page, was published under the title 'The spirit of a deceased relative started to rage.' (*Surnud sugulase vaim hakkas märatsema.*) On the same morning of 2 September at 9:03, the web portal Delfi published a summary:

Deceased relative started to rage

Torn clothes and shoes, broken clocks and radios, furniture turned over, a flying phone in the room – this is the daily life of a family in Tallinn, because for four months a furious poltergeist has been troubling their home, a three-roomed flat in an apartment house in Risti Street.

On Wednesday afternoon the armchairs and closet, which had been turned over in the morning, had been set back to their normal positions. In the corner of the corridor skis have been fixed to the wall and protected with garlic. There are three generations living in the flat – Evi, her son with his wife and their 14-year-old daughter Kristiina, as reported by the newspaper *SL Õhtuleht*.

The poltergeist has been causing trouble for the family since May 24th.

A day before that an 87-year-old relative had died in a nursing home. Earlier she had been living in the same apartment.

The old woman was very much against going to the nursing home and made numerous attempts to run away from there. Obviously, she could not accept the way she had been treated and tries to find contact with Evi's family after her death.

Today there is probably not a single thing in the Risti street apartment that is not touched by the angry spirit [*vaim*]. 'For example, I was lying on the sofa, and a cup, filled with water, came from the kitchen and threw water at me. Sometimes our pillows have been pulled away at night. The ghost [*kummitus*] has torn footwear to pieces and scattered shoes in the room,' worried Evi says.

The poltergeist furiously attacks Kristiina's bed. 'Recently it lifted the bed together with the girl. Yesterday morning, when nobody was at home, it turned over the closet,' Evi says. Evi admits that she has once seen the ghost. 'Once, when I was sleeping on the sofa in the big room, I opened my eyes and saw a hunched old woman. Obviously she is the one who has thrown water at us,' suggests the concerned woman, who has called for several psychics [*teadmamees*] to help them.

Until now nobody has been able to help the family. 'They have said that the bad energy [*halb energia*] of the old woman has entered the grandchild. When my granddaughter was at the sports camp, it was really more peaceful here,' the mistress says. In her great trouble Evi wanted to invite a clergyman to ward off the ghost but she does not have the heart to invite a Man of God into her home. 'Maybe he will be hit by a cup! What to do then?'

The woman says that there is more peace in her heart, however, as the clergyman promised to pray for the family.

Igor Volke, a researcher of anomalous phenomena says that this is a classic poltergeist case. 'There is a dead person who is not pleased with the way she had been treated. Her soul tries to express itself and punish the family,' he says.

Volke adds that in addition to the circumstances within the family the ghost's activity is supported by the sandy ground of the place, which is suitable to carry energy. He also does not know how to ward off the poltergeist.

As a media text from the yellow press this article offers a cycle of compressed narratives that focus on tension and conflict and mixes them with emotional quotes from the people involved (Hennoste 2010: 13–15). As an elaborated blend of beliefs the article presents arguments about manifestations of supernatural powers in the physical and social world. Similarly to legends the article makes us forget that we are dealing with a verbal construct of social reality. The reader gets the impression that the journalist has personally visited the devastated flat, observed the situation and now confirms the mysterious events, experienced by the eyewitness Evi, whose quotes bring strong evidence about the case. In addition, the outside expert Igor Volke, who is a leading investigator of the paranormal in Estonia, verifies the extraordinary activities of the poltergeist.

Remarkably, the article not only tells a story about strange events in a disturbed apartment but also offers a set of clues as to how to interpret them. The main belief statement, also expressed in the title, explains the poltergeist as the angry ghost of an old woman who had been mistreated during her lifetime. This opens up the first possible perspective from which to read the article – as a media version of a revenant legend, which reports the revenge of a dead person. Revenants (*kodukäija*) appear in thousands of recordings of Estonian legends from the late nineteenth and early twentieth centuries and many of them explain the haunting as a consequence of mistreating someone or breaking some other social norm. The idea of revenge is one of the oldest motifs that has generated ghost legends (Lecouteux 1987: 173). In a similar way to many traditional revenant legends the article bears a moral message about the importance of proper ethical behaviour. If the old woman had been treated fairly before her death, the dramatic consequences could have been avoided. Second, the expert Igor Volke who on the one hand acknowledges that events are caused by ghostly activities, also opens up a new materialistic perspective by referring to the physical qualities of the environment, such as the sandy ground, as a possible clue to explain the anomalous phenomena. Third, the article hints at psychological interpretations by drawing attention to the teenage girl Kristiina and her connection with the paranormal events. These three perspectives can be characterized as different frameworks of interpretation or vernacular theories, representing belief-related, (quasi)scientific and (folk) psychological or psychiatric approaches. The first perspective endorses the supernaturalist worldview, the latter two open up possibilities of inverting the poltergeist story into a set of anti-legends that destroy intrinsic beliefs and serve as ways of distancing listeners from them (Ellis 2005).

These and other lines of thought were developed in 288 comments that followed the publication of the article in Delfi. The first commentary appeared five minutes after the text was published and the last one at 1:40 in the early morning of the next day. The most active discussants wrote 19, 14 and 14 comments (some under different names, as indicated by the IP address), around 150 people altogether expressed their opinions. Gillian Bennett has noted that the 'supernatural is a topic that is debated frequently and seriously in informal situations, so that individuals are pressurized into taking sides, and they adopt the discourse by learning from those on their side in the philosophical tug-of-war' (Bennett 1999: 38). The interactive qualities of the Internet and the disguise of anonymity enables the use of the aggressive and intolerant rhetorics of warfare (Runnel 2008; Howard 2009). The two basic discourses that are triggered by legends – those of belief and disbelief – are in a strong dialogical relationship. Whereas some people confirm the supernatural and provide further evidence of proof, others undermine and ridicule these statements and offer alternative ways to look at the described events. Legends and beliefs do not address fantasy or dream worlds but the collective reality, which is shared by all members of the society. Arguments about spiritual or physical essence of this shared world do not leave anybody untouched and provoke strong reactions.

Many of the comments that followed the Delfi article did not get involved in theoretical debates but gave immediate practical advice to the disturbed family on how to restore peace in their home. The article says that Evi had called for some psychics to assist her but did not dare to invite professional clergymen to solve the problem. Commenters encouraged her to do this, although there was no agreement about who would be the most effective exorcists, as several religions and denominations are mentioned – beginning with Lutheran pastors:

tiide, 02.09.2004 09:35
I have heard that if Christians pray and command such 'evil' spirit to leave, this helps … it goes away. Why not ask some pastor to do this, as God's power is stronger than the Devil's power.

Soovitan [I recommend], 02.09.2004 09:35
I recommend to light a candle in a church for this dead relative and beg her pardon. One can also bring the candle to the grave. Also, some Catholic priest could be asked to help. Ghosts usually appear in places with small children.

Mütoloog [mythologist], 02.09.2004 11:02t
One should call for a Buddhist monk as they are said to have a remedy for wandering souls. However, the granddaughter seems suspicious, thus one cannot be sure …

abi [help], 02.09.2004 17:59
One should call for Emmanuel Kirss

abi [help], 02.09.2004 18:13
Kirss is a clergyman of the Orthodox Church of Estonia, who before now has solved problems with such invisible characters. I also know a case when reading a prayer on the grave of the restless dead helped and the haunting stopped. Sometimes souls cannot get away.

In addition to using garlic as a protective device against demonic forces other ways of pacifying the ghost without any professional help were recommended. Evidence about the positive results of such ritual solutions was confirmed by earlier personal experience or by reference to reliable sources:

adeele, 02.09.2004 12:20
they should light a candle on the grave for one week, this helps. My dead friend bothered me in my dreams for three nights (inviting me to visit her). I put a candle on her grave and peace was restored.

Tomm, 02.09.2004 18:17
The same happened with my friend's family – a poltergeist acted and the living room was haunted. They put crosses, made of rowan, above each door and peace was restored.

Lighting candles on graves is common in Estonia today to commemorate the dead after the funeral, on All Souls' Day (2 November), Christmas Eve and some other holidays. Folk belief that rowan has magical qualities and can ward off evil has been widely documented in Estonia since the nineteenth century. Several believers noted the moral message of the revenant legend about keeping high ethical standards to avoid such supernatural interventions. Practical advice – all representing the discourse of belief – were supported by bringing other evidence about supernatural powers and arguments against commentaries that manifested a scientific and sceptical worldview. Some commenters, who saw the case in the wider context of belief, brought examples of consequences of ignoring supernatural realities and expressed their systematic worldviews:

> **saturniline ring** [saturnic circle], 02.09.2004 11:55
> Risti street is near Rahumäe graveyard. It is not good to live near houses of death, mourning and pain. Hospitals, prisons, nursing homes, barracks and other places of detainment where much pain is caused are bad, bad …

Others provided more personal experience stories about similar cases, thus endorsing the same beliefs:

> **maakas** [country cousin], 02.09.2004 11:30
> A few years ago the same happened with my acquaintances but they did not trumpet the fact. However, something soaked through. There was also a girl in her early teens in the family. The spirit even wrote warnings. They were quite non-religious and honest people – I have no reason to distrust them, although I am a rather skeptical person.

> **ehh**, 02.09.2004 11:36
> the same has happened to me. It also said something like 'drink less', or that you or your neighbours are making fun. If this would have been a living human being, he would have been a world famous illusionist and would work in a circus. Three of us went to church, prayers were read and peace was restored. Such a thing makes your face look green if things start to move. You have a feeling that breaking the world record of 100 meter race would be a piece of cake at this moment.

However, the above flow of discourse of belief provoked sceptics and disbelievers to express their disagreement, such as the following anti-legend, disenchanting the world from the supernatural:

dr., 02.09.2004 14:36
Vincent and the cleaning man of a mad-house [pseudonyms of two discussants] are living proofs that this bullshit of spirits is located between one's ears ... If you think that I don't know what I am talking about, I give a classic example. After a tragedy in a family it seemed to a certain lady that the phone was constantly ringing but there was silence [when the phone was answered]. The phone continued ringing even when it was unplugged from the wall. Of course, this is not a poltergeist case but a mental disorder. This also explains sounds in the neighbouring rooms, when people hear footsteps and movements. In more severe cases sick people hear shouting and speech. These are the infamous voices in one's head, if somebody still does not understand. Thus, for you two I recommend to make at least one visit to a psychiatrist.

Medical discourse represents the authority of science and offers strong arguments against a supernaturalist worldview. A psychiatric interpretation of the poltergeist case emerged several times together with other rational views to explain the supernatural elements away. Among the 'real' causes of the poltergeist and other ghostly activities commenters mentioned alcohol, drugs, a desire for media attention and the possibly low education and psychology of the teenage girl, affected by hormonal and emotional changes. This authoritarian discourse often took plainly insistent forms, such as the following proclamation: 'drink less! go to school!' (**ci**, 02.09.2004 11: 46). However, the discourse of belief was equally compulsive, accusing the opponents of narrow mindedness and of ignoring abundant evidence that simply cannot be overlooked:

agathodaimon, 02.09.2004 17:18
you idiots who don't believe supernatural things! Damn, isn't there enough proof? you should study literature about these matters and watch some documentaries. Is everybody so narrow minded? Don't ghosts and aliens exist, because 'they are mere characters of science fiction movies such as Superman'? Damn, maybe there was no ice age either, because it was shown in a Hollywood blockbuster? There are so many cases and proofs in the world about such 'science-fiction' things that we cannot deny them. There is a website about supernatural powers where EVERY DAY up to ten news items are posted and 1–3 of them have been described in details. There are about 3,000 reports about alien abductions and real photos of extra-terrestrial creatures exist. Oh damn, this talk gets too long, go and study this on your own and you will discover a terribly exciting world.

Internet discussions and debates about the alleged poltergeist and its witnesses are much more complex than presenting simple pro and contra arguments about beliefs. Some discussants could be characterized as potential believers who were in principle ready to accept the belief-related perspective if convincing evidence could be provided. Several of them recommended installing surveillance cameras in the rooms to detect either the poltergeist or some family member in action. Others presented conspiracy theories, developed vernacular theories about social causes of the narrated events and interpreted the whole debate from a meta-discursive point of view:

> **vaatleja** [observer], 02.09.2004 10:19
> It seems that the politics of the Estonian state is going downhill. Obviously, such means are used to force people to go to churches. Believers are like castrated bulls, they never complain. The roots of this case are much deeper than it has been presented to us.

> **Eksperimentaator** [experimenter], 02.09.2004 13:49
> I inform you of what is going on. There is a group of scholars investigating the mental level of the Estonian people. This is nothing but a test for commenters. One wants to prove the old statement that a great number of DELFI commenters are – excuse me – nothing but nuts. This opinion has now been confirmed. Please continue, the more comments, the more reliable the results will be.

Certainly, there is irony in the above opinion, which is addressed to those who take the poltergeist case and its supernatural causes for granted. Other commenters remained serious and discussed the possible intentions of the family involved:

> **füüsik** [physicist], 02.09.2004 09:23
> There are several ways to explain the case. It is most likely that one aims at reducing the price of the apartment. For example, the landlord wants to get rid of his tenant and find a richer tenant. Or one (or two) members of the family want to give hell to the others. Or they are bored and want to get attention. Anyhow, it seems that residents are not as disturbed as they could have been if things would have been so bad indeed. Obviously, they have an interest in getting the media involved. 'Psychics' confirm that all happens due to the energy of the girl.

Such rational speculations reject supernatural explanations; however, they acknowledge the social power of belief, as it can be used to achieve certain goals. Imitating poltergeist activities may be an attempt to solve problems inside the family or as a symbolic extension of complicated relationships. Beliefs can also be expressed in a staged, non-verbal form and still gain strong discursive support due to their social relevance as they are widely accepted – by some people as factual truths and by others as disturbing proofs of ignorance that have to be contested. As William Hanks has noted, the social production of beliefs starts from belief ascription as part of common sense: 'I believe that you have beliefs and moreover that you also ascribe beliefs to me' (Hanks 2001). Disbelievers who believe that the others believe, have an important role in producing the discursive web of beliefs and finalizing legends with their sceptical and ironic commentaries.

The above examples of vernacular views of disbelief discuss the social functionality and psychological relevance of beliefs. Next to such socio-psychological interpretations expressions of scientific ethos appeared:

> **skeptik** [sceptic], 02.09.2004 16:19
> Phenomena exist. Experiences exist. We experience some phenomena that do not exist ... Science honestly acknowledges its own limits and the greatness of the Universe (thanks to sciences we know how big the Universe is). At the same time, science is consistent. History shows that ignorance has saucer eyes and the gaps of ignorance are filled by fairytales, myths, fears, religions, taboos, prejudices. History also shows that the beginning of science gives space to rationality, as myths, prejudices, fears, etc., withdraw. Myths, ghosts, UFOs, etc. are interesting material for the social sciences, psychology, psychiatry. No better method for gaining new knowledge has been invented.

The above statement again shows that debates about the poltergeist case hit more fundamental topics than allegedly supernatural events in a particular apartment in connection with a certain family. Expressions of belief reveal supernaturalist worldviews, which cannot be tolerated by a scientifically oriented mind that seems intoxicated by belief in never-ending progress. In contrast to expressing awe before the tangible mysteries of the universe, folklore genres here represent the discourse of ignorance, which will inevitably be rooted out to give space to true knowledge. However, the above statement makes reference to the current dominants of Estonian supernatural beliefs, such as ghosts and UFOs, in order to make its rational points. Vernacular theory concerning scientific cognition needs the supernatural discourse in order to claim the supremacy of reason.

Conclusion

The Internet gives voice to the people who are involved in developing vernacular theories that blend into the discursive web of beliefs. These responses make up a forum of contestation that accompanies and finalizes legends as a common media genre. In contrast to institutionally established discourses with monological voicing the expressive field of folklore is always heteroglot. Dominant discourses, with claims to hegemonic authority and expressing ultimate truths, generate counter arguments, become targets of attacks and are refuted. Legends are thus transformed into anti-legends, vernacular theories that are built up are at the same time critically analysed and torn to pieces by the weavers of the same discursive web. If worldviews are discussed, disbelievers have a crucial role in producing belief ascriptions and reproducing beliefs. Expressions of disbelief are thus like an ectoplasmic fluidum, emanating from the living generic body of beliefs. The discourse of disbelief is nothing more than a shadow of its dominant 'other' – the discourse of belief.

Acknowledgement

This article was supported by the Estonian Science Foundation (grant no 7516: Vernacular Religion, Genres, and the Social Sphere of Meanings) and by the European Union through the Regional Development Fund (Centre of Excellence, CECT). I am indebted to William F. Hanks for sharing with me the written version of the paper presented at the conference in San Marino in 2000. I am also grateful to the Internet portal Delfi for the kind permission to use its material and to the newspaper *Õhtuleht* to reproduce the illustration of its front page.

References

http://publik.delfi.ee/news/kuum/tsunamipiirkonnas-kummitab.d?id=9626380
http://www.delfi.ee/news/paevauudised/eesti/surnud-sugulane-hakkas-maratsema.d?id=8516115 [both accessed 29 July 2010]
Bakhtin, M. (1986) The problem of speech genres. In C. Emerson and M. Holquist (eds) *Speech Genres and Other Late Essays,* 60–102. Austin, TX: University of Texas Press.

Bauman, R. (2004) *A World of Others' Words: Cross-Cultural Perspectives on Intertextuality*. Oxford: Blackwell Publishing.

Bennett, G. (1988) Legend: Performance and truth. In G. Bennett and P. Smith (eds) *Monsters with Iron Teeth: Perspectives on Contemporary Legend III*, 13–36. Sheffield: Sheffield Academic Press.

Bennett, G. (1999) *'Alas, Poor Ghost!' Traditions of Belief in Story and Discourse*. Logan, UT: Utah State University Press.

Bergmann, J. R. and Luckmann, T. (1995) Reconstructive genres of everyday communication. In U. M. Quasthoff (ed.) *Aspects of Oral Communication*, 289–304. Berlin, New York: Walter de Gruyter.

Blank, T. J. (2009) Toward a conceptual framework for the study of folklore and the Internet. Introduction. In T. J. Blank (ed.) *Folklore and the Internet: Vernacular Expression in a Digital World*, 1–20. Logan, UT: Utah State University Press.

Bortolotti, L. (2009) *Delusions and Other Irrational Beliefs. International Perspectives in Psychology & Psychiatry Series*. Oxford: Oxford University Press.

Bronner, S. J. (2009) Digitizing and virtualizing folklore. In T. J. Blank (ed.) *Folklore and the Internet: Vernacular Expression in a Digital World*, 21–66. Logan, UT: Utah State University Press.

Brunvand, J. H. (1983) *The Vanishing Hitchhiker: American Urban Legends and Their Meanings*. London: Pan Books.

Dégh, L. (2001) *Legend and Belief: Dialectics of a Folklore Genre*. Bloomington and Indianapolis, IN: Indiana University Press.

Ellis, B. (2005) Legend/anti legend: Humor as an integral part of the contemporary legend process. In. G. A. Fine, V. Campion-Vincent and C. Heath (eds) *Rumor Mills: The Social Impact of Rumor and Legend*, 123–140. New Brunswick, NJ and London: Transaction Publishers.

Ferreira Barcelos, A. M. and Kalaja, P. (2006) Conclusion: Exploring possibilities for future research on beliefs about SLA. In P. Kalaja and A. M. Ferreira Barcelos (eds) *Beliefs about SLA: New Research Approaches*, 231–238. New York: Springer.

Hanks, W. (2001) Belief ascription and the social production of belief. Paper presented at the conference on belief ascription at the International Center for Semiotic and Cognitive Studies, University of the Republic of San Marino.

Hennoste, T. (2010) *Kommikoer ja pommikoer. Üksteist lugu Eesti ajakirjandusest. Loomingu Raamatukogu* 1/2. Tallinn: SA Kultuurileht.

Hoppál, M. (2000) On belief system. In M. Hoppál, *Studies on Mythology and Uralic Shamanism. Ethnologica Uralica 4*, 39–59. Budapest: Akadémiai Kiadó.

Howard, R. G. (2009) Crusading on the vernacular web: The folk beliefs and practices of online spiritual warfare. In T. J. Blank (ed.) *Folklore and the Internet: Vernacular Expression in a Digital World,* 159–174. Logan, UT: Utah State University Press.

Kramsch, C. (2006) Metaphor and the subjective construction of beliefs. In P. Kalaja and A. M. Ferreira Barcelos (eds) *Beliefs about SLA. New Research Approaches,* 109–128. New York: Springer.

Lecouteux, C. (1987) *Geschichte der Gespenster und Wiedergänger im Mittelalter.* Köln, Wien: Böhlau Verlag.

Mullen, P. B. (2000) Belief and the American folk. *Journal of American Folklore* 113 (448): 119–143.

Nicolaisen, W. F. H. (1987) The linguistic structure of legends. In G. Bennett, P. Smith and J. D. A. Widdowson (eds) *Perspectives on Contemporary Legend 2,* 61–76. CECTAL conference papers series. Sheffield: Sheffield Academic Press.

Oring, E. (2008) Legendry and the rhetoric of truth. *Journal of American Folklore* 121 (480): 127–166.

Paas, K. (2004) Surnud sugulase vaim hakkas märatsema. *SL Õhtuleht* 2 (September): 6–7.

Primiano, L. (2001) Oprah, Phil, Geraldo, Barbara and things that go bump in the night: negotiating the supernatural on American television. In E. M. Mazur and K. McCarthy (eds) *God in the Details: American Religion in Popular Culture,* 47–63. New York and London: Routledge.

Runnel, P. (2008) Eesti infoühiskonna meedia- ja tehnoloogiakultuur. In A. Viires and E. Vunder (eds) *Eesti Rahvakultuur,* 580–585. Tallinn: Eesti Entsüklopeediakirjastus.

Slotkin, E. M (1988) Legend genre as a function of audience. In G. Bennett and P. Smith (eds) *Monsters with Iron Teeth: Perspectives on Contemporary Legend, III,* 89–111. Sheffield: Sheffield Academic Press.

Tangherlini, T. R. (2007) Rhetoric, truth and performance: Politics and the interpretation of legend. *Indian Folklife. A Quarterly Newsletter from National Folklore Support Centre* 25: 8–12.

Valk, Ü. (2008) Folk and the others: constructing social reality in Estonian legends. In T. Gunnell (ed.) *Legends and Landscape: Articles Based on Plenary Papers from the 5th Celtic-Nordic-Baltic Folklore Symposium, Reykjavik 2005,* 153–170. Reykjavik: University of Iceland Press.

Warf, B. and Grimes, J. (1997) Counterhegemonic discourses and the Internet. *Geographical Review* 87 (2): 259–274.

Some Epistemic Problems with a Vernacular Worldview

Seppo Knuuttila[*]

The question of describing models of vernacular thinking without including conditions (entities, premises, beliefs) unnecessary for understanding within the interpretation has been addressed in the field of folkloristics for a long time, with various punctuations. At times, the so-called extended simplicity principle has been applied to the vernacular worldview, according to which the interpretative construction with the lowest number of interchangeable elements is probably the most correct. Ethnologists and folklorists have been able, and even tended to, imagine themselves as intellectually a few steps ahead of the human objects of their research, which has resulted in variously simplified interpretations of folk culture.

In the following, I examine certain questions of vernacular episte-mology with the aid of folklore material. My viewpoint is construc-tivist to the extent of not considering necessary, for example, the presupposition of the unitary nature of a vernacular worldview or the people's belief in the supernatural as an explanatory principle for their worldviews. I'm also inclined to think that there is no substantial need for the mechanically repetitive, collective hypothesis of the subject directed by tradition. It is thus a question of the criteria of the subject of research. When writing about the relationship between science and magic, philosopher G. H. von Wright has pointed out that 'the world of imagination that magic is based on, is not a bunch of suspicious "hypotheses" that could be experientially verified or disproved, but completely another *way of thinking* that is basically alien to us' (von Wright 1987: 40). In saying so, von Wright proceeded to italicize the essential research interest of folkloristics, the vernacular way of thinking concerning the world of imagination.

The interpretation of folklore as vernacular thinking manifested as knowing, feeling and doing is typical of contemporary research, which

* Seppo Knuuttila is Professor of Folklore Studies at the University of Eastern Finland.

concentrates on such epistemological questions as: how meanings are generated and where they reside, what do the stories about other realities refer to, what presuppositions does the supernatural concept of the fairy tale include, and whether the vernacular beliefs are states of mind, patterns of thought or theories about the world (Primiano 1995).

The polyphony of folklore studies and the interpretations of subjects that can change at the very basic level are not only due to the richness and inexhaustibility of folklore, but are essentially also due to the imaginative state of folklorists and folkloristics at any given time. In any case, the articulated constructions both postulate explications and produce explanations.

The multi-faceted interpretation history of oral poetry has traditionally been mediated by the idea of oral tradition as representing the world view of preceding generations. In this sense folkloristics has, especially in the twentieth century, developed as a collection of academic theories about vernacular theories, which can be seen as a constructive interpretation of both the history of mentality and its early contemporary, *Völkerpsychologie*. The exemplary stories heavily utilized in the philosophy of mind and meanings resemble myths and fairy tales through folkloristic eyes. By the following analogies I'm not aiming to present folklore stories as solutions to philosophical questions. Rather, it is interesting how the problematics generated by philosophers, for example of parallel worlds and the locations of meanings, have also occupied the minds of the storytellers. This way of reading may seem inappropriate because of the convention of placing vernacular thinking into a hierarchical context that always ends up with *us* at the present moment knowing what *they* in the past thought, and *us* assuming how *they* felt.

Examples of and for

In tradition research the requirement for empirical representativeness has been emphasized, for example, by referring to cases where one or two folklore notes have been used for descriptions of a vast subject; I recall having been warned against this kind of procedure at the very beginning of my studies in folkloristics (over 30 years ago). Things get more problematic, though, when a note, story or other text is used as an example; in this case what the sample is an example of must naturally be stated, and in which way it is an example. Sceptical remarks have been made about how 'in philosophy, examples are always misleading, since the reader is always inclined to find something familiar in them and then concentrate only on this familiar aspect' (Varto 1996: 40). But isn't it the exact purpose of an example used in this sense to make the unknown understandable through a familiar genre/form/structure, etc.? This seems to be the case especially in the scholarly texts aimed for a public broader than only the experts. Liisa Saariluoma, a literary scholar, has aimed to show, in the context of literary history, that the conviction of the exemplariness of single cases inherent in the old school exemplum thinking hasn't 'lost any of its topicality' (2001: 175–176, also 8–9).

In folkloristics, and in the related study of vernacular religion, the word *belief* refers to the traditions, perceptions and interpretations concerning the supernatural and inexplicable, unless otherwise stated. The supernatural can, however, be understood in at least two different ways: usually it is considered to be an aspect of religion, whereas references to supernatural in the sense of the inexplicable can be interpreted as intellectual contemplation without the framework of belief. Naturally it is not necessary, or wise, to deny the mental category of belief as such, but it can be bracketed when the question asked is not if people in times past used to, for example, believe in guardian spirits. Belief stories can thus be used to exemplify the vernacular interest in knowledge and epistemology.

In 1974, the philosopher Thomas Nagel published an article in which he looked into the possibility of knowing *What is it like to be a bat?* At the time he had no way of guessing, or fearing, that the text would become one of the most criticized, and also most referred to, of texts dealing with the philosophy of the mind and consciousness for decades to come. Nagel points out that the very question of how it would feel to be something else may seem scientifically inadequate and even mindless, to some (like the eliminativists), but he also underlines the fact that questions of an exemplary nature like this recurrently appear in all the studies concerned with consciousness, in all fields, with different emphases.

In folkloristics, the question of consciousness and the so called vast mind usually relates to the entity transmitted by the text, which is in every case and solely a construct, whatever other beliefs may be held of it. Thus the question of the subjective nature and objective perceptibility of experience, which was the central problem of Nagel, is left aside from the textual examination concerning the potential and location of meaning. In fact, stories of human experiences of being animals are outlined by numerous secrets and denials of expression. Significantly, losing one's speech or the capability for human expression is frequently the condition or punishment for crossing the border of species, sometimes also the loss of memory.

In the myth sources of antiquity, metamorphoses are part of the basic material of this consideration, to which every generation has contributed with its additions, details and deletions. Nevertheless the problem of crossing the border has not disappeared, meaning that the question of how it feels to be something other than one's self has remained, and remains, a myth-like enigma to the human mind.

Gregory Bateson has based the idea of noncommunication inherent in the ecology of mind on an idea according to which it is essential, literally even fundamental, that all information is not communicated from one system to another without control; in the modern world threatened by pandemics, this is almost self-explanatory. In a cultural sense and in the vernacular epistemology these limits become secrets, which may prove lethal if revealed or even when one just became aware of them. Bateson gives, as an example of a closely guarded secret, the knowledge relative to gender, which in the myths of antiquity took shape as the representation of punishment for looking/ seeing: Actaeon saw Artemis naked and was slain for it, Pentheus spied on the women's celebration of Dionysos with similar consequences (Bateson 1988: 80). This was also the case with the town elders who peeped on the bathing Sousanna. Numerous, also anthropological, sources have it that it has been equally as dangerous for women to spy on men's secrets.

Bateson gives a personal example of the interpretation of examples. While developing the research method he named the 'ecology of the mind', he gave lectures on its central ideas and used an abundance of diverse examples. The students were heard complaining, year after year, that they could not grasp what Bateson's examples were actually examples of: 'Bateson knows something he's not telling us.' In Bateson's own view, this was a case of two different ways of thinking: the students interpreted the examples inductively, from the individual to the general, whereas his own line of thinking was deductive, reflecting facts and hypotheses on the general principles of science and philosophy, and the examples he used were thus rather touchstones than proofs (1985: xvii–xviii).

Greek mythology names Teiresias as one who crossed the borders of gender-related knowledge and experience, having lived as both a man and a woman. Nowadays the arbitrariness of the interpretations of gender borders is especially emphasized; as is the viewpoint of the Teiresias stories, in which he is either a man who has lived as a woman or the other way around. The unattainability of being the other is a kind of setting of boundaries of the possible and the imperative, which in the context of folk psychology has been made visible and negotiable through the tales of metamorphosis.

Völkerpsychologie and Mentality

Völkerpsychologie, as outlined by Wilhelm Wundt and his colleagues in the late nineteenth century, was a research programme aimed at collecting material on such linguistic and enthnographic manifestations of the 'folk soul' as myths, fairy tales, stories, arts, religion, heroes, divinities, rituals (Wundt 1912). The emphasis of the research was placed on the notions and beliefs dominant in different cultures: the mentality of a community. In this sense *Völkerpsychologie* shared certain aims with the history of mentalities. These lines of research have a lot more in common than has been surmised; both have been forgotten for a number of reasons, at times even completely rejected.

It's also interesting to note that *Völkerpsychologie* has had an influence on Finnish folkloristics, though mostly indirectly. The traces must have been scary. Senni Timonen points out how it was precisely *Völkerpsychologie* that turned out to be the problem of Oskar Relander's thesis on the folk lyric. Relander had studied in Berlin between 1888 and 1889 and attended, among others, the lectures of Wundt. Relander's intention of interpreting Kalevala-metre lyric songs as the illustrated language of feelings did not fit into Kaarle Krohn's idea of the research of folk poetry, and as the thesis was transferred to aesthetics, Eliel Aspelin noted that the work lacked knowledge of aesthetic literature. As a result Relander's study was classified under the so called 'folk psychological line' (Timonen 2004: 14–15).

Völkerpsychologie has lately proven problematic in the sense that it has been used as a kind of a scientific sparring partner whose foundation can be shown to be faulty or at least unsatisfactory (Diriwächter 2004). *Völkerpsychologie*, often considered synonymous with folk and common sense psychology, essentially deals empirically with people's ways of planning and carrying out their everyday lives, understanding each other and assigning meaning to things. This kind of description resembles in many ways the methods of ethnomethodology. Applying Primiano's conceptualization (1995: 43–45) we can say that vernacular psychology is a perpetual stream of perceptions and conclusions, where the collective, traditional and ritualistic mix with the individual, ephemeral and contextual. Folklorists in particular would do well to pay attention to whether vernacular psychology is used with the meaning of world view and mentality, or of a philosophical reconstruction understood as layman theory.[1]

The problematics of the relationship between mind and body has also been the topic of wide ranging speculation in folklore, where an essential turning point can be found, with the emergence through its inner qualities, of human substance as a kind of empty entity open to all kinds of energies. For a long time the prevailing idea in vernacular thinking seems to have been that a person's characteristics are inherent in the whole body, down to the hair and fingernails. A Finnish ethnologist, Albert Hämäläinen, who has studied the psychology of spells, wrote referring, among others, to Wundt: 'The parts and excretions of the human body, a person's belongings, even substances and things (food, drink) that come to close contact with him are so called carriers of spiritual qualities (*Seelenträger*)' (Hämäläinen 1920: 136).

All cultural meanings are questions of agreement and thus negotiable. How constructed meanings relate to feelings, which are also negotiable although they are not up for discussion in the way that, for example, perceptions are, is the topic of a vast discussion. If you have seen, say, a guardian spirit, the validity of the perception can naturally be discussed, but it would make no sense for me to claim that you don't feel as if you've seen a supernatural being.

Daniel Dennett has pondered the location of the experiential mind and used a human arm as an example. He asks if a severed arm is able to feel pain, and presupposes the reader to dismiss the question as stupid, since one needs a mind to feel pain. 'Yes, arms don't have a mind despite having lots of ingredients and sequences that easily convince us of some animals' minds' (Dennett 1997: 23). The 'examples of real life', that Dennett is so fond of, usually seem aimed at disproving presuppositions normally filed under vernacular psychology. Still, for example the interpretation of 'the feeling arm' could be broadened in another direction, rearticulating the whole question. (Cf. e.g. the Sermon of the Mount: 'If your right eye causes you to sin, tear it out and throw it away. It is better for you to lose one of your members than to have your whole body thrown into Gehenna. And if your right hand causes you to sin, cut it off and throw it away. It is better for you to lose one of your members than to have your whole body go into Gehenna', Mt. 5:27.)

The location of the mind and feelings have also been pondered in folk tales, as well as the possibility of transferring animal qualities to a different species. Is it possible? The fairy tale (ATU 660) of three doctors who, through unlucky mishaps, are forced to trade their arm, eye and stomach (heart) for a thief's arm, a cat's eyes and a pig's stomach, proposes that the qualities of these beings reside in the organs. So the thief's hand steals, the cat's eyes are able to see in the dark and the pig's stomach craves slop, regardless of who is in control of the organs. It would, of course, be trivial and totally useless to explain how qualities placed like this do not correspond to physical reality; instead, it would be interesting to examine how the meanings of fairy tales implying messages like these, form in the context of being the other. Organ transplants have given new life to these ponderings and nurtures them in urban legends and literature, as well as in movies.

Similar boundary crossing motifs can be found in stories about a human being who is granted the ability to speak animal languages or act like an animal (swim like a fish, fly like a bird). This doesn't necessarily imply a belief of this having actually happened. Rather the cognitive interest of these stories lies in the question of what these border crossings, often considered dangerous, would result in.

Theory Theory

While considering the status and meaning of vernacular psychology, references are often made to the well known article by Wilfrid Sellars, *Empiricism and the Philosophy of Mind* (Sellars 1997; 1956). While criticizing the view of a world similar to perception and the so called myth of the given, Sellars describes a self-made 'myth' about the birth of the mind. According to this, our ancient ancestors only talked about things in accordance with perception, which resulted in them having neither opinions nor imagination, and even if they had some, they weren't aware of it. Until their mastermind Jones starts to develop a theory about how vocalized, public speech is preceded by 'inner speech'.

In the light of the presented 'myth', Sellars is certainly no storyteller, and thus his exemplary story is a fragmentarily illustrative presentation, among other things, about how according to the theory built after the model of speech events, semantic categories are also considered to apply to inner events like thoughts. According to Lilli Alanen's interpretation, this means that 'we've been conditioned to perceive and recognise our thoughts as kinds of chapters of inner speech, as naturally as we perceive middle-sized objects in the outer world' (Alanen 1995: 42). In the research context of vernacular psychology, stressing the constructed aspects, this kind of reasoning, where, for example, the theory of the mind is illustrated and debated via a fictional exemplary theory, has been characterized as theory theory, which obviously implies a critical standpoint (Cf. Hutto 2008: 31–40, 243–245).

In a folkloristic framework, the setting of the Jones myth could also mean examining folklore as the theory of a constructed world which is not in accordance with perception. The mastermind Jones resembles the wise guy Matti from the Finnish numskull stories, who always spots the faults in the numskull's actions and problem solving: they always go about business concretely and literally, which leads to recurring category mistakes: carrying light in a sack, sowing salt like grain, misinterpreting animal behaviour, etc. The difference between them and the Jones example is, of course, that the numskull stories construct a stupid subject ignorant of the world by the means of relatively simple comedy (it's an entirely different matter that a *numskull* is a nickname for people belonging to other regions, other gender, other ethnic groups or other races).

As an example of the dialogical nature of theory theory one can examine the presupposition of change in a vernacular world view, according to which many things that we consider to be inner qualities have previously been attributed to beings operative outside of the human. Illness and death come from the outside, even discussing their victims between themselves. Love, envy and hate are beings that can be transmitted to another person or banished. Sleep comes from outside, intoxication from booze, joy from other people's company. The subjects of these descriptions, common in old folkloristics, resemble Sellars' 'old folk' to whom the world was as perceived. This is, in a way, consonant with the dialogical principle according to which these descriptions of theory have been derived from folklore, meaning human speech and public expression. In the light of worldview and mentality it would thus be interesting to resolve the question of how the outer beings have been transformed into inner qualities; and relating to what, and in which categories, these transferences, which are usually temporally attributed to the process of modernisation, have occurred. On the other hand it is known that the power attributed to the uniqueness of gender, for example female power, has been considered an innate quality (Apo 1995: 11–49; Stark-Arola 1998: 163–166).

One of Jones' earliest ancestors was Prometheus, who stole fire (knowledge and culture, as it has also been read) from the gods to be utilized by man; and that's where man's troubles started, as after the fall from grace. People became conscious of their capability to make choices, influence their surroundings and manipulate each other. If, as the achievements of the Enlightenment are often portrayed, knowledge had replaced folk beliefs on a large scale, the transference would have occurred from the internal interpretation of folk psychology to the external, which would be the opposite direction of development – something along the lines of starting to consider feelings as 'internal' and knowledge as 'externally learned'. No doubt it is also a question of where the meanings are located, or where we have sufficient grounds to place them.

Internal Realism and Folk Beliefs

In his theory of internal realism, Hilary Putnam considered the fact that meaning does not reside inside the human head, and thus is not limited to an individual's 'inner speech', as a central starting point. Neither did Sellars assume that meaning would be formed within inner speech but within communication, because 'the concepts linked to such inner events as thoughts are essentially and primarily *bilateral*' (Sellars 1997: 262). According to Clifford Geertz' well known view culture itself is the functional and public area of symbols, a kind of reality thought aloud (see for example Geertz 1973: 3–30).

According to the central proposition of internal realism, reality can be described in several valid ways, in contrast to, for example, metaphysical realism. That the meanings don't reside inside the head refers primarily to Putnam's central thesis that the psychological state of an individual does not dictate their chosen meanings for expressions.

Like Sellars, Putnam draws on science fiction by presenting an experimental thought of a twin Earth (Putnam 1997: 366–370), where everything is as on our Earth except that the chemical compound of water is XYZ instead of H_2O. Putnam's reasoning is complicated and detailed and his argument is linked to a vast philosophical discussion on truth. The most interesting point regarding this text is that Putnam strives to show how it is, at least in principle, possible to make an exception to the rule according to which two separate linguistic expressions can have different intensions but a common extension (morning star and evening star = Venus) but not the other way around. On this Earth and the twin Earth all descriptions of water can be consistent, so no speaker's psychological state dictates the meaning of the subjects, even though they (unknowingly) refer to two different extensions, namely H_2O and XYZ (this setting shouldn't, of course, be confused with the homonym, where several concepts share a common denomination).

A similar twin Earth model has also been developed by Dennett. His Jones looks out of the windows and sees, or thinks he sees, a horse. Soon afterwards he gets a chance to travel to a twin Earth, where everything is just as it is here, only the creatures resembling horses – and it takes an expert biologist to tell the difference – are called schmorses. Dennett's question is, in which intentional state of mind is Jones: does he believe he is seeing a horse, or some other creature resembling a horse, one he's never seen before? According to Dennett, a number of his colleagues are of the opinion that Jones has to be in one of these states, whereas Dennett believes the meanings of the intentional state to be open to interpretations (Dennett 1993: 294–295). Putnam comes close to this viewpoint, though with different arguments, by stating that no individual speaker's psychological or intentional state can dictate 'what he means', nor can meaning be derived from it (Putnam 1997: 413).

Analogous to these examples are the stories of the parallel universes of the myths, fairy tales and legends. Universes which the heroes, shamans, or even just ordinary people like the storytellers may have visited. The construction of thought concerning the existence of parallel worlds and encounters with their inhabitants has also been characterized as a distinctive intentional state, with one predestined context in folk belief. This has been based on the premise that, for example, in relation to guardian spirits a person is either in a state where (s)he believes in them, or otherwise knows, as we do, that they don't really exist.

In the light of internal realism one could ask, for instance, what kind of arguments exist that make us take it for granted that celebrations can be held, and food and drink similar in both meaning and function can be consumed, both underwater and on land? In some parts the dilemma might be resolved for example by interpreting the extensions of water to be different over and under the surface, even if the intensions of water are similar. In folkloristics it has not been considered necessary to consider the possibility that the storyteller and the listener should be in a certain psychological state prerequisite for understanding what the fairy tale means, and in the light of the former, this line of speculation would have dried up anyway. Rather, it is fruitful to examine fairy tales as examples of how their fantasy, and their connections to the storytellers' (listeners') everyday reality, are articulated.

Also the forest that misleads its visitors can be considered a twin world, with certain empirical limitations. The folklore on the subject considers it pivotal to construct a border between the 'this' (the familiar) and the 'not-this' (the unfamiliar) worlds. Everything is fine, the forest is familiar, generous and soothing. Until the wanderer realizes (s)he has walked too far, or in the wrong direction, the berry-picker straightens herself, the child takes a look around. Everything is as before, only slightly different; nothing seems familiar any more. The trees, formerly friendly, are now hostile, the sun is shining from the wrong direction. Messages don't penetrate the borders of these twin lands. The one submerged underwater or lost in the woods cannot convey his whereabouts to the ones on this side of the border. Extensions are mutually exclusive, even if intensions are consistent, which is often the case in stories and experiences. A frightened human being in grave danger is no doubt in a different state of mind than the moment just before being submerged or lost, as vernacular psychology habitually assumes (Knuuttila 2005).

When philosophers conduct various experiments with thought and reasoning with the help of a 'myth' or 'science fiction', they usually aim to illustrate an abstruse or controversial theory or to point out the weaknesses of competing views. The aim of this text has been to show that it is also productive to examine the myths, fairy tales and legends inherent in folklore from an epistemological viewpoint. In folkloristics, on the other hand, the stories under scrutiny have been interpreted as parts of the worldview they portray and construct. Whenever this has been the explicit aim, the worldview has not been identified with the stories of which the study material consists. Now, is it not necessary for interpretation to fall back on such being as people directed solely by tradition, belonging to the eternal past and prejudged to be less intellectual than ourselves.

Note

1. Other presentations and interpretations of common sense/folk psychology can be found at http://plato.stanford.edu/entries/folkpsych-theory [accessed 1 January 2012].

References

ATU: Uther, H.-J. (2004) *The Types of International Folktales. A Classification and Bibliography. Based on the System of Antti Aarne and Stith Thompson. Part I: Animal Tales, Tales of Magic, Religious Tales, and Realistic Tales, with an Introduction. FF Communications No. 284*. Helsinki: Academia Scientiarum Fennica.

Alanen, L. (1994) Sellarsin semanttinen intentionaalisuuden teoria. In S. Heinämaa (ed.) *Merkitys. Filosofisia tutkimuksia Tampereen yliopistosta 45*, 39–59. Tampere: Tampereen yliopisto.

Apo, S. (2001) *Viinan voima. Näkökulmia suomalaiseen kansanomaiseen alkoholiajatteluun ja -kulttuuriin*. SKS: Helsinki.

Bateson, G. (1985 [1972]) *Steps to an Ecology of Mind*. New York: Ballantine Books.

Bateson, G. and Bateson, M. C. (1988) *Angels Fear: Towards an Epistemology of the Sacred*. New York: Bantam Books.

Dennett, D. C. (1993 [1987]) *The Intentional Stance*. Cambridge, MA: MIT Press.

Dennett, D. C. (1997) *Miten mieli toimii*. (*Kinds of Minds*, trans. Leena Nivala). Porvoo – Helsinki – Juva: WSOY.

Dennett, D. C. (1999 [1991]) *Tietoisuuden selitys*. (*Consciousness Explained*, trans. Tiina Kartano). Helsinki: Art House.

Diriwächter, R. (2004) Völkerpsychologie: The synthesis that never was. *Culture & Psychology* 10 (1): 85–109.

Geertz, C. (1973) *The Interpretation of Cultures*. New York: Basic Books.

Hutto. D. D. (2008) *Folk Psychological Narratives: The Sociocultural Basis of Understanding Reasons*. Cambridge, MA: MIT Press.

Hämäläinen, A. (1920) *Ihmisruumiin substanssi suomalais-ugrilaisten kansojen taikuudessa. Taikapsykologinen tutkimus. Suomalais-ugrilaisen Seuran toimituksia 47*, Helsinki.

Knuuttila, S. (2005) Getting lost. *FF Network for the Folklore Fellows,* 28 (June): 7–9.

Nagel, T. (1974) What it is like to be a bat? *Philosophical Review.* 83 (4): 435–450.

Primiano, L. N. (1995) Vernacular religion and the search for method in religious folklife. *Western Folklore (Reflexivity and the Study of Belief)* 54 (1): 37–56.

Putnam, H. (1997) 'Merkityksen' merkitys. (*Meaning of Meaning*) In P. Raatikainen (ed.) *Ajattelu, kieli, merkitys. Analyyttisen filosofian avainkirjoituksia,* 359–414 Helsinki, Tampere: Gaudeamus.

Putnam, H. (1988) *Representation and Reality.* Cambridge, MA: MIT Press.

Relander, O. (1894) *Kuvakielestä vanhemmassa suomalaisessa lyyrillisessä kansanrunoudessa.* Helsinki: SKS.

Sellars, W. (1997) Empirismi ja mielenfilosofia [*Empiricism and the Philosophy of Mind*]. In P. Raatikainen (ed.) *Ajattelu, kieli, merkitys. Analyyttisen filosofian avainkirjoituksia,* 201–268. Helsinki, Tampere: Gaudeamus.

Stark-Arola, L. (1998) *Magic, Body and Social Order: The Construction of Gender through Women's Private Rituals in Traditional Finland. Studia Fennica Folkloristica* 5. Helsinki: SKS.

Stich, S. P. (1983) *From Folk Psychology to the Cognitive Science: The Case Against Belief.* Cambridge, MA: MIT Press.

Timonen, S. (2004) *Minä, tila, tunne. Näkökulmia kalevalamittaiseen kansanlyriikkaan.* Helsinki: SKS.

Varto, J. (1996) Intentionaalisuus-käsitteen merkitys ja vaikutus länsimaisessa filosofiassa, erityisesti logiikan historiassa. *Filosofinen n&n aikakauslehti* 2/96. Online http://www.netn.fi/296/netn_296_varto1.html [Accessed 18 January 2010].

von Wright, G. H. (1987) *Tiede ja ihmisjärki: suunnistusyritys.* Helsinki: Otava.

Wundt, W. (1912) *Elemente der Völkerpsychologie. Grundlinien einer psychologischen Entwicklungsgeschichte der Menscheit.* Leipzig: Alfred Kröner Verlag.

Wundt, W. (1911–1920) *Völkerpsychologie. Eine Untersuchung der Entwicklungsgesetze von Sprache, Mythus und Sitte* 1: 10. Leipzig: Engelman Verlag/Kröner Verlag.

Afterword

Manifestations of the Religious Vernacular: Ambiguity, Power, and Creativity

Leonard Norman Primiano*

It is such a pleasure to be writing the Afterword to a volume representing the study of vernacular religion in everyday life. It is especially exciting for me to see the concept applied to many different ethnographic contexts and creative expressions from England to Estonia. While there have been some excellent article collections about religious belief and practice over the last 40 years by American folklorists and European ethnologists published in special issues of scholarly journals or as conference proceedings (for example, Yoder 1974; Bringéus 1994; Gustavsson and Montez 1999; Barna 2001; Fikfak and Barna 2007; Wolf-Knuts 2009), this volume remarkably represents the first English language publication of a book of such articles by a press specifically addressing folkloristic research on religion and readily available for scholars to consult, for libraries to make available, and for students to read. Considering the great interest and consistent scholarship in this general area by folklorists and ethnologists (see Primiano 1997; 2010), it is surprising that such a collection is only now emerging in the second decade of the twenty-first century. Marion Bowman and Ülo Valk deserve much credit for their gathering and editing of these articles and for their general zeal and advocacy for this publication.

Folklore and ethnology as hybrid fields belonging to both the humanities and the social sciences are frequently misunderstood and underappreciated by scholars of religion, whose foundation and methods are often textual and historical, not ethnographic. Where the study of religion in everyday life is concerned, the work of folklorists, therefore, is frequently left out of reflections and assessments by scholars in the field of religious studies. My perusal of the recently

* Leonard Norman Primiano is Professor and Chair of the Department of Religious Studies at Cabrini College, Radnor, Pennsylvania, USA.

published *Encyclopedia of Religion in America* (Lippy and Williams 2010) is an illustrative case in point. While the encyclopedia does contain an article on 'folklore' – written by myself (Primiano 2010) – its various entries on 'popular religion' (Williams *et al.* 2010) and 'lived religion' (Hall 2010), fail to consider the contributions of American folklorists who study religious people and culture. This lack of acknowledgement is especially egregious considering that folklorists have been collecting, classifying, studying, defining, and creating research methodologies about religion as it is lived for several decades, and most certainly before the interest in 'lived religion' as an approach arose among scholars of historical and contemporary American religion in the 1990s. Folklorists and ethnologists, perhaps because of their European roots, tend to be more generous in crediting former and current work in other fields, and have not hesitated acknowledging and using the scholarship of religious studies in such areas as popular religion and lived religion, as well as sociology and religious history. While the possibilities and resources for studying religion offered by scholars of religious studies, history, sociology and anthropology are considerable, they are certainly complemented and supplemented by the appreciation for subject matter, the emic sensitivity of approach and analysis, and the methodological attention to 'thick' descriptive detail offered by the field of folklore. Folklorists and ethnologists, as illustrated in this collection, are attentive to the documentation and analysis of religiosity in historical and contemporary settings and in contexts that range from rural, urban, suburban, agricultural, industrial, face-to-face, mass-mediated and generational.

'Re-thinking what Religion Means ...'

Emanating from folklore studies, the concept of 'vernacular religion' is a theoretical hybrid of several fields studying religion: folklore and folklife; religious studies; religious history; and ethnographic disciplines including anthropology, sociology, oral history and ethnomusicology. What makes 'vernacular religion' conceptually valuable, and why it has been applied by scholars in a variety of fields from folklore to theology to ethnology to art history, is that it highlights the power of the individual and communities of individuals to create and re-create their own religion. Since the publication of the definitional article on vernacular religion in 1995, however, I have been alarmed by its misuse by some scholars with otherwise good intentions who change its meaning and applicability for understanding religion. Vernacular religion is not the dichotomous or dialectical partner of 'institutional' religious forms. Vernacular religion represents a theoretical definition of another term, not just a terminological substitution for an older concept. It shifts the way one studies religion with the people becoming the focus of study and not 'religion' or 'belief' as abstractions. Religious traditions, and the institutions which can be related to them, therefore, have vernacular religion as their foundation. Vernacular religion additionally suggests an alternative reading to the institutional connection observing that 'high' tradition – when directly influencing religious belief and practice – is itself conflicted and not monolithic.

The study of vernacular religion, like the study of folklore, appreciates religion as an historic, as well as contemporary, process and marks religion in everyday life as a construction of mental, verbal, and material expressions. Vernacular religious theory understands religion as the continuous art of individual interpretation and negotiation of any number of influential sources. All religion is both subtly and vibrantly marked by continuous interpretation even after it has been reified in expressive or structured forms. Vernacular religion is rooted in the general concept that the individual theorizes even as he or she is living (Scott 1990); moreover, that this expression of thought and action is most prominently exemplified in the case of religion as it is lived. Whether universal or even regional patterns of vernacular religiosity can be noted will only be possible after further intensive research, but the concept helps our appreciation of the paradox that, if such patterns do express themselves, they will do so in contexts and occasions that are always unique to the individual, with such creativity repeated in succeeding generations (see relevant studies by Turner 1999; Hinson 2000; Sciorra 2001; Magliocco 2004; Howard 2011). The study of religion, therefore, necessitates a complete process of contextualization; a dedicated, and by necessity intensive method of detailed and nuanced gathering; structure and relevant text appreciation; and the elevation of people's own voices and aesthetic and classificatory systems, especially over the edifice of the theoretical creations of powerful scholars. Graham Harvey beautifully summarizes in his contribution to this volume the sensibility of the vernacular religion scholar, the discoveries to be made, and the energy and joy in appreciating everyday beliefs of others when – writing about his response to the multivocal qualities of 'the culture of things' – he exclaims: 'a series of casual statements and acts

...provoke[d] me to re-think what "religion" (and not only "indigenous religion") means'.

'New Wine into Old Wineskins'

It is out of this need for contextualization and the production of 'textual ethnographies' (Honko 1998: 1) that this volume's essays seek to study the expressions of religion in everyday life through the prism of genre, and especially narrative genres (though material genres are also represented). Such an orientation could prompt some questions and concerns, especially for readers unfamiliar with contemporary folkloristics who may still identify folklore with the machinery of genre compilation and description and not the contemporary conceptual-ization of genres in the field as communicative practices. In my recent encyclopedia entry on 'Folklore and American religion', I listed some of the possible cultural expressions – easily also classified as genres – of religious affiliation, observance, affection, or memory that can constitute the multitude of aesthetic forms observable in religion as it is daily lived. My list includes: artefacts, art, craft, architecture, beliefs, behaviours, private and public customs, habits, foodways, dress, ways of speaking, narratives, bodily communication, dance, music and song (Primiano 2010: 845). Narrative genres are a familiar category for folkloristic classification and analysis, but they also hearken back to the discipline's historical and philological roots and dependence on literary texts. Such an older literary focus on narrative-based genres – such as personal experience narrative, memorate, folk tale, fairy tales, saints' legends, etc. – must not take attention away from the context-centred approach in rich fieldwork on which these articles are founded. With their sensitivity to issues of context, the scholars in this collection have worked on a way to avoid any 'genrefication' of religious beliefs and, by default, religious believers.

Beginning in the 1960s, the application of what has come to be called *performance theory* – an emphasis on mode of presentation in social context versus mere collection and documentation – to the study of folklore complemented the earlier perception that tradition is a living process exhibiting both conservative/passive and dynamic/changing qualities. Performance theory further prompted folklorists to see religion in its various forms of expression as never static, but vibrant, and continuously transforming as individuals receive and adapt traditional knowledge, practices, etc. to specific circumstances, places, times, developments. The expressive culture of religion from a performance studies perspective, therefore, does more than simply reflect the worldview of a religious tradition; it actually assists in the creation of a culture, and, if needed, its reconstruction (Primiano 2010: 848). Performance theory offered a path for understanding the nuances of religious belief and related practices, as well as verbal and material expressions of religion, as artistic communication, and seeing individual proclivities for change as representative of larger societal patterns.

The articles in this collection articulate an understanding of the nature of the belief behind the variety of folklore genres delineated, and behind the religious contexts they feel are so significant. This articulation begins the fullest possible methodological promise of folklore/ethnology and religious studies: the promise of addressing the complex parameters of religion in everyday belief and practice. The real people discussed in these essays are anything but static models. The artistic communication of their religious expressive culture is not to be found merely in its manifestations or outward phenomena, but in the holistic study of these products within their attendant conscious, unconscious, aesthetic and affective processes. The articles represent a necessary first step in the contextualization of vernacular religion in these primarily European locations and these spheres of religious influence, be it in the complexities of contemporary religious pluralism in Glastonbury; the interface of religious and health beliefs in contemporary England; the fluidity of shrine building over the centuries in Russia; the contestative nature of dream narratives in a Hungarian community in Romania; the textures of women's work and time in influencing daily domestic practices both religious and otherwise in Russian Orthodox Karelia; or the nimble re-creation of a holy healer's autobiography in Hungary. Like 'new wine into old wineskins', vernacular religion need not only be found in traditional forms of narrative genres, for the next step should most certainly be the discovery of mixed genres and new religious genres not yet known.[1] One contemporary American folklorist doing noteworthy work in this area is Robert Glenn Howard (2011) who has recently published an excellent monograph studying the vernacular religious rhetoric of contemporary Christian Fundamentalism communicated via unique religious genres over the Internet. Another innovator is Finnish religious studies scholar Mika Lassander (2012) who has applied French anthropologist and sociologist of science Bruno Latour's ideas to vernacular religion approaching the study of religion in general – and contemporary Paganism in Britain specifically – in a fresh theoretical and methodological way as a complex of bidirectional influences and networked interactive processes.

All of these ethnographers of vernacular religion become historians of religion when they are attentive to, translate, and analyse the expressions cited in this book. These chapters are the pieces of the new history of world religion, built on the foundation of individual and local experience rather than on the path of institutions and functionaries of those institutions. Read as a unit, this collection displays vernacular religion interpreted in select historical and contemporary contexts from indigenous religions of hunter/gatherers, to New Age angelic spiritualities, to the contestative lives of religious people once living under atheistic governments, to creative spiritual solutions for those challenged by serious bodily illness.

Ambiguity, Power, and Creativity

Three themes stand out to me after reading these collected essays of vernacular religion in everyday life: the significance of creativity and artistry to religious life; the ambiguous nature of people's religion; and the relationship of religious creativity to forms of power in particular as contestation to that power.[2] Working with select ethnographic examples and theoretical perspectives taken from these scholars in ethnology, folklore, religious and theological studies, this text widens and deepens the contemporary study of religion as it is lived, as many of these ethnographic studies show individuals explicitly and consciously 'creating' their religion. Such religiosity can reflect the ambiguous character of vernacular religion as it communicates two or more separate and conflicting meanings. Indeed, vernacular religiosity has the potential to manifest dimensions of both confirmation and contestation, of legitimization of the hegemonic as well as resistance to such societal and cultural manifestations of power.

Vernacular religion is 'stubbornly ambiguous', using the words of Michael Candelaria (1990: 2) in his discussion of popular religiosity and its role in Latin and South American liberation theology. Candelaria asks from a political and theological perspective whether people can be conceived as either the subjects or objects of liberation (1990: 38). I ask from a folkloristic perspective whether people can be conceived as *both* subjects and objects of traditional and performed religious belief and practice; further, in which ways are people not only acted upon but themselves actors.[3] Borrowing terms suggested by British Marxist literary critic and historian, Raymond Williams, I ask how such designations as 'residual' and 'emergent' help to delineate vernacular religion's ambiguous and complex character. Such an understanding, I argue, leads one to a richer appreciation of responses to power within contexts of vernacular religious expression; moreover, such a framework allows for comprehending religious life as the sometimes subtle and sometimes dramatic amalgamation of both conformation and contestation. Such work also highlights the theoretical contributions that contemporary folklorists and religious studies can continue to make beyond this volume, and how this act of distilling the two disciplines 'into a mutually cross-pollinating theoretical and methodological approach' (Primiano 1995: 41) suggests trajectories for future theoretical exchanges and applications.

The ethnographic referents in this collection with their emphasis on generic expressions, all demonstrate the power of creative contestation, the fluidity of religious negotiation, and the capacity of choice in religious lives even in the face of hegemony. They exemplify vernacular religion and its process of absorbing, learning, accepting, changing, denying, embellishing and appreciating the spiritual and cultural parameters of religious belief and practice in one's life (Primiano 2001: 55).

Vernacular religion in its negotiating function as the occasion for individual religious interpretation carries with it the possibility that every such moment of interpretation is itself, to borrow José Limón's phrase, an 'aesthetic act of performance' (1983: 50) which is distinctly personal. It is not that each and every moment of a religious life is a unique creative performance or expressed narrative form, but that religious lives are filled with such instances, and, that taken as a whole, religious life histories illustrate this process. Because these vernacular performances, whether verbalized or physically executed, are able not only to protest but also to confirm or create a surrounding environment, culture, or society, vernacular religion too can thus represent and express the interests of both the rich and the poor, the disenfranchised and the powerful. This quality means that no predictable categorization of vernacular religion is possible. Each particular incidence of vernacular religiosity must be examined in context to determine both its confirming and contesting, preserving and transforming, residual and emergent meanings.

By way of gesturing towards the speculative potential, both creative and critical, for deepening applications of vernacular religion, let me conclude with two provocative possibilities for future research and reflection. The first offers a commentary and the second begins a future trajectory for the study of personal creativity, belief, and expressive culture.

Sociologists of religion such as Robert Wuthnow (1998) and Wade Clark Roof (1993; 1999) have theorized a shift in the religious sensibilities of Americans since the Second World War. Attachments to religious institutions representative of a 'dwelling' spirituality have made way for a more eclectic 'seeking' sense of being religious, especially starting with the baby boom generation. An important element within this seeking-oriented spirituality for Wuthnow is the negotiation by individuals of sacred beliefs and practices. Such negotiations free one 'to maneuver among the uncertainties of contemporary life and [capitalize] on the availability of a wide variety of sources piecing together idiosyncratic conceptions of spirituality' (Wuthnow 1998: 168). Wuthnow's spirituality of seeking is characterized by a deeply personal but transient religiosity with roots in traditional religious beliefs and practices; an interest in non-institutionalized religious contexts; and an eclectic, idiosyncratic, and at times isolated, spirituality fascinated with the supernatural. I would tend to agree with Wuthnow's and Roof's assessments of contemporary religion with one major exception. I firmly believe that the power of choice – what these sociologists of religion may consider a characteristic part of late twentieth- and early twenty-first-century religion – is itself a contemporary public expression of an intrinsically private activity of creative religious negotiation that could be traced diachronically if there were sufficient sensitivity to the nuances of lived religion by historians and historical ethnographers. A short example will have to suffice: I am consistently amazed in my fieldwork among faithful Catholic women who were married in the 1940s and 1950s by their statements about their use of birth control in a period ostensibly of such powerful religious hegemony over their bodies by the male institutional Church. Such statements indicate a personal negotiation of stated Catholic moral teaching by women not in the contemporary era, but 60 years ago during Wuthnow's era of dwelling spirituality (see also Tentler 2004). The spirituality of negotiation and choice needs to be examined as not only a contemporary phase of religious life, but as a vernacular process bridging historic and contemporary religion more widely in international contexts.

Finally, this sensitivity to vernacular religious processes can draw us closer to appreciating the varieties of hegemony facing humans and the subsequent creative responses to such power when contestation itself is useless. The work of folklorist Erika Brady, in fact, has brought my attention to an expressive response to a non-socio-cultural and powerful reality faced by all humans: the biological hegemony of death. Pointing to a multitude of private religious contexts perceived in personal rituals following the death of a loved one, Brady chronicles the 'Beau Geste'.[4] In these solitary, often ephemeral, traditions of mourning, 'grief ... finds a limited expression if not solace in personalized symbolic gestures in the form of burial inclusions, specifically composed graveside rituals, and other similar actions' (Brady 1988: 26). These unicultural rituals (Primiano 1995: 47–50; 2009: 116–123; 2011: 51–52) emerge out of everyday life into the grieving process as a creative private, not a communal, statement. 'The individuals almost invariably indicate that they consider their action to be their own in a special way, not typical of their community's expectations regarding behavior of the bereaved' (Brady 1988: 30). Because these actions are recounted in narrative performances, Beau Gestes are available for ethnographic collection and study (see Brady 1988: 30–33). There may even be a connection between the discreet character of this narrative tradition and the recent contemporary practices of assembling roadside memorials on highways for accident victims (Everett 2002; Doss 2008) or streetside displays of photographs and flowers for someone murdered.[5]

Contestation operates at the level of lived religion as well as at the meta-level of scholarship on religion. That is, vernacular religion as a scholarly field of study can itself be viewed as a form of contestation. As vernacular religion can be a process of contestation – of coming to a new understanding of religion – so vernacular religious 'studies' can be a contestatory process in the midst of the study of religion. Thus, vernacular religion's very presence and positioning in scholarship enable new approaches to the study of religion. Because these approaches both employ and develop long-standing methodological traditions in folklore and religious studies, they likewise will foster stimulating reflection on – and application of – the very qualities so important to lived religion: ambiguity, power, and creativity.

Acknowledgements

I am grateful to Nicholas Rademacher, Lisa Ratmansky, Laura Sauer Palmer, Anne Schwelm and Joseph Sciorra for their assistance, and especially to Nancy L. Watterson who generously read a draft of this Afterword.

Notes

1. As already noted in this book's introduction, much research about mixed and hybrid genres and the study of folkloric discourse outside traditional genres has been done in the last 40 years. Ben-Amos (1971) gave direction to this scholarship with more advanced genre theory and research about generic practices represented by Hanks (1987), Briggs and Bauman (1995) and Bauman (2004).

2. I direct readers to Jerry Pocius's assessment of 'art' (1995) as product, performance, behaviour and skill, as well as the role of artfulness and creativity in vernacular religious expression in my own work (Primiano 1993a, b; 1995; 1997; 1999; 2001; 2009; 2010; 2011).

3. This question mirrors the pattern of folklore scholarship reflected by Patrick B. Mullen (2000) who comments that folkloristic studies of belief have moved away from romantic images of the folk as wise and rationalistic images of the folk as pathological to a postmodern appreciation of people's beliefs as processual systems influenced by and confronting traditionality and modernity.

4. The term 'Beau Geste' is taken from the title of Percival Christopher Wren's 1924 novel (Brady 1988: 24).

5. Occasionally, such mourning even emerges as wide-ranging community expressions which both record a public display of affection and manifest a personal relationship to an unknown person, as in the case of the response to the death of Princess Diana (Bowman 1998; 1999; 2001; Rowbottom 1999) or the victims of the attacks on United States civilians on 11 September 2001. Kay Turner has remarked in personal communication that after her informal survey of such spontaneous memorials she preliminarily dates the 1980 murder of former Beatle John Lennon in New York City as the earliest example of this kind of display.

References

Barna, G. (ed.) (2001) Politics and folk religion: Concepts and problems. *Acta Ethnographica Hungarica*, 46 (1–2): 9–21.

Bauman, R. (2004) *A World of Others' Words: Cross-Cultural Perspectives on Intertextuality*. Malden, MA: Blackwell Publishing.

Ben-Amos, D. (1971) Toward a definition of folklore in context. *Journal of American Folklore* 84 (331): 3–15.

Bowman, M. (1998) Research note: After Diana. *Folklore* 109: 99–101.

Bowman, M. (1999) A provincial city shows respect: Shopping and mourning in Bath. In T. Walter (ed.) *The Mourning for Diana,* 215–225. Oxford: Berg.

Bowman, M. (2001) The people's princess: Vernacular religion and politics. *Politics and Folk Religion, Acta Ethnographica Hungarica,* 46 (1–2): 35–49.

Brady, E. (1988) The Beau Geste: Shaping private rituals of grief. In A. Jabbour and J. Hardin (eds) *Folklife Annual 1987,* 24–33. Washington, DC: American Folklife Center at the Library of Congress.

Briggs, C. L. and Bauman R. (1995) Genre, intertextuality, and social power. In B. G. Blount (ed.) *Language, Culture, and Society: A Book of Readings,* 567–608. Prospect Heights, IL: Waveland.

Bringéus, N.-A. (ed.) (1994) *Religion in Everyday Life,* vol. 31. Stockholm: Kungl. Vitterhets Historieoch Antikvitets Akademien. Konferenser.

Bulthuis, K. T. (2010) Popular religion and popular culture: From the colonial era to the Civil War. In C. H. Lippy and P. W. Williams (eds) *Encyclopedia of Religion in America, 3,* 1711–1717. Washington, DC: CQ Press.

Candelaria, M. R. (1990) *Popular Religion and Liberation: The Dilemma of Liberation Theology.* Albany, NY: State University of New York Press.

Doss, E. (2008) *The Emotional Life of Contemporary Public Memorials.* Amsterdam: Amsterdam University Press.

Everett, H. (2002) *Roadside Crosses in Contemporary Memorial Culture.* Denton, TX: University of North Texas Press.

Fikfak, J. and Barna G. (eds) (2007) *Senses and Religion.* Ljubljana: Institutzaslovenskonarodopisje.

Floyd-Thomas, J. (2010) Popular religion and popular culture: From the Civil War to the mid-twentieth century. In C. H. Lippy and P. W. Williams (eds) *Encyclopedia of Religion in America, 3,* 1717–1728. Washington, DC: CQ Press.

Gustavsson, A. and Montez, M. (eds) (1999) *Folk Religion – Continuity and Change.* Universidade Nova de Lisboa – Portugal Instituto de Sociologia e Etnologia das Religioes and Uppsala Universitet – Sweden Etnologiska Institutionen.

Hall, D. D. (2010) Lived religion. In C. H. Lippy and P. W. Williams (eds) *Encyclopedia of Religion in America, 3,* 1282–1289. Washington, DC: CQ Press.

Hanks, W. F. (1987) Discourse genres in a theory of practice. *American Ethnologist* 14 (4): 668–692.

Hinson, G. (2000) *Fire in My Bones: Transcendence and the Holy Spirit in African American Gospel.* Philadelphia, PA: University of Pennsylvania Press.

Honko, L. (1998) Back to basics. *FF Network for the Folklore Fellows* 16: 1.

Howard, R. G. (2011) *Digital Jesus: The Making of a New Christian Fundamentalist Community on the Internet*. New York: New York University Press.

Lassander, M. T. (2012). Grappling with liquid modernity: Investigating post-secular religion. In P. Nynäs, M. T. Lassander and T. Utriainen (eds), *Post-Secular Society*. Piscataway, NJ: Transaction Publishers.

Limón, J. E. (1983) Western Marxism and folklore: A critical introduction. *Journal of American Folklore* 96 (379): 34–52.

Lippy, C. H. and Williams, P. W. (eds) (2010). *Encyclopedia of Religion in America*, 4 volumes. Washington, DC: CQ Press.

Magliocco, S. (2004) *Witching Culture: Folklore and Neo-Paganism in America*. Philadelphia, PA: University of Pennsylvania Press.

Mullen, P. B. (2000) Belief and the American folk. *Journal of American Folklore* 113 (448): 119–143.

Pocius, G. L. (1995) Art. *Journal of American Folklore* 108 (430): 413–431.

Primiano, L. N. (1993a) *Intrinsically Catholic: Vernacular Religion and Philadelphia's 'Dignity'*. PhD dissertation, Departments of Folklore and Folklife and Religious Studies, University of Pennsylvania, Philadelphia.

Primiano, L. N. (1993b) 'I would rather be fixated on the Lord': Women's religion, men's power, and the 'Dignity' problem. *New York Folklore* XIX (1–2): 89–103.

Primiano, L. N. (1995) Vernacular religion and the search for method in religious folklife. *Western Folklore (Reflexivity and the Study of Belief)* 54 (1): 37–56.

Primiano, L. N. (1997) Folk religion. In T. A. Green (ed.) *Folklore: An Encyclopedia of Beliefs, Customs, Tales, Music, and Art*, 710–717. Santa Barbara, CA: ABC-CLIO.

Primiano, L. N. (1999) Post-modern sites of Catholic sacred materiality. In P. W. Williams (ed.) *Perspectives on American Religion and Culture*, 187–202. Malden, MA: Basil Blackwell.

Primiano, L. N. (2001) What is vernacular Catholicism? The 'Dignity' example. *Politics and Folk Religion, Acta Ethnographica Hungarica* 46 (1–2): 51–58.

Primiano, L. N. (2009) 'For what I have done and what I have failed to do': Vernacular Catholicism and The West Wing. In Winston, D. (ed.) *Small Screen, Big Picture: Television and Lived Religion*, 99–123. Waco, TX: Baylor University Press.

Primiano, L. N. (2010) Folklore. In C. H. Lippy and P. W. Williams (eds) *Encyclopedia of Religion in America*, 2, 845–852. Washington, DC: CQ Press.

Primiano, L. N. (2011) 'I wanna do bad things with you': Fantasia on themes of American religion from the title sequence of HBO's *True Blood*. In

E. M. Mazur and K. McCarthy (eds) *God in the Details: American Religion in Popular Culture*, 41–61. New York and London: Routledge.

Roof, W. C. (1993) *A Generation of Seekers: The Spiritual Journeys of the Baby Boom Generation*. San Francisco, CA: Harper San Francisco.

Roof, W. C. (1999) *Spiritual Marketplace: Baby Boomers and the Remaking of American Religion*. Princeton, NJ: Princeton University Press.

Rowbottom, A. (1999) 'A bridge of flowers'. In T. Walter (ed.) *The Mourning for Diana*, 157–172. Oxford: Berg.

Sciorra, J. (2001) Imagined places, fragile landscapes: Italian American presepi (Nativity creches) in New York City. *Italian American Review* 8 (2): 141–173.

Scott, J. C. (1990) *Domination and the Arts of Resistance: Hidden Transcripts*. New Haven, NJ: Yale University Press.

Tentler, Leslie Woodcock (2004) *Catholics and Contraception: An American History*. Ithaca: Cornell University Press.

Turner, K. (1999) *Beautiful Necessity: The Art and Meaning of Women's Altars*. New York: Thames and Hudson.

Williams, P. W. (2010) Popular religion and popular culture. In C. H. Lippy and P. W. Williams (eds) *Encyclopedia of Religion in America*, *3*, 1701–1711. Washington DC: CQ Press.

Williams R. (1977) *Marxism and Literature*. New York: Oxford University Press.

Wolf-Knuts, U. (ed.) (2009) *Rethinking the Sacred, Proceedings of the Ninth SIEF Conference in Derry 2008*. Department of Comparative Religion, Åbo Akademi University, Religionsvetenskapligaskrifter.

Wuthnow, R. (1998) *After Heaven: Spirituality in America Since the 1950s*. Berkeley, CA: University of California Press.

Yoder, D. (ed.) (1974) Symposium on folk religion. *Western Folklore* 33 (1): 77–87.

Index